New perspectives for reference service in academic libraries

New perspectives for reference service in academic libraries

RAYMOND G. McINNIS

*Contributions in Librarianship and
Information Science, Number 23*

GREENWOOD PRESS   WESTPORT, CONNECTICUT • LONDON, ENGLAND

14393

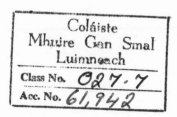
Library of Congress Cataloging in Publication Data

McInnis, Raymond G
    New perspectives for reference service in academic
libraries.

    (Contributions in librarianship and information
science ; no. 23 ISSN 0084-9243)
    Bibliography: p.
    Includes indexes.
    1. Libraries, University and college—Reference
services. 2. Research. I. Title. II. Series.
Z675.U5M32   027.7   77-94742
ISBN 0-313-20311-3

Library of Congress Catalog Card Number: 77-94742
ISBN: 0-313-20311-3
ISSN: 0084-9243

First published in 1978

Greenwood Press, Inc.
51 Riverside Avenue, Westport, Connecticut 06880

Printed in the United States of America

10 9 8 7 6 5 4 3 2

Copyright Acknowledgments

This book is dedicated to
the memory of my father
GEORGE MCINNIS
1900-1975

Contents

Contents

Figures

Acknowledgments

This book is the culmination of the thinking and research of a decade and a half; hence, it is difficult to name all of the individuals who have influenced my thinking in some way. To these unnamed people I remain grateful.

Individuals who have spent long periods discussing these topics with me include John MacGregor, Molly Mignon, Kathy Haselbauer, Enid Haag, Harry Ritter, Ed Kaplan, and Tom Frazier.

I am deeply indebted to Marian Alexander, Molly Mignon, Timothy O'Leary, Nancy Pries, Kathy Haselbauer, and Enid Haag for reading the manuscript and for their comments on it.

I owe much gratitude to Jane Clark, Florence Preder, Anne Drake, Lloyde Newman, and Joy Dabney of Western's Bureau of Faculty Research for typing the manuscript and for preparing the illustrations. Special thanks go to Marijeanne Winchell for the art work on the structured inquiry section in Appendix A.

I also extend many thanks to James Sabin, Sandra Soderberg, and Cynthia Harris at Greenwood Press for their patience, understanding, and helpfulness.

Finally, without the support and personal sacrifice of my wife, Karen, and my children, Michael and Erin, this book could not have been written. They, especially Karen, made it possible, and for this I remain humble and grateful.

Introduction

In his excellent survey of user studies, Brittain quotes Kochen's observation that a "new intellectual discipline seems to be in the making. It is the study of processes by which knowledge grows."[1] According to Brittain, Kochen draws an analogy between the way in which a growing literature organizes substantive material and the way a learner, by creating models of his environment, is able to take increasingly effective actions. Brittain notes that a similar analogy, one between information retrieval and education, is drawn by Heilprin and Goodman, who suggest that both searching for information and the process of education are subject to, and shaped by, one basic constraint—the very limited human processing capacity.[2] Central to both of these analogies is the user of information who has finite assimilation and processing capacities in the context of an exponentially expanding universe of inquiry.

Kochen tentatively suggests that the "new intellectual discipline" could be called epistodynamics: "It is concerned with lawful regularities governing the acquisition of information and its transformation into knowledge, the assimilation of knowledge into understanding, the fusion of understanding into wisdom."[3]

Shera, too, observed the development of a new discipline:

The new discipline that is here envisaged (and which, for want of a better name, has been called *social epistemology*) should provide a framework for the entire complex problem of the nature of the intellectual process in society—a study of the ways in which society as a whole achieves a perceptive relation to its total environment. . . . The focus of this new discipline should be upon the production, flow, integration, and consumption of all forms of communicated thought throughout the entire social fabric. From such a discipline should emerge a new body of knowledge about, and a synthesis[4] of the interaction between knowledge and social activity.[5]

Christ states that Shera's "theory of social epistemology . . . has never been well enough delineated to reach the functional stage."[6] Brookes also laments the failure to make some of Shera's notions operational.[7]

Other writers have made similar observations about the new discipline. Harmon refers simply to a "science of research,"[8] and Havelock speaks of the emerging "science of knowledge utilization."[9] Taylor suggests that "a new discipline deserves a new name, and I would like to put forward the claims of *catenics*, which is derived from *catena*, the Latin word for a chain. . . ."[10] Finally, Rawski speaks of the need for an "ontology of a literature."[11]

Along with labels, these people have attempted to describe the elements of this discipline. All descriptions share, to a greater or lesser degree, at least an implicit structure of information foundation. (Here, "information" is used in its loosest, most inclusive sense.) And, too, all share a common problem: none is operational, at least in a format or conception that allows such systems to be utilized in undergraduate instruction and research.

In the chapters that follow, I argue that an epistemological approach to independent research which contains elements of the approaches mentioned above can be employed in undergraduate education. If implemented sensibly, this approach can also result in greater involvement of the library in under-graduate instruction.

If I were asked to name the most important argument in this book, my immediate response would be the one positing that successful and rewarding research can be conducted by students—including undergraduates—in academic libraries. The provisions are that they be informed, first, of the underlying processes and practices of inquiry characteristic of particular disciplines; second, of the patterns of the published research literature emanating from these activities; and third, that developing and refining research skills require thoughtful attention and deliberate practice. Three related premises are that there is a tacit logic of research strategy; that this logic can be raised to the level of awareness; and that research strategy itself can be refined by its intelligent and purposeful application. In short, it is desirable that students gain the craft skills of the instructor-researcher.

Integrating Classroom Instruction and Library Research: Cooperation of Instructor and Reference Librarian

When a student research project is considered for a particular course—if it is expected to be a reasonably successful and rewarding experience—certain preparations should necessarily be made. Perhaps the biggest problem confronting classroom instructors and reference librarians alike is how to inform students rapidly of the reference sources they need to consult in order to expose them to the required material related to their research topic.

Neither the classroom instructor nor the reference librarian can solve such problems satisfactorily when each is working separately. By working together, however, considerable success can be achieved. In addition to being well acquainted with the subject, the instructor provides the stimula-tion and motivation necessary to get most students seriously concerned about engaging in research. After the students' interest is developed, it becomes the task of the reference librarian to provide the means for students to effectively engage in research. Implementing such programs requires considerable preparation, especially on the part of the reference librarian. The dimensions of the problems and opportunities confronting both classroom instructors and reference librarians are discussed in Part I.

Suggestions for the development and application of such policies and programs in academic libraries occupy the bulk of this book. For the most part, these suggestions focus on library-produced research guides.

Students' Need for Immediate Assistance

The policies and programs discussed here are basically oriented toward the immediate assistance of students and others about to engage in research. (Whatever opportunities are presented for having individual departments or instructors establish research-oriented courses should, of course, also be investigated and promoted.) The central means of giving students such immediate assistance is to inform them about how to use bibliographic research guides. This instruction can be achieved in several ways, and it is recommended that all these methods be employed. It is particularly recommended that the use of research guides be demonstrated within the context of actual research problems in which the mode of research tentatively called *structured inquiry* is employed. As experience suggests, greater impact is achieved if the demonstration focuses directly on topics related to the immediate research needs of students.

Emphasis on Structure

In seeking to achieve these goals, experience also suggests that certain notions about the production of scientific literature need to be established in the minds of students about to engage in research. Scientific literature is considered the product of disciplined inquiry in an academic setting, and thus it includes social-scientific literature. Part II addresses these matters.

To this end, the purpose and goals of inquiry in the social sciences are outlined. Particular attention is directed toward the following: that the purpose of inquiry is to explain phenomena in a specific field; that inquiry is a collective enterprise; and that scholar-researchers have certain agreed-upon precepts and conventions. Following this discussion is an examination of the primary and secondary materials with which social scientists work and of how social-scientific literature, through consensus, is turned into knowledge. The creative aspects of inquiry, including its tacit dimensions, are explored. In short, attention is directed toward the methodologies and certain aspects of their epistemological, sociological, and psychological considerations. The structural and cumulative characteristics of social-scientific literature are stressed, and two main components—bibliographic structure and substantive structure—are distinguished. It is argued that the bibliographic and substantive components of research literature can effectively be set forth in a substantive-bibliographic continuum. (This concept is developed more extensively in Part III.) The psychological structure of knowledge is then discussed.

Some of the suggested ways of graphically depicting the structure of a body of literature are considered, especially the diagrams (or historiographs) of Garfield and of Skelton, and MacGregor and McInnis' bibliographic network structures. Finally, the cognitive functions of bibliographic network structures are examined, especially in relation to Epstein's notions of learning.

Reference Works As Intermediary Sources

Once this structural grounding is established, it becomes a framework around which reference works can be introduced, but they are introduced in such a manner that their functions are related directly to the structural characteristics of the body of literature under consideration. This idea is set forth in a heuristic device called the *tripartite matrix*. In addition to the bibliographic and substantive aspects of the literature—set forth in the substantive-bibliographic continuum—the tripartite matrix includes a third component, reference works, which are conceptualized as *intermediary sources*. By considering reference works as intermediary sources, it can be seen that reference works actually provide—in a distilled or compressed format—*intermediate forms* or *stages* of the literature to which they are related. As an heuristic device, the tripartite matrix constitutes a conceptual framework designed to assist student researchers and others in developing research strategies and undertaking research projects in a logical and systematic manner, but at a pace each student can handle.

Next, the tacit dimensions of structured inquiry are discussed. Then, using diagrammatic models of the bibliographic and substantive structures, as well as illustrations from such reference materials as encyclopedias, reviews of research, and bibliographies, examples of structured inquiry are given. In these examples, the assumption is that students begin at a point where little is known about a topic, and by progressing in a step-by-step (i.e., structured) procedure, they can advance to the desired level of understanding.

It then becomes a question of whether these reference works—conceptualized as intermediary sources—function as instruments of *analysis* or of *synthesis*. That is, on the one hand, are discrete contributions to a body of literature treated analytically, where the attention is on the individual publication, typical of indexes, abstract journals, and bibliographies? Or, on the other hand, are these same discrete contributions considered together in an integrated, synthesized format, typical of encyclopedias, dictionaries, and reviews of research?

In effect, what exists is a continuum at either end of which are placed the bibliographic (i.e., analytical) and the substantive (i.e., synthetical) elements of a body of literature. Falling in divisions between these two extremes are those intermediary sources which provide various combinations of these two components of research literature.

Perhaps the most interesting aspect of the tripartite matrix of research materials is that even though a plethora of intermediary sources is produced—all of which expose various forms or stages of the literature to which they are related—taken together, their function and structure relate directly to the substantive-bibliographic continuum.

Function as an Organizing Principle

In Part IV, it is argued that in producing research guides (the emphasis is on those produced by academic libraries), greater attention needs to be directed toward the functional characteristics of research materials, especially those generally known as reference works. If their functions are to be more clearly understood, these materials should be more precisely considered intermediary sources rather than simply "reference" works. The function of intermediary sources in relation to the substantive-bibliographic continuum therefore becomes the chief organizing principle in the production of research guides.

The most important element of this concept is annotation. It is argued—and illustrated by examples—that annotation can perform both *analytical* and *integrative* functions which, if thoughtfully and deliberately executed, can assist researchers in structuring efficient research strategies. The tripartite matrix, formed by the components involved, is central to this concern and makes the concept operative.

Levels of Specificity

Finally Part V focuses on the production of research guides for area studies. After an examination of some standard research guides in the field, a new conceptual framework for the organization of research guides for area studies literature is presented. On the basis of the arguments developed in Parts II, III, and IV, it is proposed that research guides for area studies can be visualized as attempts to organize the substantive literature of particular social science disciplines related to specific geographical areas. It is argued and illustrated that the substantive literature of area studies research is necessarily embedded in the larger bodies of social-scientific literature which provides their foundation. While the notions of the substantive-bibliographic continuum and the tripartite matrix continue to be valid, a somewhat different perspective must be developed because of the different levels of specificity of treatment which area studies literature is given in the intermediary sources that give access to it. This different perspective is elucidated in the form of a series of matrices—or, more precisely, a *compound matrix.* In such a context, the analytical and integrative functions of annotation in research guides become significant aids to inquiry, especially for researchers with little or no acquaintance with the literature in the field.

Throughout, this work draws heavily from many writers within library science and from such diverse quarters as the history and philosophy of science, education, and the social sciences in general. By drawing attention to what these writers have to say, I hope to persuade academic reference librarians that many of the concepts and ideas discussed can be used in library programs designed to develop and promote increased opportunities for students and other library users to utilize library materials.

Notes

1. Manfred Kochen, "Stability in the Growth of Knowledge," *American Documentation* 20 (1969):186, as cited in J. M. Brittain, *Information and Its Users* (Bath, England: Bath University Press, 1970), p. 7.

2. L. B. Heilprin and F. L. Goodman, "Analogy Between Information Retrieval and Education," *American Documentation* 16 (1965):163-9.

3. Kochen, "Stability in the Growth of Knowledge," p. 195. This theme is pursued in greater detail in Kochen, *Principles of Information Retrieval* (Los Angeles: Melville Publishing Co., 1974), pp. 42-62.

4. Shera used "system" in the original, a term that seems preferable to "synthesis."

5. Jesse Shera, *Foundations of Education for Librarianship* (New York: Becker and Hayes, 1972), p. 112. Chapter 4, from which the passage is taken, is an extended version of "An Epistemological Foundation for Library Science" in Edward B. Montgomery, ed., *The Foundations of Access to Knowledge: A Symposium* (Syracuse, N.Y.: Syracuse University Press, 1968).

6. John M. Christ, *Toward a Philosophy of Educational Librarianship* (Littleton, Colo.: Libraries Unlimited, 1972), p. 72.

7. B. C. Brookes, "Jesse Shera and the Theory of Bibliography," *Journal of Librarianship* 5 (October 1973):233-45, 258.

8. Glynn Harmon, "Opinion Paper on the Evolution of Information Sciences," *ASIS; Journal of the American Society for Information Science* 22 (July-August 1971):240.

9. Ronald G. Havelock, *A Comparative Study of the Literature on the Dissemination and Utilization of Scientific Knowledge* (Ann Arbor, Mich.: Center for Research on Utilization of Scientific Knowledge, Institute for Social Research, University of Michigan, 1969), p. I-1.

10. Alan R. Taylor, "A Model for Academic Library Service," in *Papers Delivered at the Indiana University Library Dedication, Bloomington Campus, October 9-10, 1970* (Bloomington, Ind.: Indiana University Library, 1971), p. 19.

11. Conrad H. Rawski, "Subject Literatures and Librarianship," in L. R. Bone, ed., *Conference on Library School Teaching Methods* (Urbana, Ill.: University of Illinois, Graduate School of Library Science, 1969).

Part I

INTEGRATING CLASSROOM INSTRUCTION AND LIBRARY RESEARCH

Students don't know how to use libraries. Most can't efficiently handle the simplest bibliographic tasks they need to accomplish.[1]

Matters examined in Chapters 1 and 2 are not traditionally the concerns of academic librarians. Moreover, much of this material is explorative and speculative. The reaction of reference librarians will depend both upon their individual conceptions of the correct role of reference service in academic institutions and upon circumstances peculiar to their institutions. Such qualification is necessary because the discussion concerns, first, the professors' patterns of teaching and their processes of inquiry, and, second, the undergraduate students' comprehension and retention of subject matter— particularly how, together, these matters relate to student use of library materials and what uses students make of reference materials in connection with library-oriented research.

Relating directly to these aspects of student use of library materials is the proposal that a new approach to integrating classroom instruction and library research is both desirable and practicable. Considerations which make this proposal desirable are outlined in Part I; the practicable aspects are the subject of Parts II-V.

In developing these arguments, it is necessary to examine some of the problems facing the teaching faculty, both individually and collectively, as well as some of the solutions proposed by others. This examination is by no means comprehensive. Instead, an attempt is made to highlight those matters of which reference librarians, especially those in medium-sized academic institutions, are at least unconsciously aware. By being more consciously aware of them, it will be possible for librarians to initiate policies and programs designed to strengthen the library's function as an integral component of undergraduate education.

Chapter 1 examines the dimensions of the problem of student use of libraries from the point of view of the teaching faculty, while Chapter 2 focuses on the opportunities for increasing cooperation between under-graduate instructors in the social sciences and reference librarians.

Note

1. Allan J. Dyson, "Organizing Undergraduate Library Instruction: The English and the American Experience," *Journal of Academic Librarianship* 1 (March 1975):9.

1 The Dimensions of the Problem

It is almost an understatement to say that reference departments in academic libraries are being deluged with increasing demands from college students for various kinds of information and consultative services. Unfortunately, as Dyson concludes, the available evidence does not suggest how these increased demands can be dealt with in ways that will permit the library to become a more dynamic instrument of learning in higher education. Insufficient library faculty, book budgets eroded by inflation, and incapacity to provide effective library orientation programs are among the more conspicuous current problems. In this book, I offer some suggestions as to how reference service in academic libraries can be strengthened and intensified, particularly in the social sciences, and I give special concern to measures that will promote greater integration of classroom instruction and library research. Primarily, I focus on one of the most critical issues confronting this sector of the library profession, one which—curiously—has received little attention: the place of the classroom instructor in student use of the library. In the course of this discussion, I draw attention to the rich store of writings produced by a wide range of educators concerned with the problems of improving learning in higher education. Several publications that address aspects of this problem have appeared in the last decade.[1]

Related to the issue of the classroom instructor's role in student use of the library is that of devising ways of engaging instructors more directly in the research activities of students in the library. There are several reasons why instructors should become more concerned about students' research activities, most of which are outlined by political scientist Bayley (noted in this chapter), in his recommendations for curriculum reform.

More than any other factor, the value the classroom instructor attaches to library research determines the students' interest in use of library materials. Instructors give direction and motivation to students as to how library materials are to be used in meeting course requirements. Their influence is most often the difference between a perfunctory use of materials and a dedicated examination of the rich store of scientific literature typically available in most college libraries.

The available evidence suggests, however, that most instructor-researchers have a limited acquaintance of and appreciation for library research, especially research that is not narrowly focused on their individual interests. For example, several "user studies" have produced largely discouraging results about experienced researchers' acquaintance with research materials in their field.[2]

On the basis of this evidence, reference librarians can conclude that in general instructors' perceptions of the range, scope, and function of library reference materials, as devices for gaining access to scientific literature, are limited. Most often, however, in instructor-directed student research, the reference librarian is an awkward third party in an unhappy union of instructor and student. In such a situation, in order to increase student use of library materials, the library must place practically as much emphasis on sharpening the instructor's perceptions of the opportunities available for engaging their students in research activities as on instructing students in effective use of library materials.

How this goal can be accomplished is, of course, a vexing problem. It has no single, universal solution since so much depends upon individual circumstances. In order to obtain teaching faculty commitment to and engagement in highly motivated student library research, a sustained but, at the same time, *unstrained* effort is required. Furthermore, in order to be convincing to instructors, such programs, whatever they comprise, must provide observable, tangible results. Gration and Young have pointed out the kind of relationships between instructors and reference librarians that are needed to insure effective and realistic student use of library materials.[3]

Before suggesting ways of eliciting greater faculty commitment to and engagement in student use of the library, however, it is necessary to posit a frame of reference. This frame of reference comprises the following: the inseparability of teaching and research for enhancing the quality of instruction; the need for grounding students in the epistemological foundations of scientific literature; and the students' comprehension and retention of subject matter.

Inseparability of Teaching and Research

First, it is generally conceded that in higher education teaching and scholarly research/publication are inseparable; each contributes more or less equally to the growth and maturity of a well-rounded scholar and instructor. Indeed, the neglect of either task results in an unevenly developed individual and ultimately takes away from potential contributions in both. Perkins observes, for example, that "for the college teacher, instruction and research are both fundamental. They ought not to be separated. There is no real dichotomy between them: they are two faces of the same problem. . . . When a teacher has ceased to ask questions, when he has ceased, in other words, to cultivate the spirit of research, he has ceased to be effective. . . . Research," he concludes, "is the means by which we discipline ourselves, by which we make ourselves more careful, more accurate, and more profound."[4] Other writers have reached similar conclusions. Caws states that "inquiry is a form of self-instruction for the inquirer." He also suggests that in addition to self-instruction for the inquirer, inquiry "*may* be instruction, too, for someone else who is capable of following it." On this basis, he concludes that "the situation where instruction and inquiry are thus linked, if not identical, is the ideal of the university."[5]

Of course, not all inquiry leads to publication. Recognizing this, Ben-David suggests "that there should be some means of evaluating and rewarding success in teaching and education other than the evaluation of scholarly publications, so that capable college teachers who do not wish to publish should not feel that they are doomed to eternal academic inferiority."[6] Empirical evidence concerning the "success" of individual faculty in higher education is given by economists Siegfried and White.[7]

Similar assertions about the importance of research activities can be made about librarians. Just as the instructor who neglects research and publication fails to keep himself intellectually alive, so the librarian who fails to utilize the best of the latest developments for gaining access to scientific literature is neglecting his professional growth. Recent efforts to achieve faculty status for librarians, note, for example, the necessity of research and publication as criteria of promotion.[8]

Some—perhaps even many—in the library profession will stoutly continue to object to the suggestion that librarians are equivalent to instructors or, at best, they will admit that only by the most liberal definitions can librarians be classified as instructors. In a restricted sense this is, and probably always will be, true. The greatest and most obvious distinction between the two groups is, of course, that librarians seldom formally teach classes. On the other hand, consistent with the shifting emphasis increasingly evident in education, from *what* one learns to *how* one learns, this restrictive interpretation is slowly but inexorably changing. It should be understood, however, that the substantive aspects of particular disciplines are not being relegated to a secondary significance. The substantive components of scientific literature are, and should always remain, the primary concern of instructors, students, and librarians. In this sense, concern for methods suggests a shift in perspective, where the substantive aspects of the literature, whether theoretical or empirical, are perceived as organic substances, constantly under refinement and revision. (The significance of this property of empirical literature is discussed in Part II.) Inquiry modes of learning and research are particular manifestations of this development—but there are others.[9]

Epistemological Foundations of Scientific Literature

Of particular concern here is the increasing recognition by classroom
instructors that more stress on the epistemological aspects of scientific
literature is required.[10] Students generally have little understanding of how
the literature of a discipline is generated. I find little evidence, for example,
that they are familiar with the kind of activity involved in producing scientific literature as outlined by Price.[11] Thus, a second part of this frame of
reference necessarily concerns the structure of scientific literature.

Scientific literature, especially that derived from empirical research, is
produced for the most part in small, discrete amounts, each amount merely
adding to the accumulated body of unsynthesized subject matter. Inherent
in this view is the fact that scientific literature is an organic, dynamic com-
modity, having recognizable—but natural—structures, comprising both
bibliographic and substantive components, and certain more or less predict-
able patterns of growth. (The term *natural structures* is used because it is
more logical to assume that scientific literature evolved over time, in its
natural, diachronic structure, rather than that it existed in a synchronic state.
This argument is developed extensively in Part II.)

Man is limited in his ability to deal effectively with sizable amounts of
subject matter. In this connection, much, of course, is dependent on the
volume and complexity of the literature, as well as on the researcher's acquaintance with and experience in research procedures. Ausubel's "subject matter
sophistication" is one attempt to explain some of the factors involved in
how individuals gain an understanding of a subject.[12] Because of certain
definite parallels, some of Polanyi's claims of "tacit knowledge" also apply.[13]
Indeed, Wagener proposes that the principles underlying Polanyi's theories
of tacit knowledge have direct application to learning.[14] Unfortunately,
Wagener focuses only on the preliminary or preparatory aspects of estab-
lishing the heuristic components of learning (i.e., those aspects of learning
that encourage independent inquiry) in the relationship between teacher
and learner. Implementing such programs, in their broadest and deepest
sense, would require much additional work. In Part III, I maintain that
Polanyi's notions can be used to explain the explicit and implicit linkages
among reference works. Similar arguments, without reference to Polanyi,
are given by Oakeshott and by Caws.[15] Eble claims that ideally the teacher's
aim should be to develop understanding rather than merely to impart
knowledge: "Students will insist that learning be conjoined with doing, and
the teaching will help make that conjoining possible."[16]

It is nonetheless necessary that bodies of scientific literature be reduced to
manageable size without distorting their essential content. The instruments
derived to accomplish this task are traditionally known as reference works.
However, because they characteristically provide access to intermediate

forms or stages, in various combinations, of the components of scientific literature, I prefer to term them *intermediary sources*. The typical treatments given scientific literature in such works, almost always in a distilled form, are synthesis and analysis. Furthermore, as argued in this work, reference works, conceptualized as intermediary devices, function as the third component of a tripartite model of instruction and research. (An extensive discussion of the tripartite model of research is given in Part III.) At the same time, intermediary sources are not produced as a natural consequence of inquiry, but rather are artificial constructs. For the most part, expressed need determines the design and production of intermediary sources. This pattern is much like that in the empirical sciences as noted by Freides: "The goals and methods of science are not fixed and immutable, or imposed uniformly by designated authority, but instead evolve in largely unpremeditated fashion as the general effect of many independent actions."[17] Because of several factors, including ignorance, a crazy-quilt of reference works has developed, some of which duplicate or overlap one another and others which do not give adequate coverage.

Emanating from the structural treatment of the components of scientific literature is a heuristic model of research that can be used for demonstrating (among other things) how research is undertaken and the functional aspects of reference works. Such heuristic models will go a long way toward convincing classroom instructors that, when effectively implemented, research activities have useful cognitive functions. Also important, but little appreciated, even among librarians, is the fact that such treatment demonstrates more efficiently than any other the basic integrated or unified qualities of scientific literature, which in itself is an important feature of learning. In such a context, these two points complement and reinforce one another, resulting in a more convincing argument and more agreeably implemented program.

Implicit in the arguments concerning the epistemological foundation of learning is that the current shift in education from *what* one learns to *how* one learns will result in the recognition "that methods [will] gain the status of content." Bechtel claims (and there is much evidence available to support her claim) that heretofore such a development would have been considered "antithetical to liberal arts education."[18] For example, few oppose the suggestion that in higher education the library is really an extension of instruction and that librarians, particularly those charged with responsibility to a specific group of related disciplines (e.g., humanities librarians, science librarians), are adjunct instructors. Increasingly, following the logic of the present shift in education, it will be tacitly accepted that methods will achieve higher stature in learning. Currently, librarian's instruction consists mainly of directing students and faculty to the locations of the literature of the disciplines, with only secondary concern for the calibre of that literature.

(Such issues are the proper concern of the instructor.) At the same time, increasing importance is being attached to the bibliographical aspects of research, including the location of substantive material as an aid to understanding the substantive aspects of a literature. The so-called literature-explosion, which makes research itself more complex and difficult, is perhaps the principal reason for the shift in emphasis in learning noted above. This increasing stress on the bibliographical aspects of scientific literature in instruction is in obvious contrast to students' inability to make effective use of library materials. This issue, of course, will not easily be resolved. An approach to instruction in research strategy which emphasizes the epistemological components of scientific literature holds much promise as a means of resolving this predicament. Achieving this solution will require joint action between librarians and instructors.

Comprehension and Retention of Learning

A third current concern in education involves the comprehension and retention of learning. While some readers may question the inclusion of this factor in a discussion of the problem of research, it is nonetheless a valid one. Indeed, most instructors welcome suggestions that will ease students' problems of understanding subject matter. Specifically, as will be seen below, it is a growing concern in the social science disciplines.[19]

Ausubel has addressed the problem of comprehension and retention, especially as it relates to gaining "subject matter sophistication" which, logically, includes bibliographic as well as substantive aspects of knowledge.[20] Knapp reminds us that, along with "knowledge of bibliographic organization," a librarian is cognizant of "pattern and structure in the total system of the library." According to Knapp, this pattern and structure is analogous to the "cognitive structures" which Bruner argues must be significant components of learning. Such structures, she suggests, ought to be employed as modes of research.[21] Knapp's comments also address a weakness inherent in the current attempts of educators to apply Bruner's theories. Her comments hold true for certain recently derived library research models, namely, that they lack desirable heuristic qualities characteristic of deductive or inductive models of inquiry.[22]

In a slightly different context, though with similar intent, Foskett argues:

It is clear from the work of modern experimental psychologists such as Jean Piaget, J. S. Bruner, J. P. Guilford, and many others that classification, or categorization of items of information, plays a major role in advancing our understanding of the world around us. They have shown, however, that such classifications are multiplicative; not single hierarchies, but lattices. The fundamental problem of modern classification systems is therefore to provide a lattice-type network of terms rather than a single linear sequence.[23]

If concerns about comprehension and retention of subject matter are reasonable and necessary to provide individuals with the capability of independent inquiry, it seems logical that the librarian, being an important key to effective inquiry, will necessarily be involved in the design and production of such materials. At the same time, I agree with Knapp that the function and scope of reference materials—even though they are functional necessities in any effective library research activity—are anomalous to an ordinary understanding of the epistemological foundations of scientific literature and must be taught.[24] In Part III, for example, I suggest that the concept of reference works as artificial constructs, functioning as intermediary sources, is a worthy component of instruction in research. Not only must such matters be taught, but for maximum effect they evidently must be introduced when motivation is very high. The ineffectiveness of library orientation programs is generally attributed to the rapidity with which details are forgotten. Line, as one example, states that to:

catch the researcher at the ideal stage, when he has chosen his subject, is becoming aware of the difficulties of searching for information, but has not yet done much work on it, is extremely difficult; not the least of the difficulties being that since research students all tend to start at the same time of the year, they all tend to reach the critical stage at the same time, and even the best staffed library finds difficulty in coping with a peak demand of this kind.[25]

Knowledge of such difficulties of learning and research, it should be noted, is not limited to reference librarians. As Rundell observes with regard to research problems in history, "the human mind, being what it is, often does not absorb material lacking immediate relevance."[26] Perhaps some readers may feel that this discussion on the comprehension and retention of material focuses too narrowly on the role of inquiry, especially inquiry as library research, to be of much concern to those interested in improving instruction in higher education. As I maintain in Parts II and III, however, certain aspects of scientific literature and, concomitantly, certain heuristic models of inquiry which utilize reference works for gaining access to it can help improve comprehension and retention.

The matters noted above present the greatest promise for legitimate collaboration between instructors and librarians. Furthermore, they represent one area where librarians and instructors can jointly engage in developing programs that combine instruction and research.[27] (Such sentiments are, of course, not shared universally.)[28] In Part II, I discuss possible ways of adapting the innovative mode of instruction developed by biologist Epstein.[29] In addition, the "case-studies" method of learning outlined by Washburn has obvious parallels with the techniques of Epstein.[30]

The above postulates are a logical outgrowth of Bell's observations about missing dimensions in general education:

Training cannot deal with techniques in the narrow sense, but with the foundations of knowledge itself: i.e., how a particular discipline establishes its concepts; how these concepts, seen as fluid inquiry, need to be revised to meet new problems; how one establishes the criteria of choice of one, rather than another, alternative pattern of inquiry.

In the present phase of the organization of knowledge, one can no longer train people for specific intellectual tasks or provide a purely vocational training. In effect, obsolescence of specializations indicates that one cannot any longer educate a person for a job. One has to provide the means for intellectual mobility, for continuing education, for mid-career conceptual inquiry.[31]

"Further," he continues, "what is required is a radically new approach to teaching as conceptual innovation, conceptions that involve scrutiny of the discipline as an integral part of the imparting of the discipline itself."[32] Finally, "the emphasis in the college must be less on what one knows and more on the self-conscious ground of knowledge; how one knows what one knows, and the principle of the relevant selection of facts."[33] In a similar statement Mead notes "that we have as yet failed to recognize the new character of change is apparent in a thousand ways. Despite the fact that a subject taught to college freshmen may have altered basically by the time the same students are seniors, it is still said that colleges are able to give students 'a good education' . . . finished, wrapped up and sealed with a degree."[34]

Although such concerns seem self-evident, much progress remains to be achieved. In a recent Carnegie Foundation study of higher education, for example, Gurin is forced to conclude that "in reviewing the research literature, one is struck by the richness of the peer influence studies in contrast to the lack of studies that have imaginatively attempted to study the impact of the curriculum or other aspects of the college environment as an intellectual experience."[35] There are indications, nonetheless, that greater stress will be placed on the use of library materials in undergraduate education (see in chapter 2).

Earlier, the increasing evidence of a shift in emphasis in education from *what* one learns to *how* one learns was noted. This shift signifies that the ability to undertake independent research on almost any topic will be recognized as a legitimate skill, as part of a college education. Of greater significance is the possibility that students, rather than graduating from college convinced that they possess all the knowledge required for a career, will be aware that they are merely beginning a lifelong task of understanding their field. Wolfe and Williams, for example, suggest that "the concept of the 'student years,' that chunk out of a person's life devoted to higher education— is fading," and that it is being replaced by "the concept of lifelong education, taken when the student needs it."[36]

Change in Undergraduate Education: What Direction Will It Take?

What evidence exists that changes occurring in undergraduate instruction suggest greater student use of library materials? Before this question can be answered, certain other matters about teaching and learning must be considered. Dissatisfaction with the results of undergraduate education comes from several sources and for several reasons. The whole issue of "relevance," for example, a catchword among students in the 1960s, was often confusingly articulated, but it reflected a general unhappiness among students whose basic problem was insufficient preparation for pursuing a career.[37] Their criticisms typically resulted in curriculum changes, but according to Bayley,[38] these changes were mostly cosmetic.

Bayley's is one of the more eloquent and persuasive articles on the seemingly small value attached to teaching in higher education. Christ, who holds a somewhat similar position on the issue, sets the question of "teaching" versus "learning" in a new perspective:

A clear understanding of the focus of education within higher education today is vital for a proper understanding of independent study and the library's essential role in higher education. Succinctly stated, the contemporary focus of higher education, and it is a much criticized focus, pertains to the concept of "teaching." Within the concept may be included such concepts as teaching techniques, faculty, curriculum structure, and class organization. It is around the teacher, his teaching, and his discipline that contemporary education revolves.

Such a focus, he contends, is

educationally unbalanced. Such systematization excludes another vital educational concept—i.e., learning. It is unfortunate that through teacher-centered education the student and learning have been subordinated to the teacher and his discipline. This is regrettable because the key to a proper understanding of independent study, the library, and their place in the educational process pertains more to learning than to teaching.[39]

A new perspective is not necessary, however, for the instructor's interests in his discipline can become the central focus of student learning which includes greater library use. (This issue is explored in Chapter 2.) Although Knapp argues that "the faculty has limited understanding of the intellectual processes involved in sophisticated library competence,"[40] she maintains that methods of inquiry, loosely characterized as resembling the procedures used by scholars, can, if introduced properly, be employed as a means of research by students. While her position is valid, it requires further elaboration before it can become operational. Even so, it is a step in the right direction.

At the same time, Knapp cautions that while "faculty members are sincerely concerned about their teaching effectiveness, . . . at the moment, they are feeling guilty because they are under attack for alleged neglect of their teaching duties."[41] According to Blackburn, she notes, "librarians . . . make the faculty feel guilty for failing to get the students to use the library and feel humiliated at their own lack of ability to locate materials quickly."[42]

College Student Subcultures

The notion of student subcultures on college campuses, originally suggested by Clark and Trow in 1960, received increasing attention in the latter part of the 1960s when student unrest prevailed on college campuses.[43] Concern with student subculture as a subject of research has now diminished but the resulting analysis of the types of students making up the college student body continues to create interest.

Clark and Trow distinguish four groups of students: the academic, the nonconformist, the collegiate, and the vocational. Each group, depending on individual aspirations, views college from a different perspective. The divisions among types are not that clearcut, however, since individuals differ in their personal makeup. Some eighty-odd empirical studies, including several doctoral dissertations, have been conducted on the subject, and a considerable amount of information has been gathered. A review of many of the publications on student subcultures is given in Warren's "Student Perceptions of College Subcultures."[44]

Knapp suggests that an awareness of such groupings is an important consideration when a library is studying methods of becoming a more effective and more widely used instrument in education. Some of Knapp's suggestions about student subcultures are questionable, however, for student motivation for library use remains almost entirely in the hands of the instructors. Except in unusual cases, students, including the nonconformist (which, according to Knapp, "the library might well decide . . . is the one subculture worth courting,")[45] must be motivated to use the library by their instructors. Knapp's views on the nonconformist type may be true in some cases, but in my experience the nonconformists suspect all ideas except those that are current among their peers.[46]

Grieneeks' findings concerning "changes in student role orientation toward college" could be useful: "Many students who originally identify with the academic subculture and the values associated with the intellectual life fail to maintain their enthusiasm for that initial selection." According to her," much more attention should be given to supporting and nurturing these initial positive feelings that students express toward the pursuit of knowledge." Her evidence suggests that many students who turned away from the academic subculture "share a profound sense of disillusion and defeat in their inability to carry through with their original preferences to professional development." If a concerted effort were made, she speculates, these students could be given many of the behaviors necessary for being successful scholars.[47]

Perry holds an almost parallel position. He observes that often instructional techniques widely employed by professors also destroy or weaken the intellectual aspirations of students.[48] Kolb presents a similar argument, supported by empirical evidence. According to Kolb, characteristics of personality have a greater influence on an individual's preferred learning style than was previously believed. Given this evidence, he concludes that "the teaching process should be equally (or perhaps more) concerned with the development of the student's method of learning as with the development of his knowledge of content."[49]

Apart from such considerations is Hobbs' viewpoint that one impediment to scholarship is "to walk a lonesome road." Hobbs asserts that if the faculty took more initiative in supporting and rewarding students with encouragement and recognition for making commitments required for success in the academic subculture, perhaps greater numbers of students would remain in the academic subculture.[50] Reference librarians should consider how they can assist, or perhaps even foster, reforms that will lead to greater numbers of students remaining in the academic subculture. Such reforms will not, of course, be achieved easily or quickly, but ultimately they will produce more significant results for higher education than would be achieved by courting the nonconformist subculture.

Perhaps the greatest obstacle to the improvement of instruction in higher education is the faculty reward system.

Faculty Reward System

As noted above, Christ contends that an imbalance between teaching and learning is largely responsible for the current malaise in higher education. While Christ's proposals for change, so that students will receive from their instructors the direction and support they deserve, are somewhat unrealistic, he nonetheless focuses on the heart of the problem, i.e., that the pressure on the instructor to publish forces him in his classes to concentrate on content (usually volumes of it) rather than on *how* this content is comprehended by individual students. In other words, the reward system in higher education discourages rather than encourages attention to learning.

In this connection, the conclusions of Siegfried and White are instructive.[51] They maintain that while quality of teaching is considered, research and administrative experience are the primary determinants of faculty salary levels. Moreover, research studies appear to support the popular belief that the faculty reward system at large public universities encourages research, possibly at the expense of teaching quality. Perhaps the most radical suggestion for improving the level of instruction in higher education is that presented by Calvin, a psychologist. Although his criticisms are directed specifically at economics, they could hold for all the social sciences. He asserts that "what is needed is a completely different set of operating principles for our present undergraduate education in economics. The department of economics must be changed so that it assumes the responsibility for setting up a climate so that every student who wants to learn, can learn. . . . Undergraduate instructors should be held accountable and paid on the basis of how well their students learn." Not satisfied with just instructor accountability, Calvin also suggests that "the department administration should be deemed 'good' on the basis of how well the instructors in the department have done in raising the level of their students' peformance.[52] As attractive as his ideas may appear to those concerned with improving undergraduate learning, they are very debatable. Such reforms would, in the end, open the floodgates to interminable arguments over what constitutes learning.

Craft as a Factor in Learning

While the necessity of reform in teaching and learning is generally accepted, the direction it should take has generated much controversy. In their recent survey of the literature "Teaching Technology and Methods in Higher Education,"[53] Cohan, Rose, and Trent note the discouraging results of Dubin and Taveggia's survey of college teaching methods: "The answers are astonishingly clear, (indeed almost unique among behavioral science data in this respect): We cannot claim superiority for any among different teaching methods used to convey subject content to the student."[54]

In his discussion of college curricula, Bayley asserts that:

curriculum reform is insubstantial, superficial and so profoundly safe because it perpetuates rather than overthrows the most deeply rooted assumption in American higher education; namely, that education consists primarily in providing young men and women with knowledge. Learning is achieved, according to unspoken dogma, by students' exposure to subject matter. Schools must confront students with a variety of facts, whether they be events, observations, discoveries, theories, opinions or methods. Education is a matter of being shown, of storing, and of remembering. The prime vehicle for accomplishing this deadly serious purpose is the diversified course curriculum based upon subject matter units. . . . Only a system founded on the acquisition of factual knowledge could be organized in this fashion and could treat so cavalierly the previous educational experience of its students.

This "previous educational experience" he characterizes as one in which students have been introduced in elementary and secondary levels of education to "the fruits of man's intellectual and artistic searching in rich profusion."[55] Rather than repeat this process, albeit in greater depth, Bayley suggests that it would be more logical to have students "use purposefully and insightfully the enormous mass of information they already have." In response to his rhetorical question of what can be done to reform the curriculum, he states that

a fundamentally different view of the learning process must be adopted. It is this: the able, vigorous, creative intellect is distinguished not by what it remembers but by what it does. A creative mind is not one that knows everything; it is not a quiz-show mind. A creative mind is one that interrogates this world around it, posing questions of order and meaning, that never adopts common knowledge without reflection, that can initiate a search for answers to its own questions, and that can communicate lucidly its questing and discovery. Students should not have to defer independent work until they can compete with the best; they should undertake independent work in order to learn what it is the best are doing.

Thinking, he argues, "is a matter of using information well, not of storing it in ever vaster quantities.[56] According to Bok, "to base a college education simply on the acquisition of information and knowledge is to settle for small stakes indeed."[57] Developing the capabilities to which Bayley refers involves helping each student attain "the craft skills of the intellectual."

In anticipation of the objection that it is impossible to make all students, of whatever merit, professional intellectuals, Bayley suggests that "the intellectual, whatever his pretensions, is not someone who thinks in a uniquely different way; he is one who performs the work of the mind better than others."[58]

Bayley's concerns about instruction are, however, more difficult to resolve than we might think. For example, in his discussion of Polanyi's theories on the ideal role of the teacher, Wagener perhaps focuses on the central issue as convincingly as any other critic of teaching. In the process of learning, Wagener says, students "are prone to follow the more persuasive advocate whether he is a more competent scientist or not."[59] Moreover, according to Wagener, Polanyi argues that in order to reach that point of maturity from which an enlightened decision can be made, students must embrace one or the other positions which purport to explain a particular aspect of inquiry and "push its implications out for themselves." Put in such a perspective, it becomes difficult to understand why greater importance is not attached to the quality of instruction.

While the issues Polanyi raises about teaching include some important considerations, they would at least in part be resolved if the reforms Bayley suggests were implemented. Moreover, Bayley does not believe that his reforms, if implemented, would diminish the role of the instructor. On the contrary, "a teacher or scholar should be a model to students not because he does something mysterious and arcane but because he does what everyone needs to do, only he does it at a higher standard of accomplishment." If the "dogma that education consists of acquiring facts is overthrown and the charade of course reshuffling is brought to an end," he states that at least six results would occur.[60]

First, the mark of a successful class would be what happened to the students enrolled rather than how thoroughly or engagingly the subject matter was covered.

Second, the large lecture with its inert audience would cease to be the mainstay of college activity.

Third, teachers would not be able to "can" their courses in advance. They would *create* courses in relation both to the canons of inquiry in their fields and the capacities of individual students to do work in the field.

Fourth, the existing examination system, requiring tests at fixed intervals coinciding with the completed subject matter units, would be scrapped. Instead, tasks would be set for students requiring activity beyond sheer retention.[61] (I believe Bayley would agree that such tests would logically include an effective examination of the extent of and trends in the research literature of the topic.[62])

Fifth, rate of progress in education would be measured substantially according to what individuals accomplished in relation to their own needs, not according to how they stacked up against others.

Sixth, disparate subject matter areas would at long last be effectively related to one another. If students had to act as if facts were to be used, then mediation across subject matter boundaries would occur naturally, as it does for inquiring scholars. Students must begin to see each subject as an opportunity to practice intellectual activity by bringing their individual skill objectives into each encounter with instructors.

If such reforms were carried out, education would be viewed as the learning of a craft. The practice of a craft improves with use and is undertaken not so much to demonstrate proficiency as to show what skills need to be refined so as to achieve greater proficiency. Practice of craft, Bayley asserts, is currently undertaken in athletics, the performing arts, and the physical sciences. "In these areas students perform the work of their specialty under the eyes of their teachers. . . . Exactly like the artist and the scientist, humanists and social scientists need to practice in order to become proficient. There is time in college for basketball practice; there should also be time for history practice, sociology practice, political science practice, and literature practice."[63]

Schein, Bok, and Eble make similar points. Schein, for example, asserts that

almost all learning theories put great emphasis on the need for the learner to make some response which leads to some feedback or information as to the results of his response which, in turn, leads to a better response. Yet most college courses put a student into a passive listening and reading situation for the better part of a semester and then ask him for a single global response in the form of a test or a paper to be written. They [the instructors] provide feedback only in the form of a global evaluation such as a grade. Since there is typically no second chance, there is no incentive to use whatever feedback information was provided. If we used the learning theory, we would assign *multiple drafts* of the paper or demand frequent responses throughout the term so that the feedback could be used during the course to improve performance. In the typical course, the feedback is too little and too late.[64]

It is in the social sciences in particular that greater concern for practice is necessary. Roberts states, for example, that when compared to science, "social science theories are relatively simplified and stylized, while the role of *craftsmanship* and *tacit knowledge* are correspondingly greater."[65] "Moreover," he continues, "in almost all of the disciplines in the social sciences the *craft* aspects of social scientists' knowledge are transmitted through apprenticeship."[66] The reason for Roberts' concern is that he believes that concepts in the social sciences typically lack the precision of those in the natural sciences.

Line shares this concern. He has asserted that "the social sciences are faced with much more severe documentation problems than the pure or applied sciences. Their structure is probably not stable enough for a generally acceptable classification to be produced, and their terminology is extremely fluid."[67] According to both Roberts and Line, because of this lack of precision, craftsmanship in the social sciences must be more rigorous if they are to produce the maximum of logic and persuasiveness.

At the same time, scholars pride themselves in perfecting their craft, because more than anything else it is the element that distinguishes their activities. Ravetz, in Chapter 3 of his excellent *Scientific Knowledge and Its Social Problems*, discusses the issue of "science as craftsman's work"[68] at length and refers to similar examples in the social sciences. Craft is nonetheless a nebulous component in inquiry, particularly in its tacit dimensions. Perhaps more than anything else, it determines to what extent arguments given in explanations are convincing. Along with others mentioned in Part II, Ziman stresses this point.[69] Craft basically comprises rhetoric, writing, and a host of other arts which require painstaking effort to perfect. It is these characteristics of scholarship, of course, that account for the strong apprenticeship component in training in the empirical sciences.

Students' lack of attention to the skills of organizing materials from, in Bayley's words, "disparate subject matter areas," writing coherently, and so forth, has long been decried. While Bayley is one of the more articulate spokesmen in this area, Perry's finding that students have a desire to perfect such skills has given most weight to this concern. In his study of college students' reactions to their education, Perry reports that "one student . . . spontaneously reported as *the standout experience of four years*, a grader's marginal note beside a paragraph the student had felt to be especially meaningful: 'Nice Point.'"[70]

The blame for students' poor writing skills is usually laid at the feet of English departments, as if they have the sole responsibility for giving the whole student body writing instructions. The responsibility should be borne by *all* instructional departments of academic institutions, including the library. To this end, librarians should determine what they can do to encourage greater attention to this neglected aspect of education.

The librarians' role is, of course, determined to a large extent by particular circumstances. Since libraries are already overburdened, they should not have to assume another responsibility. The library can simply draw attention to the multitude of books and related materials concerned with the craft of writing in its broadest aspects. Library reference departments could prepare an annotated list of these materials, thus making them more effectively accessible to students. If such aids were drawn to the attention of instructors, the faculty's valuation of the library in matters of instruction would rise incalculably. Burns, et al., have prepared an excellent bibliography that can assist in this task.[71]

Craft as an element of learning and inquiry is, of course, not limited to matters of writing. In addition, there are problems such as precision and the quantity of subject matter in individual courses for which students are expected to be responsible.

As regards precision in the social sciences, the concerns of Roberts and Line have been noted in connection with the fluidity of terminology. Nagel addresses still another problem of precision in the social sciences:

The laws or generalizations concerning social phenomena made available by current social inquiry are far more restricted in scope of application, are formulated far less precisely, and are acceptable as factually sound only if understood to be hedged in by a far larger number of tacit qualifications and exceptions, than are most of the commonly cited laws of the physical sciences. . . . The issues raised for analysis by the materials selected, as well as the analysis itself, face the analogous hazard of being condemned as either irrelevant to the significant logical problems of social inquiry or as exhibiting a narrow partisan bias toward some particular school of social thought.[72]

These issues raise concern among undergraduate instructors in the social sciences, both in matters of instruction and in research. Indirectly, of course, the library is affected. Most significantly, the existence of the problems to which Nagel refers indicates why some instructors are concerned first about developing the students' capability of manipulating terms and concepts; until this capability is developed to a considerable degree, they are reluctant to permit students to undertake research in the library. (See Chapter 14 for Knapp's experience with this problem in the Monteith College Library experiment.) For those readers interested in following up the issue of precision and related problems in the social sciences, there is a wealth of literature.[73]

The problem of the quantity of subject matter which undergraduate students are expected to absorb also raises some interesting, if not difficult, issues, some of which are touched on in Chapter 2. Anticipating the problems of coming to grips with rapidly growing bodies of scientific literature (and their subsequent rapid obsolescence), Boulding observes "that we must reexamine the whole process of formal education from the point of view of what is the *minimum* knowledge, not the maximum, which must be transmitted if the whole structure is not to fall apart." He emphasizes that "any economizing of learning, therefore, is highly desirable." If, for example, "a single theoretical principle can be shown to apply over a wide area of the empirical world, this is economy in the learning process."[74] Boulding's notion, perhaps more directly than any of those previously mentioned, focuses specifically on the necessity of shifting the emphasis in education from *what* one learns to *how* one learns. In other words, he shares both Bell's and Bayley's viewpoint.

Margenau elaborates a slightly different perspective from Boulding's, but he too is concerned with the quantity of material students are expected to absorb. "True science," he argues,

is not a two-dimensional affair lacking depth, and vertical perspective as the picture puzzle implies; it has a third dimension where facts take root in rational constructs. A surface array of facts may constitute *knowledge*; the very word understanding, however, suggests, a stratum beneath that of facts, a stratum where ideas, laws, and principles unify factual experience and inspire it with scientific significance. . . . The fact-found bias, the hypnosis induced by fixation of our gaze on the obvious and the immediate, has unhappily crept into larger areas far too important for haphazard attention; among them are the teaching of science and international politics.[75]

The deans of engineering schools and medical schools, Margenau continues, are reportedly responsible for filling such courses with facts. According to Margenau, when questioned these same deans deny that such requirements are prescribed. The solution, he argues, requires a reduction of the factual matter set forth, leaving "opportunity to discuss, with student participation, the meaning of the new things learned [and such an opportunity] would open vistas in other fields."

As such, Margenau states, these are "minimum remedies whose desirability seems beyond question." More significant, perhaps, is his notion that "they need to be coupled with a shift of emphasis from induction to deduction in the teaching of elementary science. For it is deductive reasoning which allows the premises, the postulates, the principles that unify our thinking about the world to be placed most clearly in evidence, and it is unfortunate that in our elementary teaching a proper balance between induction and deduction is not often achieved."[76]

Rundell has more specific criticisms of inductive learning. He suggests that "much of the inspiration for the activities of the revisionists has been the educational theories of Jerome Bruner, as stated in the *Process of Education*." According to Rundell, Bruner contends that any child can be taught any discipline's method. Historians sympathetic to such a thesis have attempted to introduce young people to primary sources and to teach them "to reason as historians do in reconstructing the past." Such "educational theorists," Rundell maintains, suggest that what children do not work out for themselves "has little relevance and will quickly be forgotten." However, they maintain, after examining the original materials and arriving at their own conclusions, the learning that occurs will be more permanent. Rundell is alarmed by such thinking: "If this inductive philosophy dominates history teaching in the schools, the implications for the profession in both undergraduate and graduate instruction are manifest."[77]

Other applications of Bruner's theories have enjoyed considerable success. For example, Wise's *American Historical Explanations* is a historian's account of an attempt to integrate certain aspects of cognitive learning (of which inductive learning is a part) into the methodological and substantive aspects of historical research.[78] Clearly, the innovations in teaching employed by Epstein are an example of the reforms suggested by Margenau and Boulding which, at the same time, avoid the inductive trap to which Rundell alludes. Furthermore, Epstein notes his indebtedness to Bruner and to Schwab.[79] A description of a possible application of Epstein's innovations in instruction and library research is given in Chapter 16.

Knowledge, Understanding, and Wisdom

One final note on the idea of craft is appropriate here, namely, that it is necessary to make distinctions among knowledge, understanding, and wisdom. Cassidy suggests that "knowledge is information of all kinds, [which, as well as] the result of analytic activity . . . embraces the [investigation] and reporting, of experience"—although he concedes that "knowledge about" constitutes "a higher level of abstraction." Wisdom, on the other hand, "is more than understanding . . . , [for it] implies not only knowledge and understanding of knowledge, but also understanding of experience in all its subtle and noncognitive aspects."[80] This position is parallel to, among others, that of Polanyi, Ausubel, and Kochen. More attention is given the components of knowledge in Part II.

Notes

1. Sul H. Lee, ed., *Library Orientation; Papers Presented at the First Annual Conference on Library Orientation*, Eastern Michigan University, May 1971 (Ann

Arbor, Mich.: Pierian Press, 1972); P. A. Henning and M. E. Stillman, eds., "Integrating Library Instruction in the College Curriculum," *Drexel Library Quarterly* 7 (July-October 1971) (whole issue); Patricia B. Knapp, *The Monteith College Library Experiment* (New York: Scarecrow Press, 1966); Committee on the Requirements of the Academic User, *Use, Mis-use and Nonuse of Academic Libraries; Proceedings of the New York Library Association, College and University Libraries Section Spring Conference,* Jefferson Community College, May 1970 ([Albany]: College and University Libraries Section, NYLA, n.d.); John Lubans, ed., *Educating the Library User* (New York: Bowker, 1974); ACRL Bibliographic Instruction Task Force, "Toward Guidelines for Bibliographic Instruction in Academic Libraries," *College and Research Libraries News* 36 (May 1975):137-39, 169-70; and Maureen Krier, "Bibliographic Instruction: A Checklist of the Literature, 1971-75," *Reference Services Review* 4 (January-March 1976):9-26.

2. J. M. Brittain, *Information and Its Users* (Bath, England: Bath University Press, 1970), subtitled "A Review with Special Reference to the Social Sciences," is a perceptive and comprehensive survey of this literature to the end of the 1960s. The most thorough study is Maurice B. Line, et al., *Information Requirements of Researchers in the Social Sciences* (Bath, England: University Library, Bath University of Technology, 1971). Line's "Social Scientists'" Information, *SSRC Newsletter* 3 (1968):2-5 is a penetrating appraisal of problems in this area. Robert W. Friedrichs, in *A Sociology of Sociology* (New York: Free Press, 1972), pp. 7 and 17, notes the continuing stress in most of the empirical sciences on limiting the acquisition of subject matter to textbooks during the apprenticeship period. For similar opinions, see J. M. Ziman, *Public Knowledge* (Cambridge, Mass.: Cambridge University Press, 1968), especially p. 7; and Jerome R. Ravetz, *Scientific Knowledge and Its Social Problems* (New York: Oxford University Press, 1971), p. 217. Walter Rundell, *In Pursuit of American History* (Norman, Okla.: University of Oklahoma Press, 1970), is a large survey of present practices concerning the adequacy of graduate student training and research in the United States. This work suggests that recent doctoral candidates in history are not adequately grounded in research methods. Perhaps equally depressing, at least for those who visualize electronic information retrieval from data bases as a panacea, are Line's observations in "Social Scientists' Information," principally because of the fluidity of terminology in the social sciences. The comment by Beth I. Krevitt and Belver C. Griffith in *Evolution of Information Systems: A Bibliography, 1967-1972* (Washington, D.C.: ERIC Clearinghouse on Library and Information Sciences, 1973), p. 3, that "most information systems created for scientists [take] little account of either the *informal or conceptual structure of science,* which clearly guides the scientists' search for information," is a conclusion derived from an examination of the literature of information retrieval. Readers should note, however, that the use of computers for information retrieval remains an essential component of research tasks. Computers make possible certain kinds of research at such great reductions of effort and time compared to manual methods that ignoring their contribution would be unwise. What is required is that a reasonable perspective be employed, one that will allow access to data banks via computers to remain an adjunct to research, i.e., that they be considered another information source and not, in the sense noted by Krevitt and Griffith, as ends in themselves.

3. Selby U. Gration and Arthur P. Young, "Reference-Bibliographers in the College Library," *College and Research Libraries* 35 (January 1974):28-34.

4. Dexter Perkins, "And We Shall Gladly Teach," *American Historical Review* 62 (January 1957):293-4.

5. Peter Caws, "Instruction and Inquiry," *Daedalus* 103 (Fall 1974):21. For a contrary view of the necessity of research as a component of academic life, see Kenneth E. Eble, *Professors as Teachers* (San Francisco: Jossey-Bass, 1972), pp. 152 ff.

6. Joseph Ben-David, *American Higher Education, Directions Old and New* (New York: McGraw-Hill, 1972), p. 115.

7. John J. Siegfried and Kenneth J. White, "Teaching and Publishing as Determinants of Academic Salaries," *Journal of Economic Education* 4 (Spring 1973):90-9.

8. "Model Statement of Criteria and Procedures for Appointment and Promotion in Academic Rank and Tenure for College and University Librarians," *College and Research Libraries News* 34 (September 1973):192-5. Gration and Young, "Reference-Bibliographers in the College Library," pp. 30-31, suggest that "if the lack of faculty status for librarians lowers faculty perceptions of their worth, then librarians must couple their desire for faculty integration with quality performance and educational attainments beyond the basic professional degree."

9. A more active role by librarians in the instruction of students is among the reforms recommended for libraries by the Carnegie Commission on Higher Education. See its *Reform on Campus; Changing Students, Changing Academic Programs* (New York: McGraw-Hill, 1972), especially p. 50. For a discussion of the shift in emphasis from *what* one learns to *how* one learns, see Edgar H. Schein, *Professional Education, Some New Directions* (New York: McGraw-Hill, 1972), pp. 68-9, 130 ff.

10. "Scientific literature," in the context at hand, is the preferred term for the substantive literature commonly called "knowledge." By "scientific literature" is meant the substantive content of the results of disciplined inquiry. For an explanation of why this term is desirable, see Part II.

11. Derek de Sola Price, "Networks of Scientific Papers," *Science* 149 (1965):510-5.

12. David P. Ausubel, "Some Psychological Aspects of the Structure of Knowledge," in *Education and the Structure of Knowledge*, Fifth Annual Phi Delta Kappa Symposium of Educational Research (Chicago: Rand McNally, 1964), pp. 220-62.

13. Michael Polanyi, *Knowing and Being: Essays* (Chicago: University of Chicago Press, 1969), Chapter 10.

14. James W. Wagener, "Toward a Heuristic Theory of Instruction: Notes on the Thought of Michael Polanyi," *Educational Theory* 20 (Winter 1970):46-53.

15. Michael Oakeshott, "Learning and Teaching," in R. S. Peters, ed., *The Concept of Education* (New York: Humanities Press, 1967), pp. 156-76; Caws, "Instruction and Learning," pp. 18-24.

16. Eble, *Professors as Teachers*, p. 177.

17. Thelma Freides, *The Literature and Bibliography of the Social Sciences* (Los Angeles: Melville Publishing Co., 1973), p. 54.

18. Joan Bechtel, "A Possible Contribution of the Library College Idea to Modern Education," *Drexel Library Quarterly* 7 (July-October 1971):195. Evidence of such concern for methods is given by Schein, *Professional Education*, pp. 132 ff.

19. See, for example, Edith Ehrman and Ward Morehouse, *Students, Teachers*

and the Third World in the American College Curriculum: A Guide and Commentary on Innovative Approaches in Undergraduate Education (Albany, N.Y.: Foreign Area Materials Center, University of the State of New York, 1972), pp. 25-6; and William G. Perry, *Forms of Intellectual and Ethical Development in the College Years, A Scheme* (New York: Holt, Rinehart and Winston, 1968). Gene Wise, *American Historical Explanations* (Homewood, Ill.: Dorsey, 1973), pp. 44-45, notes that numerous scholars in several fields ("psychologists and philosophers and sociologists and physicists and economists and linguists and political scientists and art historians and anthropologists and literary critics and biologists and educators and clinical therapists and at least one product consultant in industry") share the view that man "intuitively tries to cope with his world and make sense out of it by patterning things, constructing schemes of reality . . . [by seeking] to impose form." As Wise observes, this view is generally labeled the "cognitive view." The core concern of these scholars is the problem of comprehension and retention. Prominent among them are Jerome Bruner, Kenneth Boulding, Thomas Kuhn, Daniel Bell, and Joseph Schwab, all of whom are cited in this book to support arguments concerning the structure and function of reference works.

20. Ausubel, "Some Psychological Aspects of the Structure of Knowledge."

21. Patricia Knapp, "The Meaning of the Monteith College Library Program for Library Education," *Journal of Education for Librarianship* 6 (Fall 1965):111-27.

22. For criticisms of the characteristics of currently popular inductive modes of inquiry, see Rundell, *In Pursuit of American History*, p. 33.

23. D. J. Foskett, "Problems of Indexing and Classifiction in the Social Sciences," *International Social Science Journal* 23 (1971):244-55. The quoted passage is on p. 247.

24. Knapp, *Monteith College Library Experiment*, p. 69.

25. Maurice Line, "Information Services in Academic Libraries," in *Educating the Library User; Proceedings of the Fourth Triennial Meeting of the International Association of Technology Libraries* (Loughborough, England: University of Technology Library, 1970), p. B-3.

26. Rundell, *In Pursuit of American History*, p. 33. Perry, in *Forms of Intellectual and Ethical Development*, makes similar observations.

27. Bechtel, "A Possible Contribution of the Library College Idea to Modern Education," p. 195.

28. For a discussion of this issue, see William A. Katz, *Introduction to Reference Work* (New York: McGraw-Hill, 1974), II. pp. 61-65.

29. Herman T. Epstein, *A Strategy for Education* (New York: Oxford University Press, 1970).

30. S. L. Washburn, "Evolution and Education," *Daedalus* 103 (Fall 1974):221-8.

31. Daniel Bell, *The Reforming of General Education* (New York: Columbia University Press, 1966), pp. 157-8.

32. Ibid., p. 164.

33. Ibid., p. 165.

34. Margaret Mead, "Why Is Education Obsolescent?" *Harvard Business Review* 36 (1958):30-4.

35. Gerald Gurin, "The Impact of the College Experience," in Stephen B. Withey, ed., *A Degree and What Else? Correlates and Consequences of a College Education*

(New York: McGraw-Hill, 1971), p. 49. For a similar conclusion, see Joseph Axelrod, et al., *Search for Relevance: The Campus in Crisis* (San Francisco: Jossey-Bass, 1969), p. 179. Perry's *Forms of Intellectual and Ethical Development*, an empirical study of the stages of intellectual growth, contains much valuable information for reference librarians. More details about Perry's finding are given in Chapter 3. See particularly note 22.

36. For more on this trend, see Gary K. Wolfe and Carol Williams, "All Education Is 'Adult Education': Some Observations on Curriculum and Profession in the Seventies," *AAUP Bulletin* 60 (September 1974):291-5; and Stephen R. Graubard, "University Cities in the Year 2000," *Daedalus* 96 (Summer-Fall 1967):817-22. The passage from Wolfe and Williams is on p. 291.

37. See Lawrence E. Dennis and Joseph F. Kauffman, eds., *The College and the Student* (Washington, D.C.: American Council on Education, 1966); Charlotte Hickman Mills, "The Wabash Project: A Centrifugal Program," *Drexel Library Quarterly* 7 (July-October 1971):371-4 (Appendix: "Suggested Readings to Orient Librarians to Today's Students and Their Search for Self in a Context of Change and Anomaly"); David H. Bayley, "The Emptiness of Curriculum Reform," *Journal of Higher Education* 43 (November 1972):591-600; and Robert G. Gregory, "Africana Archives and Innovative Teaching: The Teacher-Scholar's New Need for Research Materials," *Africana Library Journal* 2 (Winter 1971):18-20.

38. Bayley, "Emptiness of Curriculum Reform."

39. John Christ, *Toward a Theory of Educational Librarianship* (Littleton, Colo.: Libraries Unlimited, 1972), p. 94. For a similar observation, see Schein, *Professional Education*, pp. 133 ff. "Most professors tend to have only a rudimentary theory of learning and one that is likely to be based only on their own past experience and that of colleagues in their own discipline" (p. 144). Eble, *Professors as Teachers*, pp. 162 ff., argues that "teaching" and "learning" are really different sides of the same coin, a perspective that I find more convincing than Christ's. Eble argues further (pp. 182-3) that he senses a stronger interest in the improvement of instruction among professors.

40. Patricia Knapp, *The Library, The Undergraduate and the Teaching Faculty* (San Diego: The University Library, University of California, 1970), pp. 6, 39.

41. Ibid., p. 38.

42. Robert T. Blackburn, "College Libraries—Indicated Failures: Some Reasons and a Possible Remedy," *College and Research Libraries* 29 (March 1968):171-7.

43. Burton R. Clark and Martin Trow, *Determinants of College Student Subcultures* (Berkeley, Calif.: Center for the Study of Higher Education, University of California, 1960) (mimeo). Reprinted as "The Organizational Context," in Theodore Newcomb and E. Wilson, eds., *College Peer Groups: Problems and Prospects for Research* (Chicago: Aldine, 1966).

44. Jonathan R. Warren, "Student Perceptions of College Subcultures," *American Educational Research Journal* 58 (March 1968):213-32.

45. Knapp, *The Library, the Undergraduate, and the Teaching Faculty*, p. 14.

46. For a similar opinion, see Robert A. Pois, "The Lecture-Textbook Syndrome and Library Use," in Lubans, ed., *Educating the Library User*, pp. 185-6.

47. Laura E. Grieneeks, "Changes in Student Role Orientation Toward College," *Proceedings of the 77th Annual Convention of the American Psychological Association 1969* (Washington, D.C.: American Psychological Society, 1970), p. 656.

48. Perry, *Forms of Intellectual and Ethnical Development*, pp. 211-5.

49. David A. Kolb, "Individual Learning Styles and the Learning Process" (Cambridge, Mass., 1971), p. 15 (mimeo).

50. Nicholas Hobbs, "The Art of Getting Students into Trouble," in Dennis and Kauffman, eds., *The College and the Student*, as cited by Grieneeks, "Changes in Student Role Orientation Toward College," p. 656.

51. Siegfried and White, "Teaching and Publishing as Determinants of Academic Salaries," pp. 96-7.

52. Allan D. Calvin, "A Psychologist Looks at the 'Teaching' of Economics at the Undergraduate Level," in Keith G. Lumsden, ed., in *Recent Research in Economics Education* (Englewood Cliffs, N.J.: Prentice-Hall, 1970), pp. 20-3.

53. Arthur M. Cohan, Clare Rose, and James W. Trent, "Teaching Technology and Methods," in Robert M. Travers, ed., *Second Handbook of Research on Teaching* (Chicago: Rand McNally, 1973), pp. 1023-35.

54. Robert Dubin and Thomas C. Taveggia, *The Teaching-Learning Paradox; A Comparative Analysis of College Teaching Methods* (Eugene, Ore.: Center for the Advanced Study of Educational Administration, 1968), p. VIII.

55. Bayley, "Emptiness of Curriculum Reform," pp. 592-3.

56. Ibid., p. 595.

57. Derek Bok, "On the Purposes of Undergraduate Education," *Daedalus* 103 (Fall 1974):163.

58. Bayley, "Emptiness of Curriculum Reform," p. 596.

59. Wagener, "Toward a Heuristic Theory of Instruction," p. 81.

60. The following is a paraphrase of Bayley's arguments. See Bayley, "Emptiness of Curriculum Reform," pp. 596-9.

61. According to Bayley, "There are professors who deliberately—one might say defiantly—disregard matters of expression and organization in evaluating written examinations. They argue that, first, such matters are handled in other courses and therefore they cannot consider them; and that, second, one student cannot be allowed an edge because of qualities brought to the class in unequal amounts." Such problems are resolved by acknowledging that *"a term's grade should be based on a term's work, not on skills acquired before the term."* Ibid., p. 598. (Emphasis added.)

62. In another context, but nonetheless related to the issue, Borrowman voices a concern about the growing emphasis of "Performance-Based Evaluation of History Teaching"; see Merle Borrowman, "Performance-Based Evaluation of Teaching," *AHA Newsletter II* (May 1973):18-21.

63. Bayley, "Emptiness of Curriculum Reform," pp. 590-600.

64. Schein, *Professional Education*, p. 141. For Bok, see "On the Purposes of Undergraduate Education," p. 171; for Eble, see *Professors as Teachers*, p. 177.

65. Marc J. Roberts, "On the Nature and Condition of Social Science," *Daedalus* 103 (1974):47. (Emphasis added.)

66. Ibid., p. 51.

67. Line, "Social Scientists' Information," p. 3.

68. Ravetz, *Scientific Knowledge and Its Social Problems*, Chapter 3.

69. Ziman, *Public Knowledge*, and Ziman, "Information, Communication, Knowledge," in T. Saracevic, ed., *Introduction to Information Science* (New York: Bowker, 1971), pp. 76-84.

70. Perry, *Forms of Intellectual and Ethical Development*, p. 213. (Emphasis added.)

71. Shannon Burns, et al., *An Annotated Bibliography of Texts on Writing Skills* (New York: Garland Publishing Co., 1976).

72. Ernest Nagel, *The Structure of Science* (New York: Harcourt, Brace and World, 1961), pp. 449-50.

73. For more discussion of the problem of precision in social science, see Kaplan, *Conduct of Inquiry*, especially pp. 76-7, and 203-4. Rundell, *In Pursuit of American History*, provides a useful (and enlightening) survey of historians' views of methods in the social sciences. Particularly noteworthy are the opinions expressed by the more traditionally oriented historians toward the application of quantitative instruments developed in the behavioral sciences to history. This issue is explored, at least indirectly, in Part II, in connection with idiographic and nomothetic modes of explanation in the social sciences. Of greater concern in the present context, however, since it affects instruction are Landes and Tilly's observations in *History as Social Science* (Englewood Cliffs, N.J.: Prentice-Hall, 1971) that in teaching, historians are prone to "untidy" generalizations. (See especially p. 81.) Similar comments are readily available in other sources, some of which are touched on in Chapter 3.

74. Kenneth Boulding, *Eiconics* (Ann Arbor, Mich.: University of Michigan Press, 1961), p. 163.

75. Henry Margenau, *Open Vistas* (New Haven, Conn.: Yale University Press, 1961), pp. 29-30.

76. Ibid., 32-3.

77. Rundell, *In Pursuit of American History*, p. 33.

78. Wise, *American Historical Explanations*.

79. Herman T. Epstein, *A Strategy for Education* (Oxford: Oxford University Press, 1970).

80. Harold G. Cassidy, "Liberation and Limitation," in Francis Sweeney, ed., *The Knowledge Explosion* (New York: Farrar, Straus and Giroux, 1966), pp. 187-8.

2 The Dimensions of the Opportunity: The Evidence for Reform in Teaching and Learning in Higher Education

Examples of the low esteem attached to teaching in the social sciences in higher education can be derived from volumes of the recent Behavioral and Social Sciences Survey conducted under the auspices of the Committee on Science and Public Policy of the National Academy of Sciences and the Problems and Policy Committee of the Social Science Research Council.[1] However, these works also show that, for the most part, a desire to strengthen instruction prevails. Unfortunately, a viable means of implementing such desires remains elusive.[2]

Currently, "in most fully developed sciences a student is not likely to be pushed beyond acquiring textbook knowledge until he moves on to his own creative research."[3] At the same time, there is much evidence that many instructors are not satisfied with the lecture-textbook mode of learning.[4] Perhaps the best indication of such dissatisfaction is the increasing utilization of the so-called inquiry modes of learning.[5] Further, individual instructors attach varying degrees of importance to teaching, and many have published material relating to their teaching activities. The recent publication of *Teaching Sociology, Teaching Political Science, History Teacher,* and the *Journal of Economic Education* is tangible evidence of such concern. Another example is the regularly featured section of the *AHA Newsletter,* "Teaching Experiments in Undergraduate History." Each month historians describe courses they have conducted which employ innovative concepts of instruction. Nonetheless, the kind of reform discussed below will not be implemented until disciplines (through groups of instructor-researchers) officially adopt a policy of greater commitment to problems of instruction. How will library programs be affected?

Evidence of commitment to reform in teaching which affects academic libraries is not difficult to find. Area specialists appear to be the most concerned. For example, Gregory, an African historian, observes that "recent innovations in undergraduate instruction have created a new opportunity and need in American universities and colleges of a primary nature." Research in primary sources, traditionally introduced at the postgraduate level, "is now being adopted by the undergraduate teacher as an essential component of experimental teaching methodology." Gregory notes that it has generally been assumed that undergraduate students become acquainted with the important secondary sources before being introduced to the primary sources as graduate students. Such instructional activities, of course, have inevitably

determined library policy and fostered a widespread student dissatisfaction. It requires a library composed mainly of texts and compendiums of readings, and secondly of as many supporting monographs, biographies, and autobiographies as budgets will permit. Primary material is accorded the lowest priority. The system in its entirety has been subjected to severe criticism and is deemed responsible, at least in part, for the recent student dissatisfaction evident not only in the United States, but also Africa and other parts of the world. Within the last six years, partly in response to student apathy and protest, a new teaching methodology stressing the use of primary materials has evolved. . . . Courses stressing research with primary sources were introduced at Syracuse for undergraduate history majors. At the University of California, Santa Barbara, Dr. Brian Fagan . . . developed a revolutionary survey course in which students pursued individual research projects in learning the fundamentals of anthropology/archaeology. . . . The new methodology requires a library with a sizeable holding of promary material. . . . This mode of instruction, of course, entails unusual problems of concept and organization. The large undergraduate course is no longer practicable and has to be divided into small seminars. Objectives, requirements, and procedures have to be carefully delineated at the beginning of each course. Once students understand the fundamentals, however, a continued instruction or close supervision on the old model is neither necessary nor desirable. Instructors have to step down from the lectern to a level of equality with students on which together they pursue research into new subjects, draw hypotheses, and formulate conclusions.[6]

Although Gregory is one of a few among faculty publishing their concerns about acquisitions policies of academic libraries, he is not alone among them in his concern about the desirability of changing the role of the library in the education of undergraduate students. What follows is a discipline-by-discipline survey in the social sciences of what representative groups of academics consider appropriate reforms in undergraduate education. Particular attention is directed to their thoughts on independent study and other research-related activities.

Anthropology

The Behavioral and Social Sciences Survey volume on anthropology maintains that in undergraduate instruction great stimulus must be given "interfield and interdisciplinary interests":

One of the most important trends of the past twenty years has been the emergence of problems that span disciplines or require the merging of two or more subfields of anthropology. This development has not been accompanied by the disappearance of the specialized concerns of the archaeologist or cultural anthropologist; it has been additive rather than substitutive. Anthropology has been reinvigorated by the emergence of these new, field-interlocking problems. The conviction is now strong that, in spite of centrifugal tendencies generated by intense specialization, it must remain a single discipline. Nonetheless, every evidence portends a further intensification of the current blurring of the division within the profession in an expanding number of areas, as well an increasing development of intellectual problems that attract anthropologists with quite different field interests. This creative, dynamic character of the profession has important implictions that must be widely recognized by the discipline and that create opportunities upon which constructive action must be taken as promptly and fully as possible. Curriculum design and graduate degree requirements must reflect these realities. No longer can all students be expected to follow a single training pattern toward an essentially identical goal through much of their advanced program. Anthropology is now too complex, with too many specialities, too great a range of techniques, too broad a knowledge base, and too many areas of overlap with other disciplines. The objective for most graduate students can no longer be mastery of an exhaustive body of facts, concepts, and methodologies across the full spectrum of anthropology. Most, or perhaps all, newly trained professionals should possess a similar broad core of basic knowledge, embracing all four subfields of the discipline. But this requirement must not be so demanding as to prevent its being attained early in the graduate program—by the MA level or, *where broad and extensive contact with anthropology has been achieved in the BA program, even earlier.* Beyond this point great flexibility is desirable. . . .[7]

In order to achieve greater student involvement in learning anthropology, courses of independent study under faculty members or capable graduate students should be implemented.[8] Readers should note that although graduate level studies are the main focus of the discussion, concern is expressed as well for undergraduate education.

As mentioned earlier, the reward system for professors is so structured that low esteem is attached to teaching; such low esteem, of course, adversely affects the instructor's approach to teaching. The disciplines need to achieve a more desirable balance between research and instruction. This balance can be attained first by informing instructors of how it is possible to achieve greater undergraduate involvement in research activities, and concomitantly by providing a means whereby comprehension and retention of the substantive content of disciplines can be improved. Second, through curriculum change students at all levels must be made more self-sufficient in research, particularly in their ability to exploit research materials in the library.

More insight into how this balance between teaching and research can be achieved, as well as more evidence of the increasing concern for teaching anthropology at the undergraduate level, is found in Mandelbaum, Lasker, and Albert's *The Teaching of Anthropology,* a large volume of some 600 pages with 46 contributors.[9] The size of the volume and the number of contributors indicate the importance of teaching among anthropologists.

The observations of one contributor, are particularly valid, for they not only apply to the subfield of anthropology with which he is concerned (physical anthropology), but also to teaching in general: "The instructors must teach students, not subjects."[10] Mandelbaum, however, reminds us of the ever-present dilemma in anthropology as well as all disciplines: "Anthropologists are trained to be research workers, not teachers." All the papers reflect the conviction that more than any other discipline, anthropology embraces "as many phases of life as does the particular reality which is being studied [which] is in contrast with other ways of studying man, in which disciplinary boundaries are more narrowly defined and problems outside the defined limits are not seriously examined."[12]

Mandelbaum's concern for improving the quality of term papers should be of particular interest to librarians. Not unexpectedly his main concern is the quality of term papers. "Term papers," he says "are too often done in so listless a manner as to have little worth. The obvious difficulty is that of securing competent readers to help the teacher. . . . When students do more writing in anthropology courses and have their work carefully reviewed, the lasting effectiveness of the teaching will be greatly enhanced." Mandelbaum acknowledges that a call for restoration of student writing is not unique to anthropology. However, he states "it may be that anthropologists, invigorated by the record and promise of their discipline, well regarded and encouraged in various quarters, can be among the leaders in setting new standards for higher education in the United States."[13] In his discussion of teaching methods, Mandelbaum states that writing "provides students with the opportunity to exercise their own resources and stimulates them to use knowledge in a context other than that of the usual examination."[14] Nonetheless, in a statement much like one by Knapp[15] that instructors are unsatisfied with the quality of student papers, Mandelbaum takes a dim view of the ordinary term paper. "Since [students] are reporting their own observations they are less likely to paraphrase what has been written or to string together excerpts from authoritative statements." Mandelbaum highlights one other continuing problem in higher education: the practice of giving the student in the typical introductory course the sole "intellectual role [of being a] passive spectator, temporarily holding on bits of information which may be useful in passing a coded examination. He labels this practice "a common blight of American higher education . . . The resultant improvement in student learning [derived from writing thoughtfully conceived term papers] is well worth the additional time and effort which these assignments require.[16]

Lasker expresses similar sentiments about term papers. In his discussion of the introductory course in physical anthropology, he states that "if it is practicable . . . the writing of a term paper should be assigned" but in order to give such an assignment "maximum value . . . , instead of requesting merely reviews of books and articles, they [the teachers] call for some synthesis of the students' own experience in laboratory exercises with the literature of the subject."[17] Whatever kind of writing assignment is given, "everything that gives the student the experience of acting like a professional—investigating, discussing, writing, editing, and abstracting—will prove valuable in presenting physical anthropology as a science. I do not believe that this will be at the expense of acquisition of knowledge. Rather it should stimulate the mastery of the necessary grounding in fact." Finally, he echoes Mandelbaum (see note 16 above) when he states that "in the writing of term papers students should be encouraged to combine any commentary about articles they have read with an analysis of their own data accumulated in the field or laboratory."[18]

Hewes believes that anthropologists "have been doing a good job of threatening the naive ethnocentrism of our students, but perhaps less well in challenging their minds." To him, the obvious way to get students more fully engaged in undergraduate anthropology courses is to require them to "write more and better reports, based in part on *recent* journal literature." If such assignments are required, students must exercise more judgment and selection than when they use only a single book.[19]

In an article entitled "The Anthropologist in the Methodology of Teaching," French suggests that a single textbook "eliminates the tantalizing discrepancies that can encourage students to become involved in the current problems of the discipline" and that "some contact with journal literature would seem to be desirable, even in introductory courses."[20] French also stresses the position expressed throughout this volume: for the maximum of learning and retention to occur, good teaching requires active student participation.

Perhaps the most stimulating paper in the volume among many excellent papers is Casagrande's "The Relations of Anthropology with the Social Sciences." With regard to what he would expect anthropology students to derive from study in another discipline, he states:

it is important to learn not facts or the content of a discipline so much as its distinctive modes of thinking and inquiry; the theoretical frameworks employed, and from a more philosophical perspective the particular image of man that emerges from a discipline's working assumptions and its "way of knowing." At least as important then as learning the results of work in other fields is learning the kinds of questions that are posed, the concepts and methods employed, and the ways in which evidence is obtained, analyzed, and marshalled to answer the questions. . . . In cross-cutting disciplines, in addition to teaching what is distinctive to each, one might pay particular attention to what could be called "linking concepts," i.e., those that are actually or potentially useful for two or more disciplines. Prime examples of linking concepts are status and role, which serve effectively as a tri-disciplinary conceptual and theoretical bridge among psychology, sociology and social anthropology.

Personality, social structure, social systems and other global concepts as well as concepts of more limited scope, such as reference group, might also fall in this category of "linking concepts."

Casagrande recognizes that such an ambitious undertaking may raise objections from fellow anthropologists. He candidly admits that "it is ironic that we often expect our students after taking a prescribed assortment of courses in several social science fields themselves to achieve an almost miraculous integration of them when we, their teachers, are indifferent, incapable, or not inclined to do so."[21]

With regard to library research, specifically to how anthropology students can exploit library materials, discussions in the above sources demonstrate anthropologists' general lack of exposure to the range of literature in the field available in libraries. For example, the Bath University study conducted by Line reports that "demands for, and uses of, information are partly a function of real and expected availability."[22] The Bath study also finds that "in fact social scientists rarely make rational and systematic use of bibliographic tools," preferring "instead, less systematic methods. . . . The logical sequence of information, document searching, proceeding from tertiary and secondary bibliographical tools to the primary literature, is not followed."[23] The study concludes that "ignorance of existence of information . . . is largely a matter of exposure." Awareness, it suggests,

can be achieved partly by more efficient methods of exposure . . . and by user education in the use of bibliographical tools. . . . Also opportunities for multiple exposure might be required: a second or a third exposure to the same information, perhaps in different contexts, might affect judgment or relevance. The problem of unarticulated needs (due to lack of exposure and knowledge) was not limited to areas of peripheral interest; . . . in some cases researchers were ignorant of fairly large and important areas of knowledge related to their primary research interest.[24]

At least in part, these anthropologists' seeming lack of recognition of opportunities for engaging students in greater amounts of independent inquiry was caused by the relatively unorganized state of anthropology literature at the time, rather than by the anthropologists' lack of exposure. Mandelbaum's 1963 study was conducted before many of the bibliographical materials now common to anthropology were available. For example, the *Biennial Review of Anthropology* was initiated only in 1959. Moreover, the majority of other bibliographical publications for anthropology were started within the last decade. For more on these problems of anthropological research, see the articles by Amsden and Currier.[25]

Rowe has pointed out some of the problems which anthropologists encounter in using library material with regard to monographs and other related materials listed in card catalogues, he states that each subject has its own peculiar library problem, and anthropology has some especially serious ones. In the first place, the systems of organization used in most general libraries in the United States make it especially difficult for anthropologists to find the literature of their field. Library materials are organized for the reader's use in two ways: by call numbers and by subject headings in the catalogue. . . . The systems of call numbers now used in most general libraries were devised and put into practice many years ago when anthropology was generally visualized as a very small subject, and its point of view was familiar to few readers. . . . [Thus] the literature of anthropology is scattered from religion and philosophy to warfare and marine transportation. This situation may have the advantage of calling the attention of an occasional reader from another field to anthropological contributions relating to his interest, but it creates undeniable difficulties for anthropology students.

On the other hand, Library of Congress subject headings "are designed to help the 'general reader' who knows no anthropology, and the categories which are familiar to students of anthropology are either not represented at all or appear under unfamiliar names."[26]

Rowe's solution to such problems is to establish separate specialized libraries which will provide access to the literature through "analytical cataloguing." Such libraries would be so expensive, however, that few institutions would be able to afford them. (Readers should note, of course, that Rowe was writing before 1963; the G. K. Hall publishing firm made the Harvard Peabody Museum Catalog available for mass purchase in 1963.)

Economics

Economics evidently does not share the concerns of the other social sciences for enlarging the inquiry component of learning. This conclusion is based on a fairly complete examination of the literature of the teaching of economics in higher education. Economics has a rather large literature of teaching, a fact which suggests that the discipline is currently undergoing a period of intense self-examination. Its chief concern is that it tends to be sterile and unfeeling, with an almost clinical attitude toward social issues. Evidently, increasing numbers of economists want to humanize their discipline, to relate it more directly to social problems. More significantly, it is seeking to improve instruction, particularly at the introductory level. With regard to the introductory course, however, Lewis of the Ford Foundation cynically observes that in general

the simple fact is that by and large, across and throughout our profession, the teaching of the introductory course, apart from the logical problems it poses, is the very least of our concerns. *We teach this course with our left hand in our pocket,* . . . The introductory course is worth all the concerned attention we can give it, for what it can contribute to the rational, enlightened conduct of our society's economic affairs. . . . We owe it to them and to ourselves to constitute and package, and everlastingly to reconstitute and repackage our product so that everyone, in fact will buy. . . . The format of the course, its material and its emphasis should be shaken up and repatterned year after year without cease—to shake up and rethread the mind of the shaker, and to demonstrate to students that learning is for everyone, not least a restless teacher.[27]

Lewis and Orvis express similar opinions when introducing the materials listed and described in *Research in Economic Education*. They note a paucity of research on substantive content of courses:

the bulk of those studies which have been published in the *American Economic Review* have been preoccupied with a shuffling around of chapters and topics, with alternative approaches such as "problems" or "case study," and with alternative techniques and media such as programming, instructional television, and computer-assisted instruction.

While Lewis and Orvis assure us that there is a need for such articles, they state that the issue of content has rarely

been forthrightly considered in the literature. A course or curriculum must be viewed in its entirety and evaluated accordingly. Only rarely have there been coordinated attempts to evaluate or research all three dimensions of a course or curriculum in economics—the *goals, content and the techniques and resources or media*. Equally critical needs exist for more research into a host of related questions. What *content* should we teach as distinct from which *techniques or method* should we use? What are the opportunity costs (goal trade-offs) of trading-off some breadth of coverage or fewer concepts with greater depth?[28]

Lewis and Orvis's bibliography contains over 130 articles on economics education in general (including elementary and secondary levels); at least two interesting facts are apparent among the articles in this bibliography. First, there is considerable concern for retention of subject matter. Examples include two articles by Bach and Saunders,[29] and a study by Dawson and Bernstein.[30] Second, no concern is directed toward independent inquiry by undergraduates. Rather surprisingly, the volume on economics in the Behaviorial and Social Science Survey does not address the issue of undergraduate education.[31]

One promising experiment in economics instruction is that conducted by Weckstein of Brandeis University.[32] His mode of instruction, which is the same as biologist Epstein's (described in Chapter 13), is a bold departure from the traditional, but it has not received sufficient attention. This is unfortunate, for it would lend economics courses greater interest and student involvement—ingredients that, at least as characterized by Lewis, are currently lacking in the majority of introductory economics courses. My attention was directed to Weckstein by biologist Epstein in *A Strategy for Education*.[33] (Part II reports that the heuristic methods employed by Epstein and Weckstein hold much promise for learning and that the research methods students become acquainted with in these courses seem to be a subsidiary result.)

Weckstein makes the following observations about the introductory level economics courses he conducted at Brandeis University in the 1960s:

1) the text assisted presentation that is accepted as the standard is more gratifying to the compulsive needs of the instructor who is a professional economist than it is to the uninitiated student;

2) the nice division of topics and the logic of the sequence of their presentation are neither necessary nor do they conform to the needs of students who are being introduced to the subject for the first time.

3) the approach [Weckstein's] starts the beginning student of economics with the material that is a product of the working professional instead of some ersatz version, distilled of the true product, neatly ordered, and simple.

Weckstein concludes that

on the basis of performance on a standardized objective examination at the end of the semester, the class . . . did about as well as they might have been expected to after a conventional course. . . . I doubt that they are quite as well versed in the description of the tools of microeconomics as students in standard courses. But I would think they understand more about the uses of the standard tools in applied work.[34]

One reason why economics generally downplays undergraduate research is, of course, the fact that the discipline has a very broad mathematical component. Most practitioners must be grounded in the mathematics of the subject matter before any independent research can be meaningful. (Weckstein's success appears to be an exception.) The necessity of such grounding is not a characteristic of the other social sciences, although many of the more traditional-minded instructors in these disciplines might deny it.

Rich opportunities exist for undergraduate research in economics. Its core literature is blessed with perhaps the best organized bibliographical apparatus of any social science.[35] In general, it is fairly easy for undergraduate students, using the American Economic Association's *Indexes*, to gain access to the substantive literature of economics. The history of economic thought and economic history, however, do present some problems of research inasmuch as the primary sources for these areas do not fall neatly into classification schemes.[36]

Geography

The chapter on recommendations in *Geography*, that discipline's contribution to the Behavioral and Social Science Survey, makes no mention of any issues involved in undergraduate education. Clues as to this seeming unconcern with the problem can be found in Lavalle's "Assessing Recent Trends in Undergraduate Geographic Training in American Universities and Colleges." Lavalle cites the differences in teaching among private, public, doctoral and nondoctoral granting institutions. "Within the last two decades," he states, "American geographers have been involved in a serious reevaluation of their undergraduate college and university curricula." This reevaluation has been motivated by (1) "the increased demand for geographers in education, government, and industry; (2) the increasing concern on the part of many professional geographers to firmly establish geography in its rightful place among the sciences; and (3) the revolutionary changes in geographic technology."[37]

After tracing the history of the development of geography as a discipline in American universities and colleges, Lavalle concludes that "one of the most significant and recent developments in contemporary geographic curricula has been the inclusion of quantitative methodology in some of the traditional geography courses and the addition of specialized quantitative techniques courses to many geography programs." Coincident with this increased emphasis on quantification are the attempts to stress the theoretical bases of the discipline stemming from the desire to place it on a more solid scientific footing. Such changes merely reflect similar occurrences in other social science disciplines. In geography "this represents a trend away from the more traditional emphasis on the description of areas, but this phenomenon seems to be currently restricted to a small number of American institutions."[38]

When he introduced a volume of original papers presented at the American Association of Geographers' annual meeting in Kansas City in 1972, Helburn readily admits that "the inadequate response [to matters related to instruction] can be explained partly by inertia complicated by tenure." More specifically, he is convinced that the reward system is primarily "in favor of recognizing research, rather than quality of teaching."

His proposed solution is as follows:

If we can establish within the discipline a subset of geographers concerned with and skilled in the nature of geographic learning; if we can keep them in touch with each other; if we can build upon each other's research and practice, then we can make the reward system of the university work to improve geographic learning. Our success will be its own reward in the upward spiral of better learning, more interested students, higher reputation among disciplines, higher quality students, better in-

structional materials, and so on. . . . Who knows but that our lesson might be learned
and imitated by other disciplines, and colleges and universities might be saved from
fossilization.[39]

Hill, on the other hand, worries about the dangers of "fossilization." In a
paper in *Geography*, he suggests that "several signals tell us that American
academia has reached the end of the period of affluence and growth. We
need new guides to track in a new environment, one in which our reflexes
learned from the past are likely to prove nonadaptive."[40] "Creative teaching," he declares, "does more than transmit knowledge—*it generates it.*"[41]
A creative teacher

strives . . . for creative synthesis between knowing and the ways of knowing, which
is a process of having his students both learn the content of the subject matter and
learn how to learn. Content *per se* is not the measure of significance for his students;
rather it is the process of content as taught. Content (what is being learned) and
process (how learning is occurring) are strongly interpendent (but certainly not in a
simple way). The degree of subject matter learning is strongly dependent on how
well process learning is accomplished. This necessitates different teaching strategies,
materials, and experiences for different content and often for different students—his
experimentation centers on these interacting variables. . . . Acquisition of information *per se* takes low priority on his list of objectives. Learning how to better find
information ranks higher, and the ability to use it in the conceptual work of problem-
solving and decision-making ranks higher still.[42]

Ball seeks to infuse teaching with a more humanistic element, stressing in
particular that the affective component should be integrated with the "stark,
barren confines of intellectualism" that comprises the cognitive realm. "If
we were to apply the same kind of rigor for analyzing the components for
learning as we do for our own research, I think we would change a number
of things about [the traditional model of instructor]." He agrees with Grieneeks that "the trouble is that the traditional model for learning into which
we may force [students] is one designed to destroy their inherent desire,
need, and energy for learning."

According to Ball, the problem is that geography teaching gives too much
attention to content coverage. College level geography teachers "have been
unable or unwilling to see that covering material and helping students learn
are two different things." Usually, covering the material means following
the textbook, our own intellectual pursuits, or some other guide.

On the other hand,

if our concern is helping students learn, then we must cast ourselves in quite a different role—a role that, for me at least, was foreign, uncomfortable, and one for

which I was poorly trained. But, since my graduate work, if nothing else, did provide me with a model for learning, I did not feel completely helpless. Later I discovered another problem, one that I was reluctant to recognize and one that I have
not yet solved: that is, that I am part of the problem. The breaking of a behavior
and attitude pattern does not come easily, and yet I find for myself that this is essential if I am to interact with students in a way that I can assume a role of helping them
to learn.[43]

Gardner employs a slightly different argument to arrive at much the same
conclusions as Ball and Hill. He observes that though

the academic community has stressed research and teaching through a reward structure that reflects a fascination with mechanization and technological development in
society generally, research has come to be honored over teaching. *Ideally, at the
college level, both should be highly interrelated.* In practice, teaching has come to be
perceived as an impediment to productive and competitive research. . . . Time is an
important ingredient in learning process. The academic system does not accord the
same luxury to those other learners, the students. . . . Our system of formal education, specifically at the college level, is made artificial by constraints that make
information unavailable, and therefore does not give practice in the recognition
and utilization of information sources.[44]

In my opinion, Kohn's contribution addresses the problem of geography
candidly and realistically. According to him, professional geographers have
become aware that they themselves must take the lead in reforming geography
teaching. Above all, if any worthwhile change in teaching is expected to
occur "top-ranking scholars in our profession, and departments of geography
in our leading universities," must address the problems of "teacher training,
curriculum development, the preparation of appropriate teaching materials,
the development of stimulating learning activities, and good teaching at the
undergraduate level."[45]

Thus, these papers constantly reiterate the idea that many instructors in
the geography profession share with Ball, Hill, Gardner, and others the
desire to place greater emphasis on teaching. Hill claims that these instructors are "in close communication, sharing ideas and materials," and that,
not surprisingly, they "identify themselves . . . first as teachers researching
teaching." This is their "most important reference group. Many, but not all
of them, are other geography teachers. Other disciplines have similar groups."[46]
If such groups do indeed exist, and there is no reason to think otherwise,
reference librarians concerned about undergraduate education should join
forces with them. It seems far more sensible to join with these people in
implementing well-planned activities than, as Knapp suggests, to appeal to
the nonconformist student.

History

In *History as Social Science*, the history volume in the Behavioral and Social Science Survey, Landes and Tilly make the following statement on the issue of "teaching" versus "research" among historians:

In our view both groups are wrong . . . or ought to be. At the extreme, it is true, total commitment to classroom teaching would leave no time for individual research while total commitment to research would leave no time for classroom teaching. *Much of the apparent conflict, however, results from archaic and unexciting ideas of both activities.* At present most history is taught in units that bear no relation to the teacher's own research. The standard course aims to fill a box in space and time— seventeenth century England, colonial America, Ch'ing China—a box that comprises any number of topics and problems with which the teacher has little familiarity and even less concern. Such courses have their virtues, at least in principle: it is good for students of history to try to encompass the wholeness of a given society in a given period; moreover, teaching such a course is an education in itself, if—and that's a big if—the instructor makes a real effort to grasp the totality of his subject.[47]

Many historians, especially social-scientific historians, as well as increasing numbers of students, find such conventional modes of instruction "unsatisfactory and unsatisfying, in that it fails to focus on the kind of analytical problem that transcends time and place and must be studied and taught in a comparative context. *The man who works on elites and power, or the growth of cities, or social unrest, or population change, wants to, and should, teach courses that treat of such topics as he sees them from the vantage point of his own research.*"[48] Such an approach, more than any other, allows the instructor to set forth "what he is doing—to [deal with] topics that 'turn him on.'" It allows him to communicate as in no other area the excitement of the search for knowledge and rewards of discovery. Landes and Tilly add that such an approach makes it possible to convey to students the hazards of "that most perilous yet most unavoidable of historical maneuvers—*the leap from the particular to the general,*"[49] Palmer, too, is aware of these dangers. He states that "most historians succumb to the temptation to generalize beyond their immediate research despite the fact that the application of such generalizations to several cases usually results in raising doubts rather than confirming the original hypothesis."[50]

The pitfalls of generalization have long been evident to instructors and have been dutifully conveyed to students. "Yet in fact there is more untidy generalization in most conventional time-space courses than a diligent scholar can verify or refute in a lifetime. *If courses were more closely related to first-hand research, they would be more critical* and circumspect in this regard."[51]

Fortunately, Landes and Tilly conclude, "history teaching is moving in this direction, but very slowly."[52] In their examination of the discipline of

history, they make the following recommendations for training undergraduates as well as graduates in history:

1) Explicit and systematic instruction, including intensive participation by students
themselves, in problems of research design, formulation of hypotheses, logical
requirements of proof, and *the selection of appropriate research techniques.*
2) Systematic exposure of the student to the substantive findings, conceptual frameworks, and research methods of the other social sciences that seem promising for the
understanding of history or that need modification in the light of historical knowledge.
The problem is twofold: a) what contribution can the systematic use of social theory
make to the understanding of history? b) how can historical knowledge aid in the
development of social theory by providing evidence for the testing of existing theory
and by suggesting new problems for investigation?
3) Involvement of students in the creation, collection, and interpretation of sources
that are especially valuable in the study of problems of social-scientific history but
are often ignored in traditional work. In part this entails the imaginative search for
existing, but ignored sources; in part it implies the creation by the historian of the
very data he needs to carry out his inquiry. . . .[53]

Landes and Tilly next turn their attention to training in method. They
suggest that "the increasingly esoteric and technical character of social-
scientific research procedures [means that] students of history can no longer
substitute the traditional combination of common sense and self-education
for systematic preparation." Implicit in these suggestions is the recognition
that students must gain a solid grounding in research skills, especially in
exploiting materials accessible in the college library. All librarians know, of
course, that the instructors' request that students "go to the library and do
research on . . ." most often turns out to be unsatisfactory for both instructor and student. Thus, Landes and Tilly's proposed solution to the problem
is gratifying:

We therefore recommend that departments of history offer formal courses in historical method that include discussion of the appropriate literature of the other social
sciences and practical training in the use and comprehension of quantitative data;
that specialists be co-opted from the other social sciences to share in the instruction;
and that teaching materials explicitly addressed to the problems characteristic of
historical research be developed for this purpose.[54]

Concern for imparting the craft of history to undergraduate students is
not, of course, unique to those responsible for the history contribuiton to
the Behavioral and Social Science Survey. Whether history as a discipline
lends itself more readily to such matters (e.g., "Every Man His Own Historian") is debatable. Representatives of other disciplines would likely

respond to such a claim, simply by noting that historians are generally more vocal about such matters.

Remarkably, Landes and Tilly's concerns for instruction in the history volume were anticipated many years before (in 1956) in Dexter Perkins' presidential address to the American Historical Association. On that occasion, Perkins' persuasively urged that the discipline of history had to adjust to the changing needs of students in the second half of the twentieth century. Such changes, Perkins asserted, would not weaken the influence of history or eliminate it as a component in the curriculum in higher education. On the contrary, they constituted challenges to instruction and, if handled skillfully, could provide the catalyst that would ultimately strengthen the instructional contribution of the discipline. In another publication, I have noted that the arguments of Perkins and others for strengthening the place of history in the curriculum have not been widely heeded.[55] As a result, history has lost much of its appeal to undergraduates. In turn, declining enrollments have forced the termination of many positions in history departments.

It is not too late to institute the kind of reform Perkins recommends. His address, "And We Shall Gladly Teach," contains many valuable ideas about how academic libraries can encourage history instructors to lead their students to in-depth library research activities. Perkins observes that historians "have to admit (some of us reluctantly) that the trend in the American academic world is more and more vocational," a trend that is "not entirely to be deplored."[56]

Both librarians and historians are aware that, at least since the end of World War II, history has been studied entirely for its own sake and as a means of learning how to think more effectively. Indeed, for generations the history profession justified the learning of history on this basis and emphasized that such systematic patterns of thinking could be transferred to problems of everyday living after graduation. This viewpoint is even more valid today, for the knowledge and application of research procedures learned in the study of history or any other social science discipline are increasingly needed for effective functioning in our complex society. Hence, it is curious why today there is so little concern with the analytical skills that can be obtained from the study of history. One obvious reason is that the bulge of students, the advent of large lecture classes, the machine correction of exams, and the like have inevitably lowered standards of achievement for courses. Another reason is that the distorted emphasis on published research as a criterion for tenure and promotion has numbed the sensitivity of historians to the desirable role of instruction.

In order to establish a balance in such matters, Perkins suggests that both instruction and research should be part of the good college teacher.[57]

What kind of reform does Perkins suggest?

We should do better, perhaps, if, in the direction of our students, we gave more consideration to the possibility of reinterpretation of fields already covered as compared with digging away at obscure facts in an obscure area in an obscure way. Do we really need to know, to borrow from Carl Becker whether Charles the Fat was at Ingelheim or Lustnan on July, 1887? It is a fair question whether we do not sometimes kill the very spirit that we wish to foster, the spirit of exciting and excited inquiry into the past, by directing our students' attention to matters which fail to challenge them and turn what ought to be a highly intellectual adventure into a dreary kind of grabbing.[58]

Turning such sentiments into actual programs is, of course, a problem that has always vexed those inside and outside the library. This problem will continue and will become more acute. To the instructor outside the library, the problem of instructing students in effective modes of inquiry appears unsolvable. Except in unusual cases, instructors have neither the time nor the ability to provide the grounding in research needed for the type of work called for by Perkins. Within the library profession, the situation seems equally unsolvable. Generally, library orientation fails to give students the necessary instruction in research as called for by Perkins. The obvious solution is for the instructor and librarian to join forces and together establish the epistemological foundations of research in the minds of students. In this context, Perkins' concluding remarks in his address take on great significance, for they challenge both instructors and librarians to overcome the seeming impossibility of providing the required foundations for research: "I believe that the greatest challenge confronting historians today is the challenge of the classroom." By taking up this challenge effectively, historians will teach more than knowledge; they will be imparting the skills and wisdom of their craft.[59] If these ideals are to be achieved in any measure, history students must be directed beyond the classroom into their libraries, and there are countless ways in which reference librarians can assist by collaborating with history instructors.

Rundell, perhaps more specifically than any other historian, recognizes the importance of instructor-librarian collaboration: "Aside from professional shortcomings there is yet another reason for lapses in methodological training. Historians do not ensure sufficiently close coordination with librarians and archivists, who usually are competent in the technical areas where professors are weak."[60] This comment appears in a comprehensive survey on the use of original sources in graduate history training, funded by the Ford Foundation. Rundell published a briefer initial report on the subject in 1967.[61]

The Ford Foundation survey that Rundell conducted between 1965 and 1969 included an examination of the adequacy of graduate training in historical methods based on over 500 interviews with librarians, archivists, historians, and graduate students in 112 institutions. The results were somewhat discouraging: "The evidence indicates that our profession needs more and better training in historical method."[62] When these inadequately trained historians move up into the ranks of instructors, their attitudes inevitably will be reflected in the standards of achievement in research they will expect from their students in meeting course requirements. Rundell's brief survey of undergraduate training in historical method provided at several institutions provides a more optimistic note.[63] After noting that it is generally agreed that, as well as subject matter, undergraduate history majors should know something of the profession and historical methodology, Rundell presents survey results showing fifteen institutions having undergraduate history programs that include training in historical methods and research.

The findings of the Social Science Survey on history are quite pessimistic. For example, with regard to current graduate training in history, Landes and Tilly state:

Even from the point of view of "traditional history," however, present methods of historical training leave much to be desired. Problems concerning the design of research, the logical requirements of proof, the drawing of inferences from documents, or the imaginative use of new kinds of evidence—are by no means peculiar to any one kind of history. They are standard problems in the logic of research— any kind of research—and they are as relevant to the quality of work done in "traditional" as they are to more interdisciplinary forms of historical inquiry. Even so, as our survey has disclosed, much general considerations of the logic of investigation are no more a standard part of "training" of graduate students than more sophisticated attempts to make use of social theory and new research methods. Those schools that offer courses in methodology do not always require their graduate students to take them. Instead, the student is either assumed to have had this kind of instruction at some earlier stage or is left to his own devices; he is expected to learn how to write history by reading history (just as he is expected to learn how to teach by sitting in front of teachers and watching them at work). . . . In short, it would hardly be an exaggeration to say that most graduate students in history are given no "training" at all.[64]

According to Landes and Tilly, improving the training and methods historians receive entails first changes in the curriculum, especially the introduction of many more courses defined by themes and problems, alongside traditional courses; second, more emphasis on the seminar, since this mode of learning, when properly implemented, results in greater stress on research and writing; third, training in method, including discussion of appropriate literature in the sister social sciences and understanding of quantitative data; and fourth, for *undergraduate instruction* as a means of giving rudimentary understanding of the three preceding points, the introduction of varying amounts of such training.[65]

Political Science

Concern for undergraduate education is evident in *Political Science*, one of the volumes in the Behavioral and Social Sciences Survey:

Unless some skill and enthusiasm for political science as a modern social science are provided to undergraduates, the field incurs heavy costs in the kinds of students it attracts and repels, the styles students adapt, and the mutual expectations of students and faculty. . . . The style of undergraduate programs in political science effectively delays serious training relevant to research. Even worse, it makes preparation in the fundamentals of a modern scientist (such as mathematics, analysis, or other social science) either an accident of recruitment or a charge on graduate education. . . . the fact that undergraduate training in political science is not a prerequisite to graduate training is not fortuitous. The situation is directly caused by the absence of a research-related program of undergraduate instruction.[66]

The major objectives that Eulau and March visualize for the undergraduate curriculum are as follows:

1. Students with strong analytical abilities must be encouraged, which means "consciously using the undergraduate curriculum as a means of exposing the excitement of analytical political science to significant numbers of students already committed to the natural sciences, engineering and mathematics."

2. Students' natural inclinations or interests in politics must be channeled into more rigorous analytical activities "without forcing them to abandon their political passions."

3. "We must provide at the undergraduate level in political science the fundamental training in modern social problems, in the basic technology of research, and in related social sciences-training that is a prerequisite to research in political science."[67]

Recognizing that many of the problems of political science are common to other social sciences, Eulau and March recommend an interdisciplinary preprofessional undergraduate program. They state that such a program should involve "training in mathematics, computer science, statistics, theoretical analysis, research design, observational techniques, and analysis of social problems. They would provide intensive exposure to the fundamentals of the several behavioral and social sciences as an integrated collection rather than as a cafeteria of unrelated subject matters."[68] As a step toward implementing such programs, Eulau and March call for a vigorous program of funding pilot projects. Pilot projects of courses that include training in methods and research in political science are, according to Eulau and March, of interest to at least some political science teachers. It seems logical that, were it possible to get these political science teachers together with some like-minded reference librarians, some well-grounded pilot courses could be developed. If successful, these courses could in turn become models for other interested political science teachers. Much of the lack of any attempt to develop courses along lines discussed above—and, for that matter, in all of the disciplines discussed in this chapter—can be attributed to the teachers' lack of awareness of how to proceed. As noted in Chapter 1, achieving these reforms in course design is as much a problem of sharpening teachers' perceptions about the opportunities available as it is a problem of dealing with students. Once a method is found for overcoming some of the obstacles to developing courses providing training in methods and research, more political science teachers will adopt these practices for their own courses. Reference librarians can make definite contributions in the development of these courses.

Sociology

Significantly, the first recommendation listed in *Sociology* in the Behavioral and Social Sciences Survey is the strengthening of undergraduate education. The political science panel, which included Peter Caws, James S. Coleman, Paul Doty, and Albert J. Reiss, recommended

(1) that sociology departments diversify their curricula into "streams" of instruction to correspond better with the interests and career intentions of their undergraduate students; . . . (2) that empirical research be a part of undergraduate teaching from the start; . . . [and that] (3) the American Sociological Association continue and intensify its interest in undergraduate teaching as a part of its professional activities. . . . Sociology majors might be provided with a year or two of core sociological offerings, then be permitted to branch into groups, such as (a) groups with serious interest in the scientific theory and methods of sociology, and perhaps with an intention to continue work in sociology in graduate school; (b) groups intended to enter fields in which sociology is of general background value, for example, primary and secondary school teaching, social work and law; (c) groups interested in applications of sociology to public policy and social problems; and (d) groups interested in the significance of sociology as a part of the humanistic and scientific traditions of Western thought.[69]

The panel adds that smaller schools unable to present such diversified offerings might "attain the same objective by entering into collaborative interdisciplinary and 'joint-major' programs with other departments." The basic intention is to make sociology "more stimulating and more demanding." Implementing such goals requires the initiative and commitment of college and university faculties in changing curricula. Also needed are "funds for launching, implementing, and evaluating new curricula and teaching methods" for "equipment, facilities, and ancillary personnel."

With regard to emphasis on empirical research, the panel's second recommendation is that "undergraduates should collect, analyze, and interpret sociological data, as well as read or hear about others' interpretations. We recommend first-hand research, including involvement in interview surveys, participant observation, secondary analysis, and research into archives."[70]

The panel concludes that the present modes of instruction and testing in sociology leave much to be desired and that greater efforts must be made to obtain increased involvement of students in what sociologists do. A similar finding is reported by Epstein. (See the discussion in Chapter 12.)

A Call for Action

Instructors and librarians who share the concerns about higher education outlined in this chapter could attempt to cooperatively resolve some of the obstacles which stand in the way of implementing programs that encourage greater and more effective student use of library materials. Helburn, as is noted above, suggests that such a group be formed for geographers. To have librarians included in whatever attempts toward effecting such improvements in each discipline is worthy of consideration. If nothing else, it would indicate to the groups concerned that at least one group of professionals besides themselves was interested in promoting improvements in student education. If there is sufficient interest among librarians in jointly working with groups in the social sciences and other disciplines toward such improvements in education, at local, regional and national levels, exploratory inquiries by librarians should be made. The offer of joint consideration of these problems would undoubtedly be accepted readily.

There are some interesting bits of information available which support the idea of librarians working cooperatively with interested members of other disciplines. For example, Eble, an English professor long known for his concern for improving teaching in higher education, refers to findings in a survey on teaching among faculty members at the University of California at Davis. These findings suggest: (1) that teachers who were interested in teaching were better teachers[71] and (2) that one manifestation of this concern among them for improving teaching is that they enjoy discussing matters of teaching with colleagues.[72] It is members of this group who occupy positions in academic departments that reference librarians need to be aware of.

Groups of fairly active librarians are currently working toward improving student access to library materials. Most of these activities are centered on "bibliographic instruction" and library orientation. Perhaps expanding the focus of these groups to include joint actions with like-minded academics in other disciplines is the most obvious course to follow.

The best place at which to meet those individuals and groups in the various disciplines, whether social-scientific or otherwise, is at the annual meetings of a specific discipline (e.g., the annual meetings of the American Psychological Association or the American Sociological Association, or the various regional organizations of these same disciplines (e.g., the Pacific Sociological Association or the Association of Pacific Coast Geographers).

These annual meetings almost invariably include one agenda item on teaching, usually with several papers being presented. By meeting with these groups, presenting papers, making proposals, and constructively criticizing (from the standpoint of the library) proposals on improving student use of library materials, we can take those first important steps that could lead to resolving some of the problems this chapter has been concerned with.

Notes

1. Included in the survey are the following publications: *The Behavioral and Social Sciences: Outlook and Needs* (Englewood Cliffs, N.J.: Prentice-Hall, 1969); Allen H. Smith and John L. Fischer, eds., *Anthropology* (Englewood Cliffs, N.J.: Prentice-Hall, 1970): Heinz Eulau and James G. March, eds., *Political Science* (Englewood Cliffs, N.J.: Prentice-Hall, 1969); Kenneth E. Clark and George A. Miller, eds., *Psychology* (Englewood Cliffs, N.J.: Prentice-Hall, 1970); Nancy D. Ruggles, ed., *Economics* (Englewood Cliffs, N.J.: Prentice-Hall, 1970); Neil J. Smelser and James A. Dauls, eds., *Sociology* (Englewood Cliffs, N.J.: Prentice-Hall, 1969); David S. Landes and Charles Tilly, eds., *History as Social Science* (Englewood Cliffs, N.J.: Prentice-Hall, 1971); Edward J. Taafe, ed., *Geography* (Englewood Cliffs, N.J.: Prentice-Hall, 1970); and William Kruskal, ed., *Mathematical Sciences and Social Sciences* (Englewood Cliffs, N.J.: Prentice-Hall, 1970).

2. The discussion that follows is not intended to be exhaustive—merely representative. Occasionally, appropriate personal statements of influential members of the disciplines are given, since these individuals are often bellwethers of emerging attitudes. Because it is important that the statements of various disciplines regarding undergraduate education not be misunderstood, considerably more direct quotations than usual are given.

3. Robert W. Friedrichs, *A Sociology of Sociology* (New York: Free Press, 1972), pp. 7, 17.

4. See Robert A. Pois, "The Lecture-Textbook Syndrome," in John Lubans, ed., *Educating the Library User* (New York: Bowker, 1974).

5. The strengths and weaknesses of inquiry modes of learning are discussed by Raymond G. McInnis, "Integrating Classroom Instruction and Library Research: An Essay-Review," *Studies in History and Society* 6 (Fall, Winter 1974-1975):31-65; and John MacGregor and Raymond G. McInnis, "Integrating Classroom Instruction and Library Research: The Cognitive Functions of Bibliographic Network Structures," *Journal of Higher Education* 48 (January-February 1977):17-38. A more extensive discussion of inquiry learning in connection with describing a model of research methods is given in Part II of this book.

6. Robert G. Gregory, "Africana Archives and Innovative Teaching: The Teacher-Scholar's New Need for Research Materials," *Africana Library Journal* 2 (Winter 1971):18-9. The role of the librarian in the research enterprise as outlined by Gregory is analogous to Ravetz' description of the craftsman (i.e., scientist) and the "tool-expert":

Because so many of the essential tools for any field of science are so highly sophisticated, to achieve complete mastery in the use of them involves becoming a specialist in the tool rather than in the field to which it is being applied. There is thus a natural division of labor between tool-experts and their clients; and the tool experts are not merely individuals serving as auxiliaries to the clients in the work, but themselves can form a self-contained speciality, a tool-providing field. When two craftsmen with different skills are involved in the same project, they will inevitably see the work from different points of view. The different approaches will be complementary, and can correct and enrich each other; but they can also be the occasion of conflict. For each of the partners may be wanting to get something slightly but significantly different from the project. The client wants data or information, reliable by accepted standards of adequacy of his field, with a minimum of expense and delay; while the tool expert, unless he is completely subservient, will be looking for opportunities for developing particular tools in which he is interested. The two parties even perceive the situation differently, for their different interests correspond to different bodies of craft knowledge; and unless both parties enter the relation with considerable mutual comprehension and respect, only their respective incompetences will be communicated, and conflict will ensue. How conflicts work out depends on the social relations, and relative strengths, of the clients and the tool-experts individually and as recognized collectives. It must not be thought that the tool-experts' function as auxiliaries keep them in an inferior position. They are not merely essential for the work, but frequently have command of technicalities which are uncomprehensible to clients, and which also bear prestige in themselves. This is most noticeable where the tools are mathematical in character.

Jerome R. Ravetz, *Scientific Knowledge and Its Social Problems* (New York: Oxford University Press, 1971), pp. 90-1.

7. Smith and Fischer, *Anthropology*, pp. 127-8. (Emphasis added.)

8. Ibid., p. 133.

9. David G. Mandelbaum, Gabriel Lasker, and Ethel M. Albert, eds., *The Teaching of Anthropology* (Berkeley, Calif.: University of California Press, 1963).

10. William S. Laughlin, "Concepts and Problems," in Mandelbaum, Lasker, and Albert, eds., *The Teaching of Anthropology*, p. 81.

11. Mandelbaum, "Transmission of Anthropological Culture," in Mandelbaum, Lasker, and Albert, eds., *The Teaching of Anthropology*, p. 1.

12. Ibid., p. 5.

13. Ibid., p. 19.

14. Ibid., p. 54.

15. Patricia Knapp, *The Monteith College Library Experiment* (New York: Scarecrow Press, 1966), p. 41. (See note 1, Chapter 14.)

16. Mandelbaum, "Transmission of Anthropological Culture," pp. 54-5. (Emphasis added.) According to Mandelbaum, term papers can be quite simple exercises such as reports on the student's own set of kin terms, or they can be longer, more comprehensive papers, entailing repeated observations.

17. Gabriel Lasker, "The Introductory Course," in Mandelbaum, Lasker, and Albert, eds., *The Teaching of Anthropology*, p. 109.

18. Ibid., p. 117.

19. Gordon W. Hewes, "Course Design," in Mandelbaum, Lasker, and Albert, eds., *The Teaching of Anthropology*, p. 156. (Emphasis added.)

20. David H. French, "The Anthropologist in the Methodology of Teaching," in Mandelbaum, Lasker and Albert, eds., *The Teaching of Anthropology*, pp. 174-5.

21. Joseph B. Casagrande, "The Relations of Anthropology with the Social Sci-

ences," in Mandelbaum, Lasker, and Albert, eds., *The Teaching of Anthropology*, p. 471. This point is similar to that made by Schein, as noted in Chapter 1.

22. Maurice Line, et al., *Information Requirements of Researchers in the Social Sciences* (Bath, England: University Library, Bath University of Technology, 1971), p. 200.

23. Ibid., p. 216.

24. Ibid., p. 202.

25. Diana Amsden, "Information Problems of Anthropologists," *College and Research Libraries* 29 (1968):117-31; and Margaret Currier, "Problems in Anthropological Bibliography," *Annual Review of Anthropology* 5 (1976):15-34.

26. John H. Rowe, "Library Problems in the Teaching of Anthropology," in Mandelbaum, Lasker, and Albert, eds., *The Teaching of Anthropology*, pp. 69-70.

27. Ben H. Lewis, "A Retrospective Look at Undergraduate Economics," *American Economic Review* 60 (May 1970), pp. 371-3. (Emphasis added.)

28. Darrell R. Lewis and Charles C. Orvis, *Research in Economic Education: A Review, Bibliography and Abstracts* (New York: Joint Council on Economic Education, 1971), pp. 8-9. (Emphasis added.)

29. G. L. Bach and Phillip Saunders, "Economic Education: Aspirations and Achievements," *American Economic Review* 55 (June 1965):329-56; and "Lasting Effects of Economics Courses at Different Types of Institutions," *American Economic Review* 56 (June 1966):505-11.

30. George Dawson and Irving Bernstein, *The Effectiveness of Introductory Economics Courses in High Schools and Colleges* (New York: Center for Economic Education, New York University, 1967).

31. Ruggles, ed., *Economics*.

32. Richard S. Weckstein, *A Report on an Experiment in Teaching Introductory Economics* (Waltham, Mass., n.d.) (mimeo).

33. Herman T. Epstein, *A Strategy for Education* (New York: Oxford University Press, 1970).

34. As cited in Epstein, *A Strategy for Education*, pp. 70-1.

35. See John Fletcher, ed., *The Use of Economics Literature* (Hamden, Conn.: Archon Books, 1971), especially chapters by Fletcher, pp. 177-86, and R. D. Collison Black, pp. 187-8.

36. See Oreste Popescu, "On the Historiography of Economic Thought: A Bibliographical Survey," *Cahiers d'histoire mondiale* 64 (1964):168-209, as well as the chapter by Black cited in note 35.

37. Placido Lavalle, "Recent Trends in Undergraduate Geographic Training in American Universities and Colleges," in R. J. Chorley and P. Haggett, eds., *Frontiers in Georgraphy Training* (London: Methuen, 1970), p. 309.

38. Ibid., pp. 312-3.

39. Nicholas Helburn, "Introduction," in Nicholas Helburn, ed., *Challenge and Change in College Geography* (Washington, D.C.: Association of American Geographers, Commission on College Geography, 1973), pp. VI-VIII.

40. A. David Hill, "Geography and Geographic Education: Paradigms and Prospects," in Helburn, ed., *Challenge and Change in College Geography*, p. 17.

41. Ibid., p. 36. (Emphasis added.)

42. Ibid., p. 35.

43. John M. Ball, "Toward a Humanistic Teaching of Geography," in Helburn, ed., *Challenge and Change in College Geography*, pp. 6-13.

44. James Gardner, "Strategies for Relevant Learning Situations in Physical Geography," in Helburn, ed., *Challenge and Change in College Geography*, pp. 44-6.

45. Clyde F. Kohn, "The 1960's: A Decade of Progress in Geographical Research and Instruction," *Annals of the Association of American Geographers* 60 (June 1970):219.

46. Hill, "Geography and Geographic Education: Paradigms and Prospects," p. 33.

47. Landes and Tilly, Chapter 4, "The Role and Needs of Instruction," in *History as Social Science*, p. 81. (Emphasis added.)

48. Ibid. (Emphasis added.)

49. Ibid.

50. John R. Palmer, "Using Historical Research in the Teaching of American History," *Social Education* 36 (March 1972):271-2.

51. Landes and Tilly, *History as Social Science*, p. 81. (Emphasis added.)

52. For comprehensive lists of books and articles on the subject, see Alexander S. Birkos and Lewis A. Tombs, *Historiography, Method, History Teaching: A Bibliography of Books and Articles in English, 1965-1973* (Hamden, Conn.: Linnet Books, 1975); and Lester D. Stephens, *Historiography: A Bibliography* (Metuchen, N.J.: Scarecrow Press, 1975).

53. Landes and Tilly, *History as Social Science*, p. 91. (Emphasis added.)

54. Ibid., pp. 94-5.

55. McInnis, "Integrating Classroom Instruction and Library Research," pp. 31-65.

56. Dexter Perkins, "And We Shall Gladly Teach," *American Historical Review* 62 (1957):292.

57. Ibid., p. 294.

58. Ibid., p. 296.

59. Ibid., pp. 308-9.

60. Walter Rundell, *In Pursuit of American History* (Norman, Okla.: University of Oklahoma Press, 1970), pp. 34-5.

61. Walter Rundell, "Clio's Ways and Means: A Preliminary Report on the Survey," *Historian* 30 (1967):20-40.

62. Ibid., p. 39.

63. Rundell, *In Pursuit of American History*, pp. 18-20.

64. Landes and Tilly, *History as Social Science*, p. 83.

65. Ibid., pp. 91-7. (Emphasis added.)

66. Eulau and March, *Political Science*, pp. 112-3.

67. Ibid., pp. 113-4.

68. Ibid., pp. 113-4.

69. Smelser and Davis, *Sociology*, pp. 157-9.

70. Ibid., p. 158.

71. Eble, *Professors as Teachers*, p. 148.

72. Ibid., p. 148.

Part II

THE STRUCTURE OF SCIENTIFIC LITERATURE

Scientific knowledge is far more the ability and understanding of investigators than it is recorded fact.[1]

The consensus may exist chiefly in the knowledge and wisdom of experienced scholars in the field and only by implication in the published literature.[2]

The replacement of one substantive structure by another as science enlarges its grasp of its subject matter means that the existing body of knowledge is relatively ephemeral, subject to revision.[3]

A scientific library is not primarily a quarry, nor a factory, but a store. It is the "memory" in which each item is continually being rewritten as new results are transferred to it.[4]

Part II deals with disciplined inquiry as a collective enterprise of researchers in a given field. These researchers, engaged in providing systematic explanations of social phenomena, often employ models or paradigms to clarify and simplify these explanations (Chapter 3). It is established here that before the published research can be considered true knowledge, the research community must reach a consensus (Chapter 4). Next, in Chapter 5, the general subject matter of the social sciences is discussed, and two major components of scientific literature, primary sources and secondary sources, are considered. *Primary sources, the subject matter of disciplined inquiry, are pictured as fixed, or stable, components, whereas secondary sources, the published studies containing the explanations of the primary sources, are pictured as the fluid components. Primary sources are in turn divided into two groups: nomothetic and idiographic (Chapter 6). Chapter 7 examines some of the characteristic concerns of the social sciences.*

The role of creativity in the conceptualization of scientific literature is examined in Chapter 8 as background for understanding the idea of producing new literature. In the consideration of the bibliographic and substantive structures of scientific literature (Chapters 9 and 10), two parallel concepts are introduced: diachronic and synchronic structures. This discussion includes an examination of two frameworks in which scientific literature can be ordered: natural and formal structures. In addition, the cumulative-noncumulative characteristics of scientific literature are explored in this section.

Chapter 11 gives a somewhat speculative account of how individuals learn what is known in a given field, a process subsumed under the psychological structure of scientific literature.

Finally, in Chapter 12, some examples of actual or proposed modes of learning and research are outlined. These examples are based on the conceptions of the structures of scientific literature developed in the discussion.

Notes

1. R.G.A. Dolby, "Sociology of Knowledge in Natural Science," *Science Studies* 1 (1971):15.

2. John M. Ziman, *Public Knowledge* (Cambridge, Mass.: Cambridge University Press, 1968), p. 73.

3. Joseph Schwab, in *Education and the Structure of Knowledge*, Fifth Annual Phi Delta Kappa Symposium on Education (Chicago: Rand McNally, 1964), p. 34.

4. Ziman, *Public Knowledge*, p. 103.

3 How Social Scientists Know

In this discussion, anthropology, demography, economics, geography, history, political science, psychology, and sociology are all considered separate social sciences. With two exceptions, demography and psychology, no one would disagree that these are distinct disciplines. In the case of demography, some consider it a subdivision of either geography or sociology, and with regard to psychology, many prefer to call it a natural science. The merits of such claims notwithstanding, all are treated as distinct disciplines here because each has distinctive modes of inquiry and different approaches to their subject matter. An acquaintance with the individual characteristics of inquiry in each discipline enables reference librarians specializing in the social sciences to give more effective assistance to researchers.

Before examining these individual characteristics, the general features common to all the social sciences are pointed out. Rather than describe the methodology of social scientists (which has already been covered by such writers as White,[1] Freides,[2] and Hoselitz[3]), I concentrate on how social scientists know what they claim to know and relate what is known to the structure of scientific literature. What follows is necessarily brief and over-simplified; for detailed accounts, readers are encouraged to examine the numerous authorities cited.

The social sciences deal primarily with the behavior of man in his relation to his fellow man and the environment they share. Social scientists seek to understand human behavior and human institutions, and to provide a basis for planning and implementing social policies to meet human needs. Since the social sciences are concerned with human behavior, they are often called the behavioral sciences. The behavioral aspects of these sciences are most often identified as those concerned with the individual as the unit of analysis, and the social aspects as those having to do with social institutions or some group of persons.

The Goal of Inquiry: Explanation

In order to be understood, human behavior and human institutions must be reduced to manageable units of measurement or analysis. In general, such units of analysis are called social phenomena; in specific terms, they are called social variables, or simply variables. Analyses of social phenomena are advanced in the form of explanations.

Although explanation, as a term employed by social scientists, has received much attention in the field, according to Phillips there is "no firm consensus about exactly what *explanation* means."[4] Nagel,[5] Kaplan,[6] and Meehan[7] have also pointed out the lack of consensus. Problems associated with explanation in the social sciences stem both from the nature of the subject matter and from the terminology employed. Each of these aspects is covered in this chapter.

Natural scientists can for the most part achieve precisely controlled conditions: instruments accurately measure what is being investigated, results are calculated, and explanations are given. Since the controlled laboratory conditions of the natural scientist cannot be duplicated in the study of human beings, however, it is difficult, and often impossible, to obtain controlled conditions in the social sciences. For instance, since in the social sciences man is both the object of study and the observer doing the study, is it possible to obtain a control group on which valid conclusions can be drawn without imposing the observer's values? Moreover, as Berkhofer points out, "the very presence of the observer among the human beings he observes as subject may change the behavior under question."[8]

Social scientists seek to understand and explain both the internal or psychological component of human behavior and the external manifestations resulting from these internal mechanisms. The existence of an internal component as well as external behavior means that man can be studied in two different ways. The external manifestation of human behavior can be examined, and explanations can be set forth in a manner not unlike that employed by natural scientists. Or an attempt can be made to extract, measure, and interpret such internal manifestations of behavior as motives, intentions, ideals, and emotions.[9] Internal behavior is, of course, the more difficult to study, but it is claimed "that man's external behavior is explained meaningfully only when discussed in terms of such constructs as motives, intention, and even ideals and feelings."[10]

The terms used by natural scientists have quite precise meanings that can be stated in universal laws. In contrast, the terms employed by social scientists frequently possess what Nagel calls "indeterminant connotations," because social scientific terminology is derived from "everyday discussion of social questions, and is often used in formulating empirical generalizations with little redefinition of their vague common sense meanings." Sense of deprivation, morale, and role are examples of such terms. If an attempt is made to be precise, in the end "the precision is frequently achieved by way of some essentially statistical procedure," with the result that classes of individuals are designated as representative of the characteristic being studied, although they often vary widely in other characteristics which may be highly relevant to the problem under inquiry.[11]

Constructing Explanations

An explanation in the social sciences seeks rigorously to tell the why and the how of social phenomena as well as the what. Simply put, explanations seek to show the cause of particular phenomena. Social-scientific inquiry, in other words, seeks "to provide systematic and responsibly supported explanations . . . for individual occurrences, for recurring processes, or for invariable as well as statistical regularities."[12]

In contrast, in social-scientific inquiry, mere description, although it can be equally rigorous in detail, is limited to naming the characteristic features (the what) of particular phenomena. Basically, description is concerned with definition and classification. In explanation, interpretation is added to description. Interpretation, which determines the nature of the relationships among such observed phenomena as whether relationships are causative, purposive, or structural, adds to description the why of explanation.[13] In other words, "interpretation involves the reduction of explanation to the smallest number of general laws that would account for all the various specific facts described."[14] Nonetheless, description is necessarily a part of explanation. Further, according to Meehan, an explanation organizes human perceptions (or observations); at an absolute minimum, such organization means "the application of a rule or set of rules to a collection of entities." The rules which emerge from this organization "are called *concepts*," and as such, "are human creations, not natural entities, and without them man could hardly be said to think. Concepts serve to identify the entities we think about, classify entities into related sets, relate entities in time and space, define attributes and perform all of the other functions implied in the term 'organization of experience.'"[15]

When they are complete, scientific explanations are given the status of scientific laws. In order to be considered laws, relationships between phenomena must be invariable. Because of the difficulties involved in achieving the invariability demanded ("given the complexity of the phenomena and their causal factors in the field," primarily stemming from the "variety of subjective elements involved"), disciplines in the social sciences may have "to become content with something less certain than laws," and in the end, be satisfied with the prediction of probabilities "rather than the formulation of laws."[16]

Paradigms

Not unexpectedly, a research community varies on what constitutes acceptable patterns of particular modes of inquiry and explanation. To resolve this problem of variation, the most satisfactory mode of inquiry must be selected from many conventions and rules. Such a choice is, of course, subjective. As noted below, all researchers in a field are never completely satisfied. The selection amounts to choosing what Kuhn terms *paradigms* which he defines as "universally recognized scientific achievements that for a time provide model problems and solutions" to a research community.[17]

Once a paradigm is selected, scientific activity consists of "normal science," characterized by "puzzle-solving" (Kuhn's terms), by which researchers seek to provide explanations to the objects of their research. Occasionally, conventional modes of explanation are no longer satisfactory, at which time a more satisfactory paradigm must be developed. Kuhn considers the appearance of a new paradigm a "scientific revolution." Once an acceptable paradigm is developed, scientific activity returns to its "normal" state, i.e., puzzle-solving.

One of the things a scientific community acquires with a paradigm is a criterion for choosing problems that, while the paradigm is taken for granted, can be assumed to have solutions. [Largely] . . . these are the only problems that the community will admit as scientific or encourage its members to undertake. Other problems, including many that had previously been standard, are rejected as metaphysical, as the concern of another discipline, or . . . too problematic to be worth the time. A paradigm can . . . even insulate the community from those socially important problems that are not reducible to the puzzle form, because they cannot be stated in terms of the conceptual and instrumental tools the paradigm supplies. Such problems can be a distraction, a lesson brilliantly illustrated . . . by the contemporary social sciences. One of the reasons why normal science seems to progress so rapidly is that its practitioners concentrate on problems that only their lack of ingenuity should keep them from solving.[18]

This is interesting to social scientists for the following reason: "the notion of a paradigm expresses something rather important about explanation as a *process* and as an *activity*." Specifically, this notion brings together two aspects of explanation which cannot be ignored if we are to understand the behavior of a scientific investigator: "namely, the questions which he asks and the criteria which he sets up to judge whether . . . a given explanation is reasonable and satisfying."[19]

In connection with the notion of process, for example, Kuhn's conceptual framework makes evident the importance of the historical development of scientific activity in a discipline (a matter that will receive attention below). An acquaintance with the historical development of disciplines is particularly useful to reference librarians, for it is involved to a greater extent in their activity than previously has been recognized. (More attention is given this issue in Part III.)

As regards science as an activity, the explanation of a scientific paradigm by Kuhn

helps us to understand the nature of paradigm conflict, the problems . . . in choosing one mode of puzzle-solving rather than another. . . . In transforming allegiance from one paradigm to another, the scientist also transforms his own behavior. Questions which at one time did not arise, now do so because his expectations have changed. Experiences that seemed irrelevant now seem surprising and demand explanation. This general change in expectations involves a shift in the scientist's perceptions of the world around him. It involves a change in what Kuhn terms the "world view" of a scientist. His reactions to experience thus change and his conceptualization of that experience also changes. This shift in what Boulding (1956) calls the image of the investigator with respect to the world of experience is, again, an aspect of behavior in the scientific community which has tremendous implications for the prosecution of the scientist's endeavor. It must again be emphasized, therefore, that of the objectivity of science and the judgment of what is a relevant question and what [is] an acceptable answer can only be understood in the context of this prevailing image, in the context of the prevailing rules and conventions; in other words, in the context of diverse and often conflicting paradigms which themselves reflect and result form diverse behaviors, value systems, and individual philosophies.[20]

It is dangerous to oversimplify, however. It should not be assumed that scientific revolutions occur with great and sudden finality. There is no interruption of research activity during a period when accepted conventions of analysis are changing. Furthermore, even when a new paradigm is agreed upon, researchers in a given field continue to debate both large and small points, for they have varying opinions on the validity of modes of explanations and concepts. Friedrichs suggests that the existence of many conflicting modes of explanation or concepts indicates a discipline's maturity rather than its weakness.[21] College students in particular find it difficult to cope with the conflicting concepts in scientific literature. Perry suggests that "the most difficult instructional moment for the students—and perhaps therefore the teacher as well—seems to occur at the transition from the conception of knowledge as a qualitative accretion of discrete rightness (including the discrete rightness of multiplicity in which everyone has a right to his own opinion) to the conception of knowledge as the qualitative assessment of contextual observations and relationships."[22]

Are the Social Sciences Weaker Than the Natural Sciences?

Some critics claim that the social sciences, as sciences, are weaker than the natural sciences.[23] What evidence is there for this position? With regard to whether the two have equal validity, McEwen states that "social scientific analyses and natural scientific analyses are separable but congruent modes of reflective inquiry."[24] Although couched in qualifications, Nagel analogously states that, in comparison with the natural sciences, "the social sciences today possess no wide-ranging systems of explanations judged as adequate by a majority of professionally competent students, and they are characterized by serious disagreements on methodological as well as substantive questions."[25] Nonetheless, he believes that "even if the comprehensiveness of proposed explanatory premises is often small and frequently in dispute," social scientists "are able to advance explanations for a large variety of social phenomena."[26]

Inquiries into human behavior have also made evident (with the increasing aid, in recent years, of rapidly developing techniques of quantitative analysis) some of the relations of dependence between components in various social processes; and those inquiries have thereby supplied more or less firmly-grounded generalized assumptions for explaining many features of social life, as well as for constructing frequently effective social policies. To be sure, the laws or generalizations concerning social phenomena made available by current social inquiry are far more restricted in scope of application, are formulated far less precisely, and are acceptable as factually sound if understood to be hedged in by a far larger number of tacit qualifications and exceptions, than are the most commonly cited laws of the physical sciences.[27]

Meehan does not accept the premise that the social sciences are weaker than the natural sciences. He states that the explanatory capacity of the social sciences is "extremely limited" if the deductive mode of explanation is employed. Recognizing that the deductive mode of explanation (at least as presently conceived) is not always suitable for the social sciences, Meehan presents an alternative, but related, mode of explanation, which he calls the systems paradigm. He also notes that Nagel's analytical perspective on the social sciences is derived from the natural scientific tradition.[28]

Those readers who are interested in exploring the question of the validity of the literature of the social sciences or its grounds of comparison with the natural sciences should consult Machlup's article.[29] He discusses nine grounds of comparison: (1) invariability of observations; (2) objectivity of observations and explanations; (3) verifiability of hypotheses; (4) exactness of findings; (5) measurability of phenomena; (6) constancy of numerical relationships; (7) predictability of future events; (8) distance from everyday experience; and (9) standards of admission and requirements. Based on the evidence Machlup and others present, the present work accepts the assumption, with some qualification, that social-scientific literature has achieved validity.

Notes

1. Carl M. White and associates, eds., *Sources of Information in the Social Sciences*, 2d ed. (Chicago: American Library Association, 1973).

2. Thelma Freides, *The Literature and Bibliography of the Social Sciences* (Los Angeles: Melville Publishing Co., 1973) pp. 19-41.

3. Bert F. Hoselitz, ed., *A Reader's Guide to the Social Sciences*, 2d ed. (Glencoe, Ill.: Free Press, 1970).

4. Derek L. Phillips, *Abandoning Method* (San Francisco: Jossey-Bass, 1973), p. 5.

5. Ernest Nagel, *The Structure of Science* (New York: Harcourt, Brace and World, 1961), Chapter 14.

6. Abraham Kaplan, *The Conduct of Inquiry* (Scranton, Penn.: Chandler Publishing Co., 1964), Chapter 9.

7. Eugene J. Meehan, *Explanation in Social Science, A System Paradigm* (Homewood, Ill.: Dorsey Press, 1968).

8. Robert Berkhofer, *A Behavioral Approach to Historical Analysis* (New York: Free Press, 1969), p. 10.

9. Cf. Kaplan, *Conduct of Inquiry*, pp. 358-63.

10. Berkhofer, *A Behavioral Approach to Historical Analysis*, p. 8.

11. Nagel, *The Structure of Science*, p. 506. For a similar view, see Meehan, *Explanation in Social Science*, p. 38.

12. Nagel, *The Structure of Science*, p. 15. Explanation is used here in a loose general sense rather than in the precise sense as used by philosophers of science. Nonetheless, explanation is a greater problem for history than for the other social sciences because historical events must be set in chronological context so that an understanding of them can be obtained. In history, there are too many variables to be balanced one against the other to avoid this. Such difficulties are not characteristic of the other social sciences, since they can legitimately limit variables without violating their purpose. For an extended discussion of these problems, with emphasis on history, see Robert F. Berkhofer, *A Behavioral Approach to Historical Analysis*, Chapter 12.

13. Gordon J. Di Renzo, "Toward Explanation in the Behavioral Sciences," in Gordon J. Di Renzo, ed., *Concepts, Theory and Explanation in the Behavioral Sciences* (New York: Random House, 1966), p. 250.

14. Ibid., p. 250. For a more extensive examination of the distinctions social scientists make between these terms, see Robert Brown, *Explanation in Social Science* (Chicago: Aldine, 1963).

15. Meehan, *Explanation in Social Science*, p. 35.

16. Di Renzo, "Toward Explanation in the Social Sciences," p. 251. Cf. Freides, *The Literature and Bibliography of the Social Sciences*, p. 32. Not unexpectedly, there is a considerable range of positions on these matters, in the physical and biological sciences as well as in the social sciences. For example, after reading this paragraph, Timothy O'Leary (in personal correspondence in 1977) stated:

The social scientists I'm acquainted with (mainly anthropologists, sociologists, and historians) consider all scientific laws based on observation to be statistical and probabilistic in nature—this applying equally to the physical and natural sciences. The only laws that I know of which are invariable are those established by human fiat, e.g., traffic laws, religious laws, etc. These two different types of laws might also be termed "descriptive" and "prescriptive" respectively—analogous to Nagel's discussion of the laws of thought. A good reference to what I'm talking about is Hans Reichenbach's "Probability Methods in Social Science," in *The Policy Sciences*, Daniel Lerner and Harold Lasswell, editors (Stanford: Stanford University Press, 1951), pp. 121-8. . . . "Being statistical, sociological laws are not inferior to physical laws, because physical laws, too, are essentially statistical. There are only differences of degree of probability asserted in the statistical laws that are extracted from observations. And this degree of probability varies with the subject matter under investigation. Astronomy provides us with high degrees of probability for its laws and thus with highly reliable predictions; meteorology is restricted to lower degrees of probability, and its predictions cannot compete with those of astronomical phenomena. The sociologist resembles the meteorologist much more than he does the astronomer." (p. 122)

Of course, the whole question of scientific laws is much more complex than this discussion would suggest. As a beginning, see Herbert Feigl and May Brodbeck, eds., *Readings in the Philosophy of Science* (New York: Appleton-Century-Crofts, 1953).

17. Thomas Kuhn, *The Structure of Scientific Revolutions*, 2d ed., enlarged (Chicago: University of Chicago Press, 1970), p. VIII.

18. Ibid., p. 37.

19. David Harvey, *Explanation in Geography* (London: Arnold, 1969), p. 16. (Emphasis added.)

20. Ibid., pp. 17-8.

21. Robert W. Friedrichs, *A Sociology of Sociology* (New York: Free Press, 1972), p. 325.

22. William G. Perry, *Forms of Intellectual and Ethical Development in College, A Scheme* (New York: Holt, Rinehart and Winston, 1968), p. 210.

23. Cf. Meehan, *Explanation in Social Science*, p. 38.

24. William P. McEwen, *The Problem of Social-Scientific Knowledge* (Totowa, N.J.: Bedminster Press, 1963), p. 4.

25. Nagel, *Structure of Science*, p. 449.

26. Ibid., p. 503.

27. Ibid., p. 449. For an even less optimistic view of the validity of social-scientific literature, see Jerome J. Ravetz, *Scientific Knowledge and Its Social Problems* (New York: Oxford University Press, 1971), pp. 364-402.

28. Meehan, *Explanation in Social Science*, p. 9.

29. Fritz Machlup, "Are the Social Sciences Really Inferior?" *Southern Economic Journal* 27 (January 1961):173-84; reprinted in Maurice Natanson, ed., *Philosophy of the Social Sciences* (New York: Random House, 1963), pp. 158-80.

4 Knowledge as Consensus

According to Meehan, the scientific literature of a discipline is "organized experience" and the search for it is a "search for patterns of organization. The organization is always created and not discovered."[1] Producing scientific literature is therefore a creative act requiring the craft skills of disciplined inquiry.[2] Nonetheless, the publication of the results of research does not mean that they are immediately accepted as knowledge. According to Ziman, in the natural sciences published studies are considered scientific information by researchers in the field.[3] "Following the publication of a paper, there is a slow erratic process of evaluation."[4] A similar process occurs in the social sciences.[5]

The notion of consensus is intrinsic to the concept of a paradigm discussed in Chapter 3. Before published research can be considered knowledge, it must be accepted by those actively engaged in research in that field of inquiry. In the meantime, Ziman asserts, such material is "treated as an archive of what is known scientifically."[6] "A paper moves out of this limbo of tacit acceptance when it is referred to in a 'review article.' The function of this type of 'secondary' publication is to give an explicit account of the current consensus in some particular field."[7] New findings thus become part of the core of scientific literature in a field after the research community reaches a consensus on their validity.

According to Ziman, "the tentativeness of the assessment of recent work in most review articles indicates that the current scientific consensus is always *fluid*." The importance of the review article is that it "turns *information* into knowledge."[8] "Further," Ziman continues, "the purpose of the reviewing process is to achieve understanding among colleagues, rather than merely accrue information." Similar observations are made by Dolby, Freides and Ravetz.[9] According to Holroyd, "Ziman follows Kuhn in supposing that new work is normally assessed against scientific opinion rather than against immediate and thorough replication of experiments—against a collective judgment of the scientific community, rather than against empirical verification."[10]

Ziman also notes that the diverse array of research findings must be synthesized into a coherent picture in order to achieve an understanding of what is known in a given field. As these discrete findings are assembled into "comprehensible, analytically ordered and coherent systems of ideas—a consensus,"[11] a body of knowledge can be said to exist. Not unlike the fluid characteristic of new findings, "the true consensus is continually changing."[12]

In presenting a slightly different perspective of the Kuhnian notion of a paradigm, Gilbert argues that research findings are transformed into knowledge in a manner different from what Ziman visualizes. Gilbert's paper is an attempt to refute Kuhn's claims about the role of the paradigm in scientific research. Gilbert acknowledges that what he is proposing is not that different from Kuhn's arguments about the nature of paradigms in scientific inquiry. In his view, however, scientists do not adhere as strictly to the currently shared paradigm as Kuhn claims. Rather than a paradigm shared by a scientific community, Gilbert suggests that scientists "use models which have some of the functions of a paradigm for *individual* members, but . . . that there may be no feature of these models which is shared by them all. . . . Far from being fixed and unchangeable, models (unlike paradigms) are constantly changing."[13]

Gilbert proposes that statements regarding findings in research reports (he calls these statements "knowledge claims") are put forth as persuasive arguments.[14] According to Gilbert, it is necessary to ensure that the procedures, theories, and data that justify the arguments set forth will be convincing to the community of scholars in that field. This is achieved by reference to papers in the field that support the claims being made.[15] In this sense, Gilbert's position is the same as Ziman's: "A scientific paper does not stand alone; it is embedded in the 'literature' of the subject. Every argument that is presented, many of the facts that are adduced, must be supported by documentation."[16] By following the convention of citing other works in the field, Gilbert continues, the authority is established on which the author's argument is founded. "At the same time, in supporting his argument by referring to a particular knowledge claim, the author implies that he accepts the validity of that claim; in short, a citation used to justify an argument suggests that the author recognizes the cited claim as a contribution to knowledge."[17] Gilbert also notes that the citing of other papers may be designed to refute erroneous claims made in them.[18]

Apart from whether, in the final analysis, Gilbert's arguments are successful in countering or dislodging the Kuhnian notion of the paradigmatic character of scientific inquiry, his suggestions are valid about how claims made in research reports are supported by or based on other works in the field. The manner in which these claims gain acceptance among researchers in a field of inquiry is, however, also a form of consensus.

Accounts of the process of transforming research findings into knowledge in the social sciences agree that a collective consensus also determines which findings are retained and which are not.[19] Compared to the natural sciences, there are certain variations in the manner in which consensus is achieved. Knorr's findings suggest that even among the various disciplines in the social sciences the manner in which consensus is achieved varies.[20] One of the differences between the natural and the social sciences can be attributed to the fact that there are fewer formal (or, to use Freides' term, "institutional"[21]) recurrent review publications in the social sciences than is characteristic of the natural sciences. This situation does not mean, however, that compared to the natural sciences, research reviews are not published as frequently in the social sciences.[22] As one means of testing this assumption, readers can examine the frequency with which "R" symbols (the symbol used to indicate when a particular citation is discussed in a review article) appear among the entries of articles indexed in the *Social Sciences Citation Index*. (See, for example, the extract from the *Social Sciences Citation Index* in Appendix A, number 2.) As increasing numbers of periodicals designed to review recent research findings are published in the social sciences, achieving consensus will undoubtedly begin to resemble increasingly the more formalized features of the natural sciences.

Given that at the moment there are fewer review publications in the social sciences, some writers suggest that the influence of particular groups (or even individuals) is likely to be an overriding factor in determining which knowledge claims are acceptable and which are not. Unless knowledge claims can be integrated into the currently agreed upon body of knowledge in a field, they receive little or no attention. According to Bergen, for example, a social scientist's academic peers are the evaluators of the validity of particular knowledge claims. Before a social scientist acquires a reputation among his peers for sound scholarship, grounded in the currently accepted standards and norms of the field, his writings are judged to have less value than those of better known scholars. Once a social scientist acquires a certain distinction among his peers, "even his weaker publications tend to be judged more favorably than they otherwise would be."[23] Because other scholars wish to acquire similar influence among their peers, they will frequently cite the works of influential scholars in order to obtain some of the prestige they enjoy.[24]

In the social sciences, it is the nature of consensus and the fluid property of the substantive literature that seems to be little understood by librarians. An understanding of these two aspects of the social sciences is important in the retrieval of currently valid knowledge. Bry and Afflerbach, and Watson et al. have noted how a lack of awareness of the fluid property of scientific knowledge can affect the bibliographic organization of literature and literature retrieval systems.[25] The fluid characteristic of the substantive portions of social science literature is discussed in Chapter 10.

Very few librarians have addressed the issue of consensus in scientific

literature.[26] Doyle and Grimes' *Reference Resources: A Systematic Approach*
came to my attention after I had finished the manuscript for this book, but
because some misconceptions in their arguments about the precepts and
conventions of scholarly communities and the growth and structure of
scientific literature apply to the notion of consensus, I think it is instructive
to add a discussion of their book to this chapter.[27] An extensive explanation
is required for an understanding of how the conceptual framework of scientific literature that they propose as a model for conducting research is rele-
vent to a discussion of consensus.

Arranged in three parts, Doyle and Grimes' *Reference Resources* is a
research guide that attempts to combine theory with application in proposing a new orientation to research techniques. In Part I, Structure and Identi-
fication of Reference Resources, the notions of a "bibliographic chain" and
and the literature-searching process are discussed. Part II, Resource Use and
User Behavior, examines basic concepts and personal and interpersonal
information processing. In addition, five user studies in the natural and
social sciences—including Line's INFROSS survey[28]—are summarized. An
operational model and the results of an actual search are given first in Part III,
where the authors note in particular such matters as "determination of a
need," "initial question statement," redefinition, structuring search strategies,
selecting and analyzing information sources, synthesizing and analyzing,
decision-making, and evaluating. The bulk of Part III is devoted to ten
"discipline resource packages" set forth first in broad sections then, except
for general works, all subdivided into narrower fields.

Except for the general works section, all discipline resource packages are
further arranged in categories corresponding to divisions in the bibliographic
chain. Doyle and Grimes claim that researchers "must possess an awareness
of the theory of how information is created and how it 'flows' through various
formats of print material found in most libraries."[29] According to Doyle
and Grimes,

progression through the bibliographic chain is tied to time. An item of newly created
information which is sufficiently useful moves chronologically from the status of a
distinct idea through other stages of the bibliographic chain to its ultimate destination
in the generalized knowledge of an encyclopedic summary of a particular subject
field.[30]

The bibliographic chain consists of the following sequence of categories:
information residing in individuals, information created by institutions,
work in progress documents, unpublished studies, periodicals, reports
and monographs, indexing and abstracting services, bibliographic lists and
essays, annual reviews and state-of-the-art reports, books and encyclopedic
summaries. "Reference resources [i.e., the printed records of research found

in divisions of the bibliographic chain] are those informational materials which contain knowledge or surrogate references to it."[31]

Arguments throughout this book, as well as those of Ziman and Gilbert, among others, suggest a less rigid sequence in the production of scientific literature.[32] However, Doyle and Grimes also note that not all of the substantive material associated with disciplined inquiry passes through divisions of the bibliographic chain according to an arbitrary sequence, nor do all "bits of information" ultimately reach the final destination.[33]

All of these considerations concerning the working of a bibliographic chain are quite useful for orienting researchers to a particular directional flow of material in the literature of disciplined inquiry. There are, at the same time, other characteristics associated with the production of this literature that should be considered, if the concept underlying the bibliographic chain is expected to become practicable.

In particular, I don't believe that the authors penetrate deeply enough into their notion of the operation of the bibliographic chain. There are certain epistemological and sociological characteristics of disciplined inquiry missing in their arguments, and these need to be pointed out and consistently followed through if the orientation to research that they are proposing is to work satisfactorily. For example, Doyle and Grimes visualize "bits of information" being formed randomly, or at least formed with less direction and purpose than most would attribute to the intent of research. They claim that

in its initial concept a piece of information is perceived as a rather distinct entity *whose full implications are only partially realized, if at all.* As this piece of information becomes progressively integrated with other new bits of knowledge and with preexisting knowledge, it loses its unique identity and becomes a part of our intellectual fabric. It may generate its own unique set of ideas, but it usually emerges as another dimension or facet of some previously existing concept. If this newly integrated bit of information duplicates, but does not improve the previously existing concept it will, hopefully, sink into oblivion. This is, unfortunately, not always the case.[34]

Several things are missing, or at least deserve greater stress, in this argument Little evidence, if any, is given to the notion that there is a difference in the kinds of substantive materials being treated at various stages of the bibliographic chain. In the passage above note that "information" and "knowledge" are treated as if they were synonymous. Is the "piece of information" to which Doyle and Grimes refer information in Ziman's sense above? Or is it simply primary data—the subject matter that researchers seek to understand and explain—in the sense of the term in Chapter 5? There seems to be some reason for doubt. For example, following Kent, the authors note that "information has been characterized as . . . facts or figures ready for communication or use [;] . . . knowledge as an organized body of information; wisdom implies knowledge with information so thoroughly assimilated to have produced sagacity, judgment and insight."[35]

As noted at the end of Chapter 1 in this book, following Cassidy, knowledge results from analytic activity embracing the investigation and explanation of experience, not just organizing a body of information. What is lacking in Doyle and Grimes' definition, and throughout their research guide, is any notion of how information is turned into knowledge. Specific evidence of this is particularly available among entries in the "discipline resource packages" in Section III of their book. Included among "Annual Reviews" in the Social Science package are *Information Please Almanac, America Votes, Book of the States, Congressional Quarterly Almanac, Facts on File, International Yearbook and Statesman's Who's Who, Keesing's Contemporary Archives, Statesman's Yearbook, Statistical Abstract of the United States,* and the United Nations' *Statistical Yearbook.* Since all of these are considered by social scientists as sources of primary data, or primary source material, needing to be explained, including these works in the category of annual reviews and state-of-the-art reports only confuses or misinforms researchers. I also question why compilers of particular "discipline resource packages" see fit to include such strange items in the "Encyclopedic Summaries" division. For example, the United States *Statutes at Large* is neither encyclopedic nor summary; nor are the *Encyclopedia of Business Information Sources* or the *Official Congressional Directory* appropriately included in an encyclopedic category. Other items inaccurately labeled as encyclopedic summaries are the *Code of Federal Regulations,* the *Federal Register,* and *Who's Who in American Education.* If the authors had given more attention to differences in the substantive materials of inquiry, in particular noting that information (in Ziman's sense) becomes knowledge through a process of consensus, a consensus that results from the slow erratic manner in which communities of scholars in the natural and social sciences collectively evaluate scientific findings derived from empirical research, readers of their book would be better informed and better able to profit from it.

Notes

1. Eugene J. Meehan, *Explanation in Social Science, A System Paradigm* (Homewood, Ill.: Dorsey Press, 1968), p. 15.

2. Jerome J. Ravetz, *Scientific Knowledge and Its Social Problems* (New York: Oxford University Press, 1971), discusses the issue extensively.

3. Note, however, that the information to which Ziman refers must be distinguished from the primary data, or primary source material, that is the subject matter researchers seek to understand and explain. This topic is discussed in Chapter 5.

4. John M. Ziman, *Public Knowledge* (Cambridge, England: Cambridge Univer-

sity Press, 1968), pp. 120-1. For other accounts see Michael Polanyi, *Personal Knowledge* (Chicago: University of Chicago Press, 1958), especially pp. 216-9; G. Nigel Gilbert, "The Transformation of Research Findings into Scientific Knowledge," *Social Studies of Science* 6 (1976):281-306; D. A. Kemp, *The Nature of Knowledge* (London: Clive Bingley, 1976), especially pp. 81-2; and Gileon Holroyd, "On the Sociology of Knowledge," *Journal of Librarianship* 4 (January 1972):48-56. Ziman and Gilbert differ in the amount of importance each attaches to the refereeing that occurs when scientific articles are submitted to journal editors to be considered for publication. In *Public Knowledge*, pp. 111-2, Ziman claims that the publication of an article in a scientific journal "bears the *imprimatur* of scientific authenticity . . . given to it by the editor and referees whom [the editor] may have consulted." Gilbert contends that the evidence suggests that refereeing "is generally cursory and is often concerned only with ensuring that the results offered are original and that research methods used exceed a certain minimum level of technical competence." (See Gilbert, "The Transformation of Research Findings into Scientific Knowledge," pp. 293-4.)

5. See, for example, David A. Hollinger, "T. S. Kuhn's Theory of Science and Its Implications for History," *American Historical Review* 78 (1973):388. See also Dan Bergen, "The Communications System of the Social Sciences," *College and Research Libraries* 28 (1967):239-52, especially p. 243; L. E. Watson, et al., "Sociology and Information Science," *Journal of Librarianship* 5 (1973):270-83, especially pp. 277-8; and Thelma Freides, *The Literature and Bibliography of the Social Sciences* (Los Angeles: Melville Publishing Co., 1973), pp. 73 ff. Karin D. Knorr, "The Nature of Scientific Consensus and the Case of the Social Sciences," in Karin D. Knorr, et al., eds., *Determinants and Controls of Scientific Development* (Dordrecht, Holland: Reidel, 1975), pp. 227-56, is an empirical study of the notion of consensus among a group of social scientists.

6. Ziman, *Public Knowledge*, p. 120

7. Ibid., p. 122.

8. Ibid., p. 123. (Emphasis added.)

9. R. G. A. Dolby, "Sociology of Knowledge in Natural Science," *Science Studies* 1 (1971):15; Freides, *The Literature and Bibliography of the Social Sciences*, pp. 5-18; Ravetz, *Scientific Knowledge and Its Social Problems*, Chapter 7, especially pp. 233-40.

10. Holroyd, "On the Sociology of Knowledge," p. 53.

11. Ziman, *Public Knowledge*, p. 125.

12. Ibid., p. 124.

13. Gilbert, "The Transformation of Research Findings into Scientific Knowledge," p. 301. (Emphasis added.)

14. Ibid., p. 282.

15. Ibid., p. 287.

16. Ziman, *Public Knowledge*, p. 58.

17. Gilbert, "The Transformation of Research Findings into Scientific Knowledge," p. 287.

18. Ibid., p. 304, note 14.

19. Freides, *The Literature and Bibliography of the Social Sciences*, pp. 11-2, 74-7.

20. Knorr, "The Nature of Scientific Consensus and the Case of the Social Sciences."

21. Freides, *The Literature and Bibliography of the Social Sciences*, p. 75.

22. Cf. Ibid., 74-5.

23. Bergen, "The Communication System of the Social Sciences," p. 243.

24. Ibid., p. 243. This situation must be acknowledged with a certain amount of regret. Ziman discusses features of this same characteristic of peer influence that exists in the natural sciences. See Ziman, *Public Knowledge*, pp. 55-8. Although it is beyond the scope of this book to explore the ramifications of the social systems of the social sciences, there are numerous publications that interested readers can examine for an explanation. For example, as well as Bergen, "Communication System of the Social Sciences," pp. 243 ff., see Robert W. Friedrichs, *A Sociology of Sociology* (New York: Free Press, 1970, especially Chapter 2), and Norman Kaplan, "The Norms of Citation Behavior: Prolegomena to the Footnote," *American Documentation* 16 (July 1965):179-84.

25. Ilse Bry and Lois Afflerbach, "Intensive Bibliography and the Growth Pattern of the Literature," *Mental Health Book Review Index* 14 (1969): I-VI; also published in Ilse Bry, *The Emerging Field of Sociobibliography*, ed. and comp. by Lois Afflerbach and Marga Franck (Westport, Conn.: Greenwood Press, 1977), pp. 129-47; and Watson, et al., "Sociology and Information Science."

26. In notes 3 and 4 above only Bergen, Freides, Holroyd, Kemp and Watson, et al., are libarians. Kemp's *The Nature of Knowledge* came to my attention after the manuscript for this book was completed. As well as consensus, it is a timely and useful discussion of the psychology and sociology of knowledge, the philosophy of science, and other related matters of significance to librarians. Since his arguments concerning knowledge as consensus are virtually the same as those presented here, the only further comment necessary is that he does not concern himself with the problem of consensus in the social sciences.

27. James M. Doyle and George H. Grimes, *Reference Resources: A Systematic Approach* (Metuchen, N.J.: Scarecrow Press, 1976).

28. Maurcie B. Line, *Information Requirements of Researchers in the Social Sciences* (Bath, England; University Library, Bath University of Technology, 1971.) *ERIC* Document 054 806.

29. Doyle and Grimes, *Reference Resources*, p. VII.

30. Ibid., p. 4.

31. Ibid., p. 27.

32. See Ziman, *Public Knowledge*, and Gilbert, "Transformation of Research Findings into Scientific Knowledge."

33. Doyle and Grimes, *Reference Resources*, pp. 3-4.

34. Ibid., p. 4. (Emphasis added.)

35. Ibid., p. 27.

5 The Components of Social-Scientific Literature

Any discussion of social inquiry and its products first requires determining its components. This chapter presents a conceptual framework for the components of social-scientific literature.

Published explanations of social phenomena by social scientists form the permanent records of research. In general, these published records are known as secondary sources. Stored in bound volumes on shelves in libraries, these records constitute the official archives of the social-scientific community. Before the substantive content of this permanent record of research is considered knowledge, certain processes must occur. As seen in the preceding chapter, through consensus portions of this social-scientific literature (Ziman refers to it as "scientific information") are turned into knowledge. Conversely, certain portions of these permanent records, because their substantive content has become obsolete, are in effect deleted from the currently valid body of social-scientific knowledge. Taken together, these two characteristics of social-scientific literature—knowledge as consensus and its subsequent obsolescence—permit us to speak about the fluid properties of that literature. (This notion receives greater attention in Chapter 10.)

Primary sources constitute the subject matter of inquiry in the social sciences. They are often identified or distinguished by different labels among the individual disciplines. In history, subject matter is generally labeled primary sources. In other social science disciplines, however, especially those in which quantitative analysis techniques are employed, the subject matter is commonly known as social data (or simply data) and in certain disciplines such as political science, even more narrowly as time-series data or political-events data. (Narrower distinctions such as the foregoing are associated with specific methodologies employed by these disciplines.)

Social-scientific disciplines which study current social phenomena often generate data through the use of so-called instruments—devices for measuring aspects of social phenomena. These instruments are usually in the form of questionnaires, field surveys, interviews, sociometric models, statistical sampling, and so forth. The techniques employed in using instruments become the methodology of a given discipline.[1]

The term *primary sources* is preferable to data for identifying the subject matter of social-scientific inquiry because it is more inclusive. Hence, primary sources is used in this discussion.

Primary and Secondary Sources

Making a precise distinction between primary and secondary sources, though often difficult, is important, especially for those beginning study in the social sciences.[2] Without a solid grounding in what these terms denote, progress in learning can be seriously hampered.

As the subject matter of social inquiry, primary sources are epistemological elements that are fixed or stable; the original documents or data can never be changed at any time without violating their inherent integrity. Primary sources can also be viewed as the logical key to secondary sources. Since secondary sources explain primary sources, they are meaningless except in the context of the primary sources to which they refer.

What is regarded as a primary or secondary source sometimes depends, of course, upon the perspective of the researcher.[3] Once the researcher has classified a particular source as either primary or secondary, however, it stands in logical relationship to the rest of the materials accordingly. My own rule of thumb is that a secondary source becomes a primary source if the researcher is explaining or criticizing it; if, on the other hand, it is used to support an argument, it is a secondary source.

In direct contrast to the fixed quality of primary source materials, secondary source material is fluid.[4] In Chapter 3, for example, attention is directed to Kuhn's notion of a paradigm shift as a way of explaining extreme changes that occur in the substantive structure of the literature of a research field.[5] Even without extreme shifts in the paradigm, however, changes occur in the structure of that literature—principally as the result of syntheses, analyses, emendations, revisions, and so on. Given such changes, it can be said that secondary source materials are fluid.

What Are Primary Sources?

What, in fact, are primary sources in the social sciences? Members of several social sciences themselves maintain that anything can be a primary source, depending on the context. To the historian, for example, legal documents, letters, newspaper articles, legislative records, and the like are, of course, what are traditionally considered primary sources. To the sociologist, population censuses, survey questionnaires, and crime statistics are primary sources. Geographers use maps, manufacturing statistics, and traffic figures as primary sources. Such lists cover merely a fraction of what constitute primary sources for social scientists.[6]

Material, from either the past or the present, that by itself indicates little of a social incident or condition constitutes a primary source. Until a social scientist explains such primary source material and sets forth its significance in a coherent argument, it has little or no meaning. The differences between primary and secondary sources are not important. The important issue is that each of the social sciences has more or less distinct methodologies for dealing with them.[7] For our purpose, the terms *primary source* and *secondary source* are used to identify subject matter and explanation, respectively, as the two main substantive components of knowledge.

Secondary Sources as Primary Sources

To some social scientists, of course, the secondary sources of other disciplines are their primary sources. For example, for researchers in the history and sociology of knowledge, the secondary source material of other disciplines are their primary source material, the object of their inquiry. In other words, the course of the development and the relative significance of the scientific explanations of these other disciplines is the subject of explanation. The behavioral sciences are increasingly becoming the focus of historical inquiry. In this connection, Bry and Afflerbach note some of the difficulties encountered in locating original sources in the emergent subdivision of behavioral sciences, the history of the behavioral sciences:
"Among the obstacles to writing the history of the behavioral sciences as a broad intellectual movement have been specialization within separate disciplines, emphasis on recent advances at the expense of background knowledge, and neglect of primary sources."[8]
The above is only one example of a multitude of problems encountered in the social sciences. Unlike the literature of natural science, which is published in bound volumes, most of which are in periodical format and stored in libraries, social-scientific literature is published in a diverse array of sources in a variety of formats. While some of this material is stored in the library in bound volumes of periodicals (not unlike those of the natural sciences), a larger proportion is in the form of monographs and books and government publications. (As an example of the latter, the American Economic Association's bibliographies list testimony given by economists before U.S. congressional committees in the same way as research published through normal channels and, by implication, lend it the same validity.)
The greatest proportion of natural science research is published in journals, while in the social sciences a greater proportion of research appears in book format. Line speculates that the ratio of use of periodical literature and monographic literature is roughly 1:1.[9] A study in three areas of historical research in Great Britain suggests that even in a given discipline there is considerable variation in the ratios of usage of periodical and mono-

graphic literature.[10] This means that in the social sciences a considerably greater portion of shorter articles appear as chapters of books than is true for the natural sciences.[11]

In the social sciences, the substantive content of primary and secondary source materials is highly interrelated through an elaborate bibliographical structure. To the dismay of librarians, however, some researchers often encounter considerable difficulty when they attempt to gain access to specific portions of these materials. In both the natural and social sciences, these interrelations are communicated through the use of explicit references, called bibliographical footnotes or bibliographical citations. Unfortunately, the interrelations between research studies are sometimes only implied, further complicating the difficulties of researchers in tracing the course of inquiry in a field. This network of relations among research publications is called bibliographical structure, a subject that is explored in Chapter 9.

Notes

1. For extensive listings and discussions of the literature of the methodology of the social sciences, see appropriate sections of Carl M. White and associates, eds., *Sources of Information in the Social Sciences*, 2d ed. (Chicago: American Library Association, 1973); and Raymond G. McInnis and James W. Scott, *Social Science Research Handbook* (New York: Barnes and Noble, 1975).

2. Perry's findings, while perhaps only by implication, point up the importance of this distinction. See William G. Perry, *Forms of Intellectual and Ethical Development in the College Years, A Scheme* (New York: Holt, Rinehart and Winston, 1968).

3. Cf. Frank Freidel, ed., *Harvard Guide to American History*, rev. ed. (Cambridge, Mass.: Belknap Press of Harvard University Press, 1974), p. VI.

4. John MacGregor and Raymond G. McInnis, "Integrating Classroom Instruction and Library Research: The Cognitive Functions of Bibliographic Network Structures," *Journal of Higher Education* 48 (January-February 1977):22.

5. See Thomas S. Kuhn, *The Structure of Scientific Revolutions*, 2d ed. (Chicago: University of Chicago Press, 1970).

6. For an extensive discussion of primary sources, see John Madge, *The Tools of Social Science* (London: Longmans, Green, 1953) (a paperbound edition published by Doubleday [Anchor] in 1965); and "ASLIB Social Sciences Group Conference on Primary Materials in the Social Sciences," *ASLIB Proceedings* 23 (1971):166-206, 412-34. The latter covers primary sources in economics, political science, urban and regional planning, the social sciences in general, and the implications of primary sources in Maurice Line's Bath University INFROSS study: Maurice B. Line, *Information Requirements of Researchers in the Social Sciences* (Bath, England: University Library, Bath University of Technology, 1971). *ERIC* Document 054 806.

7. For a similar view, see Thelma Freides, *The Literature and Bibliography of the Social Sciences* (Los Angeles: Melville Publishing Co., 1973), p. 14.

8. Ilse Bry and Lois Afflerbach, "Bibliographic Foundations for Emergent History of the Behavioral Sciences," *Mental Health Book Review Index* 5 (1970):I-VII. The quoted passage is on p. I.

9. Maurice Line, "Information Requirements in the Social Sciences," in *Access to the Literature of the Social Sciences and Humanities: Proceedings.* Conference on Access to Knowledge and Information in the Social Sciences and the Humanities, New York, 1972 (Flushing, N.Y.: Queens College Press, 1974), p. 150.

10. Clyve Jones, et al., "The Characteristics of the Literature Used by Historians," *Journal of Librarianship* 4 (1972):137-56.

11. See Thomas S. Kuhn, *The Structure of Scientific Revolutions*, 2d ed. (Chicago: University of Chicago Press, 1970), pp. 19-20, for an account of publishing patterns in the natural sciences.

6 Nomothetic and Idiographic Aspects of Inquiry

Natural scientists refer to the published results of research stored in bound volumes of journals on library shelves as primary literature. In the social sciences, however, this literature is generally known as secondary source material. The primary source material that makes up the subject matter of these terms varies among the different social science disciplines, depending on whether the discipline is primarily nomothetic or primarily idiographic.

According to McEwen, "when a generalizing mode of analysis is used exclusively" in a discipline "without any regard for the uniqueness in the organization of singular events, it is said to be *nomothetic*." The purpose of the nomothetic discipline is to construct laws which explain characteristic patterns in social processes and events "by abstracting from them their universal, invariant, and quantifiable characteristic properties. *Idiographic* designates a way of treating in singular terms the unique, variant, non-recurrent organizations of qualitatively distinctive wholes."[1] "For most social scientists," McEwen continues, "the problem is to work idiographic considerations into nomothetic assessments; but, for the historian, the problem is to work nomothetic considerations into idiographic assessments."[2]

Plano and Riggs offer a somewhat simpler definition of the terms; nomothetic explanation, they state, is "based on general propositions applicable to classes of events or objects," while idiographic explanations "are concerned with specific propositions that explain unique or individual social phenomena. History is often regarded as essentially an idiographic discipline, while political and other social sciences that emphasize explanation by theoretical generalization are more nomothetic."[3]

Perhaps Nagel gives the most useful and simplest definitions: disciplined inquiry that is predominantly nomothetic seeks "to establish general laws for indefinitely repeatable events and processes," while disciplined inquiry that is predominantly idiographic seeks "to understand the unique and the nonrecurrent."[4] In history, textual statements "are almost without exception singular in form and are replete with proper names, designations for particular times or periods, and geographic specifications." In contrast, in most of the other social sciences, textual statements "are general in form and contain few if any references to specific objects, dates or places."[5]

Berkhofer gives more insight on these seemingly opposite modes of constructing conceptual frameworks. He believes that historians and other
social scientists

diverge in their respective interests . . . about whether . . . time can or should be
treated as processual sequence. . . . Historians are frequently thought to deal only
with the unique, whether as accidents, events, or as trends. The cumulation of these
accidents, events, and trends is said to be the domain of history proper. The social
scientist, on the other hand, seeks generalization and laws, and thus he looks to
the recurrent, whether of short or long duration, for the comparisons necessary to
establish his patterns. The historian tends to treat time sequences as unique series of
events; so he accuses the social scientist of distorting time by ripping some events
from their full context of coexistent setting and complex sequence in order to study
the recurrent and produce generalizations. In this sense, the historian sees the social
scientist as abstracting further from reality, hence warping the true nature of time,
whereas [the social scientist] perceives himself as studying a manifold complex of
concrete events and thereby preserving the true quality of time.[6]

In such a perspective, history is considered an "individualizing subject"
(i.e., idiographic), "supposedly concerned with the particular, the concrete
and the unique," while other social sciences, "as generalizing subjects"
(i.e., nomothetic), are considered to be "interested in the general, the abstract, and the repetitive." Berkhofer accurately notes that such sharp distinctions misrepresent or distort the actual practice of social scientists and
historians; he refers to several examinations of the problem.[7]

After a discussion of the issue involved in the apparent paradox of idio-
graphic-nomothetic modes of analysis, with particular attention given
problems of comparative history, Berkhofer concludes that "both history
and the [social] sciences deal with the unique and the general, the singular
and the recurrent, but the goals of the practitioners of the two branches of
knowledge result in different combinations of the two possible perspectives
on time and reality."[8]

Berkhofer notes that most historians are concerned with individual idiosyncrasies of historical figures, while the social scientist is concerned with
the motivating influences of individuals in the aggregate. The historian, he
says, seeks "to bring a wider set of events into a single framework than do
the social scientists, who only explore events insofar as they can be ordered
into repetitive series. Historians therefore investigate aspects of time not yet
amenable to 'scientific' study" because historians neither possess nor seek
generalizations on events abstracted from reality.[9]

Even though the social science disciplines are strongly divided on the
relative appropriateness of the nomothetic and idiographic modes of analysis,
they are not unwilling to make concessions. For example, Elton, perhaps the
most outspoken historian opposed to nomothetic considerations in historical
inquiry, concedes at least that "historical studies derived from sociological

influence can never be more than a small part of the whole enterprise." Such endeavors, he elaborates, are "not, of course, entirely hopeless, and the results of enquiry may be interesting. . . . Demographic studies, in particular, have very important uses and can sometimes rest on reasonably reliable figures."[10] Interestingly, Maslow, a psychologist widely known to have anti-behavioralist inclinations, calls for the infusion of more idiographic considerations by those seeking to understand and explain individuals according to scientific laws and generalizations.[11]

Another consideration that distinguishes history from the other social sciences is the problem of historical narrative: ". . . History is first and foremost a story."[12] The approach to telling the story can, of course, vary a great deal:

At one extreme is the simple chronicle that strings events one after the other like separate stones on the strand of time; at the other is the account that tries to explain each event as the result of what went before, including in the explanation such enduring circumstances, environmental and external, as influence the behavior of the actors in the story. Needless to say most histories fall not at the extremes, but somewhere between.[13]

The traditional form for historical exposition is the narrative, wherein, as explained by Berkhofer, "causal nexus is entwined in descriptive prose" with the intention of evoking, recounting, and perhaps explaining simultaneously.

In this view, the perfect historical synthesis is composed of a narrative exposition of chronologically ordered, factually true data about a part of man's past arranged so artistically that it helps to reproduce past reality in the mind of the reader at the same time as it perhaps explains man's past behavior within and by its organization. Such written history is considered both art and science by its admirers.[14]

Berkhofer notes, however, that such an ideal is no longer attainable, largely because of the increased knowledge of human behavior.[15]

Notes

1. William A. McEwen, *The Problem of Social-Scientific Knowledge* (Totowa, N.J.: Bedminster Press, 1963), p. 199.

2. Ibid., p. 200.

3. Jack C. Plano and Robert E. Riggs, *Dictionary of Political Analysis* (Hinsdale, Ill.: Dryden Press, 1973), p. 49.

4. Ernest Nagel, *The Structure of Science* (New York: Harcourt, Brace and World, 1961), p. 547.

5. Ibid., p. 548.

6. Robert F. Berkhofer, *A Behavioral Approach to Historical Analysis* (New York: Free Press, 1969), pp. 244-5.

7. Ibid., pp. 246-7. For a discussion of similar concerns as they apply to geography,

see David Harvey, *Explanation in Geography* (London: Arnold, 1969), pp. 50-3, 71-2; Richard Hartshorne, *Perspectives on the Nature of Geography* (Chicago: Rand McNally, 1959), Chapter 10; and Kevin R. Cox, "American Geography: Social Science Emergent," *Social Science Quarterly* 57 (1976):186-9. For an application to anthropology, see Robert M. Carmack, "Ethnohistory: Review of Its Development, Definitions, Methods, and Aims," *Annual Review of Anthropology* 1 (1972):227-8.

8. Berkhofer, *A Behavioral Approach to Historical Analysis*, p. 264. For similar observations, see Michael Polanyi, *The Study of Man* (Chicago: University of Chicago Press, 1959), pp. 71-99 and comment on p. 100. According to George Q. Flynn, "History and the Social Sciences," *History Teacher* 7 (May 1974):439:

One fundamental problem preventing compatibility of history and the social sciences revolves around the confusion over how an historian approaches the past. Despite its origins in the positivist revolt, history has always had a strong idealistic and romantic quality to it. Most recently articulated by R. G. Collingwood, this school insists that the historian comes to know the past by literally rethinking the ideas of historic figures. All history becomes the history of thought. Unlike the social scientist, who looks at phenomena, the historian looks through them. As W. H. Walsh puts it, "Whereas nature is all on the surface, history has both inside and outside." Obviously, this technique uses the concepts of the social sciences as they shape the intellectual mode in which the historian works. But the approach is not empirical.

9. Berkhofer, *A Behavioral Approach to Historical Analysis*, p. 267.

10. G. R. Elton, *The Practice of History* (New York: Crowell, 1969), pp. 28-9. Readers will be interested to note that Elton is the editor of a series of volumes on historical method in which one of the volumes is T. H. Hollingsworth, *Historical Demography* (Ithaca, N.Y.: Cornell University Press, 1969).

11. Abraham H. Maslow, *The Psychology of Science, A Reconnaissance* (New York: Harper and Row, 1966), pp. 8-11. Two volumes which examine the problems and opportunities of obtaining a greater integration of history and the social sciences are Edward N. Saveth, ed., *American History and the Social Sciences* (New York: Free Press, 1964), and Seymour W. Lipset and Richard Hofstadter, eds., *Sociology and History: Methods* (New York: Basic Books, 1968).

12. David S. Landes and Charles Tilly, eds., *History as Social Science* (Englewood Cliffs, N.J.: Prentice-Hall, 1971), p. 8.

13. Ibid., p. 8.

14. Berkhofer, *A Behavioral Approach to Historical Analysis*, pp. 271-2.

15. In Chapter 12 of *A Behavioral Approach to Historical Analysis*, Berkhofer provides a useful survey of the debate on the problem of narration and explanation in history. For other discussions of this issue, see Werner J. Cahnman and Alvin Boskoff, "Sociology and History: Reunion and Rapprochement," in Werner J. Cahnman and Alvin Boskoff, eds., *Sociology and History: Theory and Research* (New York: Free Press, 1964), pp. 1-18; Rudolph H. Weingartner, "The Quarrel About Historical Explanation," *Journal of Philosophy* 58 (1961):29-45, reprinted in Ronald H. Nash, ed., *Ideas of History* (New York: Dalton, 1969), II, pp. 140-57; Morton White, *Foundations of Historical Knowledge* (New York: Harper and Row, 1965), pp. 219-20; Flynn, "History and the Social Sciences," pp. 434-47; Thomas C. Cochran, "History and the Social Sciences," in A. S. Eisenstadt, ed., *The Craft of American History* (New York: 1966), II, pp. 90-109; and H. Stuart Hughes, "The Historian and the Social Scientist," *American Historical Review* 66 (October 1960): 20-46.

7 Characteristic Concerns of Individual Disciplines in the Social Sciences

This chapter presents a brief discussion of the rough dimensions of inquiry in each of the following social sciences: anthropology, demography, economics, geography, history, political science, psychology, and sociology. Excluded is education, and linguistics is included with anthropology. Readers who need fuller descriptions of the disciplines below and definitions of the disciplines not included have several good sources available.[1]

Anthropology embraces the study of human group differences and similarities, with emphasis on the so-called primitive or underdeveloped societies. It is principally concerned with

man's ways of feeling, believing, and acting, by reference to *culture* as a humanly created, transmitted, learned, and modified symbolic pattern. Accordingly, anthropologists seek to determine how such cultural patterns are externalized in social institutions, and [are] internalized in the value-orientations of persons who, as both products and procedures of culture, are motivated by the striving for culturally begotten goals.[2]

Generally, anthropological investigations have two main perspectives: the holistic, which restricts itself to the intensive examination and explanation of a particular culture, and the comparative, which seeks to compare and contrast cultural characteristics of two or more culture groups. Research done from the comparative perspective has resulted in many publications, including *Ethnographic Atlas*[3] and *A Cross-Cultural Summary*[4] which present comparative cultural data in tabular form.

The principal subdivisions of anthropology are archaeology, art of non-Western peoples, ethomusicology, folklore, mythology and religion, linguistics, physical anthropology, and social and cultural anthropology.

Demography is still in an emergent stage of development as demonstrated by the fact that it is not treated as a separate chapter in either White or Hoselitz.[5] It is rapidly achieving status as a discipline in its own right, however. For example, the *Social Science Research Handbook* observes that demography, long considered a subfield of sociology or (in its spatial aspects) a subfield of geography, has recently established itself as a distinct discipline. Centers for demographic research have sprung up all over the world; university departments of demography and centers of family planning and miscellaneous population studies have begun to appear in many parts of North America and in various European and Asian countries; and numerous journals, bibliographies, and other specialized demographic publications, are now being issued in scores of countries.[6]

Population dynamics, migration, population pressure and world resources, and population policies and population control are the principal divisions of demography.

Economics, according to McEwen, has as its primary subject matter "the allocation of scarce resources." Such a statement may appear to be too narrow and rigid, but, as McEwen explains, the motives of neoclassical and institutional economists are, at bottom, the same. Since the discipline

has been generally identified as the analysis of the allocation of scarce resources among alternative courses for meeting human needs for material goods and services . . . , [neoclassical economists treat] profit-seeking within the market process of production, distribution, consumption and exchange in isolation from other motivational and sociocultural factors, . . . [and institutional economists] analyze economic behavior as a selective adjustment of means to ends [taking] into account the impingement upon economic actions of other motivational and sociocultural factors.[7]

Hoselitz presents a more clearcut definition of economics. He states that it is "the study of the production, distribution, and consumption of material goods and services destined to fulfill the needs of persons and human groups in societies." From this perspective, economic systems can be examined in four directions: first, economic theory, which concerns itself with the general principles of human behavior within the economic system; second, methodology and measurement, "which is concerned with the ways and means of measuring more or less accurately the performance of an economic system and the magnitude of changes within the economy"; third, economic policy, "which is concerned with the steps" governments or private groups and individuals can take "to bring about certain desired results"; and fourth, economic history, "which is concerned with the equalization of exploration of the current state of the economy" which results from past developments.[8]

The principal subdivisions in economics are the history of economic thought; history of economics; international economics; private and public finance; applied economics (more often identified as business administration); and labor economics. There are, of course, many others.

Geography, like the other social sciences, investigates "both man in society and as part of the total environment which he has in part created." In this sense, geography is anthropocentric, seeking to understand and explain "human behavior to the same degree, though not necessarily in the same way," that is characteristic of the other sciences.[9]

The principal subdivisions of geography are exploration and travel, human geography, economic geography, urban geography and planning, and environmental studies. Another subdivision, physical geography, is closely aligned with geology and other physical sciences, and is only indirectly concerned with social matters; hence, it is not included in this book. While environmental studies is similarly concerned with the physical realm, the extraordinarily strong human component inherent in it dictates that it be included. It might be added that environmental studies is an emergent discipline and will probably soon become a discipline in its own right.

History, according to Broadus, can be defined to include all that has ever happened, although, more realistically, it limits its range and scope "to the *record* of that which occurred."[10] Historians seek to reconstruct and explain past human actions on the basis of evidence relating to a particular time or place. For the most part, history orders itself according to geographical or chronological divisions, with a strong bias toward European-North American perspectives.

Historians are ambivalent as to whether history should be considered a social science. (For a discussion of this issue, see Chapter 6.) The tide, however, is running increasingly in favor of history becoming a full-fledged discipline of the social sciences.[11] Historians have been reluctant to consider their discipline a social science partly because their approach to primary sources, both in terms of method and goals, is markedly different from that of other social scientists.[12] Flynn observes that the pluralist segment of historians, including Hays, Hofstadter, Cochran, and Potter, believe that "the distinction of the social scientist looking for laws and the historian seeking the unique is misleading."[13] They instead emphasize "a number of important areas of convergence between history and the social sciences."[14] In this connection, readers should note that Hoselitz omits history in his guide,[15] and that the volume on history in the Behavioral and Social Sciences Survey is entitled *History as Social Science*.[16]

Political science generally seeks to identify and explain the characteristics of political activities of social groups. McEwen states, however, that except for its broadest level, its practitioners have not achieved a consensus on the precise concerns of political science.[17] According to Plano and Riggs,

Substantively, the discipline has moved in the past century from an emphasis upon formal institutions and legal relationships to a concern for processes, the behavior of individuals and groups, and informal relationships. The preferred criteria for identifying political science subject matter have shifted from the institutional concepts of *state* and *government* to the process or relational concepts of *power, decision making,* and *political system.* Methodologically, political science has supplemented the predominantly legal, historical, and descriptive analysis of an earlier period with the methods and perspectives of modern behavioral science.[18]

Its principal subdivisions include comparative politics, international organizations, international relations, political behavior, political philosophy and ideology, and public administration.

Psychology can be described as the scientific study of behavior and experience. Reitman asserts that "the focus of psychological concern is the individual in interaction with his environment." On the one hand, such a definition suggests that psychology encroaches upon the "preserves of other specialities"; on the other hand, it indicates that psychology has much in common with other social sciences.[19] As such, the discipline can also be viewed to have a strong linkage with the biological sciences, particularly physiology.

Most psychologists seek both to explain and to predict behavior, and accordingly generalize from "observations of somatic and psychic data" derived from investigating "such functions as sensory-motor mechanisms, perceptions, learning, and psychodynamisms, as well as the personological assessments of abnormal and normal motivation."[20] In contrast, social psychologists investigate "motive-patterns, attitudes, sentiments, and role-behaviors" related to "the interpersonal transactions of individuals as they stimulate and are stimulated by other members" of particular social groups.[21]

The principal subdivisions of psychology include abnormal psychology; animal, comparative, and physiological psychology; applied psychology; clinical psychology (including treatment and prevention); developmental psychology; educational psychology; and social psychology.

Sociology is concerned with the relations in or between human groups but distinguishes itself from other social sciences by focusing primarily on the characteristics of social conduct. The discipline generally emphasizes current social phenomena in Western or developed societies. An almost limitless array of social conditions may influence actions, interrelations, and group thought patterns.

The "revolution" in sociology in the last few decades, beginning first with the work of Weber and extended largely by Parsons, Shils and Merton, consists largely in the *analytical concepts* that can be applied to *any* social system within a society, from simple pair groups, such as the family, to large complex organizations, or can be applied to the comparison of total societies, instead of using descriptive or discrete concepts whose utility is limited to the immediate phenomena observed.[22]

Sociology primarily examines such social configurations as marriage and the family, ethnic and religious groups, rural and urban residence patterns, the formation of public beliefs and opinions and the effect of the mass media, and the patterns of conformity and deviance.

Notes

1. Carl M. White and associates, eds., *Sources of Information in the Social Science*, 2d ed. (Chicago: American Library Association, 1973); Bert A. Hoselitz, ed., *A Reader's Guide to the Social Sciences*, 2d ed. (New York: Free Press, 1970); Robert N. Broadus, *Selecting Materials for Libraries* (New York: Wilson, 1973); and the volumes in the Behavioral and Social Sciences Survey, as described in Chapter 2.

2. William A. McEwen, *The Problem of Social-Scientific Knowledge* (Totowa, N.J.: Bedminster Press, 1963), p. 26.

3. George P. Murdock, *Ethnographic Atlas* (Pittsburgh: University of Pittsburgh Press, 1967).

4. Robert E. Textor, *A Cross-Cultural Summary* (New Haven, Conn.: HRAF Press, 1967).

5. White and associates, eds., *Sources of Information in the Social Sciences*; and Hoselitz, ed., *A Reader's Guide to the Social Sciences*.

6. Raymond G. McInnis and James W. Scott, *Social Science Research Handbook* (New York: Barnes and Noble, 1975), p. 34.

7. McEwen, *The Problem of Social-Scientific Knowledge*, p. 26.

8. Hoselitz, ed., *A Reader's Guide to the Social Sciences*, p. 241.

9. Norton Ginsburg, "Geography," in Hoselitz, ed., *A Reader's Guide to the Social Sciences*, p. 293.

10. Broadus, *Selecting Materials for Libraries*, p. 170.

11. See Chapter 6, note 15.

12. George Q. Flynn, "History and the Social Sciences," *History Teacher* 7 (May 1974):441.

13. Ibid., p. 442.

14. Ibid., p. 443.

15. Hoselitz, ed., *A Reader's Guide to the Social Sciences*.

16. David S. Landes and Charles Tilly, eds., *History as Social Science* (Englewood Cliffs, N.J.: Prentice-Hall, 1971).

17. McEwen, *The Problem of Social Scientific Knowledge*, p. 26.

18. Jack C. Plano and Robert E. Riggs, *Dictionary of Political Analysis* (Hinsdale, Ill.: Dryden Press, 1973), p. 67.

19. Walter R. Reitman, "Psychology," in Hoselitz, ed., *A Reader's Guide to the Social Sciences*, p. 93. See also Broadus, *Selecting Materials for Libraries*, p. 221.

20. McEwen, *The Problem of Social-Scientific Knowledge*, p. 25.

21. Ibid., p. 25.

22. Daniel Bell, *The Reforming of General Education* (New York: Columbia University Press, 1966), p. 161.

8 Creativity, Intuition, and Tacit Knowledge

As described earlier, the production of scientific literature through disciplined inquiry is a creative act requiring the craft skills of experienced researchers. Thus, a discussion of the structure of social-scientific literature requires that some attention be given to the role and influence of creativity and intuition in the production of the literature.

That the production of scientific literature is a creative act is not intended to imply that something is created out of nothing.[1] On the contrary, creating new scientific literature involves combining, synthesizing, and reshuffling "already existing ideas, facts, frames of perception [and] cognitive structures. In other words, it is the fusion of previously unconnected matrices."[2] Mills, for example, in a chapter entitled "On Intellectual Craftsmanship," states that researchers select from other published materials "this particular idea, this particular fact, for the realization of [their] own projects."[3] However, even if something new and original is merely added to a body of substantive literature and its basic framework remains intact, its structure is altered nonetheless—if only to the extent of making it larger. Most new substantive literature is produced in this manner. Small discrete amounts—after being accepted as valid by consensus—add to the accumulating body of literature. (Kuhn refers to this process as "normal science.")[4]

As the process of producing knowledge advances, however, portions of the existing body of knowledge become invalid or obsolete, and, through either deliberate or unconscious actions, these portions are deleted from it.[5] Koestler[6] gives more insight on this phenomenon by drawing attention to the observations of Bruner, McKellar, Kubie, and Bartlett. To Bruner, all forms of creativity "grow out of combinatorial activity—a placing of things in new perspectives."[7] Bruner also speaks of going beyond the information given "as being a vital part of creativity."[8]

To Bartlett, "the most important feature of original experimental thinking is the discovery of overlap and agreement where formerly only isolation and difference were recognized."

This usually means that when any experimental science is ripe for marked advance, a mass of routine thinking belonging to an immediately preceding phase has come near to wearing itself out by exploiting a limited range of technique to establish more and more minute and specialized detail. The conditions for original thinking are when two or more streams of research begin to offer evidence that they may converge and so in some manner be combined. It is the combination which can generate new directions of research, and through them it may be found that basic units and activities may have properties not before suspected which open up a lot of new questions for experimental study.[9]

McKellar argues that new information is derived from "separate items . . . not . . . merely joined, but rather fused into integrated wholes."[10] Kubie speaks of the "process of choosing from unanticipated combinations those patterns which have new significance."[11] As noted above, Koestler suggests that, along with the combining of existing bits of substantive literature, there are definite "hierarchic" sequences in the process of discovering these new combinations that are reflected in the historic, or diachronic development of the literature, resulting in a "hierarchy of cognitive structures."[12] In this sense, "the whole, the synthesis, is more than the sum of its parts, and its relational properties are to a large extent unpredictable by extrapolation from the properties of the parts." More details on the *diachronic* aspect of structure in the growth of scientific literature are given in Chapter 10.

Kaplan distinguishes between two types of logic employed by the researcher: logic-in-use and reconstructed logic. By the "logic of ___," that is, particular things or disciplines (he prefers the term *cognitive style*), he means the methodology of that group or thing. When this cognitive style is not formalized, he refers to it as logic-in-use; when it is formalized (or codified), he calls it reconstructed logic. The logic-in-use of any inquiry must prove itself; in turn, it is affected by language, culture, the state of the literature, the stage of inquiry, and other special conditions of the particular problem. A logic-in-use may precede and be superior to its own reconstruction, both in everyday life as well as in science. Conversely, reconstructed logic may either become, or otherwise influence, the logic-in-use. "For some time the most widely accepted reconstruction of science has been in terms of the so-called 'hypothetic-deductive method,' especially in a postulational form." Using in this reconstruction, Kaplan asserts, "a combination of careful observation, shrewd guesses and scientific intuition," the research derives a set of postulates governing the phenomena being investigated. "From these he deduces observable consequences" which are then tested by experiments, that confirm or negate "the postulates [; he replaces] them, where necessary, by others, and so continuing."[13]

"A reconstructed logic is itself, however, in effect, a hypothesis."[14] It is not always possible to match the hypothesis (the reconstructed logic) to the logic-in-use. In such cases, the reconstruction is an idealization of the logic of a science. Such a distinction is important, especially when considering the "context of discovery" and the "context of justification."[15] For example, everyone recognizes that imagination, inspiration, and the like are of enormous importance in science. Kaplan rhetorically asks, What role does *intuition* play? His answer is as follows:

What we call "intuition" is any logic-in-use which is (1) preconscious, and (2) outside the inference schema for which we have readily available reconstructions. We speak of intuition, in short, when neither we nor the discoverer himself knows quite how he arrives at his discoveries, while the frequency or pattern of their occurrence makes us reluctant to ascribe them merely to chance.[16]

Polanyi has devoted a great deal more of his attention to the notion of intuition than Kaplan has. Polanyi maintains that much of a researcher's success depends upon tacit knowledge, that is, upon craft skills that have been acquired through practice and that cannot be articulated explicitly. Polanyi's discussion of the personal element in all forms of disciplined inquiry gives much insight into tacit knowledge. He distinguishes between explicit knowing, such as occurs in the theoretical formulations of inquiry, and even in everyday descriptive discourse; and tacit knowing, which is unstated (and in some cases cannot even be articulated) but, is nonetheless the basis for making sense out of experience. Without acknowledging such capacity, he claims, there can be no logical explanation of certain processes that occur when extrapolating from one point, where much is known, to another point, where nothing is known for certain. In other words, "the structure of tacit knowing . . . is a process of *comprehending*: a grasping of disjointed parts into a comprehensive whole."[17]

According to Perelman, ascribing such creative characteristics to the requirements of disciplined inquiry is necessary because without the investigator's "experience, talent and technical skill," "neither the perception of the object nor the elaboration of hypotheses, nor even their verification, can be done in an entirely formal and mechanical fashion."[18] Examples of tacit skills in scientific inquiry in the natural sciences are those relating to the discovery of the causes of rain and those elucidating the nature of the relationship between brain and mind, as given by Scott and Walshe, respectively.[19]

These arguments about an individual's intuitive capacities become more convincing when a researcher is pictured as a craftsman in the traditional sense of the term. Ravetz and Ziman both stress this aspect of scientific inquiry. According to Ravetz;

Craftsman's work is done with particular objects, which may be material or intellectual constructs, or a mixture of the two: and the operator must know them in all their particularity. Their properties and behavior cannot be fully specified in a formal list; in fact, no explicit description can do more than give the first simple elements of their properties. Hence the operator's knowledge of them must be "intuitive," or of the sort described by Polyani as "tacit." It cannot be learned from books, but from a teacher by precept and imitation, and supplemented by the personal experience of the operator himself. Such a craftsman's knowledge of his objects is necessary for any sort of scientific work; even in pure mathematics, where the objects of the work are purely intellectual creations, the properties of the objects which are known from established results are not sufficiently particular and subtle to guide the work of constructing an argument for a new proof.[20]

Inevitably, questions arise that are of particular concern to those involved with the social sciences. Do craft skills also hold for inquiry in these disciplines? And if they do, how do they relate to the provision of reference service? The answer to the first question is given by Ravetz: "A different set of craft skills are involved in the production of data in fields which are 'descriptive' rather than 'experimental.'" In these, we may say that the data are 'found' rather than 'manufactured.'"[21] Ravetz directs attention to a historian and a sociologist who have made explicit the craft character of their disciplines.[22]

The second question, the relationships of these issues relating to craft skills in the use of reference materials is explored in Part III.

Notes

1. Arthur Koestler, "Evolution and Revolution in the History of Science," *Encounter* 25 (December 1965):25.

2. Ibid., p. 35.

3. C. Wright Mills, *The Sociological Imagination* (New York: Oxford University Press, 1959), p. 199.

4. Thomas S. Kuhn, *The Structure of Scientific Revolutions*, 2d ed. (Chicago: University of Chicago Press, 1970).

5. Both Bartlett and Kuhn note this characteristic of scientific literature. See note 9 below.

6. Koestler, "Evolution and Revolution in the History of Science."

7. Jerome S. Bruner, *On Knowing* (Cambridge, Mass.: Belknap Press of Harvard University Press, 1964), p. 20.

8. Jerome S. Bruner, "Going Beyond the Information Given," in *Contemporary Approaches to Cognition*, a symposium held at the University of Colorado (Cambridge, Mass.: Harvard University Press, 1957), pp. 43-69.

9. F. C. Bartlett, *Thinking* (New York: Basic Books, 1958), pp. 136-7. Readers will note that this observation is much like Kuhn's suggestion that theories or modes of explanation are used only as long as they are operative; see Kuhn, *The Structure of Scientific Revolutions*, p. 6.

10. Peter McKellar, *Imagination and Thinking* (New York: Basic Books, 1957), p. 13.

11. L. S. Kubie, *Neurotic Distortion of the Creative Process* (Lawrence, Kan.: University of Kansas Press, 1958), p. 151.

12. Koestler, "Evolution and Revolution in the History of Science," p. 36.

13. Abraham Kaplan, *The Conduct of Inquiry* (Scranton, Penn.: Chandler Publishing Co., 1964), pp. 8-10.

14. Ibid., p. 10.

15. Ibid., p. 13. For a similar observation, see Kuhn, *The Structure of Scientific Revolutions*, pp. 1, 8.

16. Kaplan, *The Conduct of Inquiry*, p. 14.

17. Michael Polanyi, *The Study of Man* (Chicago: University of Chicago Press, 1959), p. 28. Thomas Kuhn acknowledges his indebtedness to Polanyi's notion of the "tacit dimension" of scientific inquiry in his *Structure of Scientific Revolutions*, p. 44, note.

18. Chaim Perelman, "Polanyi's Interpretation of Scientific Inquiry," in Thomas A. Langford and William H. Poteat, eds., *Intellect and Hope* (Durham, N.C.: Duke University Press, 1968), p. 235.

19. William T. Scott, "The Gentle Rain—A Search for Understanding," pp. 242-74; and Francis Walshe, "Personal Knowledge and Concepts in the Biological Sciences," pp. 273-314, in Langford and Poteat, eds., *Intellect and Hope.*

20. Jerome R. Ravetz, *Scientific Knowledge and Its Social Problems* (New York: Oxford University Press, 1971), pp. 140-1.

21. Ibid., p. 78.

22. See G. R. Elton, *The Practice of History* (New York: Crowell, 1969); and Mills, *The Sociological Imagination.* In the latter volume, an appendix, "On Intellectual Craftsmanship," is an account of the author's own style.

9 The Bibliographical Structure of Scientific Literature

Upon undertaking research in any discipline, one soon becomes aware that secondary sources (i.e., published works) are linked in a network of inter-dependent relationships. Each research study on a given topic is supported by, and adds to, the existing information produced in earlier studies of that topic. (Simultaneous with the accumulation of these studies, of course, is the process of turning this information into knowledge.) The published works in this network are connected by explicit links (i.e., direct references, commonly known as footnote references, from one source to another) or, less frequently, by implicit links, where relationships are tacit rather than expressed directly. Whether linked explicitly or implicitly, the framework that is formed is known as the bibliographical structure of the literature.

As seen in Chapter 4 although the convention of bibliographical citations is a subject of considerable controversy, it is generally agreed that the pur-pose of referring to earlier contributions in a body of literature is to eliminate the necessity of showing in detail how particular arguments or assumptions are justified. It communicates to readers the previous studies which provide a foundation for the new information in the work at hand:

> The citation of references validates many of the claims . . . [made in a] paper and embeds it in the preexisting consensus. The orderliness of this process, the intellectual structure implicit in the library, the catalogue, the index, the encyclopedia, the treatise, give meaning to the research of the past and motive for research in the future. The mere accumulation of miscellaneous details is not enough to provide such order and meaning.[1]

The chapter in which this passage appears, "community and communica-tions," deals with the pattern of communication characteristic of a community of researchers; this chapter is recommended as an excellent introduction to citation behavior and patterns. Articles by Kaplan, Price, and Mitra are also useful for understanding the function of references.[2]

The bibliographical structure of a body of literature is necessarily very complex, especially for topics that have been the object of extensive critical scrutiny. The form assumed by the bibliographical structure is dictated by the chronological sequence of the publication of research studies.

Elsewhere I have argued that the content of scientific literature is fluid, that is, constantly changing, and that the bibliographical structure of a body of literature is fixed or stable; individual contributions are permanently set in the chronological sequence in which the publications appear.[3] (The fluid characteristic of substantive literature will be examined in the next chapter.) The fixed (i.e., bibliographical structure of the literature) is, of course, fluid at its expanding outer limits or frontier, where new studies are added to it. Nonetheless, it is the fixed or stable property which allows the mode of inquiry known as empirical or scholarly research ("gaining access to the network") to take place. According to Overhage:

The public printed record of the results of scholarly research is the universal device that transcends the barrier of space and time between scholars. It makes the recent advances of human knowledge accessible . . . throughout the world. Wherever there is a library, *any person who has learned the language* may participate in the outstanding intellectual adventures of his time. *The same record extends into the past; through an unbroken sequence of communications, the scholars today can trace the origin and growth of a new concept in different periods and in different countries: By standing on the shoulders of a giant he may see further.*[4]

Aside from suggesting a framework or structure of footnote references leading backwards in time, this statement also supports the argument that disciplined inquiry is basically a communication system.

Several attempts have been made to graphically representing the bibliographical structure of a body of research literature. In general, these attempts have been more or less successful. Garfield's work in this area is the most widely known, particularly his concepts of the historiograph (Figure 1) and the primordial citation. According to Garfield, the historiograph describes "a graphic display of citation data that shows key scientific events, their chronology, their interrelationship, and their relative importance" related to development of a field of research.[5] Undeniably, its most significant function is to demonstrate the influence of particular individuals in the growth of a research field. Both Garfield and Brittain have noted that several attempts were made earlier to treat citations statistically as a method of tracing the development of research.[6] The pattern assumed by citations indicates the nature of the scientific research front where an intense amount of investigation is being conducted at a particular moment.[7] Garfield's primary focus is on the use of graphic analysis of citations in literature networks for the enlightenment of experienced researchers. In theory, his method orders citation data so that the influence of the particular researchers can be perceived immediately.

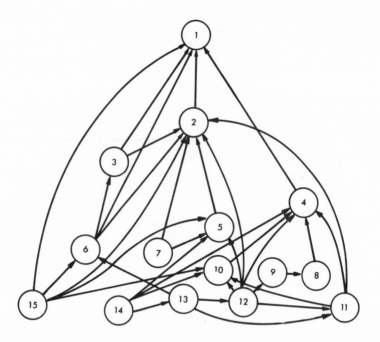

Figure 1. Garfield's Historiograph: Citation Relationships of a Bibliography on Staining Nucleic Acid. For bibliography, see Appendix B.

SOURCE: Reprinted by permission from *Toward a Theory of Librarianship* by Conrad Rawski (Metuchen, N.J.: Scarecrow Press, Inc., 1966), p. 383. Copyright © by Conrad Rawski, 1966.

Critics of Garfield's graphical depiction of citation networks claim that it presents difficulties in instruction, especially for undergraduates with little prior knowledge of the bibliographic and substantive components of research literature. For example, the use of lines (especially lines crossing lines) to show influence in the graphics tends to confuse rather than enlighten students; for that matter, it often confuses the experienced researcher as well.[8] Garfield recognized this deficiency of historiographs: "As the lines increased, the clarity of the diagram decreased."[9] Another criticism about lack of detail on how it was constructed also affects the practical application of Garfield's technique, as employed in his paper "Citation Indexing, Historio-Bibliography and the Sociology of Science,"[10] is given by Skelton, et al.[11]

Besides examining Garfield's efforts, Skelton conducted an experiment with historiographs (using hand-drawn networks) in a field in the social

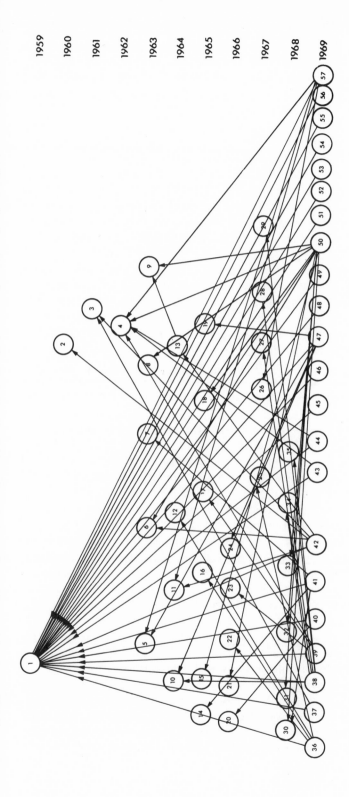

1959
1960
1961
1962
1963
1964
1965
1966
1967
1968
1969

Figure 2. Skelton's Citation Network: Short-term Memory Citation Network. For bibliography, see Appendix C.

SOURCE: Barbara Skelton et al., *The Use of Citation Linkages and Networks for Information Retrieval in the Social Sciences* (Bath, England: University Library. Bath University of Technology, 1973), p. 17.

sciences and achieved roughly the same results, but with less deficiencies. Unlike Garfield, who "gives little detail of the precise procedure he followed,"[12] Skelton gives a detailed description of the criteria used for including or excluding citations in the historiographs developed in the experiment. Skelton's study confirms the promise that historiographs hold for the social sciences, both as an effective means of information retrieval and as a teaching or study aid. With regard to the latter use, she states that "packages" could be developed according to detailed specifications ("Groups of articles can be identified that deal with particular aspects of a subject"[13]) so that the information given to a student would be directly relevant to his needs. "Packages developed in this manner could be used for programmed learning courses."

As shown below, such a mode of learning has several parallels with the techniques of Epstein, Weckstein, and Washburn. Garfield's and Skelton's achievements with historiographs help to overcome some of the basic epistemological deficiencies encountered in other types of information retrieval. According to Krevitt and Griffith, "most systems created for scientists [take] little account of either the *informal or conceptual structure of science*, which clearly guides the scientists' search for information."[14] Although Bry and Afflerbach make a similar statement, they are concerned more with effectively retrieving "secondary" publications,[15] a problem that is discussed in Part III.

MacGregor and I were convinced that the use of charts or matrices to demonstrate the bibliographical structure of substantive literature was valid, but that the use of lines to show relationships created confusion, at least for instruction purposes. We therefore attempted to develop another means, without the seemingly inherent confusion. Several principles of epistemology seemed worth depicting. We wanted first to demonstrate for undergraduate students that footnote references had a definite function and were not simply window dressing, and, second, that their relationship was reciprocal and not simply one-directional, i.e., that footnotes illustrate a two-way relationship.

Every research paper is simultaneously both a source of and a recipient of influence in relation to other studies in the network. For example, if Jones cites Smith, there are two ways to relate to that information. One is to emphasize Jones as the source of a citation to Smith: Jones → Smith; the other is to emphasize Smith as the recipient of a citation from Jones: Jones ← Smith. In the following illustrations, such relationships are evident.

We replaced Garfield's system of lines with a procedure of cross-referencing and listing citations through the symbolic notation of ovals. (Such shapes were selected because they occupied less space, but other symbols might be more satisfactory.) The advantage of this method is that, although it is somewhat more complex to construct than the historiograph, it is more easily read than Garfield's crossing lines and is therefore easier to utilize for instructional purposes.

Our method makes explicit what is only implicit in Garfield's and Skelton's historiographs: that the citations in a literature network are reciprocally related to one another. Our method demonstrates graphically (and statistically) how ideas in published research can influence other researchers to produce new information. Perhaps more significantly, it demonstrates both statistically and graphically the indebtedness of researchers to earlier studies. In the end, of course, it is the researcher, the teacher, or the learner who determines the importance of items in a literature network. The numerical count of subsequent citations, it must be acknowledged, can be a useful aid in this task.

In the Figure 3, clustered around the individual studies are symbols representing footnote references. Each symbol represents a citation by a given paper to another paper in the network. In actual practice, it is instructive if symbols representing each reference are identified. (Magnified portions are enlargements, with the symbols identified.) In the Figure 4, a more significant perspective about the progress of research on the topic is made more immediately and is graphically evident. Clustered around those studies which were cited (in the Figure 3) are symbols representing studies which cited these earlier studies. The importance of the key source, by statistical count, is readily observable. However, by manipulating the footnote references of this literature network according to various citing papers/cited works and cited works/citing papers configurations, other interesting evidence emerges. For example, in addition to the key source, it is possible to identify who were the most careful in examining the preceding literature and what types of studies should be examined in order to obtain an account of the progress that has occurred.[16]

While these diagrams are obviously comprehensive, they do not depict the total body of literature relating to the study of student subcultures. It should be especially noted that the search was limited to three referents: the names of two sociologists, Burton R. Clark and Martin J. Trow, and their concept "student subcultures." Unless a study contained these three elements, it was eliminated from the illustration. As we have seen in connection with the creative characteristics of producing new information, researchers do not limit themselves to such restrictions. They must be aware of any other material which either supports or negates what is being argued. By learning such fundamental matters as are contained in our illustrations, however, we believe that students can obtain a firmer foundation for understanding the more complex characteristics of literature networks.

The idea of the primordial citation is central to the concepts of the historiograph and bibliographic network structures. (MacGregor and I believe that for instructional purposes, the term *primordial citation* is unneces-

BIBLIOGRAPHICAL STRUCTURE
CITING PAPER/CITED WORK

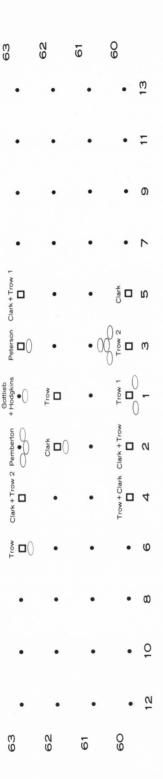

Figure 3. Clark and Trow Student Subculture Network: Citing Paper/Cited Work. Each balloon represents a footnote reference by a given paper in the network to another paper in the network. In actual practice, symbols identifying each reference are entered into the balloons. Magnified portion shows enlarged sample. For bibliography, see Appendix D.

SOURCE: Adapted from John MacGregor and Raymond G. McInnis, "Integrating Classroom Instruction and Library Research: The Cognitive Functions of Bibliographic Network Structures," *Journal of Higher Education* 48 (January-February 1977): 32. Reprinted by permission.

BIBLIOGRAPHICAL STRUCTURE
CITED WORK/CITING PAPERS

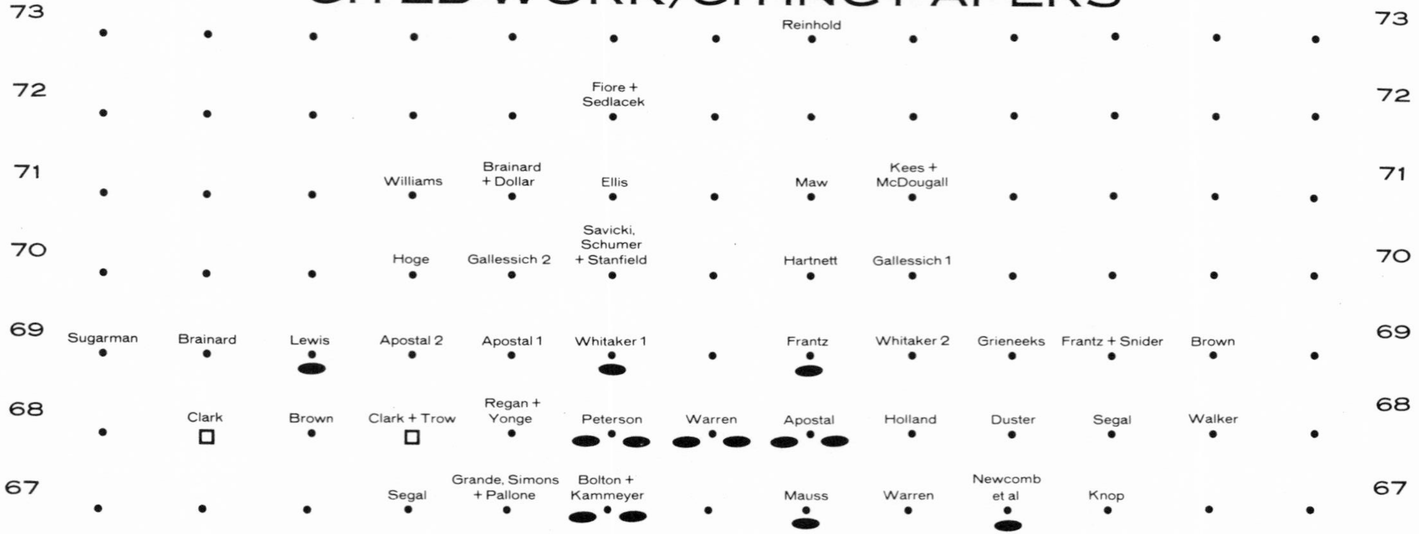

73 72 71 70 69 68 67

Reinhold

Fiore + Sedlacek

Kees + McDougall · Ellis · Maw

Savicki, Schumer + Stanfield · Gallessich 1 · Hartnett

Brown · Frantz + Snider · Grieneeks · Whitaker 2 · Frantz

Walker · Segal · Duster · Holland · Apostal

Knop · Newcomb et al · Warren · Mauss

Williams · Brainard + Dollar

Hoge · Gallessich 2

Apostal 2 · Apostal 1 · Whitaker 1 · Warren · Peterson · Regan + Yonge

Brown · Clark + Trow

Segal · Grande, Simons + Pallone · Bolton + Kammeyer

Lewis

Clark

Brainard

Sugarman

73 72 71 70 69 68 67

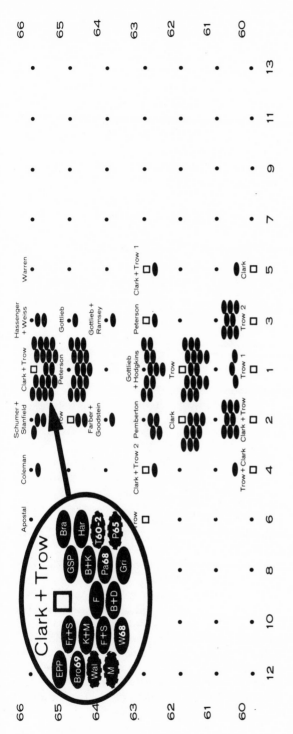

Figure 4. Clark and Trow Student Subculture Bibliographic Network: Cited Work/Citing Papers. Each balloon represents a citation of a given paper in the network by another paper in the network.

Note: The principal reason for the greater number of citations to Clark and Trow (1966) than to Clark and Trow (1960) is that the 1960 paper was available only in mimeographed form. The 1966 paper is identical to the 1960 version, and for all practical purposes, the two should be regarded as a single key source. In the magnified portion, several items have irregular edges, a means used to indicate an "implicit" reference.

SOURCE: Adapted from John MacGregor and Raymond G. McInnis, "Integrating Classroom Instruction and Library Research: The Cognitive Functions of Bibliographic Network Structures," *Journal of Higher Education* 48 (January-February 1977): 32. Reprinted by permission.

sarily abstract for the idea conveyed; therefore, in our experiments, we
have substituted the more easily comprehended term *key source*.) The key
source is the first, or base, study in the framework of the historiograph, and
it is the foundation upon which all subsequent studies linked to it are built
(for example, Clark and Trow, 1960, in Figure 3.) Linkage with the primordial citation or key source is communicated through either an explicit or
implicit footnote reference. The most dramatic example of the key source is,
of course, the appearance of an important original breakthrough. As noted
earlier, Kuhn considers this a paradigm shift.

Following a paradigm shift, there is a slow, erratic—and often acrimon-
ious—restructuring of the substantive literature in that field of inquiry.
Kuhn, in *The Structure of Scientific Revolutions*, gives the most well-known
account of this phenomenon. Because of his own study, he has created a
revolution in the explanation of the characteristics of scientific inquiry.
Hence, in turn his *Structure of Scientific Revolutions* has become a key
source in its own right.[17]

Notes

1. John Ziman, *Public Knowledge* (Cambridge, Mass.: Cambridge University
Press, 1968), pp. 103-4.

2. N. Kaplan, "The Norms of Citation Behavior: Prolegomena to the Footnote,"
American Documentation 16 (1965):179-84; D. J. de Sola Price, "Networks of
Scientific Papers," *Science* 149 (1965):510-5; and A. C. Mitra, "The Bibliographic
Reference: A Review of Its Role," *Annals of Library Science and Documentation*
17 (1970):117-23.

3. Raymond G. McInnis, "Integrating Classroom Instruction and Library Re-
search: An Essay Review," *Studies in History and Society* 6 (1974-1975):31-65; and
John MacGregor and Raymond G. McInnis, "Integrating Classroom Instruction and
Library Research: The Cognitive Functions of Bibliographic Network Structures,"
Journal of Higher Education 48 (January-February 1977):17-38.

4. Carl F. J. Overhage, "Science Libraries: Prospects and Problems," *Science* 155
(February 17, 1967):804. (Emphasis added.)

5. Eugene Garfield, "Historiographs, Librarianship, and the History of Science,"
in Conrad Rawski, ed., *Toward a Theory of Librarianship* (Metuchen, N.J.: Scarecrow Press, 1973), p. 382. Important distinctions between "reference" and "citation"
analyses are made by Jones, et al.: "Citation literally means each occasion upon
which a work is cited in the footnotes, whereas a reference is the actual work cited.
Thus in a citation analysis each citation must be recorded, while in a reference analysis each work cited is recorded only once. Most citation studies have not made this
distinction clear and some errors may have been introduced as a result." See Clyve
Jones, et al., "The Characteristics of the Literature Used by Historians," *Journal of
Librarianship* 4 (July 1972):137-56, especially p. 138 and note 3. The experiment
discussed below, according to Jones, et al., is a "reference" analysis.

6. J. M. Brittain, *Information and Its Users* (Bath, England: Bath University
Press, 1970).

7. Price, "Networks of Scientific Papers," pp. 510-5.

8. MacGregor and McInnis, "Integrating Classroom Instruction and Library Research," p. 29, note 17.

9. Garfield, "Historiographs, Librarianship, and the History of Science," p. 385.

10. Garfield's article appears in the *Proceedings of the 3rd International Congress of Medical Librarianship* (Amsterdam: Excerpta Medica, 1970), pp. 187-204.

11. Barbara Skelton, et al., *The Use of Citation Linkages and Networks for Information Retrieval in the Social Sciences* (Bath, England: Bath University of Technology Library, 1973). This work is also available as ERIC Document 078 868.

12. Ibid., p. 27.

13. Ibid., p. 15.

14. Beth I. Krevitt and Belver C. Griffith, *Evaluation of Information Systems: A Bibliography, 1967-1972.* (Washington, D.C.: ERIC Clearinghouse on Library and Information Sciences, 1973), p. 3. (Emphasis added.) Cf. also L. E. Watson, et al., "Sociology and Information Science," *Journal of Librarianship* 5 (1973):270-83.

15. Ilse Bry and Lois Afflerbach, "'Intensive Bibliography' and the Growth Pattern of the Literature in the Behavioral Sciences," *Mental Health Book Review Index* 4 (1969):I-VI.

16. For readers interested in following the course of inquiry of student subcultures, two papers are recommended: Jonathan Warren, "Student Perceptions of College Subcultures," *American Educational Research Journal* 5 (March 1968):213-32; and Robert A. Ellis, et al., "The Collegiate Scholar Education for Elite Status," *Sociology of Education* 44 (Winter 1971):27-58.

17. The amount of interest accorded Kuhn's work has been phenomenal. The book "has become a major text for interdisciplinary discourse and has been acclaimed by the *cognoscenti* that reads Lévi-Strauss, Piaget, Erikson, Laing, Lukács and Chomsky." David A. Hollinger, "T. S. Kuhn's Theory of Science and Its Implications for History," *American Historical Review* 78 (1973):370-1. Although Hollinger's study focuses principally on history, it is an excellent appraisal of and introduction to the Kuhnian "revolution." For another thoughtful assessment of the implications of Kuhn's theory, see the preface and Chapter 1 of Robert W. Friedrichs, *A Sociology of Sociology* (New York: Free Press, 1972). The second enlarged edition of Kuhn's book is also an excellent introduction to the controversy: Thomas S. Kuhn, *The Structure of Scientific Revolutions*, 2d ed. (Chicago: University of Chicago Press, 1970). See also Theodore Kisiel, with Galen Johnson, "New Philosophies of Science in the USA: A Selective Survey," *Zeitschrift fur Allegemeine Wissenschaftstheorie* 5 (1974):146, 156-67, and bibliographies of Kuhn's writings, his critics, and his influence on various disciplines, pp. 188-91; and Gernot Böhme, "Models for the Development of Science," and Roy MacLeod, "Changing Perspectives in the Social History of Science, in Ina Spiegel-Rösing and Derek de Sola Price, eds., *Science, Technology and Society* (London: Sage Publications, 1977). (Both of these last chapters have relatively comprehensive, recent bibliographies.)

10 The Substantive Structure of Scientific Literature

In the previous chapter, it is argued that graphics can demonstrate that a bibliographical structure exists for a specific body of scientific literature. Implied in this idea is the fact that the bibliographical structure forms the framework upon which the substantive content of that body of literature is supported. That is, each piece of research related to the topic is embedded in the preexisting consensus.[1] Just as it can be argued that a bibliographical structure of scientific literature exists, it can be argued that a substantive structure also exists. By substantive structure is meant that shape assumed by the cumulation of the content of published studies as a consensus is achieved. (Often in referring to what is here called substantive structure, philosophers of science and others interested in the topic speak of cognitive structures of disciplines—that is, the currently valid body of knowledge in particular fields.) Thus, it is an idiosyncratic process. It must be acknowledged, of course, that whatever shape a body of scientific literature assumes in the memory structures of practitioners in the field depends upon the ability to conceptualize subject matter concretely.

Natural and Formal Structures of Scientific Literature

One of the difficulties inherent in any discussion of the structures of scientific literature hinges on the differences between the concept of natural structure and those of formal structure. Barron and Narin state that "since the research literature is the fundamental medium of reporting research knowledge, it is reasonable to assume, a priori, that the structure of the literature in a field will reflect the structure of the knowledge in that field."[2] Similarly, Brittain and Line assume, a priori, a structure of scientific literature.[3] Since the shape taken by the substantive content of the literature occurs through natural processes, rather than by design or manipulation, it seems logical that this configuration of the literature be called natural structure. Ziman has addressed the problem in the following way:

the pattern assumed by the literature has its own internal logic, which is not at all the theoretical logic of the subject. The historical order and connectivity that it indicates are not at all the categories and logical relations into which the field will eventually settle. For example, some particular paper, clever but only partially correct, may dominate the subject for a number of years, and then be put right, or otherwise superseded, so that it scarcely warrants further mention except in the history books. On the other hand, a beautiful and important research may lie neglected and forgotten . . . and then suddenly be seen as a great well of knowledge.[4]

Formal structure refers to the idea of ordering a naturally structured body of substantive literature in hierarchical flowchart-like schemes, similar to what Ziman above names "the theoretical logic of the subject."[5] Although this method is sometimes useful for depicting knowledge, it is necessarily arbitrary and temporary inasmuch as it fits the needs of a particular situation at a particular time, and a different arrangement for that same body of knowledge may be needed in another situation.

As seen in Chapter 8, much of the activity of researchers engaged in producing new explanations or understandings of what is known in a field involves combining existing bits of information or, for that matter, even knowledge, into new configurations. Often, such combinations involve utilization of material from other fields. Such a process, of course, requires considerable understanding and skill on the part of the researcher. Occasionally, less experienced researchers can exhibit such insights, in part at least because they may not be as fixed in their perceptions as those deeply immersed in the subject. Be that as it may, with regard to the notion of natural structure, Koestler suggests that there is a definite hierarchical sequence of combinatorial processes "which results in a hierarchy of cognitive structures." He adds that such processes occur both *in the development of the individual* and in the historical development of the science."[6]

As will be argued below in this chapter, the concept of a natural structure of substantive literature is central to the notion of the fluid property of that literature. In other words, the substantive literature of a given field assumes a definite cognitive structure,[7] for the most part as a consensus among the community of researchers actively engaged in inquiry in the field.[8]

Substantive Structures of Literature

The concept of a substantive structure of scientific literature presents several problems. Specifically, how is it possible to argue, on the one hand, for a bibliographical structure of scientific literature that includes papers contributed to the development of that body of literature and, on the other hand, for a substantive structure of that same literature that includes only that subject matter that is considered valid? This seeming paradox can be explained in the following way.

Implicit in the arguments concerning creativity and intuition is the notion that along with the formation of new configurations of substantive literature, there exists both a diachronic and a synchronic structure.[9] As the etymology of these words would suggest, synchronic structure is the shape assumed at a given moment by a body of substantive literature as a consensus is achieved; and diachronic structure refers to the shape assumed by a body of substantive literature as it develops through time. That is, the diachronic structure of a body of substantive literature embodies the entire subject matter that figured in the development of its current or consensual shape.

Kuhn describes this characteristic of the advance of knowledge in the sciences. He states that the textbook approach to educating scientists has tended to make the historical progress of scientific inquiry almost imperceptible. (He also claims that a somewhat similar situation occurs coincidentally in "history, philosophy and the social sciences.")[10]

Both the layman's and the practitioner's knowledge of science is based on textbooks and a few other types of literature derived from them. Textbooks, however, being pedogogic vehicles for the perpetuation of normal science, have to be rewritten in whole or in part whenever the language, problem-structure, or standards of normal science change. In short, they have to be written in the aftermath of each scientific revolution, and once rewritten they inevitably disguise not only the role but the very existence of the revolutions that produced them. Unless he has personally experienced a revoution in his own lifetime, the historical sense either of the working scientist or the lay reader of textbook literature extends only to the outcome of the most recent revolutions in the field.[11]

Historians of science, on the other hand, are asking a new kind of question and are tracing different, *"often less than cumulative*, developmental lines for the sciences." From such inquiry has emerged a better concept of the tortuous, uneven pattern of development characteristic of scientific inquiry. The historians' main concern is the "attempt to display the historical integrity of that science in its own time."[12] Central to these investigations is an awareness of the diachronic structure of the literature in a particular field. Few original contributions remain intact; much is discarded and forgotten as it becomes revised or outmoded. Thus, diachronic structure means the entire contributions to the development of a body of scientific literature. Put another way, the diachronic structure of a literature is the entire body of substantive content associated with the entire bibliographical structure of that same literature.[13]

It is in the diachronic sense, then, that scientific literature can be said to be cumulative. Admittedly, this conception of scientific progress is at odds with the conventional view of the cumulative characteristic of scientific literature. On the other hand, based on the above arguments concerning the concept of synchronic structure of literature, scientific literature is noncumulative. Only those portions of its substantive content that are valid by consensus remain as the core of that literature.[14] (Knowledge accepted as valid through the consensus of the community of researchers can be said to constitute the synchronic structure of that literature.) Moreover, as a body of literature, not only is it noncumulative but, as seen in Chapter 3, it is almost always in an untidy, diffuse state, with the consensus often existing only in the collective memory structures of the researchers and others associated with that field of inquiry.

Given such a perspective, it can be argued that knowledge is fluid; that is, its fluidity is the mechanism by which it accommodates additions and revisions, or put another way, it fluctuates to mirror at a given moment what is perceived as valid. As new material is contributed, the literature is frequently modified beyond recognition or is discarded altogether. The rate of fluidity, and therefore the size of the body of relatively fixed elements that make up the core of the currently valid knowledge in the discipline, vary among the disciplines. Among the social sciences, anthropology and geography and, to a lesser extent, economics are more fixed and cumulatively stable. Nonetheless, shifts in emphasis, new primary sources, more precise measuring instruments, and the like, result in constant additions and alterations in the literature. This does not mean, however, that obsolescent matter will not be recovered at some future date, when its validity is suddenly restored.[15] In other words, the structure (or shape) literature assumes at a given moment is its synchronic structure, while the shape it has taken while it has evolved is its diachronic structure.

Schwab, Bell, Koestler, and Ziman have noted this characteristic of scientific literature having both diachronic and synchronic structures. At the same time, bibliographical structure is an integral part of the substantive structure and, to a certain extent, provides its form. And yet, it is argued above, the bibliographical structure of scientific literature is fixed or stable; individual contributions are permanently set in the chronological sequence in which the publications appear. At first, it may appear paradoxical that in this conception of knowledge there are such opposing forces, that is, both fixed and fluid components. In this conception, they are viewed not as in opposition but rather as complements; that is, bibliographic structure and substantive structure are integrated, although they operate on different levels within the same plane. They are separable for analytical purposes; yet, each is fused to the other.

Such distinctions between bibliographic and substantive structure and diachronic and synchronic structure are, of course, analytical. The bibliographic and diachronic structures are actually integral parts of the substantive and synchronic structures of any field of scientific research. Indeed, bibliographic structure is its key, providing convenient access to the substantive components of that literature. The implications of this concept of the components of scientific literature are explored in the next chapter in connection with another structural perspective of scientific literature, the psychological structure of knowledge.

Notes

1. John Ziman, *Public Knowledge* (Cambridge, England: Cambridge University Press, 1968), p. 103.

2. Paul Barron and Francis Narin, *Analysis of Research Journals and Related Research Structure in Education* (Chicago: Computer Horizons, 1972), p. 1. This work is also available in ERIC Document 072 787.

3. J. M. Brittain and Maurice Line, "Sources of Citations and References for Analysis Purposes: A Comparative Assessment," *Journal of Documentation* 29 (March 1973):72-3.

4. John M. Ziman, *Public Knowledge*, pp. 59-60.

5. Ibid., p. 59.

6. Arthur Koestler, "Evolution and Revolution in the History of Science," *Encounter* 25 (December 1965):36.

7. Ibid.

8. Joseph J. Schwab, "The Concept of the Structure of a Discipline," *Educational Record* 43 (July 1962):200; Daniel Bell, *The Reforming of General Education* (New York: Columbia University Press, 1966), pp. 156-78; and Ziman, *Public Knowledge*, pp. 30-62, 102-26.

9. For somewhat similar views, see Ilse Bry and Lois Afflerbach, "'Intensive Bibliography' and the Growth Pattern of the Literature in the Behavioral Sciences," *Mental Health Book Review Index* 4 (1969):I-VI; and Conrad H. Rawski, "Subject Literatures and Librarianship," in L. R. Bone, ed., *Conference on Library School Teaching Methods* (Urbana: University of Illinois, Graduate School of Library Science, 1969). Bry and Afflerbach use the terms *extensive dimension* and *intensive dimension* to characterize the bibliographic and substantive properties of scientific literature.

10. Thomas S. Kuhn, *The Structure of Scientific Revolutions*, 2d ed. (Chicago: University of Chicago Press, 1970), p. 165.

11. Ibid., p. 137.

12. Ibid., p. 3. (Emphasis added.)

13. See Koestler's remarks, Chapter 8, note 1, on the same matter.

14. Ziman, *Public Knowledge*, p. 60.

15. Since completing this chapter, two different sources confirming this argument have come to my attention. See Theodore Kisiel, with Galen Johnson, "New Philosophies of Science in the USA: A Selective Survey." *Zeitschrift für Allegemeine Wissenschaftstheorie* 5 (1974):166, especially note 67; and D. Alasdair Kemp, *The Nature of Knowledge: An Introduction for Librarians* (London: C. Bingley, 1976), pp. 123-40.

11 The Psychological Structure of Knowledge

A conception of the structure of substantive literature similar to the one being discussed here has been elaborated by several psychologists and others. This concept is concerned with the ability to conceptualize subject matter concretely, and it appears to be well grounded in common sense. For example, according to Wise, a historian, "the facts of our experience don't come to us naked and isolated, they come stuck together; what mind does with experience—when it's working as we want it—is transmit information for us from fact into meaning." Further, Wise asserts, "we don't merely *aggregate* experiences, . . . we *integrate* them, . . . ordering them into forms and patterns."[1] Similarly, Charters, a social psychologist, states that individuals

never meet situations in a totally naive fashion. The human being confronts the next moment of his life with reasonably stable, well-structured concepts and expectancies that allow him to bring order to what otherwise would be intolerable chaos. . . . The concepts he applies are the ones that seem to have worked for him in the past in bringing him food, fun, freedom from guilt, or other things he has sought. . . . These enduring modes of perceiving and cognizing are what contemporary social psychologists mean, in part, by the term *attitude*. . . . A fundamental ingredient in a person's cognitive system—you might say the building block of cognitions—is the concept. Concepts are the differentiations the person makes as he surveys events before him. . . . The successfully educated person . . . is the one whose conceptual schemes are articulated, rigorous and powerful.[2]

Much the same point is made by Wise (although he refers to it simply as learning) and by Freides.[3] Similar statements run through the arguments of, among others, Bruner, Bell, Kuhn, and Schwab. The ideas of Wise, Charters, and social psychologist Ausubel on how information is assimilated by individuals are closely parallel.

Before examining Ausubel's arguments, it is useful to recall (see Chapter 1) Kolb's assertion that individuals have preferred learning styles which are individually the desired way new substantive material increases.[4] That is, it is a characteristic of cognition that what is learned must be added to what is already known in a manner appropriate to an individual's learning style; otherwise, extreme difficulties in comprehension and retention are encountered. Hence, there is a distinction between the formal organization of subject matter and the internalized representation of it in the memory structure of individuals.

Ausubel distinguishes these two structures of substantive content with respect to four of their principal attributes: meaning, process of organization, arrangement of component parts, and maturity of subject matter. As noted above, psychological meaning, i.e., internalized representation, is always idiosyncratic: "Meaning depends not only on the learner's possession of the requisite intellectual capacities and ideational backgrounds, but also on his *particular* ideational content. When an individual learns logically meaningful propositions, therefore, he does not learn their logical meaning *but the meaning they have for him.*"[5] Reconciliation, or matching the logical and psychological structures of knowledge, Ausubel asserts, occurs in an individual's mind in the "terminal stages of subject-matter sophistication." According to Ausubel:

Only after an individual develops mature cognitive capacities and acquires an expert, specialized knowledge of a subject does his psychological structure of knowledge in that discipline correspond (although in somewhat less systematized form) to the logical structure of knowledge in that same discipline. In any case, he can at this stage easily reorganize this psychological structure in terms of the topically most homogeneous and systematic ordering of relationships between component facts, concepts, and propositions. This degree of parallelism between the logical and the psychological structure of knowledge does not exist during earlier stages of intellectual development and subject-matter sophistication. . . . It is evident therefore that the following degree of interdependence prevails between the logical and the psychological structure of knowledge: on the one hand, the psychological structure of knowledge is a derivative of subject-matter content abstracted from the logical structure of knowledge, and psychological meaning is an idiosyncratic elaboration of logical meaning; on the other hand, the logical structure of knowledge is a topically systematized reorganization of the psychological structure of knowledge as it exists in mature scholars in a particular discipline.[6]

Ausubel's "logical structure" seems to be analogous to the concepts of natural and synchronic structure. There is, for example, no doubt about their equivalence in the mind of a researcher-instructor deeply immersed in and familiar with the substantive content of his area of specialization. Further, recall Garfield's and Price's arguments concerning the function of bibliographical citation discussed in Chapter 9. Garfield suggests that references to discrete contributors can be used as "shorthand" referents to the substantive content of a literature, while Price speaks metaphorically of published papers being "scholarly bricklaying."[7] In light of these considerations, it does not seem unreasonable to conclude that the psychological structure of a literature held by individuals roughly approximates a combination of the bibliographic structure and substantive structure of that literature.

What are the curriculum or instructional implications of this concept of knowledge? Does it imply a mode of inquiry and learning that contains obvious cognitive and heuristic utility? Certainly, considering the success Garfield, Skelton, Epstein and Weckstein, and Washburn have achieved, the answer to these questions is yes. Moreover, the weaknesses of the traditional method of representing bodies of knowledge by bibliographies, comprehensive or selective, have been noted by Garfield, Freides, Ravetz, and Bry and Afflerbach.[8]

Bry and Afflerbach, it should be noted, are not directly concerned with instruction, but if their recommendations regarding "intensive" bibliography were ever implemented, the resulting bibliographic reorganization inherent in their system would have obvious implications in the classroom.

Notes

1. Gene Wise, *American Historical Explanations* (Homewood, Ill.: Dorsey Press, 1973), pp. 14-5.

2. W. W. Charters, "Knowledge and Behavior: A Framework for the Educative Process," in James Shaver and H. Berlak, eds., *Democracy, Pluralism and the Social Studies* (Boston: Houghton, Mifflin, 1968), pp. 308-9.

3. Wise, *American Historical Explanations*, p. 15; Thelma Freides, *The Literature and Bibliography of the Social Sciences* (Los Angeles: Melville Publishing Co., 1973), pp. 261-2.

4. David A. Kolb, "Individual Learning Styles and the Learning Process" (Cambridge, Mass., 1971) (mimeo).

5. David P. Ausubel, "Some Psychological Aspects of the Structure of Knowledge," in *Education and the Structure of Knowledge*, Fifth Annual Phi Delta Kappa Symposium on Educational Research (Chicago: Rand McNally, 1964), p. 223. (Emphasis added.)

6. Ibid., pp. 226-7.

7. Eugene Garfield, "Primordial Concepts, Citation Indexing, and Historiographs," *Journal of Library History* 2 (1967):235-49; and Derek J. de Sola Price, *Little Science, Big Science* (New York: Columbia University Press, 1963), pp. 64-5.

8. Garfield, "Primordial Concepts, Citation Indexing, and Historiographs," p. 241; Freides, *The Literature and Bibliography of the Social Sciences*, p. 261; Jerome R. Ravetz, *Scientific Knowledge and Its Social Problems* (New York: Oxford University Press, 1971), p. 79; and Ilse Bry and Lois Afflerbach, "'Intensive Bibliography' and the Growth Pattern of the Literature in the Behavioral Sciences," *Mental Health Book Review Index* 4 (1969):I-VI.

12 Inquiry as a Mode of Learning: Substantive and Cognitive Considerations

This chapter gives several examples of reported modes of learning that their originators believe have been successful or are potentially successful. Their success stems largely from their originators' conviction that each mode of learning contributes additional dimensions to what is learned, beyond the merely substantive content. (For the most part, the term *cognitive structure* is used to identify their perspective of learning.)[1] Moreover, without the teacher's enthusiasm and dedication to how a subject is learned, as opposed to what is learned, these particular modes of instruction and learning would not be as effective.[2]

As observed earlier, some of the underlying principles of these modes of learning are presently, at best, only implicitly linked to accepted modes of inquiry in the library. However, incorporating in them some dimension of inquiry seems but a logical extension of their utility. Further, it is a legitimate function of concerned reference librarians to direct the attention of potentially interested instructors to such matters. Obviously, such a task will be neither rapidly nor easily accomplished; it will require considerable personal dedication and conviction and long periods of seemingly unproductive effort. Thus, interested librarians will be well advised to be prepared to enjoy limited successes, and not to look forward to brilliant, immediate achievements.

The first example of a mode of instruction and learning is drawn from biology. Rather fortuitously, it was rapidly adopted by a discipline of the social sciences, economics; both instructors involved in these experiments in teaching are convinced that it can be utilized effectively in a wide range of disciplines in all fields of inquiry. As is noted later in this chapter, one of the critics of the system, Schwab, claims that as a system of learning it is merely another application of a mode of learning he and others have long advocated.

Epstein's Research Studies Method

In an attempt to make the introductory course in biology at Brandeis University more stimulating, Epstein departed from the traditional format of combining lectures and laboratory exercises during the academic year 1968-69.[3] As a classroom exercise, Epstein had his students examine and discuss a series of papers on a narrow biological topic explicitly linked, so that there was "a distinct thread of development from one paper to another."[4] Epstein calls this method of teaching experience-based learning or the research studies method. At the outset, Epstein did not consciously recognize that his method essentially involved discussing at least a partial literature network. He did, however, consider the structure of knowledge to be a useful curriculum component, and in this connection he refers to the work and theories of Conant and Bruner.[5] (As noted by Morgan, Bruner derived his ideas about using the structure of discipline as a curriculum component from Schwab.)[6]

Epstein explains that his intent was "to design a course to teach what a biologist does when he's doing his biology. If the student can learn an answer to this question for any one biological problem, it should not be hard to explain biology in general, because the essentials of particular problems differ little from one field of life to another."[7] At first glance, this statement appears to contradict what was said in Chapter 1 of this book about the pitfalls of inductive learning. By setting forth the principle underlying Epstein's method, however, it is evident that this inductive mode of inquiry is not inconsistent. In a review of Epstein's book, Schwab draws attention to an observation Comte made in the nineteenth century:

Every science can be viewed according to two modes of development—the historical and the dogmatic. According to the first, one considers the science successively, following the order by which the human mind has really acquired the knowledge. . . . According to the second, one presents the system of ideas as they would be conceived today by a mind which . . . is concerned with remaking the science as a totality.[8]

Schwab accurately asserts "that the first mode treats original works (research papers) with primary emphasis on the manner in which the science has been formed." As explained, there are definite parallels between the underlying principles of this mode of learning and the diachronic structure of scientific literature discussed above. Moreover, such statements about their historical development apply to almost all disciplines, and are consistent with the growing shift in emphasis from *what* one learns to *how* one learns. Put another way, the general epistemological and methodological principles of various disciplines can be learned inductively, and at the same time deductive modes of learning can increasingly be introduced into the content of courses. Epstein's basic purpose is simply "to have the students themselves recreate the research; to let them read through a set of research papers."[9]

According to Epstein, digressions are central to the process of learning in which the research studies method is employed. Indeed, digressions constitute a major portion of the activities of the course, for they enable the instructor to help students understand the theory and facts underlying the concepts and methods of each of the papers. Epstein cautions, however, that digressions must be carefully selected and controlled so as not to depart very far from the thread of the topic of inquiry. A familiar principle of psychology, he asserts in this connection, is that one absorb related information rapidly and firmly when learning a particular body of material. Bruner, along with others, Epstein notes, contends "that knowledge acquired with other knowledge of importance to the individual is very likely to remain with him because it is tied up with the memory of important information."[10]

Perhaps the most remarkable result of Epstein's classroom activities, is that in the first week, after only three one-hour class sessions, "the students had gone through the definitions and explanations of perhaps 75 terms." Indeed, this was a significant accomplishment "because most of the students appeared to have understood and perhaps even learned many or most of the terms in a situation in which the focus was on something else." Epstein considered this progress remarkable, for "to put the matter directly, what might have been the result if the students had been asked to learn the meanings of 75 terms without having the research paper to support the learning?"[11]

Several important conclusions can be derived from Epstein's teaching methods; these conclusions suggest how his methods can be more directly related to inquiry modes of learning. First, while Epstein speaks of the structure of a discipline as the central component of this method of learning, he does not explicitly state that the papers discussed constitute at least a partial network of literature. The evidence he presents to justify the method, however, demonstrates the implicit linkage of these papers. "We select about ten papers in a subject in which there is a distinct thread of development from one paper to another."[12] The linkage between papers leads Epstein to speak of the higher retention rate resulting from "structured learning." Second, he does not seem eager to have students undertake their own research in the library. Indeed, he states that "no review papers, no text-like materials, and no popular articles (such as from the *Scientific American*) can be used during the first two-thirds of the semester."[13] Instead, during digressions in class, he provided the explanations his students needed to understand how statements in a given paper could be justified.

Assuming that students have proper grounding in research methods, independent student research in the library would be equally satisfactory, and in many respects could even strengthen the retention rate. Any instructor interested in employing Epstein's methods of learning should at least be open to the idea of independent research. However, in cases where independent research cannot be instituted in the introductory course, instructors could incorporate independent modes of inquiry in subsequent courses and thereby take advantage of the grounding students received in the introductory courses.

The results Epstein obtained suggest that his innovations in classroom instruction should be taken very seriously. In a related study, the economist Weckstein, also of Brandeis, gave an identical test to two groups of economics students, one of which was taught according to traditional methods and the other according to the research studies method. (The topic of the special class was evaluating Mexican land institutions.) All students in the special group did about as well as the standard group, "that is, they *all* studied and mastered at least 60 percent of the material in the regular course while studying something else."[14] (The average grade for the standard group was 66.) Of greater significance perhaps is that "the retention rate . . . of the [special] students appeared far superior to that of a regular [economics] principles course."[15]

In a review of Epstein's book, Schwab cites two important contributions of the mode of learning: (1) "the extent to which participation by students in the solution of significant problems challenges of them to renewal of interest and marshalling of energy," and (2) "primary sources (research papers) constitute accessible occasions and effective springboards for posing problems of scientific enquiry and inviting participative solutions."[16]

In his section on recommendations for the reform of modes of instruction, Epstein refers to Conant's case-study method. According to Epstein, "Conant method gives a combined historical and conceptual development of some of the great insights in science. For example, one such topic is the development of the idea of the atom and the molecule. . . . [Conant] selects out the experiments and speculations that eventually led to the postulation and subsequent proof of the existence of atoms and molecules." Epstein is critical of this method on the basis that it "shows how some important concepts were evolved but gives the students little idea of what scientists actually do or what the scope of science may be."[17]

Washburn's Case-Studies Method

Washburn believes that the case-studies method is a viable mode of instruction and learning.[18] His proposed method can be termed an elaboration of Conant's, even though he seems unaware of Conant's previous work in this area. Washburn proposes that while a particular topic (one of the examples he uses is the discovery of continental drift) is being studied, students can simultaneously study the historical background of the topic, with emphasis on why the scientific community initially refused to accept the idea.

Ziman outlines the issue of continental drift briefly in his discussion of knowledge as consensus:

As I have suggested, we often observe some powerful ideological principle at work, some peculiar bias in the theoretical consensus. A fascinating example, is the rejection of the hypothesis of Continental Drift for some fifty years after it was first put forward on a serious scientific basis by Wegener at the beginning of the century. This is a long story, which should be carefully studied by those who interest themselves in the history of science, for there are lessons to learn from it. . . . What happened was that Wegener advanced his hypothesis on the basis of such evidence as the geographical fit between the coast of Africa and South America, and the similarities of the flora and fauna of the southern continents. This evidence is quite intelligible to the layman, and plausible enough, but it was rejected by the leading geologists of the day, who were not very interested in or knowledgeable about the geology of the Southern Hemisphere and who thought that the whole thing was too radical. They were backed up by Jeffreys, a Cambridge mathematician, who calculated, on the basis of seismological evidence, that the earth must be too rigid to allow for such drastic phenomena. The subject was, then, not quite closed, but dropped into the limbo of cranky and speculative notions. Only a few individual scientists continued the search for further evidence; in the main centers of geological teaching and research it became almost heretical to admit to belief in Wegener's hypothesis. . . . After the Second World War, an entirely new technique, the study of the magnetism of the rocks, began to produce quite new evidence in favour of Continental Drift. After a further series of debates, this evidence began to convince the younger generation of geologists and geophysicists, and it may now be said to be a well-established scientific theory. Some of the old school of geologists still stand out against it, but the multiplication of evidence of all sorts is now so rapid that it cannot be long before their conservatism will appear stubborn rather than cautious.[19]

Immediately, of course, one speculates on what a fascinating bibliographic network structure (or historiograph) would emerge from the literature on continental drift, in contrast, say, to the normal configurations characteristic of most bibliographic structures. Further speculation suggests that a detailed analysis of individual contributions to this structure would reveal as much about human nature as it would about the difficulties of advancing a scientific field. It would show the extent to which scientific activity, its appeals to rational thought processes notwithstanding, is infused with personal and social idiosyncrasies. Ziman, in a postscript to the above account, concludes:

The point of this story, is however, that much of the evidence *now* put forward on behalf of Continental Drift *does not* depend on the new geophysical techniques. Had an effort been made, 50 years ago, to look seriously for conventional geological evidence, many very strong arguments could have been made in its favour. *It has not been difficult in recent years to persuade the other Cambridge mathematicians to produce calculations refuting Jeffreys and supporting the theory*—and so on. Why were such investigations not put in train long ago? The theory is obviously of prime importance with tremendous consequences for all kinds of major geological structures. According to the picture of science as the accumulation of the independent investigations of individuals, an imaginative hypothesis on this scale should have been the leitmotif of innumerable researches, which would have verified or falsified it in detail many years ago. The inhibition of these studies is a clear sign of the power of the climate of opinion, of the effective consensus of geological science having rejected the hypothesis and excluded it from accepted Public Knowledge. The influence of the mathematical argument (which was probably not understood by most of those who assumed it was valid) is particularly interesting; there is nothing like an abstruse mathematical proof to convince the lay public, even against apparent factual evidence.[20]

According to Washburn, the example of continental drift is one of many opportunities where courses could be

built on cases that illuminate the kinds of contributions the sciences and humanities can make. . . . [Underlying] the case-study approach to understanding the nature of the world and man is the assumption that survey courses give only a superficial statement of the conclusions of a traditional piece of knowledge. In contrast, the cases would delve deeply into an important problem and would show how it was related to technical information, history, and literature. *The essence of the well-chosen case would be its ramifications.*[21]

Washburn's comments have important implications for instruction in higher education. Implementing such programs, Washburn speculates, would involve the cooperation of two or more traditionally structured academic departments. These innovations would not require major changes in the organization of the institution. With the support of colleagues and administration, it could be done by a relatively few people. The most likely candidates, at least at the beginning, are the types of instructors interested in involving students in more independent study discussed at the end of Chapter 1. At the same time, Washburn notes, not all courses need be organized in this way. Some instructors could continue to use the traditional pattern of study, and case-study courses would compete with conventional courses, including surveys. The significance of case-study courses would be that "they would attempt to give the opportunity for general understanding of knowledge through the analysis of selected materials."[22]

Continental drift, Washburn suggests, would involve geology, history, and philosophy. Other examples he gives are evolution and genetics which, are fascinating, although sadly neglected topics for study from several interdisciplinary perspectives, notably biology, history, and psychology. In my own experience with genetics research, before my work with DeLorme on the compilation of *Antidemocratic Trends in Twentieth Century America*, I was unaware of the extent to which the idea of racial and ethnic supremacy was based on inconclusive scientific evidence.[23] In connection with the antidemocratic sentiments that emerged from the eugenics movement of the late nineteenth and early twentieth centuries, two representative selections were included in our text: portions of Madison Grant's *The Passing of the Great Race* and Alleyne Allord's "Democracy and the Accepted Facts of Heredity" in a 1918 issue of *Journal of Heredity*. Together, these documents provide insight into the attitudes of various strata of American society toward the problems of an increasingly pluralistic society. (Readers will recall that these publications appeared in a period of intense immigration to the United States.) Both documents are replete with references to scientific literature justifying separation of the races. I began to recognize certain implications for teaching research techniques. First, it suggested the need to caution students about the most effective use of older, well-known encyclopedias and related reference works, and second, to encourage community college history instructors to utilize library reference works in their class assignments to compensate for the lack of primary and secondary resources. (Concern about the lack of resources in community college libraries is considerable, as a perusal of issues of *History Teacher* and *AHA Newsletter* will confirm.)

My concern about the need to be cautious in the use of older reference works was reinforced during the writing of the *Social Science Research Handbook*.[24] As a reference librarian, I (and no doubt most of my colleagues) approach the ninth and eleventh editions of the *Encyclopaedia Britannica* and the *Encyclopedia of the Social Sciences* with apprehension. Although these works contain valuable information, much of it is obsolete. Nonetheless, much of the information is still useful, especially for historical purposes. (The statistical data alone in the eleventh edition of the *Encyclopaedia Britannica* make it one of the most valuable sources of historical statistics in an academic library.) Thus, explaining the usefulness of works that are obsolete poses a real dilemma.

The solution to this dilemma would be to treat these works as primary sources. They do, after all, reflect the values of society and patterns of thinking which were dominant during the periods in which they were written. In addition, the content of various articles on similar topics expose the changes that have occurred in these areas during intervals between publication of the encyclopedias. Furthermore, some types of articles are of more lasting value than others. On the one hand, for example, terms, events, and people requiring only narrative descriptions (such as *anarchism*) are still fairly reliable in the ninth and eleventh editions of the *Encyclopaedia Britannica* and the *Encyclopedia of the Social Sciences*. On the other hand, terms and concepts (such as *eugenics*) where much advance has occurred, and which require more than narrative descriptions, are only partially reliable and, in some cases, downright misleading. History instructors have generally approved of this method of treating the two encyclopedias as primary sources; in some cases, it has sharpened their perceptions of the uses that can be made of older reference materials.[25]

With regard to the second implication—demonstrating to community college history instructors how library reference works can compensate for the lack of primary and secondary sources—pertinent details are as follows.[26] Many reference works currently available in most community college libraries are rich sources of primary materials for the study of history. Among them are the eleventh edition of the *Encyclopaedia Britannica*, the *New Larned History*, the *Encyclopedia of the Social Sciences*, and the *International Encyclopedia of the Social Sciences*. If these particular works are not in the library, they should be purchased.

As an example of how reference works can compensate for the lack of other sources, the partial bibliographical structure of the primary, secondary, and reference sources for eugenics can be depicted graphically[27] by setting forth in chronological order items mentioned in the bibliographies at the end of the reference book articles on Eugenics, Sterilization, Immigration, and Intelligence. The significance of these items is verified simply by noting a reference to them in some recent and reputable secondary sources concerned with the history of the eugenics movement. The only value of such a chart is to direct attention to the primary sources considered important both at the time particular reference works were published and at present. Determining the importance of individual primary sources still remains the task of those engaged in historical research; this point must, of course, be stressed to the student.

The above example, perhaps with some adaptation, suggests practicable means of making operational portions of Washburn's proposed innovations in learning patterns. In addition, certain elements in these examples can be applied to the mode of learning advocated by Epstein. The number of examples of such applications is, however, virtually limitless. Reference librarians encounter similar instances at work almost daily. If placed in different perspective rather than simply as run-of-the-mill reference questions, they could be used to help students develop effective techniques in research.

Discovering the formula for drawing instructors and librarians into closer collaboration remains a formidable obstacle however. At present, there is little such cooperation, and there is not much hope of achieving it in the near future. The modes of learning advocated by Epstein and Washburn would provide the ideal conditions for making instructor-librarian collaboration a reality.

But even assuming that these ideal conditions can be achieved, unresolved problems will remain. The greatest problem is how to realistically and effectively reconcile the instructor's aspirations of what students should acquire (both substantively and cognitively) from their research activities with the obvious constraints under which reference librarians must operate. On the one hand, library tours, or even more elaborate library orientations, obviously are of little value in giving students a command of effective research techniques. With their general ignorance of the library's resources, they cannot gain the effective access to the substantive literature that their instructor visualizes as desirable. On the other hand, more elaborate modes of instruction in research techniques are beyond the capacity of reference librarians, who are also confronted with the problem of merely fulfilling their functions as members of reference departments. (Increasing numbers of positions for orientation librarians have been created, but few of their individual experiences have been reported.)

As the literature suggests, the situation remains bleak, with little prospect of improvement;[28] therefore, efforts to make improvements, however small, should continue. Given such discouraging conditions, the following proposal for improvement is presented not as a magic formula but as a method that should be tested by others in other contexts. Indeed, any innovative method that might strengthen reference service in academic libraries should be encouraged. With these thoughts in mind, below I present a concept of the function of reference works in a perspective that can be quite easily and rapidly comprehended by anyone seriously engaging in research.

Based on the framework of the structure of substantive literature characteristic of the empirical sciences as developed in this chapter, this concept of the function of reference works attempts to place in an analytical perspective a model of research strategy that will allow students, when sufficient grounding is required, to gain access to the required material through a logical, coherent procedure. The operative phrase in the above sentence is, of course, *when sufficient grounding is acquired.* By dissecting the epistemological components of knowledge, certain principles of research can be set forth with greater clarity. Basic operations in research are more easily comprehended, and conceptions of what directions to follow are more effectively visualized. To date, reference librarians have seldom delved to any extent into the component parts of substantive literature (at least in the social sciences) with which they work. (An obvious exception is Freides, *Literature and Bibliography of the Social Science*, which holds much promise for developing a stronger epistemological foundation for library science as a discipline.)[29] On the other hand, because practitioners work with the components of substantive literature as a matter of course, they are acutely aware of them. By relating matters having to do with research in the library more closely to the actual circumstance of the researcher, a more rapid and effective integration of their investigations with those of librarians will be achieved. (Whether the model of inquiry is can be applied by others in a wide range of circumstances remains to the reader.) Such a method is consistent with the admonition of Gration and Young, that reference librarians responsible for giving service to students and faculty in particular disciplines must be generally well informed about these specific fields of inquiry.[30]

If reference librarians do not have this knowledge, their ability to provide effective service is strained and fragmented. At the same time, reference librarians must continually keep abreast of developments in the particular disciplines. Hence, they should have a broad familiarity with the sources that provide access to the currently valid substantive literature of these fields. They should also follow the trends and developments in these fields in the publications that are almost exlusively devoted to such functions. Thus, they will be better able to assist researchers, of whatever level of experience or intensity of need, guiding them to ideal specific research strategies with more precision and confidence. This steadily increasing command of literature in these areas, particularly the materials which give access to the literature, is reflected in the improved quality of service provided.

The task of informing oneself to this extent is a long process, requiring considerable individual capability and capacity. To those who consciously and deliberately seek to perform at a high level of achievement, progress does, however, occur with regularity. In addition, the satisfaction of acquiring a command of such capabilities has its own stimulations and rewards which, in turn, encourage greater levels of achievement. Of course, acquiring this level of expertise requires that the individual have an inherent interest in the subject matter involved. Given such an interest, achieving an increasing level of expertise has its own momentum and is more or less self-sustaining. And more than this, those outside the library profession—experts in their own fields—will realize that underlying the library profession is an enormous amount of substantive content which makes it, in its own right, an honorable and exacting discipline.

Notes

1. See Arthur Koestler, "Evolution and Revolution in the History of Science," *Encounter* 25 (1965):33; and Fred Schwartz, "Introduction," in Fred Schwartz, ed., *Scientific Thought and Social Reality: Essays by Michael Polanyi* (New York: International Universities Press, 1974), p. 6.

2. See Chapter 1, pp. 14ff, and Wise's observations in Chapter 12.

3. In one of the courses he conducted, Epstein used several papers on the DNA basis of heredity. One can only speculate on Epstein's reaction to the prospect of the availability of Garfield's historiograph for this same subject. See Herman T. Epstein, *A Strategy for Education* (New York: Oxford University Press, 1970), p. 115; and Eugene Garfield, et al., *The Use of Citation Data in Writing the History of Science* (Philadelphia: Institute for Scientific Information, 1964).

4. Epstein, *A Strategy for Education*, p. 34.

5. Ibid., pp. 8, 11. Perhaps Conant's work relates more directly to Washburn, since both use a case-studies method. For Washburn, see note 18 below.

6. Kathryn P. Morgan, "Some Philosophical Difficulties Concerning the Notion 'Structure of a Discipline,'" *Educational Theory* 23 (Winter 1973):74.

7. Epstein, *A Strategy for Education*, p. 11.

8. Cited by Joseph J. Schwab, "Teaching Science as Enquiry," *Science* 170 (1970): 1394.

9. Epstein, *A Strategy for Education*, p. 12.

10. Ibid., p. 15.

11. Ibid., p. 19.

12. Ibid., p. 34.

13. Ibid., p. 40.

14. Ibid., pp. 70-1, 78-9.

15. Weckstein's conclusions concerning his course are given on pp. 35-36.

16. Schwab, "Teaching Science as Enquiry," p. 1394.

17. Epstein, *A Strategy for Education*, p. 8.

18. S. L. Washburn, "Evolution and Education," *Daedalus* 103 (Fall 1974):221-7.

19. John M. Ziman, *Public Knowledge* (Cambridge, Mass.: Cambridge University Press, 1968), pp. 56-7.

20. Ibid., p. 57. (Emphasis added.)

21. Washburn, "Evolution and Education," pp. 222-5. (Emphasis added.)

22. Ibid., p. 223.

23. Roland L. DeLorme and Raymond G. McInnis, eds., *Antidemocratic Trends in Twentieth Century America* (Reading, Mass.: Addison-Wesley, 1969).

24. Raymond G. McInnis and James W. Scott, *Social Science Research Handbook* (New York: Barnes and Noble, 1975).

25. Those readers interested in following the results of these comparisons are referred to McInnis and Scott, *Social Science Research Handbook*, pp. 88-92.

26. For a full discussion of this example, see Raymond G. McInnis, "Integrating Classroom Instruction and Library Research: An Essay Review," *Studies in History and Society* 6 (1974-1975):31-65.

27. See ibid.

28. For a review of the literature, see Geoffrey Ford, "Research on User Behavior in University Libraries," *Journal of Documentation* 29 (March 1973):85-106.

29. Thelma K. Freides, *The Literature and Bibliography of the Social Sciences* (Los Angeles: Melville Publishing Co., 1973).

30. Selby U. Gration and Arthur P. Young, "Reference-Bibliographers in the College Library," *College and Research Libraries* 35 (January 1974):28-34.

Part III

THE EPISTEMOLOGICAL FOUNDATIONS OF REFERENCE SERVICE: The Logic of the Concept "Intermediary Sources"

A relatively unexplored problem in librarianship and the emerging discipline of information science is the nature of the relationship between the structure and the transmission of knowledge, on the one hand, and the array of bibliographic devices which has been developed to facilitate access to that knowledge on the other.[1]

In Chapter 13, reference works are pictured as artificial constructs, (that is, devices designed to give order and coherence to a body of scientific literature), much as Ziman describes them (see Chapter 9). Thus, it is evident that aspiring researchers seeking to obtain an adequate foundation in effective modes of inquiry must be informed about the various instruments available which give order and coherence to scientific literature. Structured inquiry is proposed as one mode of inquiry for providing such a grounding.

In structured inquiry, reference works are conceptualized as intermediate forms or stages of the scientific literature with which they are concerned. In Chapter 14, structured inquiry is set forth in an inquiry model called the tripartite matrix. As shown in Chapter 15, by arranging the bibliographic and substantive components of scientific literature at either end of a continuum, the functions of reference works combine logically with these two components to form a three-part matrix.

Before this model of inquiry is extensively developed, attention is directed to current suggested modes of inquiry which contain characteristics similar to those in the tripartite matrix. An example of structured inquiry is then presented (Chapter 16).

Next, in Chapter 17, the tacit dimensions of inquiry, including those contained in structured inquiry, are explored. In particular, the role of tacit knowledge in modes of inquiry employed by reference librarians and other experienced researchers is noted. Finally, Chapter 18 presents a commentary on Knapp's notion of the substantive-bibliographic continuum.

Note

1. Daniel B. Bergen, "Foreword," in Edward B. Montgomery, ed., *The Foundation of Access to Knowledge: A Symposium* (Syracuse, N.Y.: School of Library Science, Syracuse University, 1968), p. 1.

13 Reference Works as Artificial Constructs

Because man's ability to deal effectively with sizable amounts of substantive material is limited, it is necessary to construct devices which assist in giving order and coherence to scientific literature. In particular, I am concerned with the problem of setting forth this concept in an instructional perspective so that inexperienced researchers can comprehend at an early juncture how such materials can be used to develop more effective research strategies. I have tentatively termed this proposed mode of research *structured inquiry*.

Intermediate Forms or Stages of Scientific Literature

In Chapters 9 and 10, it is proposed that social-scientific literature, similar to scientific literature, comprises two main structural components: substantive structure and bibliographic structure. In retrieval, researchers seek either substantive or bibliographic portions of these structures, or some combination of both, associated with a given field of inquiry. The ultimate goal of inquiry is to gain access to the substantive portions of a body of literature, but because this component is fused to the bibliographic structure of that literature, the bibliographic component cannot be avoided. If the required portions of these epistemological components of scientific literature are to be retrieved efficiently, bodies of substantive literature must be reduced or distilled to manageable size, without distorting their essential content. Such distillation should also be ordered in a logical, coherent arrangement, so that inquirers at all stages of research can locate the information needed with minimum time and effort expended. The importance of this point is discussed in Part II, particularly in connection with the notion of the psychological structure of knowledge that is continuously evolving in the minds of researchers, whatever the extent of their knowledge in their particular field. The sources devised to give distilled treatments of the substantive and bibliographic structures of a literature perform definite cognitive functions for all levels of inquiry. This is as true for the specialist in another field searching for data to support arguments in his personal research, as well as the student-learner seeking merely to inform himself in the area, as it is for the expert in the field pursuing a specific course of inquiry.

The instruments devised to accomplish this task are traditionally known as reference works. However, inasmuch as their function is to provide access to varying amounts or different combinations of the two components of scientific literature, they should be considered *intermediary sources* (i.e., basically, reference works function as intermediate forms or stages of scientific literature). This term embeds reference works more deeply into the epistemological foundations of the literature—both the substantive and the bibliographical elements—with which they are associated.[1]

No Preexisting Grand Design

Although individual reference works are produced in response to specific needs, none is produced because of some preexisting grand design. Freides, for example, has argued that "the goals and methods of science" are not "fixed and immutable, or imposed uniformly by designated authority, but instead evolve in largely unpremeditated fashion as the general effect of many independent and individual actions." It can be argued that similar conditions determine the production of reference works. Perceived need is the greatest—but not the only—factor in determining that a particular reference work is produced.[2] While some general overall scheme does indeed determine what kind of reference works are produced in a particular field, not occasionally chaotic, unpremeditated policies and whimsy are responsible. Reference librarians often find that sources providing substantive or bibliographic information are fragmented and give uneven coverage of a given field. In the process of assisting a researcher, they frequently discover obvious gaps in the array of reference works in an area of inquiry; thus, the effort to gain access to the information required becomes both irksome and time-consuming. Freides states the matter succinctly: "The communication structure of the social sciences has many deficiencies."[3]

Artificial Constructs

Two typical treatments given the substantive and bibliographic components of scientific literature in reference works are synthesis and analysis. If, as stated above, reference works are not produced as a natural consequence of or according to a preexisting design for inquiry, they must logically be considered artificial constructs. They are devices artificially produced to help give order and coherence to a body of literature (as well as to communicate what is known scientifically), so that all inquirers, regardless of their familiarity with the discipline, can gain access to it as rapidly as possible. While librarians and even many outside the profession are aware of these functions, their potential use in all levels of inquiry, particularly in instruction, has not been sufficiently recognized.[4]

Reference works are produced because of the obvious cognitive functions they perform. It is in this sense that reference works conceived as intermediary sources are at once both functional necessities and artificial constructs, and that their relationship to the notion of intellectual craftsmanship becomes obvious. This idea is at least implied in the arguments of Bayley, Bell, Bok, Eble, and Schein (see Chapter 1), that undergraduates be given instruction in modes of inquiry rather than simply be taught a particular subject matter. Bell, for example, maintains that education for undergraduates ideally blends "general education" and "specialism." He contends that such an education embodies and exemplifies general education through disciplines, while at the same time extending the context of specialism so that the ground of knowledge is explicit. The common bond of general education and specialism is the emphasis on "conceptual inquiry."

To this extent, in the reconciliation of liberal education and specialism, training cannot deal with techniques in the narrow sense, but with the foundations of knowledge itself: i.e., how a particular discipline establishes its concepts; how these concepts seen as fluid inquiry need to be revised to meet new problems; how one establishes the criteria of choice for one, rather than another, alternative pattern of inquiry. In effect, general education is education in the conduct and strategy of inquiry itself.[5]

A similar notion is implicit in Ravetz's and Ziman's discussion of the importance of craftsmanship in scientific inquiry, particularly in their contention that the craft skills of a discipline are developed during the apprenticeship period in the training of practitioners.[6]

Necessity of Instruction

The proposition that reference works, conceptualized as intermediary sources, are actually artificial constructs, merits more detailed examination, especially in connection with instruction in their use. By describing them in such terms, their functions are more easily comprehensible to students.

Although reference materials are heuristic devices designed to order the bibliographic and substantive components of scientific literature in a logical and coherent arrangement, their actual existence is not self-evident. That is, if potential users are to be able to integrate reference materials into logical, coherent modes of inquiry, they need to be informed of the existence, function, and—most significantly—possible applications of these materials to their own immediate problems of inquiry. While these materials are functionally necessary in attempts to give order to a literature, their production is not a natural or automatic concomitant of the operations involved in producing scientific literature. Seldom do the producers of the scientific literature in a field also produce the reference materials in that field. Bergen, among others, notes that the relationship between the structure and communication of scientific literature, on the one hand, and the array of inter-mediary sources developed to facilitate access to that literature, on the other, is a phenomenon that has not been widely examined. As Brittain states, "it is doubtful if bibliographic devices have always been developed with the idea of facilitating access to knowledge, or that knowledge comes first and bibli-ographic devices later, or that knowledge production takes place inde-pendently of bibliographic devices." Thus, many factors operate in the pro-duction of reference works. "In principle," Brittain continues, "there is general agreement that bibliographic devices should facilitate access to knowledge but in practice many bibliographic devices have appeared as the result of commercial interests."[7] Freides makes a similar observation: bibli-ographic devices "have tended to develop independently of each other, in response to specific needs and possibilities as these were perceived at various times by particular groups and individuals."[8] Thus, because of the unpre-dictable factors associated with the production of reference works, even though such works ultimately fall into more or less definite patterns of function and structure, it can be argued that they are artificial constructs.

The notion of reference works as artificial constructs acquires its greatest significance when addressing the problem of instruction. For example, in a study of research competence among a selected group of Monteith College students, Knapp concluded "that high-level library competence calls upon a wide range of knowledge and skills and *that it probably involves a particular kind of mental quality*."[9] She is forced to acknowledge, however, that even "a particular kind of mental quality" is insufficient to acquiring an accept-able level of library research competence. "This level of competence is not just 'picked up' by the bright student. *It must be taught*."[10]

The Tripartite Matrix as an Inquiry Model

At least one important perspective on modes of inquiry, including those relating to instruction, emerges from the arguments above. That is, reference works, conceptualized as intermediary sources, can function as a third component of a tripartite matrix. Indeed, it is as the third component of scientific literature that the epistemological foundations of reference works become most evident. It seems self-evident that without reference works the production of knowledge would be difficult, fitful, and hesitant. If no attempt were made to distill scientific literature into an ordered and coherent format, following the course of inquiry in a given field would present tremendous difficulties. Becoming familiar with a body of literature would be fraught with much greater obstacles than is presently the case. Lacking an orderly arrangement of the literature, students would have to depend much more on training by masters. Under such conditions, instruction would tend to be rigid and dogmatic, creativity would be discouraged, and fewer new discoveries would be made. Not knowing specifically what others in the same field were doing, researchers separated geographically would duplicate each other's research. Inevitably, communication through invisible colleges would prevail, in a pattern not unlike the communication network developed following the growth of scientific investigation in the Renaissance.

Notes

1. Evidently, the use of the term *intermediary sources*, or simply *intermediaries*, as a means of identifying reference works is quite new. In my own reading, I have encountered only one other writer who uses this term explicitly to identify the functions of reference works: Marcia Bates, "Rigorous Systematic Bibliography," *RQ* 16 (Fall 1976):9, suggests that "bibliographies are intermediaries." Nonetheless, as the discussion below indicates, many writers have at least implied that what are considered reference materials perform such functions. For example, much of Wilson's discussion on forms of "bibliographical control" implies the notion that bibliographies function as intermediary sources. See Patrick Wilson, *Two Kinds of Power* (Berkeley, Calif.: University of California Press, 1968), especially Chapter IV.

2. Cf. Thelma Freides, *The Literature and Bibliography of the Social Sciences* (Los Angeles: Melville Publishing Co., 1973), p. 54.

3. Ibid., p. 265.

4. This fact is lamented in Frederick Holler, "Library Material Without Instruction—A Disaster?" *Journal of Education for Librarianship* 8 (Spring 1967):38-49.

5. Daniel Bell, *The Reforming of General Education* (New York: Columbia University Press, 1966), p. 159. For a sympathetic examination of the implications of Bell's proposals for learning, with particular emphasis on history, see G. Douglas Nicoll's "Liberal Learning, History, and the 'Bell Thesis,'" *Liberal Education* 58 (1972: 317-27.

6. See Jerome J. Ravetz, *Scientific Knowledge and Its Social Problems* (New York: Oxford University Press, 1971), especially Chapter 3, and John M. Ziman, *Public Knowledge* (Cambridge, Mass.: Cambridge University Press, 1968), especially Chapter 4. A similar argument is given by Freides, *The Literature and Bibliography of the Social Sciences*, pp. 263-4.

7. J. M. Brittain, *Information and Its Users* (Bath, England: Bath University of Technology Press, 1970), p. 155.

8. Freides, *The Literature and Bibliography of the Social Sciences*, p. 135.

9. Patricia Knapp, *The Monteith College Library Experiment* (New York: Scarecrow Press, 1966), p. 77. (Emphasis added.)

10. Ibid., p. 69. (Emphasis added.)

14 Current Notions of the Function and Structure of Reference Works as Intermediary Sources

In Chapter 1, considerable attention is directed to some of the obstacles to closer integration of classroom instruction and library research at the undergraduate level. At least three factors contribute to this situation. First, many instructors do not attach sufficient value to student research, assigning them only a limited amount to fulfill course requirements. The instructors' reluctance to assign more research stems in part from their own limited grounding in research procedures. (Studies that confirm this proposition are cited at the beginning of Chapter 1.)

A second factor, as noted by Knapp, is the instructors' dismay with the quality of students' written assignments. Some instructors, she states, are inclined to conclude that "students tend to be uncritical in their choice of sources of information, . . . [and] therefore, they must be told what to read."[1] Nonetheless, a minority of instructors in each discipline in the social sciences do attach considerable importance to developing their students' skills in research procedures. They believe that actual experience in research, including the self-discipline required to write up their findings, is at least as valuable to students as the substantive content of courses.

It is at this juncture that we are confronted with the third factor which discourages a greater emphasis on student research. As noted in Chapter 1, most of the methods so far devised for engaging students in library research have proven to be unsatisfactory to instructors and students alike. Dyson's comments, quoted at the beginning of Part I, puts the situation in sharp perspective. This third factor derives from an incorrect and incomplete conception—held by instructors and students—of, first, the structure of the literature in the social sciences and, second, the relationship between reference materials and the substantive materials to which they are related. Arguments concerning the former issue are extensively developed in Chapter 2. The argument is not that instructors are not acquainted with the structure of the literature in their field; rather it is that they are insensitive to the necessity of preparing students for research by informing them about the structures of literature or are unwilling to take the time to do it. In order to demonstrate their functions and structures more concretely for instructional purposes, it is necessary that reference works be related more directly to the bibliographic and substantive structures of the literature with which they are associated.

By depicting reference materials simultaneously as functional necessities and as artificial constructs designed to order scientific literature in logical, coherent arrangements, the cognitive function of reference materials becomes more apparent. That is, by setting forth these relationships in a perspective that demonstrates concretely what is unconscious, or at best, only vaguely perceived, the function and structure of reference materials come to be viewed as keys to more explicit and direct modes of thought and action in developing research strategies. (A considerable portion of such an understanding hinges upon an acceptance of the arguments developed in Chapter 8 concerning intellectual craft, intuition, and tacit knowledge.)

This notion of the structural-functional characteristics of reference materials has three related premises: first, there is a tacit logic of research strategy; second, this logic can be raised to the level of awareness; and third, research strategy itself can be refined by its intelligent and purposeful application. Most significantly, by employing such a perspective in library instruction programs, reference works will be more deeply embedded in the epistemological foundations of the literature to which they are related. Their characteristic as intermediary sources will become more immediately self-evident. By viewing reference works as intermediary sources, literature searching will be made an intrinsic part of inquiry and will not be regarded as an extraneous task. Freides makes a similar point when she says, "Literature searching is an intrinsic part of scholarship, and should not be regarded as an extraneous mechanical chore."[2] Before presenting these arguments as propositions, some of the current suggestions for achieving this end (that is, making literature searching an intrinsic part of scholarship and learning), as well as some of the obstacles to implementation, will be examined.

Knapp's System of "Ways"

By far the most ambitious and elaborate attempt to integrate classroom instruction and library research is Knapp's Monteith College Library experiment. While most of the library profession likely considers it a failure, some of its results and conclusions deserve some attention.[3] Certainly, Knapp's reflections and speculations point to the many pitfalls, as well as opportunities, of such experiments. For example, in her speculation on the potential applications of the notion "structure of the literature," in which she visualizes how reference materials would be employed as a component in modes of inquiry, Knapp states that she:

became painfully conscious of the lack of conceptual unity in [a system designed to teach library competence] which consists of an introduction to the classification [system], to the card catalog, and to certain important reference books of certain types, such as bibliographies, indexes, encyclopedias and dictionaries. . . . These basic reference sources constitute just one facet of the bibliographic organization which the library encompasses. Another facet, and one of crucial importance in the academic world, is the organization of scholarly communication.

She concludes that library instruction at the college level requires a "unifying theoretical concept" which demonstrates in a logical, concrete perspective how the library "embraces the bibliographic organization of scholarship"[4] (that is, how it conceptually integrates these two seemingly disparate realms).

Knapp's arguments are put in sharper perspective by Polanyi. As mentioned in Chapter 8, Polanyi contends that tacit knowing occurs when seemingly disjointed parts are understood to constitute a "comprehensive whole":

When we comprehend a particular set of items as parts of a whole, the focus of our attention is shifted from the hitherto uncomprehended particulars to the understanding of their joint meaning. The shift of attention does not make us lose sight of the particulars, since one can see a whole only by seeing its parts, *but it changes altogether the manner in which we are aware of the particulars. We become aware of them now in terms of the whole on which we have fixed our attention.*[5]

More attention is given below to how Polanyi's notion of tacit knowing can contribute toward a "unifying theoretical concept" of library materials.

Knapp proposes that what draws these seemingly divergent facets of inquiry into a logical and coherent system "centers on the intellectual processes involved in the retrieval of information and ideas from the highly complex system our society uses to organize its stored records."[6] She suggests that as part of teaching effective use of library materials, greater stress be placed on the methods and materials researchers use in producing scientific literature. This suggestion is in line with the concerns of those educators who believe that the emphasis in education should shift from *what* one learns to *how* one learns. It also is consistent with the idea that how libraries treat materials is in large part dictated by the format of the material (i.e., books are listed in the card catalog, articles and government publications are not, and so forth).

Freides, Knapp, and Shera, among others, have observed that, in contrast to the open communication patterns of scholarly inquiry, the library is a relatively closed system. As they point out, adjustments to changes in research approaches occur very slowly because the nature of library operations is dictated largely by the format of the materials and by the technologies and communication devices proven most effective in providing access to materials in a library. The library system is too unwieldy to accommodate the shifts in the communication patterns of disciplines. In contrast, the structure of the literature, especially new configurations in its bibliographic structure (i.e., research fronts), are fluid and unpredictable.[7]

In view of the relatively closed character of the library system, Knapp suggests that library orientation programs should be reformulated: "If it is to be effective the library program must be not merely presented in the context of 'content' courses, but truly consistent in goals and methods, in tone and style, with the overall educational program in which it occurs." In essence, she is proposing a shift away from the traditional concept of the library as a place to acquire facts and skills toward the ideal of visualizing knowledge as consensus, "where the student is encouraged to question authority." In such a context, the library is not "the place to find the 'right' answer or the 'definitive' source."[8] Realistically, of course, such a shift could not be achieved without the explicit cooperation of the classroom instructor. Hence, the integration of classroom instruction and library research must increase if Knapp's method is to be realized. She, too, observes that a change in instructor attitudes would be necessary.[9] Such considerations aside, it must be recognized that, without formulating a viable mode of inquiry adaptable by students around which such a program can be formulated, significant change in faculty attitude is not likely to occur.

To this end, Knapp visualizes the library as a system of "ways" and thus relates it to the pattern of inquiry employed by the practitioner:

The term "ways" in the sense of method implies knowledge and understanding of the interlocking organization of the library and scholarly communication. Knowing the way to use the library . . . means, on the one hand, understanding the nature and degree of bibliographic control characteristic of any discipline is likely to depend on the maturity of the discipline, the extent to which its work is cumulative, the economic support society is willing to give it, the social structure in which its practitioners work. It means appreciating, on the other hand, that there are communication needs and purposes common to all disciplines. It means knowing and being able to use the tools of scholarly communication, the tools of library organization, and the tools which connect the two.[10]

While Knapp's proposed "unifying concept" does not penetrate deeply enough into the epistemological foundations of scientific literature as a means of teaching about its structure, she does recognize one of the keys to an effective program of instruction in modes of inquiry. She states: "The more important contribution of the pilot project lies in the fact that it convinced us of the feasibility of illustrating the *same key concepts and processes with a variety of experiences and materials*," when "concepts and processes [are stressed] rather than specific library tools."[11]

Freides' "Tuning In"

While both Freides and White, et al., are not concerned with the problems of teaching research procedures to undergraduates to the same extent as Knapp, they have addressed the issue of integrating the seemingly divergent facets of scholarly communication and library organization into modes of inquiry. Freides' concept of inquiry in part builds upon Knapp's ideas.[12] Freides speaks of "literature searching as tuning in"[13] by which she means that "the bibliographic tools of scholarship may be viewed as comprising a system whose structure and organization parallels that of the scholarly literature."[14] By taking advantage of the parallels between the bibliographic tools of scholarship and the scholarly literature—"tuning in"—students can avoid the "approach which separates the processes of searching from the processes of learning about a subject."[15] Through this method, a student can "locate a discussion at the level of generality corresponding to [his] degree of acquaintance with the topic, and read that before seeking further references."[16] In this way, the search proceeds by stages where each forward step is informed by the researcher's increasing skill in developing search strategies and acquaintance with the topic. There are obvious similarities between this mode of inquiry and the observations concerning how learning occurs (Wise refers to it as the "cognitive" view) of Ausubel, Bell, Bruner, Schwab, and Wise. The parallel features of Freides' "tuning in" and my own structured inquiry as a system of demonstrating the principles of research are examined in Chapter 18.

White's "Bibliographic Expertise"

In his discussion of the "structure of the information system," White states that "while books[17] are of infinite variety, our more common information needs gradually build into the literature of a given discipline a discernible inner structure that, although not the same in detail as the bibliographical structure of another discipline, has points of correspondence with it too marked to be dismissed as accidental."[18] The "bibliographical structure" mentioned here is the structure or interrelatedness that occurs among bibliographies in a given field, and not the bibliographic structure (discussed in Chapter 9) that provides the framework of literature networks. As used by White, the term *bibliography* includes abstracting services and bibliographical reviews, as well as bibliographies in the narrower sense (i.e., listing of works on a particular subject).

To his question, "If guidance in the use of the literature is desired and needed, how is it to be given?" White answers that "there is growing agreement along three lines." Only two are pertinent to this discussion.

First, social control over ever-accumulating information hinges less on bibliographical control and supporting technologies than on *bibliographic expertise*. It is the latter that creates the system and makes it work. Second, the importance of subject bibliography has spiraled upward as the physical corpus of social science has grown, but its development as a branch of study has lagged. . . . Discontent with traditional practice is arousing interest in finding a better way.[19]

Let's focus for the moment on the problems of integrating classroom instruction and library research. Any system of instruction in student research, whether it is called a system of ways, tuning in, developing bibliographic expertise, or structured inquiry, has to be viewed by instructors as an effective adjunct of teaching. The principal obstacle to achieving integration is apparently the seeming anomaly between the library as a closed system and the fluid system of substantive literature to which it provides access. By devising effective means of instructing students in modes of inquiry which overcome this obstacle, the problem of convincing greater numbers of instructors that integrating classroom instruction and library research can be more satisfactorily achieved is reduced.

Mohamed's Call for Curriculum Reform

Can instructors be convinced that classroom instruction and library research can be satisfactorily integrated? It is possible, or at least definite steps in that direction can be taken if, first, the library profession heeds Shera's urging that librarians inform themselves more thoroughly about the nature of the epistemological components, research methods, and published records of inquiry.[20] Perhaps the most promising method of achieving this end is that proposed by Mohamed. He calls for a shift in emphasis in the profession from its traditional "passive custodial function" to a "dynamic information service."[21] Typically, he states, instruction in reference service has been centered around "generalized reference techniques and bibliographical tools." Little concern has been directed toward relating the material examined in courses in reference service to the structures of the literature, the modes of inquiry, and the communication problems of research. To a large extent, Whitten echoes Mohamed's lament when he states that conventional courses in reference service, as they relate to the social sciences, fail to provide an understanding of how these materials fit into actual research activity.[22]

Achieving integration does not mean that library students will be required to have a thorough acquaintance with the subject matter of the disciplines. Instead, concern would be directed to the structural patterns and research methodologies common to all the disciplines. (Specialized knowledge of any discipline would, of course, be an asset.) Armed with such an understanding, librarians would be more acutely aware of the research problems confronting both experienced and inexperienced researchers. In the social sciences, Freides has provided us with the best model for achieving what Mohamed is proposing for the library science curriculum.[23] More than anyone else, Friedes has demonstrated that it is possible to distinguish definite structural and functional patterns among the materials designed to give order and provide access to social-scientific literature.

Implicit in both Mohamed's and Freides' discussions is the idea that reference works should be considered intermediary sources to the literature with which they are associated. In effect, they argue that reference works provide, in distilled format, intermediate forms or stages of a literature. By placing the functions of reference materials in such a perspective, the reference materials are embedded more deeply into the structure of the literature to which they provide access. By making these properties of reference materials more explicit and concrete to librarians, they in turn will be better able to perform the "dynamic information service" visualized by Mohamed.

A Practicable Application

The principles inherent in a "dynamic information service" are at least implicit in the methods proposed by Frick.[24] She maintains that, if bibliographic instruction is to be usefully applied, it must be directly related to the underlying structure of the literature which students are seeking. Her proposals are an actual application of linking the functions of reference works to the literature in a perspective demonstrating their underlying function as intermediary sources of that literature. The result, as Frick suggests, is that students are given a more solid grounding in developing research strategies. My own experience with similar methods suggests that these conclusions are valid.

Before moving to the next chapter, I want to point out how the term *intermediary source* is used in the rest of this book. In many cases, reference, which encompasses activities and functions such as reference work, reference source, and reference department, is a more desirable term than intermediary source. For example, one intuitively bridles at the phrase "Intermediary Source Department." Hereafter, when discussing social-scientific literature, the term *intermediary source* is used to define or identify that type of device traditionally known as a reference work. The criterion for defining reference works in this fashion is whether they provide intermediate forms or stages of a larger body of social-scientific literature.

In the discussion that follows, textbooks present a special problem. Just as a particular encyclopedia article or review of research is often a pioneering synthesis of what is known in a given field, textbooks also provide useful distillations of what is known in a field. Their purpose, however, is fundamentally pedagogic, that is, they instruct a particular group at a particular level of understanding. As such, although they can often serve in a manner not unlike the encyclopedia or the review of research, within the scope of the current discussion, their contribution to the production of knowledge is considered to be only marginal.

Notes

1. Patricia Knapp, *The Monteith College Library Experiment* (New York: Scarecrow Press, 1966), p. 41.

2. Thelma Freides, *The Literature and Bibliography of the Social Sciences* (Los Angeles: Melville Publishing Co., 1973), p. 262.

3. See, for example, comments by Robert T. Blackburn, "College Libraries—Indicated Failures: Some Reasons and a Possible Remedy," *College and Research Libraries* 29 (1968):171-7.

4. Knapp, *The Monteith College Library Experiment*, p. 81. Asian scholar Skinner perceptively observes that librarians and scholars tend to differ "on the nature of the bibliographic unit. . . . Librarians must keep tabs on physical publications as such—this book, this pamphlet, this journal—and their tendency therefore is to take the physical publication as the bibliographic unit. Scholars, by contrast, tend to take each discrete product of scholarship as their unit—not this journal but this article, not Smith's books, but Lee's paper in Smith's book." G. William Skinner, ed., *Modern Chinese Society: An Analytical Bibliography* (Stanford, Calif.: Stanford University Press, 1973), I, p. XVI.

5. Michael Polanyi, *The Study of Man* (Chicago: University of Chicago Press, 1959), p. 29. (Emphasis added.)

6. Knapp, *The Monteith College Library Experiment*, pp. 81-2.

7. Freides, *The Literature and Bibliography of the Social Sciences*; Knapp, *The Monteith College Library Experiment*, pp. 82-3; and Jesse Shera, "An Epistemological Foundation for Library Science," in Edward B. Montgomery, ed., *The Foundations of Access to Knowledge: A Symposium* (Syracuse, N.Y.: School of Library Service, Syracuse University, 1968), p. 10.

8. Knapp, *The Monteith College Library Experiment*, p. 88.

9. Ibid., p. 106.

10. Ibid., pp. 82-3.

11. Ibid., p. 90. (Emphasis added.)

12. For example, in dedicating her book *The Literature and Bibliography of the Social Sciences* to the memory of Patricia Knapp, Freides acknowledges her for having shown "the way."

13. Freides, *The Literature and Bibliography of the Social Sciences*, p. 262.

14. Ibid., p. 135.

15. Ibid., p. 263.

16. Ibid., pp. 263-4. Cf. John M. Ziman, "Information, Communication, Knowledge," *Nature* 224 (October 25, 1969):318; reprinted in Tefko Saracevic, ed. and comp., *Introduction to Information Science* (New York: Bowker, 1970), p. 83.

17. *Modes of communication* more precisely suggests the sense White intends.

18. Carl M. White and associates, eds., *Sources of Information in the Social Sciences*, 2d ed. (Chicago: American Library Association, 1973), p. 7.

19. Ibid., p. 5. (Emphasis added.)

20. Shera, "An Epistemological Foundation for Library Science," p. 9.

21. Oli Mohamed, "Structure of Knowledge and 'Resources' Programs in Librarianship," *Journal of Education for Librarianship* 16 (Summer 1975):3.

22. Benjamin Whitten, "Social Sciences Bibliography Course: A Client-oriented Approach," *Journal of Education for Librarianship* 16 (Summer 1975):26.

23. A variation of the notions of Freides and Mohamed is presented by Conrad H. Rawski, "Subject Literatures and Librarianship," in L. R. Bone, ed., *Conference on Library School Teaching Methods* (Urbana, Ill.: Graduate School of Library Science, University of Illinois, 1969), pp. 92-113. Although Rawski's proposals contain elements that are definitely parallel to Freides, I believe they are developed in an unnecessarily abstruse and abstract manner.

24. Elizabeth Frick, "Information Structure and Bibliographic Instruction," *Journal of Academic Librarianship* 6 (September 1975):12-4.

15 The Substantive-Bibliographic Continuum and the Functions of Intermediary Sources

In part II, it is argued that scientific literature comprises two main structural components: bibliographic structure and substantive structure. Each of these two components, however, is fused to the other. It is further suggested that the bibliographic structure is fixed, while the substantive structure is fluid. The fixed characteristic of scientific literature is related to its diachronic structure, i.e., how a body of literature developed through time. Related to the diachronic structure is the notion of synchronic structure, i.e., those portions of scientific literature that, by consensus among the scholars in a field, constitutes what is currently valid in that field.

The next two chapters develop a tripartite matrix, or model, of inquiry which employs intermediary sources in a relationship to the bibliographic and substantive components of scientific literature. It demonstrates concretely how intermediary sources are designed to expose portions of these components. Essentially, intermediary sources provide intermediate forms or stages of the substantive and bibliographic elements of scientific literature. The arguments that follow are an elaboration of those contained in the MacGregor and McInnis article in the *Journal of Higher Education*.[1] The method is called structured inquiry, a term suggested by a colleague outside the library profession. The previous chapter noted that research strategy has a tacit logic that can be raised to a level of awareness to make its purposeful application more concrete and deliberate. It is toward this end that the concepts and procedures employed in structured inquiry are proposed.

Five Divisions

In the tripartite matrix developed here, the two structural components of scientific literature are placed at either end of a line or continuum (see Figure 5). Superimposed on the continuum are the functions of intermediary sources which provide access to or otherwise expose either substantive portions or bibliographic portions, or different combinations of both, of the scientific literature of a field of research. This component constitutes the third part of the tripartite matrix.

TRIPARTITE MATRIX

2 —————— 1 —————— 0 —————— 1 —————— 2

SUBSTANTIVE STRUCTURE ————— BIBLIOGRAPHIC STRUCTURE

Subject (Substantive) Information	Primarily Subject Information, Secondarily Location Information	Combination of Location & Subject Information	Primarily Location Information, Secondarily Subject Information	Location (Bibliographical) Information
Glossary Dictionary (providing only definitions)	Dictionary, Encyclopedia, or Statistical Compendia [Primarily subject matter with less emphasis on bibliography].	Comprehensive Encyclopedia (with extensive bibliographies) Reviews of Research	Abstracts Annotated Bibliography [Primarily location information with brief analysis of subject matter].	Card catalog Bibliography Index Citation Index

Figure 5. Tripartite Matrix

SOURCE: Adapted from John MacGregor and Raymond G. McInnis, "Integrating Classroom Instruction and Library Research: The Cognitive Functions of Bibliographic Network Structures," *Journal of Higher Education* 48 (January–February 1977): 24. Reprinted by permission.

Readers should observe that the five divisions on the scale of functions of intermediary sources are ordinal divisions, i.e., the properties ascribed to each division are general or rough characteristics of the works that are considered to belong in that division. Moreover, reference works, conceptualized as intermediary sources, are produced separately by diverse groups and individuals in an unpremeditated fashion, and (recalling Freides above) not according to a fixed or immutable authority. It is in this sense that intermediary sources are considered artificial constructs designed to reduce portions of scientific literature to a manageable size in a logical and coherent arrangement. Where the needs for individual research problems are perceived from different perspectives, inevitably the content of particular intermediary sources will vary, even though basically they perform a similar function. Further, by moving from one end of the continuum toward the other, the properties of each successive division acquire increasing amounts of the characteristics of the epistemological component at that end of the continuum.

At the substantive end (on the left) of the continuum are those intermediary sources which, as a rule, provide only information about the subject matter of topics. For the most part, they are glossaries, dictionaries, and lexicons of concepts and other terms associated with the social sciences in general or particular disciplines.[2] Winick's *Dictionary of Anthropology* and Theodorson's *Modern Dictionary of Sociology* are examples of items concerned with one discipline falling in this division.[3] The information provided about particular entries in these sources is typically a very compressed or distilled explanation of how a particular term is used or what is known scientifically about it. As a rule, there is little concern for the individuals responsible for coining the term or for employing it in a particular way so that it acquires a new connotation.[4]

Several observations can be made of what treatment substantive material is given in works that fall in this division. In most cases, the concern is, first, for the synchronic aspects of topics and, second, as Freides suggests, for "terms in relation to a larger body of knowledge."[5] Because of space limitations, considerations of the substantive structure of the topic are necessarily minimal. Therefore (especially to the researcher not well acquainted with the topic), the substantive structure is difficult or impossible to detect. Given such conditions, theoretical or empirical considerations of the topic that are operative at the time of writing are likewise often implied and are seldom made explicit. (This is less often true for terms to which considerable importance is attached. Even in these sources proportionately greater space is given to explanations of theoretical and empirical aspects of such terms.) Finally, it should be understood that the fluid property of scientific literature, which is characteristic of the left end of the continuum, is also difficult or impossible to detect. Particular sources in this division focus on the more general and permanent characteristics of particular concepts and terms, but even these, according to Kuhn, can "often be less than cumulative."[6] Although Kuhn made this observation with regard to the natural sciences, because of the greater fluidity of the social sciences, it is truer of them.[7] Successive editions of individual sources in this division, it is expected, would reflect such changes and would thus help to justify the notion that it is toward the left end of the continuum that the fluid characteristic of scientific literature is more evident.

In the next division, moving to the right, are those intermediary sources (most often known as dictionaries) which provide primarily substantive information but secondarily, bibliographic or location information.[8]

Substantive information in the intermediary sources in this division is also given in a compressed, distilled format, similar to its treatment in the division on the left. In general, however, greater space is given to explanations of concepts and terms; as a result, there is greater evidence of the characteristics of the substantive structure that can only be given minimal attention, or implied, in the division on the left of the continuum. Bibliographic information, since it is given only secondary emphasis, is often sketchy, being limited for the most part to individuals considered the key sources or principal contributors of what is known scientifically about the topic.

Perhaps the best example of an intermediary source that falls in this division is Gould and Kolb's *Dictionary of the Social Sciences.*[9] Others that come readily to mind are *General Ethnological Concepts,*[10] Volume 1 of the *International Dictionary of Regional European Ethnology and Folklore,* Mitchell's *Dictionary of Sociology,*[11] and to a lesser extent the *McGraw-Hill Dictionary of Modern Economics.*[12] In Gould and Kolb, for example, about 270 noted U.S. and British social scientists define and explain about one thousand concepts, using the following format: A, the generally accepted meaning of the term; B, its historical background or a more extensive explanation. Paragraphs C, D, E, and so on, are used where "controversies and divergencies of meaning have been explored, [with an] attempt made to place them in their perspective."[13] Given such treatment, users are thus provided with brief accounts of both synchronic and diachronic characteristics of individual terms, as well as *key sources* or other principal contributors who had a hand in giving particular meaning or different connotations to them.

In the center of the continuum are those intermediary sources which provide more or less equal amounts of bibliographic and substantive information.[14] Nonetheless, since articles are the work of many individuals who have differing interpretations of how each topic should be treated, the amount of attention given each component varies considerably. The understanding to be derived from the foregoing is that sources which fall in the center of the continuum can be expected to furnish both bibliographic and substantive information. Such an understanding is especially useful, as is seen below, when a technique of structured inquiry is employed.

Examples of intermediary sources in this division for the most part consist of comprehensive encyclopedias (with extensive bibliographies provided at the end of articles) and reviews of research. The preeminent example of a comprehensive encyclopedia is the *International Encylopedia of the Social Sciences*.[15] Its articles are perhaps the best examples of the intermediary source which is concerned with both substantive and bibliographic components of social-scientific terms. Characteristically, comprehensive encyclopedias falling in this division stress theoretical aspects of the topic being considered, while reviews of research usually give greater emphasis to the empirical aspects of these same topics. Thus, it is often useful to make joint use of these two types of intermediary source (illustrations of such joint use are given below and in Appendix A.)

In addition, in those intermediary sources which are here called reviews of research (they, are perhaps as often entitled handbooks or guides or advances in), considerably greater stress is given current trends and developments occurring in the research fronts of topics. The practice seems to be to call recurrent review publications either *Annual Review of* . . . or *Advances in* . . . , while single volumes or multiple-volume sets are most often entitled *Handbook*. In most of the social sciences, there are journals that devote all or a great proportion of their pages to review articles, and it is not uncommon for individual scholarly journals to contain occasional review articles. (Significantly, the *Social Sciences Citation Index* provides a key to locating reviews of research in recurrent review publications and scholarly journals).[16] Thus, reviews of research are correctly considered important links in the production of knowledge through consensus (see Chapter 4).[17] Reviews of research assume that researchers have some or considerable acquaintance with the topics therein.

In sum, the discussion in review articles often begins at, or otherwise overlaps with, where an article in a comprehensive encyclopedia leaves off. Thus, more recent empirical findings are noted, and, as a result, researchers are given greater proportions of recent parts of the bibliographic structure of the topic than is characteristic of an article in the comprehensive encyclopedia.

Before discussing the divisions on the right of the continuum, let us briefly review some important considerations of the left side and center of the continuum. It is important to recognize that the sources from the left end to the center predominantly contain or stress the more fluid, substantive, comprehensive, and synthetic aspects of a research topic. Implicit in discussions of topics in any source in these divisions is the diachronic aspects of the topic, that is, how the currently valid portions of it have emerged from a process of consensus of the community of researchers working in that field. Space limitations in these intermediary sources, as noted above, allow little concern for such considerations. Nonetheless, through an understanding of the processes involved in the production of knowledge, in experienced researchers can develop more purposeful and intelligent modes of inquiry in which intermediary sources in these divisions can make significant contributions. In explaining how particular substantive portions of the literature developed, articles (in intermediary sources in the center division and the division left of center) often note the key source (or, to use Garfield's term, *primordial citation*) as well as other important contributors. Thus, to a greater or lesser degree, the general outlines of the bibliographic structure of the topic emerges. As mentioned in Chapter 10, there is a definite correlation between the bibliographic and the diachronic structure of a literature.

Moving from the center of the continuum to the divisions on the right produces a dramatic change in the epistemological elements of scientific literature exposed by intermediary sources which perform the functions ascribed to the respective divisions. Intermediary sources in these divisions provide primarily bibliographic or location information, and secondarily information about the substantive content of individual elements (i.e., primary and secondary sources) in the structure of the literature of a topic. In other words, in contrast to divisions of the continuum to the left, divisions on the right provide access to the more fixed, bibliographic, discrete, and analytic aspects of the structure of scientific literature. For example, in the first division to the right of center intermediary sources expose primarily location information of discrete publications in a literature's bibliographic structure, but as a secondary function give brief analyses or abstracts of these publications. Perhaps the best examples of sources that fall in this division are the abstract journal and the annotated bibliography. (It is beyond the scope of this discussion to examine these examples in great detail. Readers who desire more complete information can consult several excellent sources.)[18]

In the divisions at the right end of the continuum are those intermediary sources that provide almost exclusively bibliographical or location information. Such sources include card catalogs, bibliographies, indexes, and citation indexes. (The implications of the unique contributions of citation indexes will be discussed in Chapter 16.) In general, intermediary sources in this division list citations representing discrete items which constitute the bibliographic structures of bodies of literature.

Information about the subject matter contained in individual items listed in these sources is, at best, minimal; such information simply serves to indicate the content. Substantive content is not given.[19]

Before discussing how the system works in actual practice, a few clarifying observations should be made. Except for citation indexes, the intermediary sources in the divisions on the right of the continuum pose at least two problems for the concept of bibliographic structure (these problems relate to the concerns expressed by Knapp, Freides, White, Mohamed, Rawski, and Frick in Chapter 14): first, what is known scientifically in a specific research area? Second, following the arguments of Bell, et al., noted in Chapter 13, what is the relative significance of the individual contributors to the production of this knowledge?

The first problem arises from the manner in which information about discrete elements in the structure of a particular field of research is organized in intermediary sources falling on the right of the continuum. Detecting relationships and linkages between citations in bibliographies and other intermediary sources in these divisions is (except for citation indexes) at best difficult, especially for researchers who are not well acquainted with the topic. Garfield, for example, accurately points out that even "in conventional bibliograph[ies], a simple chronological listing of publications gives [only] the faintest hint of the historical development of a particular subject."[20] Similar observations are made by Line and by Freides.[21] The materials contained in intermediary sources in the divisions on the right of the continuum are not often arranged in the chronological order to which Garfield refers. Rather, the arrangement is more frequently according to subject, with other mechanisms such as subject and author indexing provided to facilitate locating particular items on narrow aspects of the topic. As carefully as indexes may be prepared, experience suggests that only to a limited extent do they facilitate finding materials in the sense to which Garfield refers. (A closer examination of this problem is presented in Part IV.)

The second problem subsumes two considerations: the adequacy of the searcher's understanding of how scientific literature is produced (i.e., its basic structural characteristics); and the searcher's acquaintance with the bibliographic and substantive aspects of the topic being researched. If searchers have an inadequate or incomplete conception of the structure of scientific literature (see Chapters 9-11), a name or subject listing in an index or bibliography will give only a fragmented view of how these separately listed materials are in fact interrelated. There is, in other words, little or no basis for differentiating among the references to discrete elements in a field of research and determining how they are linked or related.[22] Even in the sources in the division to the right of center where abstracts and annotations add analytical information about discrete items concerned with the topic, a problem still exists. Namely, these items have to be placed in an order that reflects their significance (i.e., so that the logical development of the topic's synchronic structure is evident).

What are the implications of these structural considerations? If searchers have an inadequate understanding of the structure of scientific literature, they cannot use reference works to their full potential (even when they are conceptualized as intermediary sources). Thus, only after inexperienced researchers develop a concept of the cognitive structures of scientific literature characteristic of experienced researchers can they be expected to refine research strategies in which the functions of reference works are recognized as intermediate forms of the scientific literature to which they provide access.[23] Citation indexes, the intermediary sources which are most deeply embedded in the structures of the literature, are especially confusing and frustrating instruments of research when users are not acquainted with the epistemological principles underlying their structure and function.

Divisions on the continuum are not rigid; indeed, individual intermediary sources often perform more than one function. Basically, the divisions serve merely as guides to developing research strategies; as such, they are intended to inform researchers of the functions of the different types of intermediary sources and to make them aware of potentially available research devices in a given field. Through such an understanding, the difficulties of selecting appropriate intermediary sources for specific research problems can be reduced, and the underlying logic of reference works can be made more self-evident. Thus, by employing a tripartite model of inquiry which depicts scientific literature as comprising two components and which stresses the functional characteristics of reference works (as intermediary sources), searchers are given a greater awareness of the functions of individual sources. This awareness can help dispel some of the confusion caused when intermediary sources are given titles that do not explicitly indicate the designated functions of particular works.[24] Even so, facility in using intermediary sources for their intended purposes still requires an acquaintance with them, or to use White's term, *bibliographic expertise.*

Finally, certain tacit dimensions are attached to the refinement of effective research strategies. In Chapter 8, considerable attention is given to the significance of creativity, intuition, and tacit knowledge in disciplined inquiry, and in this chapter the "tacit logic" of research strategy is mentioned. Not yet introduced into the discussion is the part these aspects of research play in structured inquiry. They do figure in any form of inquiry, and they are especially important if inexperienced researchers are to develop self-sufficiency in most research tasks. Tacit logic, then, is part of the craftsmanship that researchers develop as they become more proficient.[25] Before considering the role of tacit logic (in Chapter 17), the results of using structured inquiry as a research strategy are demonstrated with an actual example (see Chapter 16).

Notes

1. John MacGregor and Raymond G. McInnis, "Integrating Classroom Instruction and Library Research: The Cognitive Functions of Bibliographic Network Structures," *Journal of Higher Education* 48 (January-February, 1977):17-38.

2. For an explanation of how general-purpose dictionaries relate to the social sciences, see Thelma Freides, *The Literature and Bibliography of the Social Sciences* (Los Angeles: Melville Publishing Co., 1973), p. 103.

3. Charles Winick, *Dictionary of Anthropology* (New York: Philosophical Library, 1959), and George A. Theodorson, *Modern Dictionary of Sociology* (New York: Crowell-Collier-Macmillan, 1969).

4. Cf. Freides, *The Literature and Bibliography of the Social Sciences*, pp. 102-3.

5. Ibid., p. 103.

6. See Chapter 10, note 12.

7. Cf. Maurice Line, "Social Scientists' Information," *SSRC Newsletter* 3 (1968): 2-5.

8. The suggestion that bibliographic information is also location information is of considerable importance for bibliographic instruction. That is, the function of a bibliographic citation is both to identify a discrete epistemological element in a body of literature and to show its location in the published (or unpublished) records of research. Cf. Eugene Garfield, "Primordial Concepts, Citation Indexing, and Historio-Bibliography," *Journal of Library History* 2 (1967):244; and Patrick Wilson, *Two Kinds of Power* (Berkeley, Calif.: University of California Press, 1968), p. 58.

9. Julius Gould and William A. Kolb, eds., *Dictionary of the Social Sciences* (New York: Free Press of Glencoe, 1964).

10. Ake Hultkrantz, ed., *General Ethnological Concepts* (Copenhagen: Rosenkilde and Bagger, 1960).

11. G. Duncan Mitchell, *Dictionary of Sociology* (Chicago: Aldine, 1968).

12. Douglas Greenwald, ed., *McGraw-Hill Dictionary of Modern Economics*, 2d ed. (New York: McGraw-Hill, 1973).

13. Gould and Kolb, eds., *Dictionary of the Social Sciences*, p. XII.

14. The phrase "equal amounts" is not intended to suggest that bibliographic information occupies the same amount of space as the substantive information. As noted above, bibliographic citations, which are symbols used to identify substantive contributions to the published record of research, necessarily occupy proportionately less space than the substantive portions of the literature which they represent. However, since together the bibliographical citations listed in articles in the intermediary sources in the center division of the continuum constitute the rough or broad outlines of the bibliographic structure of the substantive material contained in the article, each of these two epistemological components are in general about equally represented.

15. David L. Sills, ed., *International Encyclopedia of the Social Sciences*, 17 vols. (New York: Macmillan, 1968).

16. For more extensive discussions of the individual characteristics of such publications, refer to appropriate sections of Raymond G. McInnis and James W. Scott, eds., *Social Science Research Handbook* (New York: Barnes and Noble, 1975); Carl M. White and associates, eds., *Sources of Information in the Social Sciences* (Chicago: American Library Association, 1973); and Freides, *The Literature and Bibliography of the Social Sciences*.

17. Patricia Knapp, *The Monteith College Library Experiment* (New York: Scarecrow Press, 1966), pp. 93-4, makes a similar observation and suggests that greater use should be made of reviews of research in bibliographic instruction.

18. For extensive discussions of the purpose and function of abstract journals in

research, see Robert L. Collison, *Abstracts and Abstracting Services* (Santa Barbara, Calif.: ABC Clio, 1971; Harold Borko and Charles L. Bernier, *Abstracting Concepts and Methods* (New York: Academic Press, 1975); and V. A. Winn, "A Case Study of the Problems of Information Processing in a Social Science Field: The OSTI: *SEA* Project," *ASLIB Proceedings* 23 (1971):76-88. Besides abstracts, Freides' *Literature and Bibliography of the Social Sciences* extensively discusses the function and structure of annotated bibliographies.

19. Cf. Patrick Wilson, *Two Kinds of Power* (Berkeley, Calif.: University of California Press, 1968), p. 74.

20. Garfield, "Primordial Concepts, Citation Indexing, and Historio-Bibliography," p. 241.

21. Maurice Line, "Social Scientists' Information," pp. 2-5; Freides, *The Literature and Bibliography of the Social Sciences*, p. 263. Freides' discussions of bibliographies, indexes, and card catalogs are particularly recommended.

22. Cf. Freides, *The Literature and Bibliography of the Social Sciences*, p. 263.

23. Cf. Wise and Ausubel, in Chapter 11, notes 3, 5-6; Patricia Knapp, "The Meaning of the Monteith College Library Program for Library Education," *Journal of Education for Librarianship* 6 (1965):111-27; and Freides, *The Literature and Bibliography of the Social Sciences*, p. 261.

24. Perhaps the best example of a confusing title is Alfred M. Freedman and H. I. Kaplan, eds., *Comprehensive Textbook of Psychiatry* (Baltimore: Williams and Wilkins, 1967). Upon examining it, most will agree that it is a review of research, or an encyclopedia; it would be utilized more readily if its title reflected its content.

25. Cf. Jerome R. Ravetz, *Scientific Knowledge and Its Social Problems* (New York: Oxford University Press, 1971), pp. 75-108.

16 An Example of Structured Inquiry

The example of structured inquiry presented here can be used by experienced researchers who want information on a particular research topic, and more importantly, by inexperienced researchers to learn how different intermediary sources can reveal both the bibliographic and substantive structures of a research topic. This mode of learning is not unlike that proposed by the cognitive psychologists and other concerned educators mentioned in Chapter 11. For example, Koestler, it will be recalled, suggests that ideally learning occurs in a hierarchical sequence of cognitive structures,[1] and Ausubel maintains that learning also involves the elements of meaning, process of organization, arrangement of component parts, and maturity of subject matter (see Chapter 11 above).

In structured inquiry, individuals develop an increasingly complex and comprehensive understanding of what is known scientifically about a topic. The sequence in which this understanding is achieved is roughly parallel to the sequence of the development of the substantive literature on that topic. In other words, attention is directed to both the diachronic and synchronic characteristics of the topic's literature.[2]

Structured inquiry also seeks to help researchers by providing procedures that combine the processes of literature searching and learning about a subject. In this sense, these procedures are not unlike those recommended by Knapp and Freides in Chapter 14. In combining these two processes, searchers begin their inquiry at, in Freides' words, "a level of generality corresponding to [their] degree of acquaintance of the topic." (See Chapter 14.) Hence, by employing a structured mode of inquiry, searchers can intelligently and purposefully internalize the cognitive or psychological structures of a topic much as mature scholars can. This is done by progressing from simplified, generalized formulations of a topic to more complex, less organized, expanding frontiers where new research findings are being added to it.

Certain qualifications must be made at this point. For example, if a searcher lacks an understanding of the mathematical or statistical basis of specific concepts in the social sciences, reaching an adequate understanding of the subject matter becomes difficult or even impossible. Thus, readers must recognize that these arguments apply only to substantive literature that searchers can understand without possessing skills such as mathematics or statistics. Apart from such considerations, research strategy in this mode of inquiry essentially means progressing from a point where the more permanent cumulated literature on a topic is accessible in relatively compact distillations to a point approaching its expanding research frontier. At the frontier of research, the substantive literature consists only of discrete elements, accessible in undifferentiated analytical fragments but nonetheless embedded in the topic's bibliographical structure.[3]

As the processes of literature searching and learning about a subject take place certain other developments occur. Recall for a moment that Epstein's intent was to design a course to teach what a biologist does when he's doing his biology (see Chapter 12). He suggests that this base of understanding can be used as a foundation on which to build more complex and comprehensive acquaintance with biology in general because the essentials of particular problems differ little from one field to another. A similar process occurs in structured inquiry, so long as the underlying principles of the tripartite matrix are adequately understood. As inexperienced researchers employ the recommended methods of inquiry, they simultaneously become acquainted with principles of research techniques and materials that can be applied to other research tasks. Several educators, including Epstein, have drawn attention to this phenomenon: "Knowledge acquired with other knowledge of importance to the individual is very likely to remain with him because it is tied up with the memory of important information."[4]

In effect, when the structured inquiry method is employed, reference materials formerly considered separate are now understood by inexperienced researchers to be components in a communication system linked either explicitly or implicitly, all of the components giving organization and coherence to particular bodies of scientific literature. By employing the tripartite matrix, we seek to inform researchers, especially inexperienced ones, about the structure and function of intermediary sources that are universal across disciplines. That is, the structure and function of intermediary sources fall into a definite pattern. Armed with an understanding of this pattern, determining independently which type of intermediary source should be expected to provide needed information for a specific problem does not appear to be difficult. This skill is refined by experience however. According to Phenix, "The logic of structural [similarity] is of great importance for pedagogy because it points to those common features of studies that can be transferred from one discipline to another, thus eliminating the unnecessary duplication of learning and facilitating insight into relationships."[5] Structured inquiry is designed to promote general self-sufficiency for research and at the same time, to avoid the necessity of tediously learning the individual characteristics of countless numbers of reference works— which unless constantly reinforced is not retained.[6]

Principles of Structured Inquiry

In the example of structured inquiry given here, the searcher is assumed to be a student with little or no acquaintance with the methods or instruments of research. He is introduced to the topic (the Clark and Trow typology of student subcultures) by an intructor's lecture in an introductory course in sociology. The topic stimulates some interest, and when the instructor gives the class a research assignment, the student selects it as the topic for his research.

Posing hypothetical research projects according to a particular theme or research problem: (1) encourages students to think about the practical time-saving aspects of well-grounded research procedures; (2) generates higher interest level; and (3) results in greater retention of methodology (if, of course, students employ these procedures in their own research projects). In particular, it fosters an appreciation of the following four principles. (1) A concept of the ideal of structured inquiry, where students progress from a limited understanding of or acquaintance with a topic to increasingly complex and less organized states of its literature. As noted earlier in this chapter, at least at the beginning of the instruction in modes of inquiry, this means advancing on a topic from its generalized formulation (characteristic of the distilled, synthetical treatments in encyclopedias and reviews of research) to its more complex, less organized expanding frontiers (characteristic of intermediary sources that give analytical treatments of discrete elements of the same substantive literature).

(2) A general attitude of self-sufficiency, encouraging students to consider a specific research problem or obstacle as a question that needs to be answered, before the general research can proceed satisfactorily.[7]

(3) An understanding of the different formats in which information and knowledge are published, including how effective research embraces the use of substantive material in a diverse array of formats and employs a diverse array of strategies. The purpose of this mode of instruction, comprising lectures, illustrations, and exercises, is to demonstrate that scientific literature is both tightly interrelated and interdependent, regardless of the format in which discrete contributions to a given body of literature are published. Concern should be directed toward differentiating between information and knowledge, and between primary sources and secondary sources (see Chapter 5 above). It should be emphasized to the students that gaining access to the discrete elements of a body of literature requires developing a variety of research strategies, each intended to expose particular components of it.

(4) The purpose of the lectures, illustrations, and exercises, which is to demonstrate that a research problem, if executed thoroughly and carefully, involves a large number of small activities that together contribute to the successful completion of a research project.

Most researchers start their research with at least a modicum of acquaintance with it, but without sufficient l ibliographic information, the names of important researchers associated with it, or a logical approach to library research procedures. Keeping this fact in mind, the intent of the example of research being developed here—the Clark and Trow typology of student subcultures—is to demonstrate a research strategy based on the epistemological foundations of scientific litrature discussed in Chapters 9 and 10. Central to this method is the importance of locating the authors of the principal studies on a given topic. In Chapter 9, it is argued that such studies can logically be considered key sources or, according to Garfield, primordial citations. Such studies have had more impact than others on the research advances on the topic and, because they are more frequently cited than others, provide ease in tracing other citations comprising the bibliographical structure of the topic. (As noted in Chapter 9, Garfield calls these structures historiographs, while MacGregor and I prefer to call them bibliographic network structures.) The purpose of concerning students with the principles of bibliographic network structures is to help them visualize the interdependent characteristics of scientific literature, especially how an individual study is embedded in the literature of the topic.[8]

Figure 3, which presents two perspectives of the bibliographic structure of the Clark and Trow student subculture typology, demonstrates graphically how each successive study is in reality built on the preceding ones, with— by statistical means—attention directed particularly to the importance of Clark and Trow's papers in which the concept originated.

Once the principles of bibliographic structure are introduced, the other, more abstract structural characteristics of scientific literature can more easily be presented. Of course, the primary concern is for substantive structure, since it is the subject matter that any mode of inquiry is attempting to expose. An integral part of both substantive and bibliographic structure is the diachronic and synchronic aspects of the topic, and thus these are also important considerations. It is important, however, that all of these concepts be made as concrete as possible.

By employing this or similar diagrams in an instructional program, it becomes less difficult to introduce the concept of substantive structure without confusing students, especially when the concepts of diachronic and synchronic structure are also noted. In my own experience, I have discovered that if the example of the literature network concerns a topic closely related to the subject of students' own immediate research, these techniques have greater impact.

Introducing the Continuum

When instructing students in the techniques of structured inquiry, it should be stressed that the three epistemological components of scientific literature of which the tripartite matrix is made up are integral parts of an elaborate communication system. Central to introducing this concept in a logical and coherent manner is the notion of the key source, for it is the key source which unifies the system. By keeping initial attempts at research confined to studies linked with the key source, it is possible to keep the assignment within controllable limits.

Because numerous literature networks are vast, even assignments associated with key sources should be made with caution. In some instances, the influence of individual papers (based on the number of times these papers are cited by others) is indeed enormous. For example, Garfield notes that every year the article by D. H. Lowry et al., "Protein Measurement with the Folin Phenol Reagent," *Journal of Biological Chemistry* 193 (1951):265-75, is cited by other scientists between 2,400 and 2,500 times.[9] Similarly, in the *Social Sciences Citation Index*, each year's listings under such names as B. F. Skinner and K. Deutsch present a formidably complex citation pattern. An even more dramatic illustration is the number of citations received by Glueck and other influential criminologists in the post-World War II period covered by the *Criminology Index*. Even if the citation statistics given in the *Criminology Index* are inaccurate and somewhat misleading (see Part IV), they nonetheless suggest the vastness of certain literature networks and the importance of certain key sources. If turned loose on any of these confusing masses of papers, inexperienced researchers would soon give up in hopeless frustration. Thus, definite direction must be given at the beginning of any program designed to acquaint beginning researchers with the techniques of inquiry. In such circumstances, it is ideal if instructor and librarian enjoy a close relationship to insure that students take on research projects they can handle.

Such concerns aside, exposing students to the bibliographic and substantive structures of literature networks serves definite cognitive functions.[10] Moreover, by focusing on these characteristics of structured inquiry, instructors will find greater appeal to the suggestion that engaging students in such exercise is useful for instructional purposes in addition to acquainting them with an efficient mode of inquiry. It is in this sense, for example, following Freides, that literature searching can be considered an intrinsic part of learning rather than as a separate, mechanical aspect of it (see Chapter 14).

Developing the Clark and Trow Student Subculture Literature Network: Encyclopedias and Reviews of Research

In structured inquiry, students (in this case sociology students) are taught that the type of intermediary source which offers the most promise in exposing the key sources associated with a field of sociological research is one that falls in the center of the continuum. Intermediary sources that fall in the center also provide a brief account of what is known scientifically about that same field of research. As noted above, these arguments are made more convincing if they are accompanied by actual examples—admittedly a task that requires considerable preparation on the part of the instructor in the use of library materials.

The more thoughtful and careful the preparation and the more lucid and logical the presentation, the more students will benefit and respond accordingly. If the demonstration of recommended research procedures relates directly or closely to the subject matter that the students are expected to examine, the greater the impact of the exercise. More than anything else, conducting a demonstration of this kind of research demands prior consultation with the instructor. For the purpose of this discussion, it is assumed that the instructor fully accepts structured inquiry as the mode of inquiry the students will employ.

In the interest of keeping this discussion brief, except for a few comments about citation indexes and abstract journals, the details of how individual works are used will not be presented here. It should be understood, however, that in demonstrating these materials, considerable attention should be directed to how such works are located, how they are typically organized, and how they are most efficiently used. (These matters are examined in Part IV.)

Let us turn first to the *International Encyclopedia of the Social Sciences* and the article "Educational Organization Subcultures." Here it is mentioned that Burton R. Clark and Martin Trow have distinguished four types of student subcultures that flourish in varying quantities on different college campuses (see Chapter 1 above). In the bibliography that accompanies the article is a reference to the chapter "The Organizational Context," published in 1966 by Clark and Trow.[11]

Let us next examine an intermediary source which also falls in the center of the continuum: Faris' sociological *Handbook*.[12] The article "Educational Subcultures" in Faris' *Handbook* also discusses the determinants of student subcultures and refers to an unpublished 1960 work by Clark and Trow,[13] a 1962 book by Clark,[14] and a 1963 article by Clark (an abridgement of a 1962 article) in collaboration with Broom and Selznick.[15]

"College Environments," an article in the *Encyclopedia of Educational Research*,[16] notes a typology of student subcultures described in two papers by Trow in 1960.[17] The article also points out that Trow's concept was used by the Educational Testing Service in its 1965 College Student Questionnaire, constructed by Peterson.[18] In addition, there is a reference to Peterson's 1968 revision of the questionnaire, wherein he discusses the concept.[19] Finally, Volume II of the *Encyclopedia of Education,* in the article "Student Subcultures," contains a discussion of the Clark and Trow typology of student subcultures, as well as a reference to Clark and Trow's 1966 paper.[20]

In assessing the information these intermediary sources have provided, we find that as well as brief discussions of the concept we repeatedly find references to the key people in the field: Clark and Trow. (See Figure 6.) Since the purpose of the exercise is to demonstrate the kind of information that can be derived from these intermediary sources, the sequence in which the foregoing works are examined should not concern us here. In using these works, students will become aware of their relative strengths and weaknesses in a manner that will have greater impact on them.

Citation Indexes

According to the principles of structured inquiry, once the researcher has gathered the substantive and bibliographic information available from encyclopedias and reviews of research, he can expand his location (i.e., bibliographic) information in order to gather the names of other researchers not cited in the foregoing works. This is the principal function of citation indexes.[21] Citation indexes are relatively comprehensive listings of footnote citations which (1) indicate the explicit linkages among primary and secondary sources and (2) provide a more efficient source of significant citations than can be generated through a search of the literature by using other types of intermediary sources. Garfield states that "citations display all the properties of word indexing terms because citations are, in fact, alternative and *usually unambiguous* symbols for concepts traditionally codified by headings."[22]

If some of the papers exposed in the foregoing discussion of encyclopedias and reviews of research were examined, however, several references to earlier studies would be uncovered. For example, in Figure 3, the footnote symbols clustered around each paper represent references to previous studies in the literature network. While these citations allow searchers to trace the course of inquiry on a topic backwards in time, it was not until citation indexes appeared that it became possible to advance with the course of inquiry using, it should be noted, the same names. In particular, as noted above, by using the explicit linkages which the names provide, searchers can confine themselves to studies related to the key sources and thus keep the initial assignment within controllable limits.

After acquiring skill in these initial research exercises, searchers can refine and enlarge their research efforts, and more creatively include a broader range of studies that are outside the bibliographic structure of a body of scientific literature. More significantly, the use of citation indexes depends especially upon an understanding of the concept key source. The key sources located in the foregoing intermediary sources, for example, are the cited sources in citation indexes (Figure 7). At the time the bibliographic structure of Clark and Trow's typology of student subculture was constructed, only the 1973 *Social Sciences Citation Index (SSCI)* was available; hence, the *Science Citation Index (SCI)*, beginning 1967, was used as a substitute. Unfortunately,

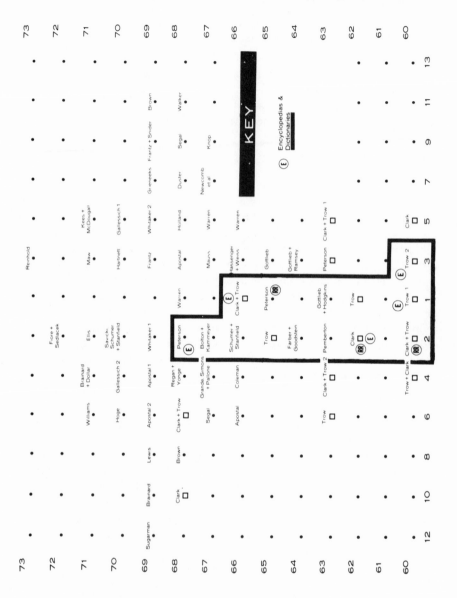

Figure 6. Student Subculture Bibliographic Network Exposed in Encyclopedias and Reviews of Research

SOURCE: Adapted from John MacGregor and Raymond G. McInnis, "Integrating Classroom Instruction and Library Research: The Cognitive Functions of Bibliographic Network Structures." *Journal of Higher Education* **48** (January-February 1977):35. Reprinted by permission.

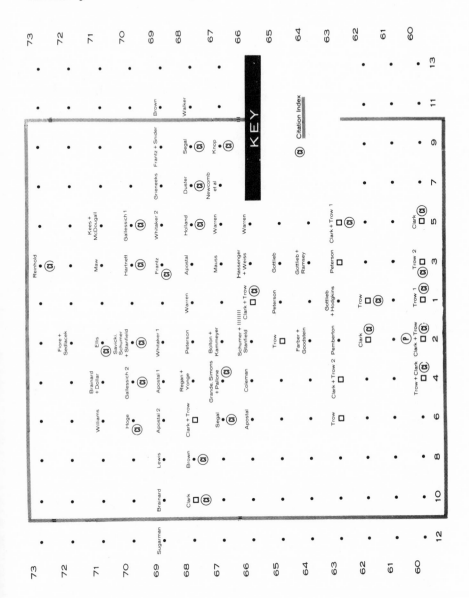

Figure 7. Student Subculture Bibliographic Network Exposed by Citation Indexes

SOURCE: Adapted from John MacGregor and Raymond G. McInnis, "Integrating Classroom Instruction and Library Research: The Cognitive Functions of Bibliographic Network Structures." *Journal of Higher Education* 48 (January-February 1977):35. Reprinted by permission.

the journals indexed in *SCI* are less likely to contain articles on the sociology of education; thus, it is not as satisfactory as the *SSCI* in generating citations to Clark and Trow. Accordingly, if the SSCI extended to an earlier date, say to the early 1960s when the student subculture network was constructed, several of the citations generated by other means would likely have been exposed by it.

Such temporal limitations in the coverage of citation indexes point out that not all research undertaken by students and others can be accommodated to citation indexes. However, by understanding the underlying principles of citation indexes, student researchers can become more thoroughly grounded in the general process of research. It can be said, then, that citation indexes serve definite instructional and cognitive functions beyond their basic function as bibliographic indexes.

The use of citation indexes by inexperienced researchers can present several problems. Students should be cautioned to exercise judgment about whether citations listed under a given name appear as if they are citations that are contained within the particular network of literature in which they are interested. An especially confusing practice in citation indexes is its placement of the citation of people with the same surnames and initials in one sequence. Thus, often listed below such common names as Clark are citations of works of two or more people with the same name and initials.

Such considerations aside, citation indexes have definite advantages which can make their use a means of refining any mode of inquiry to more effective levels. Perhaps better than any other example of intermediary source, citation indexes contribute to the concept of the substantive-bibliographic continuum and the functional characteristics of reference works. The reasons are that, (1) uniquely among instruments of research, the citation index is as rich as the footnote references of the articles indexed in it, and (2) it mirrors more precisely the communication patterns of scientific literature. Gray goes so far as to suggest that if "*SSCI* continues along its present course, progressively expanding its source journal base, it could within a very few years become the master index in the social sciences, one exerting total bibliographical control over the entire structure of the social science litrature."[23]

Several characteristics of the *SSCI* support the notion of the substantive-bibliographic continuum. First, articles that are basically reviews of research or bibliographies have an "R" symbol included as part of the citation. (See the extract from the *SSCI* in Part 2 of Appendix A.) These review articles provide in a compressed or distilled format a synthesis (or, what is described above as an intermediate form or stage) of a portion of a body of scientific literature. In other words the function of such review articles is similar to that attributed to reference works, conceptualized as intermediary sources, which fall in the middle of the continuum. By being aware that such treatment is given indexed articles, users of the *SSCI* can gain access to these special formulations of social-scientific literature. Similar arguments can be made for articles that are basically bibliographical; although the same "R" symbol is used to distinguish them, these fall in either of the two divisions of the continuum to the right (see Chapter 15).

Second, since articles, including review articles and bibliographies, are currently listed (beginning in 1974) in the *Source Index* portion of *SSCI*, with all cited references for each article given below the citation of the article, another perspective emerges: that is, that intermediary sources provide symbolic representation (or intermediate forms or stages) of scientific literature. Bibliographic citations both identify and symbolize subject matter.[24] It can therefore be said that the subject matter of an article is symbolically represented by its citation of the article and by the materials the author cited to support the arguments in his article. By using such formulations of articles, the *SSCI* is in effect giving, in an intermediate form or stage, the substantive content of the article.

Third, by being aware that such treatment is given the substantive content of discrete elements in scientific literature listed in the *SSCI*, searchers can rapidly identify or confirm the key sources in a topic of research. Using the tripartite matrix as an aid to inquiry, the implicit linkages (i.e., those unstated or tacit relationships between items in divisions of the continuum) of such intermediary sources as encyclopedias and citation indexes are made more explicit, allowing a more purposeful and intelligent development of research strategy. (Recall that intermediary sources fall into definite patterns of structure and function, even though as artificial constructs [see Chapter 13] each is produced separately and independently by diverse individuals or groups.) More significantly, by concretely informing inexperienced researchers about these characteristic structures and communciation patterns of scientific literature, they will be better prepared and more self-sufficient to undertake research.[25]

In assessing what parts of the bibliographic structure of the Clark and Trow typology of student subcultures literature network was exposed by the *SSCI*, about one-third of the total number of the citations were found to be included (Figure 7). It can be said, then, that on the whole it is a fairly efficient intermediary source, especially since a very narrow topic is being traced.

Abstracts

Having exposed a considerable number of citations in the literature on the Clark and Trow typology of student subcultures, researchers are informed of another intermediary source which can narrow down the located citations to those with the greatest relevance to their own needs. This is the most useful, although not the primary or traditional, function of abstract journals. However, abstracts present difficulties for several reasons: (1) there is a time lag between the publication of an article in a journal and the publication of its abstract in an abstract journal; (2) some abstract journals have uneven and fragmented coverage of portions of the literature; (3) locating abstracts or annotations of individual items in literature's bibliographic structure is a time-consuming, often frustrating task; and (4) the abstract does not always accurately represent the content of an article. Unfortunately, the first two difficulties were factors in the construction of the Clark and Trow student subculture literature network.

For example, only one or two of the citations were exposed by *Sociological Abstracts*[26] and only a few more by *Psychological Abstracts*.[27] Although the reasons for such limited coverage of this particular body of literature never became entirely clear, one seemed to be that a considerable portion of the studies in the Clark and Trow student subculture network is published in specialized educational counseling journals not included in either service.

The matter became more puzzling when a manual search of the Educational Resources Information Center (ERIC) *Research in Education*[28] and *Current Index to Journals in Education*[29] failed to expose more than ten citations in the network. (A computer search also failed to expose more items.) *Research in Education* does not, of course, cover articles but would expose research conducted on student subcultures not published in journals. Likewise, although we were able to consult only a few applicable years in *Sociology of Education Abstracts*, the few citations exposed in the networks suggest that its coverage is not comprehensive.[30] Not until *College Student Personnel Abstracts* was consulted did citations in the network become exposed in significant numbers.[31]

The intent of this discussion is not to draw attention to the inadequacy of the above abstract journals in the particular research project (a similar research project more centrally focused in the sociology of education probably would have exposed greater numbers of citations), but to point out that abstract journals are best considered as secondary rather than primary devices for *locating* citations. The reasons for the limited coverage in these abstract journals are beyond the scope of our concerns here: namely, informing experienced researchers of the potential functions of abstract journals.[32]

In this project the position was taken that although abstract journals can be used for locating papers on a particular topic, they are more efficiently employed as selection devices.[33] In this sense, the abstract's information on the content of papers is most useful selecting from them for more detailed examination those publications located by other means. Other reasons why abstract journals are in most cases better employed as selection devices rather than as location devices are that (1) particular abstract services vary in the extent in which they cover the literature of particular topics; and

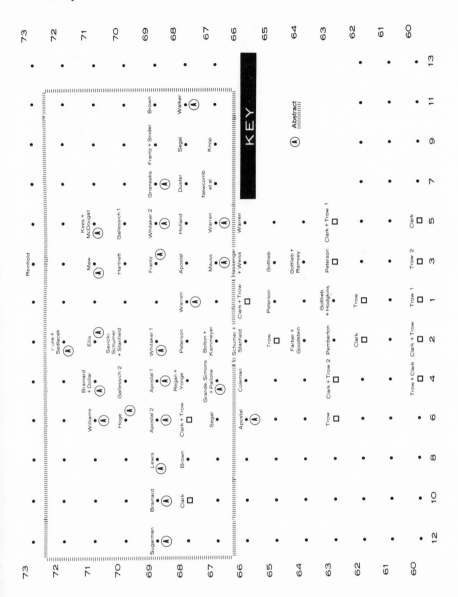

Figure 8. Student Subculture Bibliographic Network Exposed by Abstract Journals

SOURCE: Adapted from John MacGregor and Raymond G. McInnis, "Integrating Classroom Instruction and Library Research: The Cognitive Functions of Bibliographic Network Structures." *Journal of Higher Education* 48 (January-February 1977):35. Reprinted by permission.

(2) the interval between the publication of a paper and the publication of its abstract is often erratic. Both of these charactristics of abstract publishing are in themselves instructive to inexperienced researchers.

In sum, if researchers, especially inexperienced ones, are aware of the existence and function of abstract journals, purposeful and intelligent use can be made of them when the need arises. Lacking acquaintance with these intermediary sources deprives researchers of an important link in the communication system of inquiry.

Similar inconsistencies and ambiguities occur in all devices produced to aid research, and learning about these deficiencies is an important part of becoming an effective researcher, whatever mode of inquiry is employed. (White's argument about developing bibliographic expertise perhaps best describes what is needed.) Moreover, in the social sciences "the real potential of abstract services has never been realized, largely because of the general lack of planning and funding to publish virtually complete abstracting of scientific litrature."[34] As noted by Brittain, very few studies have attempted to relate information requirements and demands to the available material in a discipline or to local conditions of availability and access.[35] This point, principally because of time limitations, is most significant to undergraduate students. Most of their research assignments must be completed by a certain date. The day-to-day activities of reference librarians are often filled with attempts to help students obtain specific materials, which for one reason or another cannot be physically located within the time limits in which they are working.

As Figure 8 illustrates, at a practical level abstract journals serve both as devices to locate citations and as a means of determininmg the substantive content of citations located by other means. While such a statement contradicts some of the foregoing discussion, if *College Student Personnel Abstracts* had not been included as one of the intermediary sources used in constructing the bibliographic structure of the network, several of the later citations would not have been exposed. *College Student Personnel Abstracts* was included for instructive purposes, to illustrate what Line calls the "classical model of research, where the researcher undertakes a thorough review of the literature."[36] By demonstrating that a purposeful search often does expose additional citations, students are made aware of the value of thoroughness, *if* such a search is required. In the research which they conducted, a thorough search of every possible source, principally because of time limitations, would be impractical. Also of importance, of course, is the type of articles exposed. For example, Warren (1968), on the Clark and Trow typology literature network illustrated in Figure 3, is a useful and comprehensive review article (See Appendix D.) Unfortunately, because it was published in a journal not covered by a citation index, it was not exposed. Ellis (1971) was, and since Warren is cited by Ellis, it is logical to assume

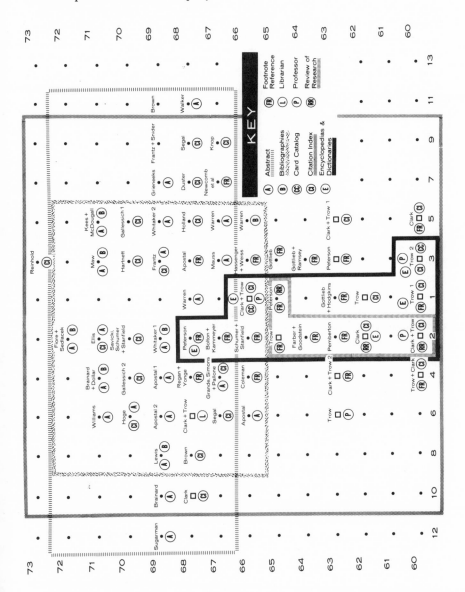

Figure 9. Composite View of All Sources Exposing Student Subculture Bibliographic Network

SOURCE: Adapted from John MacGregor and Raymond G. McInnis, "Integrating Classroom Instruction and Library Research: The Cognitive Functions of Bibliographic Network Structures." *Journal of Higher Education* 48 (January-February 1977):35. Reprinted by permission.

that searchers would eventually have discovered the Warren review article. (See Appendix D.)

A notion of how additional citations might be exposed is given in Figure 9. In actual practice, citations are exposed in many different quarters, including footnote references of individual papers, bibliographies, professors, and reference librarians. Thus, in order to fill out the bibliographic network as shown, as well as the sources of citations from Figures 6 through 8, the other sources which exposed individual citations are also shown in Figure 9.

One final note: The student research experiment involving the literature of the Clark and Trow studies of student subcultures on college campuses reported in this chapter was conducted during the academic year 1974-75.[37] MacGregor, the instructor of the sociology class with whom the experiment was conducted, is no longer with Western Washington University. In the meantime, I have become convinced that using structured inquiry handouts (see Appendix A) presents greater flexibility while achieving the same instructional purposes that the experiment with MacGregor did. At the same time I remain convinced that the procedures used and the results achieved in constructing the Clark and Trow college student subculture literature network (see Figures 3-9) are worth sharing with students as part of their introduction to library research procedures. At the very least, showing students these illustrations achieves two objectives: (1) it demonstrates that following the suggested procedures is a useful and efficient method for completing the literature-searching portion of a research project in psychology or sociology; and (2) together the two topics covered by the different illustrations ("stereotypes" in Appendix A and "Clark and Trow student subcultures," in Figures 3-9) each illustrates and reinforces similar principles of structured inquiry from different perspectives.

Notes

1. See Chapter 8, note 12.

2. See comment by Comte, Chapter 12, p. 109 above.

3. John Ziman, *Public Knowledge* (Cambridge, Mass.: Cambridge University Press, 1968), p. 73.

4. Herman T. Epstein, *A Strategy for Education* (New York: Oxford University Press, 1970), p. 15.

5. Philip H. Phenix, "The Architeconics of Knowledge," in *Education and the Structure of Knowledge* (Chicago: Rand McNally, 1964), p. 54.

6. Cf. Patricia Knapp, *The Library, the Undergraduate, and the Teaching Faculty* (San Diego: Institute on Training for Service in Undergraduate Libraries, 1970), p. 70. This is also available as ERIC Document 042 475.

7. Cf. G. L. Gardiner, "Empirical Study of Reference," *College and Research Libraries* 30 (March 1969):130-55.

8. Cf. Ziman, *Public Knowledge*, p. 58.

9. Eugene Garfield, "Citation Indexing, Historio-Bibliography, and the Sociology of Science," *Proceedings of the 3rd International Congress of Medical Librarianship* (Amsterdam: Excerpta Medica, 1970), p. 187-203.

10. See John MacGregor and Raymond G. McInnis, "Integrating Classroom Instruction and Library Research: The Cognitive Functions of Bibliographic Network Structures," *Journal of Higher Education* 48 (January-February 1977):17-38.

11. Burton R. Clark and Martin Trow, "The Organizational Context," in Theodore Newcomb and Everett Wilson, eds., *College Peer Groups: Problems and Prospects for Research* (Chicago: Aldine, 1966), pp. 17-70.

12. Robert Faris, ed., *Handbook of Modern Sociology* (Chicago: Rand McNally, 1964).

13. Burton R. Clark and Martin Trow, "Determinants of College Student Subcultures" (Berkeley, Calif.: Center for the Study of Higher Education, University of California, 1960) (mimeo).

14. Burton R. Clark, *Educating the Expert Society* (San Francisco: Chandler Publishing Co., 1962), pp. 202-43.

15. Leonard Broom and Philip Selznick, *Sociology*, 3d ed. (New York: Harper and Row, 1963).

16. R. L. Ebel, ed., *Encyclopedia of Educational Research*, 4th ed. (New York: Macmillan, 1969).

17. Martin Trow, "Cultural Sophistication and Higher Education," in *Conference on Selection and Educational Differentiation, Berkeley, 1959* (Berkeley, Calif.: Field Service Center and Center for Higher Education, University of California, 1960), pp. 107-23; and "The Campus Viewed as a Culture," in Hall T. Sprague, ed., *Research on College Students* (Boulder, Colo.: Western Interstate Commission for Higher Education, 1960), pp. 105-24.

18. Richard Peterson, *College Student Questionnaire and Technical Manual* (Princeton, N.J.: Educational Testing Service, 1965).

19. Richard Peterson, *College Student Questionnaire (Technical Manual)*, rev. ed. (Princeton, N.J.: Educational Testing Service, 1968).

20. Joseph F. Kauffman, "College Student Profile," in L. C. Deighton, ed., *Encyclopedia of Education* Vol. 2 (New York: Macmillan, 1971), pp. 217-21.

21. Melvin Weinstock, "Citation Indexes," in Allen Kent and Harold Lancour, eds., *Encyclopedia of Library and Information Science* Vol. 5 (New York: Marcel Dekker, 1971), pp. 16-40, is an extensive discussion of the principles and uses of citation indexes. The annual *Social Sciences Citation Index Guide and Journal Lists* (Philadelphia: Institute for Scientific Information) contains an extensive list, as well as reprints, of articles on a wide range of applications of citation indexes. Elizabeth Miller and Eugenia Truesdell, "Citation Indexing: History and Applications," *Drexel Library Quarterly* 8 (April 1972):159-72, is another useful discussion.

22. Eugene Garfield, "Primordial Concepts, Citation Indexing, and Historiographs," *Journal of Library History* 2 (1967):243. (Emphasis added.)

23. Richard A. Gray, [review of *SSCI*] in *American Reference Books Annual* 7 (1976):151.

24. Eugene Garfield, "Citation Indexing, Historio-Bibliography, and the Sociology of Science," p. 196; Thelma Freides, *The Literature and Bibliography of the Social Sciences* (Los Angeles: Melville Publishing Co., 1973), p. 259 and Marcia Bates, "Rigorous Systematic Bibliography," *RQ* 16 (Fall 1976):9.

25. Similar to the manner of indicating review articles, citation indexes are the most efficient means currently available for locating book reviews,—a "B" symbol in a citation indicates a book review—in the social sciences. Unfortunately, the policy of indicating book reviews was discontinued in the *Science Citation Index* in 1967.

26. *Sociological Abstracts* (New York: American Sociological Association, 1952).

27. *Psychological Abstracts* (Washington, D.C.: American Psychological Association, 1927- .)

28. *Research in Education* (Washington, D.C.: U.S. Government Printing Office 1966-).

29. *Current Index to Journals in Education* (New York: CCM Corporation, 1969-).

30. *Sociology of Education Abstracts* (London: Pergamon, 1965-).

31. *College Student Personnel Abstracts* (Claremont, Calif.: College Student Personnel Institute, 1965-).

32. Although considered outside the needs for instructing undergraduates in general research procedures, Oscar K. Buros, ed., *Seventh Mental Measurements Yearbook* (Highland Park, N.J.: Gryphon Press, 1972), pp. 112-6, contains a large list of studies. The "College Student Questionnaire," the instrument developed by Peterson for the Educational Testing Service, and based on the Clark and Trow typology, resulted in numerous tests of variables by doctoral candidates.

33. Cf. Winn's conception of the purpose of *Sociology of Education Abstracts*: "It was not conceived of primarily as a tool for the purpose of tracing relevant documents but as a medium for the dissemination of knowledge about sociological research into education." V. A. Winn, "A Case Study of the Problems of Information Processing in a Social Science Field: The OSTI:*SEA* Project," *ASLIB Proceedings* 23 (February 1971):76.

34. MacGregor and McInnis, "Integrating Classroom Instruction and Library Research," p. 28. See also Thelma Freides, "Bibliographic Gaps in the Social Science Literature," *Special Libraries* 67 (February 1976):68-74; J. M. Brittain, *Information and Its Users* (Bath, England: Bath University Press, 1970), pp. 143-5; and Maurice Line, *Information Requirements of Researchers in the Social Sciences* (Bath, England: University Library, Bath University of Technology, 1971), 1, p. 216.

35. Brittain, *Information and Its Users*, p. 88.

36. Line, *Information Requirements of Researchers in the Social Sciences*, 1, p. 226.

37. The experiment is more fully reported in MacGregor and McInnis, "Integrating Classroom Instruction and Library Research."

17 The Tacit Logic of Structured Inquiry

Implicit Linkages Among Intermediary Sources

The tacit dimension is inherent in any mode of inquiry. That is, because explicit instructions in a given intermediary source about where a particular fact or concept can be found in another intermediary source are seldom included in the information provided, searchers are left to their own devices to find needed material. For example, there is an unstated but recognized interdependency between the explanations of social patterns of marriage and the family in Christensen's *Handbook of Marriage and the Family*,[1] and the various configurations in which citations of the literature are arranged in the *International Bibliography of Research in Marriage and the Family*.[2]

The concept of unexpressed linkages between intermediary sources is put in sharper perspective by O'Leary. In the introduction to the latest edition of the *Ethnographic Bibliography of North America*,[3] he states that the bibliographies for each tribal group are designed "to make the coverage . . . more congruent to that of the forthcoming *Handbook of North American Indians*," an encyclopedic work of twenty large volumes.[4] "The fit between them is not particularly close at times, because of the different classificatory systems and emphases of the two works." Nonetheless,

the articles in the *Handbook* will complement this bibliography very directly, in that much of the literature is given a critical discussion in these articles. In addition, the articles themselves will provide extensive bibliographies on the ethnic groups and subject fields discussed. Since the individual bibliographies will have been prepared by experts on these groups and fields, it is inevitable that there will be much in them which is not found in this bibliography. Of course, the converse will also be the case. Therefore, it will behoove the conscientious investigator to peruse both the present bibliography and those in the *Handbook* articles, in order to be certain [that the bibliographical structures of the ethnic groups and subjects are discovered].[5]

The linkages between articles or topic divisions in intermediary sources are therefore implicit. As searchers gain greater experience and skill, utilizing these materials in the manner they are intended—even though linkages between them are understood—becomes part of their search strategy.

Librarians' Tacit Knowledge of Structured Inquiry and
the Substantive-Bibliographic Continuum

All experienced reference librarians know the sequence of reference works to consult for tracing a research topic embedded in the scientific literature of the field. The typical pattern followed is structured inquiry or, in Freides' words, "tuning in." The object is to progress from a point where an intermediary source provides a particular form or stage of the literature of the topic to the particular formulation of the literature which the researcher needs.

By education and experience, reference librarians are prepared to think of the logical locations of these materials. This capability is part of their craft, and accordingly, in giving reference service they often act at different levels of awareness in determining the best intermediary source, or combination of intermediary sources, to consult for solving a particular reference problem. This ability constitutes the reference librarians' tacit knowledge of structured inquiry.

It must be acknowledged, however, that librarians have varying levels of expertise as regards this capability. For instance, House reports that even experienced reference librarians vary widely in thoroughness of research.[6] Such evidence notwithstanding, even the most ill-prepared reference librarians have more knowledge of what strategy to employ in a search than most researchers outside the library. The researcher who does employ a search strategy which approaches the standard inherent in Line's notion of the "classical model of research" (see Chapter 16) is unusual. As Line's Bath University study concludes, even most scholars who normally would be expected to have a command of the requirements of research, upon questioning exhibit surprising gaps in their knowledge of available reference materials in their field of inquiry: "The results of the investigation show that in fact social scientists rarely make rational use of bibliographic tools. Instead they prefer less systematic methods."[7]

With regard to the strategy employed by experienced reference librarians, the following example is instructive. If the researcher has merely heard of the concept "student subcultures" but is fairly well informed about the substantive literature in related areas, the following sequence may appear the most logical. First, an encyclopedia article gives, in a distilled format, an account of what is known scientifically about "student subcultures" and the names of people prominently associated with developing the concept. From here, it may be logical to proceed to a more recent review of research which concisely outlines the research advances of the last decade, the last five years, and so forth. Or, it may seem obvious that an abstract journal is necessary or that the most recent research may be traced with the aid of a citation index.

Except in unusual situations, such as where elaborate audiovisual programs are used, most of these procedures are recommended orally (perhaps with demonstrations included). The librarian proceeds step by step (i.e., in a structured sequence) from one intermediary source to another, the specific strategy being directed by the clues (information) gathered in successive intermediary sources.

In following these procedures, there is no conscious awareness of the substantive-bibliographic continuum of intermediary sources, i.e., those that give access to primarily one component of scientific literature or to various combinations of the components. Nor, since particular intermediary sources consulted seldom give explicit instructions as to what other sources can be consulted for more information, is there any direction from some immutable authority. In short, the librarian, pursues a pattern developed by a tacit logic.

The foregoing evidence, perhaps better than any other, supports Knapp's contention that acquiring an acceptable level of library competence is not just "picked up" by the undergraduate student. "It must be taught." The above evidence also suggests that many researchers believed to be acquainted with research procedures and materials would benefit by being better informed. On the other hand, according to Winn, "a balance has to be struck between 'educating' the user in the use of information services and developing information services to accord with his requirements and habits of information seeking."[8] Even if the ideal of developing information services in accord with researchers' needs is feasible, instruction for inexperienced researchers will continue to be required.

In the case of social-scientific literature, the most promising method of achieving this desired level of competence among both experienced and inexperienced researchers is to set forth the research materials typically available in academic libraries according to their *patterns* of giving coverage and access to the structural components of the literature. (Similar arguments can be made for the literature of the natural sciences and the humanities.) Once the concepts of the bibliographic and substantive structure of the literature are understood, the functions of reference works, conceptualized as intermediary sources, can be introduced in a context where their underlying logic becomes evident. Not all research problems are, of course, immediately eliminated. Manipulation of these materials still requires practice and refinement, especially among students who have had little or no experience in research. Further, finding those research materials currently not in the literature network (e.g., primary sources) creates other kinds of problems for researchers attempting to develop search strategies.

Sharpening Researchers' Awareness of the Tacit Logic of Inquiry

Sharpening researchers' awareness of the tacit logic of inquiry depends on a number of factors. First, potential researchers must have the opportunity to become grounded in the structure of scientific literature. Second, they must have the means of becoming informed fairly rapidly about the kind of intermediary sources available in their library. Third, students must be motivated by the knowledge that their instructor considers the system to be viable. As regards this third point, readers will recall that throughout this book, the desirability of integrating classroom instruction and library research has been emphasized, the principal reason being that if students are given the motivation for using the library effectively by the classroom instructor they will attach greater importance to the task.

Finally, the fourth factor is exposure. In the Bath University study, Line states that social scientists' "ignorance of the existence of information . . . is largely a matter of exposure." Increased awareness, he contends,

can be achieved partly by more efficient methods of exposure . . . and by user education in the use of bibliographical tools. . . . Also opportunities for multiple exposure might be required; a second or third exposure to the same information, perhaps in different contexts, might affect judgments of relevance. The problem of unarticulated needs (due to lack of exposure and knowledge) was not limited to areas of peripheral interest; . . . In some cases researchers were ignorant of fairly large and important areas of knowledge related to their primary research interest.[9]

An exercise for library school students conducted by Whitten in a social science bibliography course provides an unwitting collaboration of Line's arguments. In the exercise, library school students were to give bibliographical assistance to faculty engaged in research projects in departments and research institutes at the University of Southern California. One of the results of having students work with faculty researchers "was the extent to which it became clear that the faculty often did not know exactly what they wanted when they originally set the assignments" ("it was only when the students began to bring them citations for evaluation that the real topics began to emerge"), and the astonishment of the faculty "at the number and good quality of citations found in sources and with techniques they would not have thought of or known about themselves."[10]

Instructional Purpose of the Clark and Trow Literature Network

The graphical illustrations of different configurations of the literature of the Clark and Trow typology of student subcultures were constructed with such instructional purposes in mind. By using most types of intermediary sources typically available, it was intended to demonstrate for sociology students how all research devices contribute to the successful completion of a research exercise—even though, in actual practice, students may not make use of all of them in any single research assignment. However, if the functions of specific types of intermediary sources (in the context of their pattern of exposing individual or combinations of components of scientific literature) are drawn to their attention, students are made aware of these research materials in a way that can be applied to other situations.

Polanyi's Concept of Tacit Knowledge

Polanyi's most significant distinction for the concept of tacit knowledge[11] is that between focal and subsidiary awareness. Focal awareness is the ordinary kind of fully conscious awareness of a specifiable object. In contrast, subsidiary awareness is the peripheral noticing of features of an object that are not attended to in themselves but are seen as pointers or clues to the object of focal attention. According to Polanyi, it is "well-known *that the aim of a skillful performance is achieved by the observance of a set of rules which are not known as such to the person following them.*"[12] Polanyi gives many examples, and Wagener's interpretive descriptions of Polanyi's theories are simple and direct.[13]

In any given context, there are some factors of which we are aware because we are directing attention to them. In other words, we are *focally aware* of them. In the same context, there are also factors we are aware of, even though we are not focusing on them. That is, we are *subsidiarily aware* of them. For example, when a person is pounding a nail with a hammer, attention is focused on the nail. The person is only subsidiarily aware of the hammer. If, however, attention is switched to the hammer, the person becomes focally aware of the hammer and subsidiarily aware of the nail.

In such examples, "the cognitive context is brought into being by the knowing subject 'attending from' that which he is subsidiarily aware and 'attending to' that of which he is focally aware."[14] In pounding a nail, the person *attends from* the hammer, of which he is subsidiarily aware, and *attends to* the nail, of which he is focally aware.

Things look different and sensations feel different when seen or felt as clues to something else, than when they are attended to directly. The kinds of differences that occur depend, of course, on the type of subsidiary element being considered, but in all cases we can say that the knowledge gained by subsidiary awareness is tacit. To speak in the indicative mode about such elements would require focusing attention on them and then they would no longer be the relied-on subsidiary elements in question.[15]

Ravetz, in describing science as a craft, offers another example:

Craftsman's work is done with particular objects, which may be material or intellectual constructs, or a mixture of the two; and the operator must know them in all their particularity. Their properties and behaviour cannot be fully specified in a formal list; in fact, no explicit description can do more than give the first simple elements of their properties. Hence the operator's knowledge of them must be "intuitive," or of the sort described by Polanyi as "tacit." It cannot be learned from books, but from experience, derived from a teacher by precept and imitation, and supplemented by the personal experience of the operator himself.[16]

When we apply the foregoing principles to library research, experienced reference librarians can be said to be subsidiarily aware of the pattern or sequence of intermediary sources they consult when they are engaged in assisting a researcher. Their focal awareness is directed to the subject of the inquiry. By instructing students about the functions of reference works from the perspective of the tripartite matrix, stressing particularly the notion of reference works conceptualized as intermediary sources, it is possible to facilitate learning about their functions and the implicit linkages between them. Through this system, student researchers can be assisted to become more subsidiarily aware of intermediary sources and more focally aware of the subject of their inquiry. In this context, as argued in Chapter 8, tacit knowing is a process of understanding, a grasping of disjointed parts into a comprehensive whole, of visualizing disjointed parts as a logical system.

Analogy Between the Craft Skills of Scientists and Library Research

An analogy can be made between these arguments and those of Ravetz concerning the skills of "the matured craftsman of scientific inquiry." According to Ravetz,

the matured craftsman of scientific inquiry will be working on technical problems which are peculiar to himself and some colleagues, and which change fairly rapidly with the development of his field; and so there is no substitute for his personal, largely tacit knowledge of the tools which have become nearly continuous extensions of the sensory, motor, and intellectual equipment within his body. The transmission of such knowledge will then be largely through a close personal association of master and pupil, and the explicit precepts of the refined methods of tool-using have meaning only in the context of the solution of sophisticated technical problems. The informal and largely tacit precepts of method are not restricted to the tools in the solution of technical subsidiary problems of a scientific inquiry. The scientist's craft also includes the formulations of problems, the adoption of correct strategies for the different stages of the evolution of a problem,[17] and the interpretation of general criteria of adequacy and value in particular situations.[18]

In support of his position, Ravetz refers to Oakeshott's observations:

In every [refined ability] there is an ingredient of knowledge which cannot be resolved into information, and in some skills this may be the greater part of the knowledge required for their practice. Moreover, [these] abilities do not exist in the abstract but in individual examples: the norms by which they are recognized are afterthoughts, not categorical imperatives, and each individual has what may be called a style or idiom of its own which cannot be specified in propositions.[19]

Oakeshott suggests that "the inheritance of human achievements into which the teacher" initiates his students is "knowledge." As interpreted by Oakeshott, "knowledge is to be recognized as manifolds of abilities, in each of which there is a synthesis of 'information' and 'judgment.'" These "two components of knowledge ('information' and 'judgment') can both be communicated [i.e., taught] and acquired, but cannot be communicated or acquired separately—at least, not on separate occasions or in separate lessons.'"[20] (Judgment is intended here to have a connotation similar to that ascribed to wisdom in Chapter 1.) Although I am speaking of aspects of teaching and learning in general, the implications for synthesizing information and judgment in teaching and learning how to undertake inquiry—in its broadest sense—are obvious.

Just as Ravetz suggests that the tools of a mature scientist become almost continuous extensions of the sensory, motor, and intellectual equipment of his body, analogously reference works can be considered extensions of reference librarians. The library is, in effect, a laboratory filled with research instruments. Through education and experience, reference librarians develop a tacit logic for giving assistance to researchers. Ordinarily, the strategies employed in giving this assistance cannot be precisely articulated. Experience has proven that each situation demands slightly altered patterns for tracing a problem to a solution, peculiar only to that situation. Because of these peculiarities, explaining or otherwise transmitting the general pattern of research employed is difficult. A further complication is that patterns of research strategy are altered with the development of new types of intermediary sources. Consider how, for example, the appearance of the *Social Sciences Citation Index* has altered the pattern of giving reference service in the social sciences. In the passage quoted above, Ravetz notes that a similar phenomenon occurs in the scientific laboratory when a new research instrument is introduced.

The reconstructed logic (Kaplan's term, as defined in Chapter 8 above) of structured inquiry (i.e., formalizing or codifying it as a mode of inquiry) makes researchers aware of its potential use, but developing and refining procedures associated with structured inquiry still require practice. Such considerations become more logical and convincing when they are considered from the perspective of what Kaplan terms logic-in-use, i.e., the informal methods of inquiry that individuals employ in research. Within the conceptual framework of the tripartite matrix, particularly in relation to the notion of the bibliographic-substantive continuum of functions of intermediary sources, reconstructed logic merely serves as a guide to selecting a research strategy.

According to Kaplan, intuition in any logic-in-use is "preconscious" and "outside" the inference schema for which there are available reconstructions (see Chapter 8 above). Intuition is said to occur when no one, including the discoverer, can specify how the discovery was made, but its occurrence cannot be "ascribed merely to chance." As argued in Chapter 8, developing the skills required for inquiry is analogous to those developed by craftsmen.[21] According to Ravetz, such skills are not learned in books but are acquired by precept and imitation. In connection with inquiry, such skills will be more easily comprehended and better retained if they are learned within the context of an actual research problem.

By integrating a mode of inquiry with learning, inquiry will be recognized as a logical part of learning rather than as a separate and mechanical task. Such teaching, through precept and imitation, "which is sometimes dismissed as an inferior sort of teaching, generating inflexible knowledge because the rules of what is known remained concealed, is emancipating [the student] from the half-utterances of rules by making him aware of a concrete situation."[22]

Does Instruction Have Any Lasting Effects?

Concrete evidence that students employ such patterns of research strategy in other situations is difficult to obtain. Later observation of the research habits of students working in the library who have been introduced or otherwise exposed to these concepts suggests that they are indeed applying the principles learned in the demonstration. Not all students, after being introduced to the system, follow the prescribed procedures, however. Just as often, certain students will seek out a reference librarian who, they have discovered, can more quickly produce the required source of information. Before these students were introduced to library materials in this structural-functional context, they were not aware that such materials existed. Thus, some satisfaction can be derived from the fact that, although these students are not themselves going to the extra effort of locating the required materials, they are applying a tacit logic in determining what to ask the librarian to locate for them. These students are at least partially making the heuristic leap (to use Polanyi's term) from their perceived need to solve a particular research problem and the intermediary source (or sources) which lead to solving it.[23]

While such an act is basically intuitive, it is improved by instruction or demonstration. In effect, using the pattern of the functions of intermediary sources on the continuum of the tripartite model of inquiry, students are inferring which type of source is likely to contain the information they need.[24]

Conclusions

By introducing library reference materials as integral components of the underlying structure of social-scientific literature, a conceptual framework for developing a mode of inquiry is provided. (In this context, reference works are conceptualized as intermediary sources, where each provides in a distilled format a special form or stage of scientific literature.) This proposed mode of inquiry is called structured inquiry. Without such a concept, some sort of tacit logic must be employed by researchers in developing research strategies. This tacit logic is dependent almost entirely on intuition and experience, with the result that such strategies are, to use Line's phrase, "less than systematic."

Introduced as components of the tripartite matrix outlined above, intermediary sources can be visualized by researchers as performing specific and important functions in exposing particular portions of the scientific literature of a given field of inquiry. Such an understanding raises their awareness of how a tacit logic can more systematically be employed in a mode of inquiry. Tacit logic, in this context, refers to those thought processes which enable researchers acquainted with the tripartite matrix, as a model of inquiry, to visualize the particular intermediary source, or combination of them, required for solving a particular research problem. For example, when a researcher encounters an unfamiliar term he will seek out a dictionary *likely* to have an explanation of it.

If the student has an understanding of the underlying principles of the tripartite matrix, he will know that in all likelihood there will be a dictionary available that will provide, in a compressed format, an account of what is known scientifically about that term. (Student researchers must understand, however, that not all dictionaries in a special field consistently explain all terms and concepts considered relevant to a particular context.)

Notes

1. Harold T. Christensen, ed., *Handbook of Marriage and the Family* (Chicago: Rand McNally, 1964).

2. Joan Aldous and R. Hill, eds., *International Bibliography of Research on Marriage and the Family, 1900-1972*, 2 vols. (Minneapolis: University of Minnesota Press, 1967-1974).

3. George P. Murdock and Timothy O'Leary, *Ethnographic Bibliography of North America*, 5 vols. (New Haven, Conn.: HRAF Press, 1975), p. XIV.

4. William C. Sturtevant, ed., *Handbook of North American Indians*, 20 vols. (Washington, D.C.: Smithsonian Institution Press, forthcoming).

5. Murdock and O'Leary, *Ethnographic Bibliography of North America*, p. XXXVI.

6. See David E. House, "Reference Efficiency or Reference Deficiency," *Library Association Record* 76 (November 1974):222-3. G. L. Gardiner, "Empirical Study of Reference," *College and Research Libraries* 30 (March 1969):130-55, is a critical examination of attempts to study what reference service involves. Gardiner notes that to date such studies have not succeeded, and he suggests that a more promising approach would be that reference service is a special case of problem-solving.

7. See Maurice Line, *Information Requirements of Researchers in the Social Sciences* (Bath, England: University Library, Bath University of Technology, 1971), I, pp. 193-231. The quoted passage is on p. 216.

8. V. A. Winn, "A Case Study of the Problems of Information Processing in a Social Science Field: The OSTI: *SEA* Project," *ASLIB Proceedings* 23 (February 1971):83.

9. Line, *Information Requirements of Researchers in the Social Sciences*, II, p. 202.

10. See Benjamin Whitten, "Social Science Bibliography Course: A Client-oriented Approach," *Journal of Education for Librarianship* 16 (Summer 1975):30-1.

11. The following discussion owes much to articles by Jerry H. Gill, "The Case for Tacit Knowledge," *Southern Journal of Philosophy* 9 (Spring 1971):48-59; William T. Scott, "Tacit Knowing and *The Concept of Mind*," *Philosophical Quarterly* 21 (June 1971): 22-35; Jerome R. Ravetz, *Scientific Knowledge and Its Social Problems* (New York: Oxford University Press, 1971); James W. Wagener, "The Philosophy of Michael Polanyi as a Source of Educational Theory," Ph.D. dissertation, University of Texas, 1968; and the writings of Polanyi.

12. Michael Polanyi, *Personal Knowledge* (Chicago: University of Chicago Press, 1958), p. 49. (Emphasis added.)

13. See Wagener, *The Philosophy of Michael Polanyi*, pp. 46-66.

14. Gill, "The Case for Tacit Knowledge," p. 49.

15. Scott, "Tacit Knowing and *The Concept of Mind*," p. 24.

16. Ravetz, *Scientific Knowledge and Its Social Problems*, p. 140.

17. Ravetz describes science as essentially problem-solving.

18. Ibid., p. 103.

19. Michael Oakeshott, "Learning and Teaching," in R. S. Peters, ed., *The Concept of Education* (New York: Humanities Press, 1967), p. 169.

20. Ibid., p. 170.

21. Cf. Wagener, *The Philosophy of Michael Polanyi*.

22. Oakeshott, "Learning and Teaching," p. 175. See also Ann Diller, "On Tacit Knowing and Apprenticeship," in Michael J. Parsons, ed., *Philosophy of Education 1974; Proceedings of the Thirtieth Annual Meeting of the Philosophy of Education Society*, Boston, April 1974 (Edwardsville, Ill.: Philosophy of Education Society, 1974), pp. 59-67.

23. Michael Polanyi, as cited by Wagener, *The Philosophy of Michael Polanyi*, p. 61.

24. A recommended method for setting forth intermediary sources for particular disciplines in the social sciences, so that students can locate required materials by themselves, is given in Parts IV and V.

18 A Comment on Knapp's Notion of a Substantive-Bibliographic Continuum

Knapp's suggested continuum has considerable similarity to the substantive-bibliographic continuum proposed here.[1] Careful analysis will show, however, that her model of inquiry is not entirely consistent with the present tripartite matrix, particularly in the way the three epistemological components of scientific literature are considered. Further, Freides consistently speaks of literature and bibliography as the two principal components of scientific literature, which more or less follows the notions of Knapp.[2] Thus, there are obvious differences between Knapp's arguments and those developed here. Though subtle, the distinctions need to be recognized.

The two structural components of scientific literature, bibliographic and substantive, are implicit in Knapp and Freides. By making such distinctions more explicit, especially in their relation to the intermediary sources that provide access to them, their proposed modes of inquiry become more internally consistent and logically complete. Such an observation is particularly true with regard to the concept of diachronic and synchronic structures of scientific literature developed in Chapter 10.

Let's briefly examine Knapp's continuum. In connection with the Joyce assignment in the Monteith College Library experiment, Knapp arranged to have students use a set of bibliographical sources.

We asked each student to examine a set of three items. One was a non-selective, non-annotated bibliography, such as the *Annual Bibliography of English Language and Literature*; the second was an encyclopedia article or a selected, annotated bibliography, in short, a publication which provided a limited bibliography but information of some sort; and the third was one of the collateral readings to be found on the Joyce shelves in the library.[3]

At that moment, it occured to her that

although the three categories of bibliographical sources set up for the assignment are not clear-cut, they do fit into a continuum between high coverage of the literature with low direct provision of information at the one end and low coverage of the literature with high provision of direct information at the other. It follows that the usefulness of any source on this continuum depends on the amount of information the user brings to his search. The scholar can use the exhaustive bibliography effectively because he knows something of the literature of the subject; the neophyte can use the encyclopedia article with profit because it offers background information and a highly selected bibliography, *provided* he understands that what he has is merely a good starting place for serious study.[4]

Although Knapp's continuum contains "three categories of bibliographical sources" that have some resemblance to those in the tripartite matrix being developed here, it is not consistent in distinguishing the various epistemological components contained in it. For example, in her third division (on the end) is placed "one of the collateral readings to be found on the Joyce shelves in the library," or what is ordinarily considered a collection of discrete secondary sources. Although I recognize that it is open to debate, in the tripartite matrix being developed here, items contained in a collection of "collateral readings" are considered to constitute discrete components of both the substantive and the bibliographic structure of the topic, and *not* as intermediary sources. Recall that intermediary sources give access to or otherwise expose a special form or stage in analytical or synthetical formulations, of either bibliographic or substantive information of a topic (or combinations thereof). As the third part of the tripartite matrix, only what is generally considered an intermediary source is found in each division.

However, since the subject, the literature of Joyce, is outside the social sciences, generalizations must be made with caution. Bell argues, for example, that the structure of literature (in its generic sense) in the humanities does not follow the patterns characteristic of the natural sciences or the social sciences.[5] Basically, the literature of the humanities does not reflect the same cumulative-noncumulative characteristics as those of the natural and social sciences (see Chapter 10). Such considerations aside, the "collateral readings" are epistemologically inconsistent with the properties ascribed to intermediary sources occupying divisions of the third part of the tripartite matrix.

Next, in the middle division are grouped an "encyclopedia article" and "a selected, annotated bibliography." The encyclopedia article provides a synthesis of the current valid substantive elements of the topic—i.e., current when the article was written. In addition, it *usually* provides a select bibliography directly linked to the substantive elements discussed in the article. In contrast, the "selected, annotated bibliography" gives an analytical treatment of discrete contributions to the literature of the same topic and, except for the annotations, gives treatment to each item similar to that accorded items in Knapp's first category. Simply put, the synthetical treatment of the substantive and bibliographical components of a topic in an encyclopedia article is inconsistent with the analytical treatment given these same components in an annotated bibliography.

In the end, such differences are of little importance, especially if the underlying motives for proposing them are directed toward the same goal, namely, to devise more effective means for the processes of inquiry to be understood and applied. Furthermore, Kolb's findings (see Chapter 1 above) concerning the different preferred modes of learning among people suggest that there should be several models of inquiry to choose from, so that the method most agreeable to them can be selected.

Notes

1. This similarity was also noted in John MacGregor and Raymond G. McInnis, "Integrating Classroom Instruction and Library Research," *Journal of Higher Education* 48 (January-February 1977): Note 8.

2. Thelma Freides, *The Literature and Bibliography of the Social Sciences* (Los Angeles: Melville Publishing Co., 1973), pp. 260-1.

3. Patricia Knapp, "The Meaning of the Monteith College Library Program," *Journal of Education for Librarianship* 6 (1965):123.

4. Ibid., pp. 123-4.

5. Daniel Bell, *The Reforming of General Education* (New York: Columbia University Press, 1966), p. 174.

Part IV

THE PRINCIPLES AND APPLICATIONS OF RESEARCH GUIDES IN THE SOCIAL SCIENCES

The two sorts of power now roughly described might be contrasted as "exploitative control" and "descriptive control." "Exploitative control" is a deliberately somewhat rough or severe term for the ability to make the best use of a body of writings, "descriptive control" a not very adequate term for an ability to line up a population of writings in any arbitrary order, to make the population march to one' command.[1]

In the preceding chapters, it is argued that if research undertaken by students is to be successful and satisfying, it is desirable that they first be given a well-grounded understanding of both the structure of scientific literature and the structure and function of reference works (see especially Chapter 14). Central to this task is the necessity of devising a means of informing students about how reference works function as intermediary sources where they expose—in a distilled format—the network and content of published studies which make up a body of scientific literature. In this context, reference works, conceptualized as intermediary sources, are seen to expose various forms or stages of portions of bodies of scientific literature.

Basically, intermediary sources perform either analytical functions, exposing discrete elements of a body of literature (i.e., the individual studies of which it is comprised), or synthetical functions, exposing synthesized *portions of that same literature (i.e., the discrete contributions, which taken together form a larger body of literature). Thus, intermediary sources are a means of reducing or distilling a body of literature to manageable size, without distorting the essential content.*

Chief among the examples of intermediary sources which perform analytical functions in this process are the abstract journal and the bibliography. Chief among the examples of intermediary sources which perform synthetical functions in the process are the encyclopedia and the review of research. In addition, the latter (to a greater extent than the former) is part of the mechanism developed for assessing and sifting those valid substantive portions of social-scientific literature contained in new publications as well as for screening from the older body of that same literature those portions that have become obsolete. Hence, intermediary sources which perform synthetical functions are the means by which a community of researchers communicates which portions of the literature, through consensus, have been accorded the status of knowledge. This description is oversimplified, since the development of a literature seldom achieves such idealized tidiness.[2] Nonetheless, without such a conceptual framework of how knowledge is produced, potential researchers cannot have a secure ground from which research can be conducted.

Notes

1. Patrick Wilson, *Two Kinds of Power* (Berkeley, Calif.: University of California Press, 1968), p. 25.
2. John Ziman, *Public Knowledge* (Cambridge, Mass.: Cambridge University Press, 1968), pp. 122-3.

19 Library-Produced Research Guides

It is appropriate now to explain how these research materials can be introduced and set forth in library-produced research guides. In this connection, the reader should recall the observation that a recommended method of instructing students in sound research methods is to introduce these materials in the context of an actual research problem.[1] When the illustrated research problem is closely related to the students' immediate research needs, the demonstration will have even greater impact on them. Introducing the intermediary sources of a literature in this manner provides a concrete demonstration of how students can make use of them and what sorts of results they can expect to achieve.

The concern in Part IV is with how these materials are presented to researchers (i.e., how reference works, especially those conceptualized as intermediary sources, are arranged and described in library-prepared research guides).

Reference librarians, instructors, and students should be aware of at least two matters.

First, students should be cautioned that they cannot expect to use these materials without giving considerable time and effort to refining their research procedures. Students should be advised that developing sound research habits requires practice and experience. They should be assured that, as is true of any other task that requires skill, their first attempts at research, although clumsy and discouraging, will become more effective and rewarding as their research methods are refined. (Ideally, such advice should come from both instructors and librarians.) White's claim that "bibliographic expertise" must be developed is particularly fitting here. Developing such bibliographic expertise is made less difficult and confusing if researchers are acquainted with the principles underlying structured inquiry.

It is in the context of structured inquiry that the second observation can be made. Specifically, students should be informed that their ability to conduct research effectively is determined to a large extent by how thoroughly they come to understand the subject matter of their research topic. Structured inquiry allows researchers—particularly those with little or no prior acquaintance with the topic being investigated—to advance from a general or sketchy level of understanding to a more detailed consideration of the less well-organized and refined forms and configurations of the literature on that same topic. In addition, by using this mode of inquiry, advances occur at a comfortable pace for the researcher.

To a certain extent, this argument resembles that offered by Freides (see Chapter 14). Freides' primary concern is for the instruction of library school students. She gives little attention to effective ways of presenting these materials to students in library-prepared research guides.

Undergraduates have a special need to be informed rapidly and effectively of which intermediary sources give access to scientific literature. In the introduction to the third edition of the *Ethnographic Bibliography of North America*, O'Leary discusses the problem of rapidly informing researchers—especially inexperienced ones—of scientific literature sources. Specifically, O'Leary addresses the problem of going beyond the retrospective listings of studies on particular North American Indian tribal groups. Although his observations were made specifically for the *Ethnographic Bibliography*, they apply to the problem at hand. In distinguishing between the relative strengths of Walford,[2] Winchell and Sheehy,[3] White,[4] and McInnis-Scott,[5] O'Leary notes that the orientation of McInnis-Scott "is toward the immediate assistance of students engaged in research, while that of White and associates is toward the scrutiny of the general social science information system and the evaluation of its major products."[6] (In his discussion, O'Leary does not ignore Winchell and Walford; he considers them "standard general guides to the reference literature.")

Time constraints dictate that students be assisted quickly in locating needed substantive materials. While, as White suggests, it is desirable that students become well informed about the general social science information system, it is not a practicable or realistic expectation. Indeed, giving students a general understanding of the structure of scientific literature and the structure and function of reference works which expose that literature is addressed in Parts II and III. Such a general understanding is, at best, only a beginning. If a more detailed scrutiny of the social science information system and its major products is desirable, it remains as a goal we all wish to achieve. In the meantime, the problem that remains is to inform students rapidly of specific intermediary sources which expose needed substantive literature. Apparently, O'Leary concurs that it is desirable that students be informed rapidly of the materials they can consult for their immediate research needs. A similar intent is at least implied in the comments of the social scientists surveyed in Chapter 2.

Central to any arrangement of research materials designed to permit students engaged in research to locate specific items quickly is the relation of intermediary sources to the substantive-bibliographic continuum of scientific literature. As mentioned earlier in the context of the substantive-bibliographic continuum, particular functions of intermediary sources fall into five divisions. Intermediary sources in each division provide access to or otherwise expose a particular combination of the substantive and bibliographic components of social-scientific literature. Considered together as an integrated system, the two structural components of that literature (i.e., bibliographic and substantive) and the functions of intermediary sources constitute the tripartite matrix.

Notes

1. See Chapter 16. Actual examples are given in Appendix A.

2. Arthur J. Walford, ed., *Guide to Reference Materials,* 3d ed. (London: Library Association, 1973).

3. Constance M. Winchell and Eugene P. Sheehy, eds., *Guide to Reference Books,* 8th ed. (Chicago: American Library Association, 1967). Three supplements compiled by Eugene P. Sheehy covering the years 1965 through 1970 have also been issued. A ninth edition, edited by Sheehy, covering to late 1974, was published in 1976.

4. Carl M. White and associates, eds., *Sources of Information in the Social Sciences,* 2d ed. (Chicago: American Library Association, 1973).

5. Raymond G. McInnis and James W. Scott, eds., *Social Science Research Handbook* (New York: Barnes and Noble, 1975).

6. George P. Murdock and Timothy O'Leary, eds., *Ethnographic Bibliography of North America* (New Haven, Conn.: HRAF Press, 1975), I, p. XXXV.

20 Preliminary Observations

Before extensively discussing the principles and problems of organizing and describing intermediary sources in guides to research (especially those prepared for individual libraries) within this conceptual framework, a few preliminary observations will be useful. These preliminary observations, posed as rhetorical questions, point out the importance of both organization and annotation in the production of research guides, including those prepared for local use by academic libraries.

First, *is there a more effective way research guides can organize intermediary sources of a particular discipline?* Organizaion means the manner in which particular materials, in relation to the substantive-bibliographic continuum, are arranged so that their functions are made evident. This notion parallels arguments by Wilson. According to him, bibliographical organization is a "structural problem" closely related to "bibliographical control." In theory these "two notions are distinct, but in practice one cannot talk of control without talking of organization, for one of the chief ways in which we control things is by taking advantage of the organization they exhibit."[1] In the context of organizing research guides, both general and specific coverage of disciplines must be taken into consideration by researchers, or what in effect amounts to at least two or more levels of specificity of coverage of the literature.[2] (Figure 10 attempts to illustrate the notion of such relationships. This notion is developed more extensively in Part V. See Figures 22 and 23.)

In order to effectively inform researchers about what is available and, perhaps, what is not available, in a given field of inquiry, it is desirable that they be able to scrutinize a wide assortment of materials in several levels of coverage. Thus, such matters as scope and range of coverage of the literature, which are actually matters of annotation, cannot entirely be separated from concerns for organization. For the moment, however, the basic issue is the relation of the organization of bibliographies of intermediary sources (i.e., research guides) to the substantive-bibliographic continuum of social-scientific literature.

The manner in which intermediary sources are organized largely determines how individual researchers approach a particular field of inquiry.

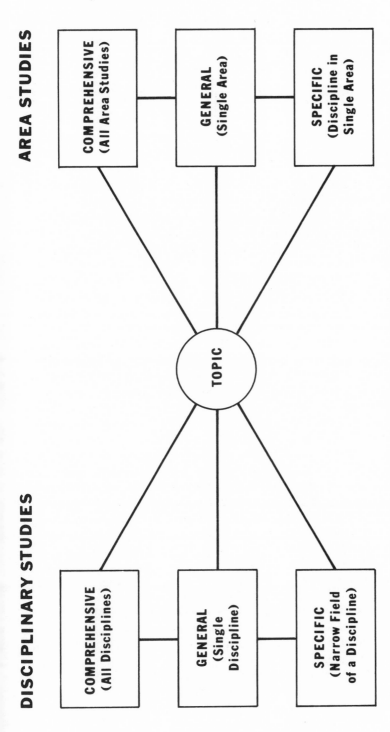

Figure 10. Conception of Suggested Levels of Specificity of Intermediary Sources for Disciplinary Studies and Area Studies (I)

SOURCE: Raymond G. McInnis and James W. Scott, *Social Science Research Handbook* (New York: Barnes and Noble, 1975), p. xiii.

This is especially true for inexperienced researchers. If intermediary sources which expose either bibliographic or substantive components or various combinations of social-scientific literature are separated into such categories as (1) periodical indexes, (2) abstracts, (3) current (I prefer Freides' "recurrent") bibliographies, (4) retrospective bibliographies, (5) handbooks, (6) dictionaries, (7) encyclopedias, and (8) reviews of research, the researchers' task of scrutinizing this array of materials is made unnecessarily confusing and time consuming. It is an artificial and unnecessary separation of research instruments which expose either bibliographic or substantive components of social-scientific literature.

Certain qualifications about the types of literature exposed must be recognized. Some research devices exclusively expose methodological works or statistics sources. Others such as maps and atlases expose illustrative material. Still others expose information that does not fall in the realm of social-scientific literature, at least as social-scientific literature is considered in this discussion. For example, since for the most part the *Reader's Guide to Periodical Literature* exposes subject matter that does not fall strictly in the realm of social-scientific literature, perhaps some argument can be submitted for not including it among other bibliographic devices which do. (For my own part, I prefer not to make such fine distinctions for research guides and simply include these with other intermediary sources that have similar functions.) A discussion of the type of literature exposed by the *Reader's Guide* should not be allowed to cloud the issue at hand: *Is there a more efficient way of organizing intermediary sources?*[3]

The organization of intermediary sources in research guides is more important than is generally acknowledged and merits greater consideration. For example, recall for a moment the discussion in Chapter 8 of Kaplan's arguments concerning logic-in-use and reconstructed logic. Briefly, he suggests that there is a difference between the informal methods in which researches in the social sciences are conducted and how they are subsequently written up according to a formally structured format. An analogous situation prevails in the construction of a bibliography of the intermediary sources of a particular discipline. The answer to the rhetorical question, "How are bibliographic research guides typically organized?" is: bibliographic guides' especially those prepared by librarians, are organized according to the compiler's reconstructed logic of how these materials should be arranged so that users can effectively gain access to required substantive materials. The organization of materials in these bibliographies most often reflects what the compiler visualizes as the "classical" mode of inquiry. In such cases, the basic assumption is that typically research is conducted according to "prescribed patterns."[4]

On the other hand, what implications does logic-in-use have as a guide to organizing materials? *Is it possible to organize materials in such a way— without, of course, violating the basic principles of bibliography—that re-*

flects more closely the typical informal methods most researchers employ?
Knapp's arguments about a system of "ways" directly address this issue
(see Chapter 14). She suggests that the research process rather than specific
library materials should be emphasized, including demonstrating—contrary
to the popular view—that the organization of library resources embraces
the bibliographic system of scholarship. Structured inquiry, is an example
of a mode of inquiry in which process is the organizing principle. It is with
such motives (i.e., process as the organizing principle) in mind—especially
concerning the assistance of students—that I suggested above that research
materials be introduced to potential researchers in the context of an actual
research problem.[5]

To some skeptical readers, such an assertion immediately raises another
question. *How is it possible to anticipate actual research problems in the
process of compiling for students a library guide to research materials?* As
experience suggests, through collaboration of individual classroom instructors, it is indeed possible to incorporate these elements in library-prepared
research guides, especially in a manner that encourages structured inquiry
as a mode of research.

The key is to introduce to both instructors and students the multitude of
intermediary sources available—(and to suggest the existence of others of
related interest) that are concerned with special treatments of the substantive
and bibliographic components of a particular body of social-scientific
literature. Thus subsumed as part of anticipating actual research problems
students will encounter is that evaluative annotations about each source
will be given on research guides. Ideally, the comments will indicate the best
sources for beginning a search, the sources that can be used in combination,
the areas of research literature that are less well covered by intermediary
sources, the sources whose functions are different from what titles suggest,
and so on. In this sense, the organization of a research guide and the annotation of individual sources in it are not considered separate. By giving
such advice, librarians are ultimately raising the level of bibliographic
instruction which, given their education and experience, they are best prepared to give. By requesting the collaborative efforts of classroom instructors, librarians are acknowledging the potential contributions of experienced
researchers and at the same time are demonstrating that they are sympathetic
to their needs.

Such instruction is designed to relate directly to the three premises outlined
in Chapter 14: a tacit logic is involved in research; this logic can be raised to
a higher level of awareness; and research strategy can be refined by intelligent and purposeful application. When put into application, such aspirations can be realized. The experience of Frick and of others confirms that
these aspirations are not unique.[6] Not infrequently, these efforts are a revela-
tion to instructors as well as a boon to students.

Let me give an example involving a faculty member experienced in research.

A colleague in Western Washington University's History Department, concerned about the dismal quality of undergraduate writing and research—but not yet convinced that structured inquiry could be employed both as a means of teaching research methods and as an adjunct to instruction—was conducting research on Friedrich Engels and the East European nationality problem. His purpose was to present a revision of the accepted explanation. Over several months he patiently surveyed the existing literature on the topic, using a method not unlike the classical mode of research noted above. He recalls that particular stress was given to what the card catalog could expose.

Fortuitously, Kernig's *Marxism, Communism, and Western Society* was placed on the library's reference shelves.[7] After being informed of the set's existence, he consulted it, knowing that as a review of research it would likely contain a distillation of what was known of his research topic. Imagine his surprise when he discovered that the bibliography of the article was almost a duplication of the one he had just compiled. The text of the article itself contained a portion of the explanation for which he was suggesting a revision. Ever since this incident, he has been firmly committed to engaging his students in structured inquiry as a mode of research in his courses. In addition, as part of the course, he requires his students to read appropriate articles in several works similar to the above. The students are thereby introduced not only to the subject matter, but to the functions of encyclopedias as well.

The instructor's training as an historian had not included coverage of the research materials of which Kernig's *Marxism, Communism and Western Society* is representative. As noted in Chapter 2, this lack in the training is quite widespread. Thus, preliminary to, or in conjunction with, the preparation of research guides, instructors must often be informed of the existence of a rich array of research materials. Of course, not all instructors are receptive to such information.

The trick is to set forth intermediary sources of a particular discipline imaginatively, where both experienced and inexperienced researchers are pleasantly made aware of items they did not know existed, or simply had visualized as having a much more limited use.

After a format of arrangement has been selected, what is the best mode of annotating the items which a research guide contains? Here annotation means the manner in which particular materials, in relation to the substantive-bibliographic continuum, are explained, so that not only are their specific functions made evident but their relative strengths are noted.[8] Of greater value developing sound research strategy are the recommended combinations in which specific items can be used. The major problem in designing research guides is to produce a research instrument that is logically integrated and internally coherent, so that definite patterns of inquiry are almost self-evident to researchers. Such a view is, of course, biased toward structured inquiry and its reliance on the tripartite matrix—where the recommended procedure is to progress from sources providing distilled, generalized treatments of a topic's literature to those sources that perform basically analytical functions, where that topic's literature is in less well-organized forms.

For example, is a citation-annotation format of setting forth research materials superior to an essay format? Here the concern centers on how works which narrowly focus, say, on the literature of a subdivision of a discipline, can be brought to the attention of researchers, without danger of neglecting those intermediary sources which give comprehensive coverage to the same discipline. This was the particularly vexing problem encountered in producing the *Social Science Research Handbook*. The solution arrived at (i.e., present materials in an analytical and integrated format, with liberal use of cross-references) seems to have satisfied the critics. While no one objected to it, and some even lauded it, as a solution to drawing attention to both general and specific materials it needs much improvement. Apart from such concerns, however, employing the system in a large volume presents fewer problems than are usually encountered in library-produced guides to research materials which have to be more modest in size and scope.

My original concern about the pattern of literature coverage among these publications is how, for the benefit of researchers, they can be linked or otherwise brought together so that their relationships in literature coverage become more self-evident. When the typical citation-annotation format of arranging items alphabetically by author is used, illustrating these patterns is, at best, awkward. This obstacle can be partially overcome by demonstrating how the research guide is used in an actual problem related to the students' immediate research needs. Such a demonstration requires preparation, of course, but it is worthwhile.

How much detail should be given of the structure and content of each item? Unfortunately, this has received little attention. As noted in Chapter 14, Knapp, Freides, White, and others have all been concerned with this problem. Implicit, if not explicit, in all of their arguments is the necessity of instruction as a means of developing competence in research. The problem of developing this competence, especially where the notion of research as a process is stressed, is nowhere more evident than with regard to how the structure and function of particular intermediary sources are presented. Experience suggests, for example, that instructions given in an annotation about how to use specific sources can actually ease the initial problems researchers encounter with particular research materials.

Further, is it possible to inform researchers that related materials in other disciplines are also often useful for specific research needs, without constructing an overly complex and confusing array of materials? Answers to these and related questions necessarily will be loaded with qualifications. The following questions are of primary concern. How well are the primary users acquainted with research procedures? What is the intensity of the needs of researchers? Do the resources of a library adequately reflect the substantive literature exposed by intermediary sources contained in a research guide?

What conclusions can be drawn from this discussion? The foregoing brief observations merely make overcoming the difficulty of instruction in library use more perplexing. If these suggestions are implemented, only partial solutions can be achieved to problems library users encounter, even in the context where structured inquiry is recommended as a model research procedure. At best, demonstrating a particular research strategy with an actual research problem merely scratches the surface of the potential uses to be made of items in research guides. (As a small measure of success, we can at least appreciate that after such instruction students' requests for assistance become more sophisticated and complex.) For the most part, the degree of success achieved can be attributed to the amount of thought and effort put into the production of library research guides. The results achieved by Frick and Whitten verify this statement, but the library literature is full of other examples.

Thus, it seems logical that numerous suggestions illustrating patterns of literature coverage be built into the body of library-produced research guides for particular disciplines. As a model for constructing research guides, the essay format of annotating items included provides greater flexibility. Attention can be directed to numerous related items with greater ease. Generally, however, in library-prepared research guides the citation- annotation format is employed; this suggests that it is the preferred model.

Some reference librarians may consider such concerns academic or even superfluous. At the same time, following convention, all reference librarians are concerned about making the library a more effective and dynamic instrument of learning. Given the problems library users typically encounter in using the library, it only seems logical that many such attempts to provide better access to library resources will be considered.

The most significant implication of an active program of producing research guides for library users is that, without one, instructors remain unconvinced that the library, especially library research, can become more fully integrated with course requirements. Lacking the availability of research guides, instructors remain skeptical of engaging their students in research in the library.The dismal results of the majority of students persist as a constant reinforcement of this attitude. Instructors either become resolved to other means (outside the library) of engaging their students in research or delete research exercise from their course requirements.

On the other hand, by demonstrating to instructors and, in turn, the students, that the library genuinely has their interests at heart, the results can indeed be greater commitment to engaging students in research in the library and more effective use of library materials. The library must take the lead if these results are to be realized.

Notes

1. Patrick Wilson, *Two Kinds of Power* (Berkeley, Calif.: University of California Press, 1968), p. 3.

2. When dealing with the literature of a narrow field of research for a particular geographical area, it can be argued that there are actually five or six levels of specificity in literature coverage.

3. I am not suggesting that the bulk of the periodicals indexed in the *Reader's Guide*—since they do not contain what is considered social-scientific literature—contains unreliable material. On the contrary, I believe that the information in periodicals in the *Reader's Guide* should be considered valid. However, except for a small number of journals indexed in it, the subject matter exposed does not have the same structure and function of the social-scientific literature published in scholarly journals which communicate new findings of empirical research. A stronger argument can be made for the subject matter exposed in the *Reader's Guide* being considered primary source material. (Such an argument is, of course, dependent upon the perspective of individual researchers; see Chapter 5.) For a more extensive discussion of the *Reader's Guide*, see Raymond G. McInnis and James W. Scott, *Social Science Research Handbook* (New York: Barnes and Noble, 1975), p. 7. Cf. also Thelma Freides, *The Literature and Bibliography of the Social Sciences* (Los Angeles: Melville Publishing Co., 1973), pp. 2-3.

4. Benjamin Whitten, "Social Science Bibliography Course: A Client-oriented Approach," *Journal of Education for Librarianship* 16 (Summer 1975):26.

5. See Chapter 16. See also Chapter 14, note 4.

6. Chapter 14, under "A Practicable Solution."

7. C. D. Kernig, ed., *Marxism, Communism and Western Society*, 8 vols. (New York: Herder and Herder, 1972).

8. Cf. Wilson, *Two Kinds of Power*, p. 3.

21 Function as an Organizing Principle

Let's return to the rhetorical question posed in Chapter 20 concerning an effective means of organizing intermediary sources in the social sciences. The most important organizing principle is function, but consideration should be given the fact that coverage of portions of the substantive literature of a topic occurs on at least two levels. First, there are general intermediary sources where coverage of a topic's literature is treated along with that of many other topics. *Sociological Abstracts*,[1] the *International Bibliography of Sociology*,[2] Faris' *Handbook of Modern Sociology*,[3] and Lindzey and Aronson's *Handbook of Social Psychology*[4] include coverage of many subdivisions of sociology. Second, as is discussed in greater detail below, some intermediary sources are specifically devoted to a narrow topic. (Alcoholism and marriage and the family are the examples given.)

Such matters cannot be overemphasized, for when dealing with researchers, especially inexperienced ones, few details concerning their research can be taken for granted. Too often it is discovered that they neither know *nor* understand even what appears simple and self-evident. Even some experienced researchers have some surprising gaps in their knowledge of the most common intermediary sources, including the *International Encyclopedia of the Social Sciences*. Furthermore few researchers, even the most experienced, are aware of the extent to which particular sources provide information or assistance. When these sources are set forth in a broader perspective, researchers' perception of the several other kinds of information or assistance it can provide is increased. The chief examples illustrating this problem are Hultkrantz's *General Ethnological Concepts*,[5] Murdock's *Ethnographic Atlas*,[6] and the McGraw-Hill art encyclopedia.[7]

The limited perception of the potential usefulness of the aforementioned works results either from the context in which they are published or their titles. Hultkrantz's ethnological dictionary, for example, is not entitled as such; therefore, it receives limited attention. A much greater problem in its use, however, is that it is part of a set devoted to a particular geographical area. (*General Ethnological Concepts* is the first volume of the *International Dictionary of Regional European Ethnology and Folklore*.) Until the fuller

Figure 11. Outline of Arrangement of Library-Produced Sociology Research Guide, Western Washington University.

Section I: Works covering Sociology in general, arranged by type

    I.a   Atlases and Gazetteers. p. 1
    I.b   Bibliographies. p. 1
    I.c   Bibliographies of Bibliographies, p. 7
    I.d   Biographical Dictionaries and Directories. p. 8
    I.e   Book Review Citations. p. 8
    I.f   Encyclopedias, Dictionaries, and Reviews of Research. p. 8
    I.g   Handbooks, Yearbooks, etc. p. 14
    I.h   Methodological Works. p. 15
    I.i   Statistics Sources. p. 19

Section II: Works devoted to subdivisions of Sociology

    II.a   Social Structure. p. 23
    II.b   Social Change. p. 29
    II.c   Public Opinion, Communication and Mass Media. p. 32
    II.d   Social Pathology, Social Deviance, Social Control, and Social Policy, p. 34

Section III: Government Documents. p. 45

Section IV: Pamphlet Materials. p. 45

coverage of anthropological terms in *General Ethnological Concepts* is pointed out, its usefulness is almost completely overlooked.

Murdock's *Ethnographic Atlas* is perhaps more curious, since it is not an atlas at all, but rather a tabulation of data about selected ethnic groups of the world derived from the Human Relations Area Files. Even among librarians its misleading title can lead to mistaking its intended purpose.[8]

The *Encyclopedia of World Art* is perhaps the best source in the English language for information on research on archaeology and the art of non-Western peoples. Yet, because its inclusiveness is not made evident, even by standard research guides, researchers make limited use of it.[9] In the end, then, the way in which intermediary sources are organized (*and* analyzed) does much to communicate the several perspectives from which researchers can usefully perceive their potential functions in the social sciences. (Problems of analyzing specific items are treated in Chapter 22.)

Figure 11 outlines the arrangement of a library-prepared research guide for sociology used at Western Washington University. The guide is relatively simple, particularly the second section. There are sound reasons for employing a relatively simple organization scheme, most of which are directly related to the tripartite matrix, especially the substantive-bibliographic continuum. Recall that there are five divisions on the continuum into which, according to what combinations of substantive or bibliographic components of social-scientific literature are exposed, the particular functions of intermediary sources fall. For the most part, in Section I of Figure 11, intermediary sources in the five divisions of the substantive-bibliographic continuum which give general or inclusive coverage of sociology literature can be put in either the Bibliographies or the Encyclopedias, Dictionaries, and Reviews of Research categories. The Biographical Dictionaries and Directories, Handbooks and Yearbooks, Methodological Works, and Statistics Sources categories are for research materials that provide information on specialized aspects of inquiry.

In Section II, intermediary sources are arranged according to very broad subdivisions of sociology. The use of fewer rather than numerous divisions leads to some initial confusion by researchers. It is not self-evident where certain works might be listed.

The advantages of using fewer, general subdivisions rather than numerous, specific ones, however, outweigh the weaknesses. It should be remembered that most users of the bibliography are unacquainted with any specific works. If numerous specific, narrow categories are used, other more general items might be overlooked when the research guide is being examined for particular aids to research. Thus, by imposing a simple, rather loose structure on the organizing scheme, users are forced to examine greater numbers of items. Ultimately, individuals have a greater opportunity of seeing the wealth of materials exposed by individual intermediary sources. Another consideration is that intermediary sources devoted to narrow subdivisions of a discipline, say sociology, often cover topics of that subdivision rather unpredictably.

One of the strongest reasons for this ambiguity in coverage of the literature is the current stimulus toward interdisciplinary research, particularly research relating to specific geographical areas. Sociologists, anthropoligsts, and geographers, to name a few, make wide use of each other's research. For the most part, as will be seen in Part V, in research guides devoted to particular geographical areas, the second section is arranged according to specific disciplines, with items giving exclusive (or a major portion of) coverage to the literature of that discipline for that geographical area included in particular divisions.[10]

Notes

1. *Sociological Abstracts* (New York: American Sociological Association, 1952-   ).

2. *International Bibliography of Sociology* (Paris: UNESCO, 1959-   ).

3. R.E.L. Faris, ed., *Handbook of Modern Sociology* (Chicago: Rand McNally, 1964).

4. Gardiner Lindzey and E. Aronson, eds., *Handbook of Social Psychology*, 5 vols. and index (Reading, Mass.: Addison-Wesley, 1968-1970).

5. Ake Hultkrantz, ed., *General Ethnological Concepts* (Copenhagen: Rosenkelde and Bagger, 1960).

6. George P. Murdock, *Ethnographic Atlas* (Pittsburgh: University of Pittsburgh Press, 1967).

7. *Encyclopedia of World Art*, 15 vols. (New York: McGraw-Hill, 1959-1968).

8. See, for example, James M. Hillard, *Where to Find What: A Handbook to Reference Service* (Metuchen, N.J.: Scarecrow Press, 1975), p. 108.

9. For example, rather curiously, the *Encyclopedia of World Art* is *not* cited by either Carl M. White and associates, eds., *Sources of Information in the Social Sciences*, 2d ed. (Chicago: American Library Association, 1973), or in Volume two of Arthur J. Walford, ed., *Guide to Reference Materials*, 3d ed., 3 vols., (London: Library Association, 1973), which covers the social sciences.

10. For a graphic illustration of what is meant by the foregoing, see Figure 22.

22 Annotation as an Analytical Function and as an Integrative Function

The substantive and bibliographic components of social-scientific literature are emphasized in preceding portions of this book in order to demonstrate how reference works which expose these two components (when conceptualized as intermediary sources) can be linked to each other so that their natural or inherent relationships become more self-evident. In this connection, a research model is developed in which the tripartite matrix is the organizing principle. By using the tripartite matrix as a central part of a mode of instruction in research, a step is taken toward reducing what inexperienced researchers consider a sprawling admixture of diffuse elements into an intelligible process. Drawing on the research of others on these same problems, structured inquiry, becomes concrete. The amalgam created from the three components informs researchers of the natural patterns of scientific inquiry and communication.

Producing bibliographic research guides in which these ideals are realized is, of course, a touchstone to which reference librarians all aspire. In the preceding chapter, organization is seen as an important element in achieving these ideals. At the same time, organization, no matter how thoughtfully it is executed, must be supported by annotation. Annotations that are precise, compact, imaginative, and stimulating aid in making a research guide a dynamic instrument of research.

Just as function is the most significant principle of guides, so it is the chief concern of annotation in research guides. In this context, as well as such concerns as the content, structure and purpose of particular intermediary sources, annotation refers to how these works can be used in combination to provide more complete coverage of, or more efficient access to, the substantive literature of a research topic. Annotation is therefore seen to have both analytical and integrative functions. Indeed, it is from the perspective of both the analytical and integrative functions of annotation that the inseparability of organization and annotation becomes most evident. This inseparability, in the end, stems from the cognitive functions which organization and annotation perform in research guides. The awareness of the importance of this aspect of annotation is not often very acute.

Perhaps the best means of clarifying the foregoing distinctions of the functions of annotation is to give some examples. One of the most personally instructive experiences of producing the *Social Science Research Handbook* has been that frequent discovery that so-called narrow fields of inquiry are replete with intermediary sources that fall into all or several of the five divisions of the substantive-bibliographic continuum. Occasionally, all of these materials are produced by the effort or under the aegis of one individual. Such an individual combines both the capacity to visualize the need for these intermediary sources and the drive necessary to produce them. For example, Keller, the director of the Rutgers Center on Alcohol Studies, has edited the dictionary on alcohol[1] and the retrospective bibliography;[2] he also edits the leading journal on alcohol, a major portion of which is devoted to abstracting the current literature.[3]

More frequently, diverse individuals have independently produced particular intermediary sources which, when the pattern of the coverage of the literature in question is examined, fall into all or most of the five divisions of the substantive-bibliographic continuum. Of the intermediary sources on the study of marriage and the family, for example, the following publications fall into several of the divisions of the continuum. (Of course, given the quantity of research conducted on marriage and the family, numerous types of intermediary sources would be expected.) Aldous and Hill's retrospective bibliography, in two volumes, covers 1900-1972.[4] The same research institute with which Aldous and Hill are associated—the Department of Family Social Science at the University of Minnesota—produces a biennial listing.[5] Goode's *Social Systems and Family Patterns*, a unique analytical bibliography of the literature of marriage and the family, provides brief substantive information about individual studies; this suggests that it falls in the division to the right of center of the continuum.[6] Christensen's *Handbook of Marriage and the Family* provides encyclopedic coverage of the field.[7]

While perhaps not as narrowly focused as the above examples in sociology, similar patterns of literature coverage can readily be pointed out in other disciplines. Previous to undertaking the *Social Science Research Handbook* project, I was only dimly aware of this characteristic pattern of coverage in the literature of a specific field of inquiry.[8] After recognizing this pattern, I realized the importance of developing a reference collection in the social sciences in which, where possible, intermediary sources falling in the five divisions of the continuum were purchased. Following the acquisition of these volumes, of course, the means of informing library users of these materials and the character of their coverage of the literature were considered.

As emphasized earlier, the most important link in any program designed to encourage student use of the library is the classroom instructor. In general, I have discovered that when the tripartite matrix is introduced to instructors, many acquire a keener interest in research—for themselves as well as for their students. Structured inquiry as a mode of instruction in research is particularly attractive to instructors. The underlying logic of the system is self-evident to them, not only as a mode of research but also as a means of informing their students of the process of social-scientific inquiry and communication. In their view, structured inquiry, particularly in the context of the tripartite matrix, is also an aid to lectures and other classroom activities.

Such considerations aside, format had to be devised for these research exercises which would allow students to be informed about intermediary sources and at the same time permit ready access to and use of them. On the one hand, when a citation-annotation format is used—a format which typically arranges items according to broad subjects and then alphabetically by author—drawing attention to these coverage patterns is problematical. If evaluative comments and suggestions are not inserted in annotations, researchers do not often see the desirability of using certain combinations of intermediary sources (which to reference librarians is an obvious strategy). On the other hand, by employing an essay treatment, where a number of intermediary sources are set forth in an analytical and integrated format, rapidly locating individual items is occasionally time consuming. True, there is always danger of overemphasizing these relationships to the extent that the research guide becomes unnecessarily confusing and difficult to use. Avoiding either extreme requires thoughtful consideration. There are methods, nonetheless, by which library users can be informed about the literature coverage patterns of intermediary sources in a particular field.

Analytical Functions of Annotation

Central to the development of any annotated research guide is an analysis of the structure and function of the works included. Annotations should be precise, compact, imaginative, and stimulating; at the same time, they should inform researchers of the strengths and weaknesses of specific works. Writing informative annotations requires considerable acquaintance with the materials being annotated and if the annotator has actually used the materials, some of this experience can be incorporated in the annotations. Experience derived from use, more than any other factor, prepares an individual to analyze specific materials accurately and realistically and to avoid any misleading declarations of how a particular work can assist users when it really cannot. Even with care, however, an abundance of errors seems to crop up.

The research guide should simply and directly inform users of the scope and range of individual intermediary sources, but in a manner relating first to the intensity of their needs and second to their level of acquaintance with research procedures. Not unexpectedly, both of these concerns present considerable difficulties which are not easily resolved.

Figure 12. Annotation for *Annual Review of Sociology*

      I.f

Ref.   1. *Annual Review of Sociology.* v. 1-   Palo Alto, Annual
HM 1   Reviews, Inc. 1975-
A78
1975   Each of the approximately fifteen articles of a volume is the
work of a specialist, and provides in a synthesized, distilled
format a survey of recent advances in narrow fields within the
discipline. Coverage is according to a framework consisting
of ten broad categories: differentiation and stratification;
political sociology; social processes; institutions; individual
and society; formal organization; urban sociology; demography; policy; theory and methods. These are, in turn, subdivided into narrow areas. References for the approximately
3,000 items noted per volume given at the end of articles in
which they are discussed. Indexed in *SSCI* (I.b.12).

Figure 13. Annotation for *Social Sciences Citation Index*

      I.b

Periodical   12. *Social Sciences Citation Index.* Philadelphia, Institute for
Index   Scientific Information, 1972-

      Issued three times a year, the *SSCI* gives another dimen-
sion to research procedures in the social sciences. Based
on the principle that the names of people can be substituted
for the subjects with which they are associated, it provides
the opportunity for advancing from earlier research to
more recent studies on the same subject. As well as sociology, such subjects as area studies, demography, anthropology, history and political science are covered. *SSCI*
consists of three separate but related indexes: the *Source
Index*; the *Citation Index*; and the *Permuterm Subject
Index*. Except in unusual cases, the object is to converge
on the *Source Index* from either the *Citation Index* or the
Permuterm Subject Index.

Of the three, the *Citation Index* is the largest and most
useful, but for a clear understanding it is better to describe
first the *Source Index*. In the *Source Index* are arranged
alphabetically by author's name articles that appear in
1000-odd periodicals. Along with the names, information

given includes article title, abbreviated title of periodical, volume, date, page of issue and number of footnote references. In addition, since 1974, the footnote references of each article are listed in abbreviated citation format in the *Source Index*. In the *Citation Index*, also arranged alphabetically by author's name, are articles cited by the authors listed in the *Source Index*, with the *citing author's name* (from the *Source Index*) listed below. Because authors appearing in the *Source Index* ordinarily cite numerous studies, the *Citation Index* is several times larger than the *Source Index* and gives an efficient means of exposing new articles on the subjects covered by known authors. (Approximately 100,000 citations are listed annually.) Finally, in the *Citation* and *Source Indexes*, any type of communication other than an ordinary article that reports research (e.g., review of research, book review, letter, editorial, etc.) is distinguished by a set of symbols. The symbols and other aspects of using *SSCI* are described inside the front cover of each volume.

The *Permuterm Subject Index* serves when researchers do not know a specific author concerned with a topic for which information is required. By pairing *two* words derived from the titles of articles listed in the *Source Index*, users are led to articles in the *Source Index* which *may* be on those subjects. (As a method, it is not as efficient as using names of people.)

In general, the *SSCI* is useful for tracing trends and developments resulting from the publication of particular research studies, but it is also useful for exposing reviews of research in such titles as the *Annual Review of Sociology* (I.f.1), *Current Sociology*, specialized articles listed in *Social Science Information* (I.h.15), and book reviews.

Figure 14. Annotation for *Advances in Experimental Social Psychology*

II.a

Ref.   1. *Advances in Experimental Social Psychology*. New York,
HM 251   Academic Press, 1964-   .
A35
               WWSC holds v. 1 to date.

The purpose of this series is not unlike the *Annual Review of Sociology* (I.f.1). Articles (four or five annually) in these volumes examine the literature on a narrow field of research in experimental social psychology and attempt to set forth, in a compressed or distilled format, a synthesis and note trends and developments. Can often serve as a useful updating of research reported in the *Handbook of Social Psychology* (I.f.14). Recent articles include: "Social Support for Nonconformity"; "New Directions in Equity Research"; and "Distribution of Rewards and Resources in Groups and Organizations." Each volume has a subject index. Full citations of numerous works examined are given at the end of each article.

The first case, intensity of needs, refers to those of undergraduates, whom I consider the primary users of the library-produced research guides at Western. Since estimating the intensity of undergraduate needs is always an uncertain task, I have tried combining experience and intuition. In the second case, a fairly close association with classroom instructors is the greatest assistance in determining the students' level of acquaintance with research procedures.

The following five examples from the research guide for sociology used at Western Washington University attempt to fulfill the above criteria.

The first example, the *Annual Review of Sociology* (Figure 12), is in the Bibliographies section, with a "see reference" in Encylopedias, Dictionaries, and Reviews of Research directing users to the main entry. Because of its strong bibliographical emphasis, this placement seemed logical. However, if one simply reverses the order of the citations, the same desirable linkage can be achieved.

In the second example, the *Social Sciences Citation Index* (which is also in the Bibliographies section), because of the difficulty users typically have with it, considerably greater detail of its function and structure is given (see Figure 13).

The next three examples (Figures 14, 15, and 16) are from the Social Structure section. There are either direct or implied linkages with several other works on the research guide, including the *Annual Review of Sociology* (Figure 12) and the *Social Sciences Citation Index* (Figure 13). Where possible, to conserve space, the features that are parallel with another source are used as a means of providing more detail.

Titles of recent articles are noted in order to suggest the scope of coverage. An attempt is made to avoid technical or jargon words, especially where they are not necessary.

Equally important in informing users of the structure and content of particular works is informing them briefly in advance of how a particular work can most efficiently be used. The time consumed in simply discovering how

Figure 15. Annotation for *Small Group Research*

II.a.

Ref.   10. McGrath, Joseph E. and Altman, Irvin. *Small Group Re-*
HM 131   *search: A Synthesis and Critique of the Field.* New York,
M27   Holt, Rinehart and Winston, 1966.

              In three sections. In the largest, further subdivided into
              three parts, some 2,600 studies—books, articles from
              psychological and sociological journals and government
              supported research reports—of small group behavior pub-
              lished up to and including 1962 are listed. In this same
              section, over 200 of these studies are annotated according
              to an elaborate format which includes: a brief statement of
              the central problem; a digest of methodology employed;
              review of major findings; and "study variables" (i.e., "a
              list of the major classes of variables used in the study"). A
              "Catalogue of Relationships Between Variables" contains
              an analysis of these same 250 studies according to the
              authors' "Operational Classification System" of 31 variable
              classes. Finally, 50 pages of comment on the literature of
              small groups, descriptions, methodology, what is known
              scientifically, and so forth, is given. No indexes. For more
              recent material use jointly with *SSCI* (I.b.12).

Figure 16. Annotation for *Handbook of Leadership*

II.a

Ref.   18. Stodgill, Ralph M. *Handbook of Leadership.* New York,
HM 141   Free Press, 1974.
S83
              An attempt to assemble "all the published evidence on a
              given topic and [summarize] the findings . . . It is intended
              for the serious reader who wants to know what results
              have been obtained, who did the research, and what con-
              conclusions can be drawn from the accumulated evidence"
              (Preface). More than 5,000 items were examined, but only
              those with a direct bearing on leadership were included in
              the survey, with particular concern for research validated

by several investigators, using different research designs and methodologies, and obtaining similar results. Arranged according to seven broad categories, then under appropriate subdivision: Leadership Theory; Leader Personality and Behavior; Leadership Stability and Change; Emergence of the Leadership Role; Leadership and Social Power; Leader-Follower Interactions; and Leadership and Group Performance. For example, the last category is subdivided into democratic and autocratic patterns of behavior; permissive leadership; follower-oriented and task-oriented leadership; the socially distant leader; participative and directive patterns of behavior; consideration and initiating structure; and leadership and group survival. On p. 6 are given a listing of 48 reviews of research on leadership. Works discussed in the text are cited in full in the bibliography. Author and subject indexes.

to approach a particular intermediary source is irksome, even infuriating. Indeed, some computer-produced volumes are almost incomprehensible without assistance from someone experienced in their use. At the very least, by preparing potential users of annotations of library-produced research guides as to what to expect when encountering particular works, the library does much to allay the apprehensions of researchers making their first, hesitant steps in inquiry. (For that matter, such feelings are sometimes characteristic of experienced researchers.) Computer-produced works falling in the difficult-to-use category include Wall's *Author Index to Poole's Index to Periodical Literature*,[9] Murdock's *Ethnographic Atlas*,[10] Textor's *Cross-Cultural Summary*,[11] the *Ekistics Index*,[12] Taylor's *World Handbook*,[13] Banks' *Cross-Polity Times-Series Data*,[14] and, of course, the *Social Sciences Citation Index*.[15]

In addition to relieving the apprehension of the initial encounter, details given about suggested uses lead to greater use of these materials, thereby justifying their purchase. Banks' *Cross-Polity Times-Series Data* is a case in point. Its very title is so forbidding that, except to those acquainted with terms and techniques of comparative study of social institutions, it appears to be too formidable a research instrument for most researchers. Once the researcher learns its purpose, structure, and the like, however, it can be used for what it is—as a compendium of historical and social statistics and other data on over 150 countries. Indeed, it is sometimes the only source for certain historical statistics. While the recent spate of volumes covering this area of research is lessening dependence on *Cross-Polity Time-Series Data*, both because it gives easy access to specific facts and because it cites sources of data, it continues to serve as an excellent ready-reference source. At the same time, unless the contents of the volume is drawn to the attention of researchers in nontechnical terms, it sits on the shelf unused. Substantially more use is made of it when it is included with other sources of historical and social statistical data in library-prepared research guides.

The *Criminology Index*

Determining how to treat some of the above-mentioned items in library-produced research guides can be problematical. Perhaps the best example is Wolfgang's *Criminology Index.*[16] This work attempts to combine discrete contributions to a given field of inquiry over almost three decades into the natural, logical structures in which they developed. Produced with the assistance of a computer, it is closely patterned on the *Social Sciences Citation Index (SSCI)*. All of its sections have counterparts in the *SSCI*, but unfortunately not all are as well conceived or executed. However, since the *Criminology Index* comprises books and chapters of books and articles published in the period covered, there are necessarily certain differences between it and the *SSCI*. The *Criminology Index* consists of three separate but interrelated indexes: the Source Document Index, the Criminology Citation Index, and the Subject Index.

In the Source Document Index articles are listed separately from books, research reports and dissertations. The entries for articles give the author(s) name(s) and institutional affiliation(s), title of paper, journal title, year of publication, and page on which the article begins. The publisher, place of publication, and names of all contributors are added for books, research reports, and dissertations. Much as is done in the Source Index in the *SSCI*, individual works are classified according to type, and the number of footnote references is given. (A list of symbols used for this purpose is given in the first of four illustrated keys to the elements employed in the various sections.) For collected articles published in book form, unfortunately this means *all* the references in the volume, without regard to the chapters in which they are contained. "See references" direct users from the names of authors of chapters of books to the volume in which they are contained. Treating chapters of books that are legitimate contributions in their own right in a different manner than articles is not logical. Treating chapters and articles alike would require more effort on the part of the compilers, and too they may have encountered restrictions that did not allow it. Three changes in organization would have eliminated some of the difficulty.

First, by treating chapters in the same manner as articles (i.e., separate entries), with volume title and page indicated, users would be able to determine more precisely how a particular item relates to the research topic being traced. In recognition of such difficulties each entry is given a five-digit number that can be matched with the equivalent entry in other sections. Even using these numbers, however, is difficult or nonproductive.

Second, by integrating the two lists, a more accurate picture of the literature would emerge. All entries of an individual would appear in one alphabetical sequence; the need for "see references" would be eliminated; and more significantly, relationships between discrete items in the Source Document Index would be put in sharper focus with related items in other sections of the *Criminology Index*. For example, paired words derived from chapter titles would direct users from the Subject Index to the Source Document Index.

Third, the use of chapter titles (or even portions of them) would facilitate advancing from the Criminology Citation Index to the Source Document Index, and the use of numbers could be eliminated. The number of footnote references indicated would relate directly to the work at hand (i.e., chapters), and not to the total number of the volume. When dealing with books consisting of chapters by individual authors, part of the problem occurs because the compilers are often confused about who is the cited author. Sometimes it is impossible to discover in which volume a cited work appears, while in other instances the editor of a volume is given as a cited author.

The Criminology Citation Index portion lists authors alphabetically and *all* their cited works chronologically, and—following the pattern of *SSCI*—those authors who cited these works. This index is divided into three separate parts: anonymous works, general works, and legal documents. Of the three, the general works section is the most useful. The first and third are quite confusing, principally because there is no table of abbreviations to identify the extremely brief citations given corporate works. It is in the linkage between the general works section of the Criminology Citation Index and the Source Document Index that the compilers' intended purpose becomes most obvious: researchers are "able to address questions of originality, criticism, development and application of an idea, concept or technique" of a work or topic over the period covered.[17]

Some entries are necessarily large (one entry for Glueck, for example, occupies several pages). This requires considerable diligence and determination when tracing a thread of inquiry, but the method produces results more rapidly, and with greater rewards, than does the conventional method.

When lacking an author's name, researchers can turn to the Subject Index. (This method is similar to that employed in the Permuterm Subject Index portion of the *SSCI*.) By using paired words derived from titles of books (but not individually authored chapter titles which, as noted above, are a more precise indication of the subject) and articles, researchers are led to the author's work in which these words are used in the titles. (The subject approach is less efficient than when authors' names are used for tracing the pattern of inquiry on a topic.)

An obvious gap in the massive set is the apparent failure to point out bibliographies or reviews of research. As mentioned above, among the symbols used to indicate the type of work, only the type of format is indicated. Doleschal's reviews of the literature of criminology, published in *Criminal Justice Abstracts*, are treated strictly as articles, often without the subtitles which indicate they are review articles.[18]

Thus, we are confronted with a research instrument that is difficult to use. Even so, it should be suggested as a research aid because of its potential usefulness in exposing the literature of a field of inquiry for which the coverage by other sources is fragmented and uneven. Since it is based on the principles of the widely used *Social Sciences Citation Index*, the problem of indicating its structure and possible uses is made easier. Moreover, the *SSCI* is the logical means of advancing from where the *Criminology Index* ends. Figure 17 is an attempt to inform users of library produced research guides in psychology and sociology about the *Criminology Index*.

Integrative Functions of Annotation

If a citation-annotation format is considered the best means of meeting the research needs of a particular group of students, introductory headnotes in each division of the research guide can be used to draw attention to items that can be used jointly. Another means of suggesting to student and other users the desirability of using several sources in combination is to stress such matters in a general introduction to the research guide, where a conceptual framework of particular research strategies is set forth, with examples. Or the text of an annotation of a particular item can suggest what other sources covering the same topic can be consulted. Obviously, each of these techniques is compatible with the other, and all of them can be used to achieve specific instructional ends.

Let's examine how White employs the first technique. The example is Koch's multivolume *Psychology: A Study of a Science*.[19] The Koch set is a major synthesis of what is known scientifically in psychology. Logically, White groups Koch with citations to nineteen other "syntheses" of the literature of psychology, under the heading Handbooks. Rather than provide annotations for each, White chooses to supply a headnote at the beginning which describes the basic purpose of all works cited under the Handbooks heading in the psychology chapter. In the headnote, it is suggested that such works are "important aids to scholarship," being useful for "advanced study," for "taking stock of the subject," and "for planning and conducting research."[20]

Figure 17. Annotation for the *Criminology Index*
II.d.

Ref.   46. Wolfgang, Marvin E., *et al.*, *Criminology Index: Research*
JX   *and Theory in Criminology in the U.S., 1945-1972.* New
1975   York, Elsevier, 1975.
R4
                A computer-produced index, closely patterned on the *SSCI*,
                (I.b.2). All its sections have counterparts in the *SSCI*, but
                unfortunately not all are as well conceived or executed.
                Since, as well as articles, the *Criminology Index* comprises
                books, chapters of books and government studies published
                over almost three decades, there are necessarily certain
                differences between it and the *SSCI*. It consists of three
                separate but interrelated indexes: the *Source Document
                Index*, the *Criminology Citation Index*, and the *Subject
                Index*. In the *Source Document Index* articles are listed
                separately from books, reports, and dissertations. Full
                citations are given for articles. The publisher, place of
                publication and names of all contributors are added for
                books, reports and dissertations. A see reference and five-
                digit number, which matches that in the main entry, directs
                users from the names of author of chapters of books to the
                volume in which they are contained. Some 3,000 articles
                and 500-odd books are listed. The *Criminology Citation
                Index* portion lists authors and *all* their cited works chron-
                ologically, and—following the pattern of *SSCI*—those
                authors who cited these works. The *Criminology Citation
                Index* is divided into three separate lists: anonymous works;
                general works; and legal documents. Of the three the general
                works section is the largest and most useful. The first and
                third are quite confusing, principally because there is no
                table of abbreviations to identify the extremely brief cita-
                tions given works that cannot be identified by a personal
                name. It is in the linkage between the general works section
                of the *Criminology Citation Index* and the *Source Docu-
                ment Index* that intended purpose of this set is most obvious:
                researchers are "able to address questions or originality,
                criticism, development and application of an idea, concept
                or technique" of a work or topic over the period covered.
                Some entries require considerable diligence when tracing a
                particular idea, but the method produces results more
                rapidly and with greater rewards than does the conventional
                one.

Since White's orientation "is toward the scrutiny of the general social science information system and the evaluation of its major products,"[21] the prime users of his research guide are assumed to possess considerable knowledge of research. The typical user of White will be acquainted with the general structure and function of individual works listed under a heading such as Handbooks. Therefore, in the interest of economizing on the space consumed by intensive analysis of each work, it is considered sufficient to employ (in this subdivision of the chapter on psychology) a citation format, preceded by a descriptive headnote. By treating such works in this manner, White efficiently achieves the underlying purpose of his research guide: to scrutinize the information system of the social sciences and evaluate its major products. In this sense, then, White's research guide is "didactic" in the manner described by Freides. According to Freides, "the primary aim of these works is not to create new routes of access to the literature or to add to the body of accessible writings, but rather to aid the reader in selecting from a plethora of available materials."[22]

White's intent, however, is not to provide a guide whose basic purpose is to instruct researchers with little or no prior acquaintance with the function and structure of intermediary sources. Nonetheless, the method he employs in the example above can be applied in library-produced research guides where the intent is to instruct students about the structure and function of a group of intermediary sources similar to those considered by White. Merely by annotating each item in such a grouping, attention can be appropriately directed to those items researchers might use in particular situations. The headnote can give students additional information, as well as suggest particular research strategies.

The second technique, that of suggesting an integrated use of intermediary sources by stressing such matters in the general introduction to the research guide, is perhaps the most novel (and controversial) of the three. The primary objection to this technique is that it is separated from the main body of the research guide. Unless users read it along with appropriate sections of the research guide, an introduction, no matter how excellent, cannot be relied upon as a device for focusing attention from one item to another.

Thus, in the end, the second technique is most satisfactorily used in a more formal situation where a group of students is using the research guide in an assignment to meet course requirements. In such a context, it is assumed that students will read the introduction as part of the preparation for their library research. The introduction can reinforce and supplement the conceptual framework on which the research exercise is based. An example of this method is given in Figure 18.

The degree of success achieved in the example shown in Figure 18 depends to a large extent on the classroom instructor. If the instructor attaches con-

Figure 18. Introduction to Library-Produced Sociology Research Guide.

Introduction

This list of selected materials concerned with research in sociology is part of a series of mimeographed research guides prepared for numerous subjects in the social sciences by the Reference Department of the Wilson Library. Designed to assist in more effective use of the Library's resources, each research guide describes materials useful for obtaining information about a subject's *primary* and *secondary sources.*

For individuals unacquainted with research procedures and materials in sociology, the following paragraphs briefly outline an efficient mode of inquiry.

Some Helpful Suggestions

1. Successful and rewarding research requires considerable acquaintance with how sociological literature is produced, how it is organized, and how it is retrieved.

2. Skill in conducting research is acquired through purposeful and intelligent refinement.

3. Do not hesitate to ask a reference librarian for assistance in solving any research problem.

Principles of Developing Research Strategy

The research method outlined here is called *structured inquiry.* According to this method it is possible to progress in a step-by-step (i.e., structured) procedure from a point where little is known about a topic to the desired level of understanding of it.

The *structured inquiry* method is based on the following concepts:

1. *Primary Sources.* The material or data of sociology, including information generated from questionnaires, surveys and other similar instruments designed to measure certain socioeconomic characteristics called variables. The design and use of these instruments is called methodology. Until the data generated with these instruments are explained they have little or no meaning. (Section I.h. of this research guide describes sources of methodological works used by sociologists.)

2. *Secondary Sources.* The modes of communicating the significance or meaning of primary source materials; these include articles in periodicals, chapters of books, entire books, and special research reports. As secondary sources are published, bodies of literature develop.

3. *Key Sources.* Certain secondary sources are important, influential publications—usually a report of original research on a topic—which

Figure 18 (continued)

establish a conceptual focus or direction of inquiry. Subsequent investigators will indicate their indebtedness to key sources by referring to
them in their published research, a convention that gives a pattern, or
structure, to how a topic's literature develops. For example, on the
"Structured Inquiry" handout (available in the Reference Department)
typical pages from various encyclopedias, dictionaries and the like
show the importance of the classic 1933 study of "stereotypes" by
Katz and Braly. Most other research on stereotypes refers to this study
(e.g., the 1974 papers by Koslowski, Kutner, and McMillen, illustrated
on pp. 7-8 of the handout).

4. *Substantive Information.* Refers to the subject matter contained in
the body of primary and secondary sources associated with a particular
research topic.

5. *Bibliographic Information.* When research in sociology is reported
in a publication it is necessary to show how those findings are supported
by or related to the literature on that topic (e.g., the footnotes at the
bottom of pages or at the end of articles in sociological journals). References to specific primary and secondary sources are made with a convention or device called a *bibliographic citation.* A "shorthand" referent
for a specific primary or secondary source, a bibliographic citation is
a means of *identifying* or *representing* the subject matter contained in a
specific publication. Its usuage makes giving more details unnecessary,
but tells researchers where that material is *located* in the library. (See
Figure 2 for examples of bibliographic citations of such materials, and
instructions on how to locate these materials in the library.)

6. *Intermediary Sources.* The *third* component of research literature,
these are reference works and related publications with similar functions
designed to reduce the literature of research topics to manageable size
in a logical and coherent arrangement. A topic's two components
(subject matter and bibliographic data)—made up of many individual
studies—are compressed or distilled into compact articles or bibliographic entries, which in effect are *intermediate forms* or *stages* of the
larger body of literature which they represent. Intermediary sources
can inform researchers briefly about a topic or be used as an aid to
further research.

Intermediary sources treat the substantive and bibliographic components of research literature in two different ways, according to
whether individual publications on a topic are treated in an analytical
format (e.g., citation indexes, abstract services, and bibliographies),
or whether individual publications of this same topic are treated in an
integrated, synthesized format (e.g., encyclopedias, dictionaries, reviews of research). The former provide primarily bibliographic or
location information, the latter primarily substantive information.

Figure 18 (continued)

Subject (Substantive) Information	Primarily Subject Information, Secondarily Location Information	Combination of Location & Subject Information	Primarily Location Information, Secondarily Subject Information	Location (Bibliographical) Information
—2—	—1—	—0—	—1—	—2—
SUBSTANTIVE STRUCTURE			BIBLIOGRAPHIC STRUCTURE	
Glossary Dictionary (providing only definitions)	Dictionary, Encyclopedia, or Statistical Compendia [Primarily subject matter with less emphasis on bibliography].	Comprehensive Encyclopedia (with extensive bibliographies) Reviews of Research	Abstracts Annotated Bibliography [Primarily location information with brief analysis of subject matter].	Card catalog Bibliography Index Citation Index

Figure 1. Functions of Intermediary Sources

Figure 18 (continued)

These functions are illustrated by Figure 1, which is based on the following assumptions:

1. That the functions of intermediary sources fall into *five* divisions.

2. That these divisions containing types of intermediary sources can be arranged on a *continuum*, according to whether they provide primarily substantive information or location (bibliographic) information, or some combination of these two (see Figure 1).

The Production of Sociological Literature

Sociology is a collective enterprise. Using certain agreed upon precepts and conventions, sociologists, as communities of researchers, attempt to understand and explain human behavior. Sociology distinguishes itself from other social sciences by focusing primarily on characteristics of social conduct between groups of people in developed societies. For the most part sociologists investigate such social configurations as marriage and the family, ethnic and religious groups, rural and urban residence patterns, patterns of conformity and deviance, the formation of public beliefs and opinions, and the effect of mass media.

The shared precepts and conventions employed by sociologists in research and publication ensure that the published results are added to the accumulating body of literature associated with a particular research topic. These conventions give a *pattern* to the literature which aids in conducting inquiry.

How to Begin. Researchers begin by consulting encyclopedias and reviews of research selected from this research guide which provide *both* substantive and bibliographic information (that is, identify key sources and other important publications) on a topic. Since these intermediary sources are limited in the amount of substantive and bibliographic information provided, it is necessary to turn to sources which provide primarily bibliographic information on that same topic which *lead* to more substantive information in other publications. Suggested combinations of intermediary sources are often given in annotations; otherwise, it is up to researchers to determine which of the intermediary sources on this or another research guide will best suit their needs. The "Outline of Arrangement" following this introduction indicates how this research guide is organized.

An Example. In the "Structured Inquiry" handout (available in the reference Department) is illustrated how it is possible to examine a sequence of intermediary sources described in this research guide falling in *all* divisions of the continuum in Figure 1. By following this sequence, researchers advance from very brief accounts of what is known about "stereotypes" to increasingly complex, less well-organized formulations of the research literature on that topic.

Figure 18 (continued)

Types of Intermediary Sources

 a. *Dictionaries, Encyclopedias, Reviews of Research.* Often the best point at which to begin research on a topic, dictionaries, encyclopedias, and reviews of research attempt to set forth in articles or chapters brief details about the subject matter, the substantive content of the literature, on a range of topics. Concern is also directed in some to important contributors (the key sources), and to the works of numerous other researchers. (These types of intermediary sources fall in divisions in the center and on the left end of the continuum in Figure 1.) On pp. 1-6 of the "Structured Inquiry" handout is shown the kinds of information given in these sources, including the importance of the key source, Katz and Braly.

 Among examples of these types of intermediary sources on this research guide are: the *International Encyclopedia of the Social Sciences* [I.f.12]; Faris' *Handbook of Modern Sociology [I.f.7]*, Lindzey's *Handbook of Social Psychology* [I.f.14]; the *Annual Review of Sociology* [I.f.1]; Perlin's *Handbook for the Study of Suicide* [II.d.34]; Menditto's *Drugs From A to Z* [II.d.28]; Keller's *Dictionary of Words About Alcohol* [II.d.23]; Glaser's *Handbook of Criminology* [II.d.15]; Kanfer's *Helping People Change* [II.b.5]; and Stodgill's *Handbook of Leadership.* Note in this connection, however, that the *SSCI* [I.b.12] and the *Monthly Bibliography of Medical Reviews* [I.b.6] are *keys* to the locations of review articles which give useful treatments in synthesized format of recent published research on specific topics.

 b. *Bibliographies, Indexes, Citation Indexes.* Publications related to a particular topic are assembled as a list of bibliographic citations in a single intermediary source. Such treatment reduces a topic's literature to manageable size, but allows convenient access to individual items listed. (These types of intermediary sources fall in the division on the right end of Figure 1.)

 Among examples in this research guide are: the *Social Science Citation Index (SSCI)* [I.b.12] (illustrated on p. 7 of the "Structured Inquiry" handout); *International Bibliography of Sociology* [I.b.4]; Morrison's *Collective Behavior* [I.b.7]; *International Bibliography of Research in Marriage and the Family* [II.a.2]; Glenn's *Social Stratification* [II.a.7]; and Driver's *Sociology and Anthropology of Mental Illness* [II.d.9]. The *SSCI* [I.b.12] also is a source of bibliographical articles.

 c. *Abstracts, Annotated Bibliographies.* Primarily these are bibliographies, but as an aid for selecting specific publications on a topic, brief summaries or abstracts are given about the substantive content of each entry. (These types of intermediary sources fall in the division on the right of center in Figure 1.)

Figure 18 (continued)

Among examples on this research guide are: *Sociological Abstracts* [I.b.13] (illustrated on p. 8 of the "Structured Inquiry" handout); *Human Resources Abstracts* [II.d.19]; *Journal of Studies on Alcohol* [II.d.21]; *Crime and Delinquency Literature* [II.d.8]; *Bibliography on Ethnicity and Ethnic Groups* [II.a.22]; Straus' *Family Measurement Techniques* [II.a.19]; and *Work Related Abstracts* [II.a.23].

Other Sources to Consult

In addition to this research guide, similar ones having selected materials on other subjects or on major geographical areas of the world have been prepared. Because of the interrelated nature of the social sciences, particularly in connection with specific geographical areas, subject and geographical research guides should be used jointly. Assume, for example, that someone is interested in comparing certain social variables of African and American blacks. By examining "African Studies" (no. 4) and "American Studies" (no. 11) those sources which contain substantive information in sociology for each of the geographical areas can be selected, and used jointly with appropriate intermediary sources selected from this research guide.

Using the Card Catalog

Attention should also be directed to the Card Catalog. Books held by Wilson Library are listed in the Card Catalog by author, title and general subject. (See examples of typical book citations [nos. 2 and 3] in Figure 2.) Cards are arranged alphabetically in a "word-by-word" sequence. (The Library of Congress' *Subject Headings* and supplement volumes, which list in a dictionary format many of Wilson Library's subject headings and suggested cross references, is available in two locations on the main floor: on a stand near the Card Catalog and near the Information Desk in the Reference Department.) The dictionary-style format of the Library of Congress' *Subject Headings* volumes gives an efficient method for determining appropriate subject headings to consult when access to the Card Catalog by subject is required.

A brief description of the Card Catalog and the procedures for finding books in the Wilson Library is one of several handouts available in the Reference Department or at the Circulation Desk. Other handouts give details about the organization and use of periodicals, microtext materials, and other special services and collections in the Library. These guides and other bibliographies and library aids prepared by the Reference Department are listed on a blue mimeographed sheet available in the Department.

Figure 18 (continued)

EXAMPLES OF TYPICAL FORMATS OF BIBLIOGRAPHICAL CITATIONS

1. FORMAT FOR ARTICLE IN PERIODICAL

A. ①Sapir, E. ②The Na-dene Languages. ③A.A., ④n.s. XVII, 535-58, 1915

| ① Author of Article | ② Title of Article, often enclosed in quotation marks | ③ Title of Periodical | ④ Volume number, followed by page numbers of article and date of publication |

B. ①Sapir, Edward. ②"The Na-dene Languages." ③American Anthropologist, ④n.s. 17(1915):535-558

To obtain issue of periodical ③ containing article ② by author ① Sapir, consult Wilson Library Periodical Card Catalog under title of periodical ③. Cards in Periodical Card Catalog indicate Wilson Library holdings and location of particular periodicals.

2. FORMAT FOR CHAPTER IN BOOK

A. ①Hunter, Floyd. ②"Methods of Study: Community Power Structure." ③In Michael Aiken and Paul E. Mott, eds. ④The Structure of Community Power. (New York, Random House, 1970), 228-223.

| ① Author of Chapter | ② Title of Chapter | ③ Editors of Book | ④ Title of Book | ⑤ Series Name and Number |

B. ①Stanton, Max E. ②A Remnant Community: The Houma of Southern Louisiana. ③In J. Kenneth Morland, ed. ④The Not So Solid South. ⑤(Southern Anthropological Society. Proceedings, No.4) Athens, Ga.; Southern Anthropological Society, 1971, 82-92

To obtain a chapter ② by author ① consult Wilson Library Card Catalog under either editors' name ③, title of book ④, or series name ⑤. Author ① or title ② not listed in Card Catalog.

3. FORMAT FOR BOOK BY ONE OR TWO AUTHORS

A. ①Benedict, Ruth. ③Patterns of Culture. (Boston: Houghton Mifflin Co.) 1934.

| ① Author | ② Second Author | ③ Title of Book |

B. ①Berelson, Bernard, and ②Steiner, Gary A. ③Human Behavior: An Inventory of Scientific Findings. (New York: Harcourt, Brace & World, 1964)

To obtain a book by one or more author consult Wilson Library Card Catalog under first author's name ①, names of other authors, ② or title of book ③.

Figure 18 (continued)

4. FORMAT FOR GOVERNMENT PUBLICATIONS

A. ①U.S. Congress. House. Committee on Ways and Means. ②Medicare-Medicaid Reimbursement

Policies, 94th Cong., 2nd sess., 1 March 1976.

          Author (i.e., government   Title of
①agency responsible for   ②Publication
          publication)

B. ①Washington(State). Office of Program Planning and Fiscal Management. ②State of Washington

Pocket Data Book, 1975. (Olympia: 1976)

To obtain a government publication ask for assistance in Government Documents
Division on Fourth Floor East of Wilson Library.

5. FORMAT FOR NEWSPAPER REPORT

A. ①Harsch, Joseph C., ②"Mr. Reagan and the GOP," ③Christian Science Monitor, ④Aug. 12, 1976, p. 31

   ① Author ②Title of   ③Title of   ④Date of
             Report   Newspaper   Report

B. ②"Viking finds Mars Oxygen is Unexpectedly Abundant," ③New York Times, Sunday, August 1, 1976, p.l.*

* (no author)

To obtain a newspaper report, consult Newspaper title section in Wilson
Library Periodical Card Catalog. Cards in Newspaper section of Periodical
Card Catalog indicate Wilson Library holdings and location of particular
newspapers. Newspaper section precedes A's of Periodical Card Catalog.

6. FORMAT FOR DOCUMENT IN MICROFICHE

A. ①Kent, Calvin A. and Johnson J.W., ②Indian Poverty in South Dakota. Vermillion, S.D., 1969.(South

Dakota, University, Vermillion Institute of Indian Studies, Bulletin. No.99) ③ERIC ED042529

  ①Author of   ② Title of   ③Microfiche
     Document   Document   Number

B. Washington. State Legislature Joint Committee on Education. Subcommittee on Indian and

Migrant Education. ②a report to the Washington State Legislature. Olympia: Washington State

Legislature, 1970. 25p. ③ERIC ED053841

Each of these citations has appeared above. (6.A. is similar to 2.B.; 6.B is
similar to 4.A.) In both cases, the items have also been published in microfiche
format, indicated by the microfiche no. ③ ED042529. Material in this collection
is housed in the ERIC Center of Wilson Library. There are, in addition, other
similar collections of materials on microfiche in various places in the Library.

Figure 19. Annotation for *Psychology: A Study of a Science*

I.c   13

BF   20. Koch, S., ed. *Psychology: A Study of a Science*. New York,
38   McGraw-Hill, 1958-1963.
P8
v.1-6   Prompted by the American Psychological Association's deci-
                sion in 1952 on the need for a thorough and critical examina-
                tion of the status and development of psychology. An ambi-
                tious work of a projected seven volumes (the seventh is not
                yet published) and over eighty expert contributors. Each
                study, volume, essay, is a self-contained unit. Volumes I-III,
                labeled *Study I, Conceptual and Systematic*, consists of the
                following titles: *Sensory, Perceptual and Systematic Formula-
                tions* (1959); *General systematic formulations, learning and
                general processes* (1959); and *Formulations of the Person and
                the Social Contexts* (1959). The three volumes in *Study II*,
                labelled *Empirical Substructure and Relations with Other
                Subjects*, are entitled: *Biologically Oriented Fields* (1962);
                The Process Areas, the Person and Some Allied Fields (1963);
                and *Investigations of Man as Socius* (1963). The broader
                themes of each volume are appropriately subdivided into 80-
                odd narrower, but related, topics, each an authoritative
                survey, in a synthesized, distilled format not unlike the *Amer-
                ican Handbook of Psychiatry* (II.d.4), assessing what is known
                about the topic at the time of publication. In *Study I* 34 topics
                ("systematic formulations") are intensely analyzed. The empha-
                sis of *Study II* is on the exploration of interrelations among
                the parts of psychology (as a field of knowledge) and on the
                place of psychology within the field of scientific activity. The
                numbers of works examined by each of the authors in articles
                range from just over 30 to almost 300, and thus even though
                this work is somewhat dated, it can be used jointly with such
                similar reviews of research as the *Handbook of Social Psy-
                chology* (II.g.5) or the *American Handbook of Psychiatry*
                (II.d.4). Or, if the older volume covers areas lacking in the
                narrower more recent works, it often can aid, by referring to
                a significant older name, in tracing advances that have occurred
                since publication by using the *SCI* (I.a.13) and the *SSCI*
                (I.a.14). Name and subject indexes for each volume but no
                cumulative indexes.

siderable importance to the method (in this case, structured inquiry) and reiterates to students the desirability of viewing the research exercise as an integral part of the course, then the use of an elaborate introduction is justified.

The third technique, by which suggestions for developing research strategies are given within the text of the annotation, is perhaps the most efficient. For example, Figure 19 illustrates to psychology students how Koch's multi-volume work can be used jointly with other works. In other words, it is an attempt to enlarge the conventional purpose of annotations, allowing researchers to visualize the opportunities available for obtaining better access to the substantive literature of their research topic by articulating a particular work with others. By employing this technique, researchers, especially inexperienced ones, can logically and efficiently advance from the information on a research topic given in an earlier work to later works which assess more recent stages of the same topic.

In this sense, the annotation goes beyond the technique employed by White. In other words, the underlying purpose of such annotations is to expand the "didactic" purpose of the research bibliographies noted by Freides.

In addition to directing the attention of users to related items described in the research guide devoted to a particular subject, it is often desirable to direct them to other sources, for specific coverage of a narrow topic. Such instances occur most often in connection with area studies. It is for such a context, for example, that Figure 23 (see Part V) was devised. The figure attempts to illustrate two principles. First, there is a genuine interdependence between studies of a discipline in a particular geographical area and the larger body of scientific literature of that discipline. That is, sociological research conducted in, say, Latin America, necessarily is based upon the larger body of sociological literature accumulated from the study of *all* societies. It is in the interest of sociologists of Latin American societies to apply those concepts and methodologies from the general body of sociology literature, so that the results of their own studies can be added to that body.

The second principle derives directly from the first. It concerns the interdependence between the research instruments produced to link what is known in the general core of literature with the accumulating body of literature for the same discipline in a particular geographical area. Not unexpectedly, attempts to articulate these two seemingly disparate areas of inquiry cause problems for librarians as well as for researchers. Part V will consider some of these problems.

Notes

1. Mark Keller and Mairi McCormick, eds., *A Dictionary of Words About Alcohol* (New Brunswick, N.J.: Rutgers Center on Alcohol Studies, 1968).

2. Mark Keller, ed., *International Bibliography of Studies on Alcohol* (New Brunswick, N.J.: Rutgers University Press, 1960-   ).

3. *Journal of Studies on Alcohol* (New Brunswick, N.J.: Rutgers Center on Alcohol Studies; 1940-   ).

4. Joan Aldous and R. Hill, eds., *International Bibliography of Research on Marriage and the Family*, 2 vols. (Minneapolis: University of Minnesota Press, 1967-1974).

5. David H. L. Olson and Nancy S. Dahl, eds., *Inventory of Marriage and Family Literature* (St. Paul, Minn.: Family Social Science, University of Minnesota Press, 1975-   ).

6. William J. Goode, *Social Systems and Family Patterns: A Propositional Inventory* (Indianapolis, Ind.: Bobbs-Merrill, 1971).

7. Harold T. Christensen, ed., *Handbook of Marriage and the Family* (Chicago: Rand McNally, 1964).

8. Raymond G. McInnis and James W. Scott, *Social Science Research Handbook* (New York: Barnes and Noble, 1975).

9. C. Edward Wall, *Author Index to Poole's Index to Periodical Literature* (Ann Arbor, Mich.: Pierian Press, 1971).

10. George P. Murdock, *Ethnographic Atlas* (Pittsburgh: University of Pittsburgh Press, 1967).

11. Robert B. Textor, *A Cross-Cultural Summary* (New Haven, Conn.: HRAF Press, 1967).

12. *Ekistics Index* (Athens, Greece: Athens Centger of Ekistics, 1955-   ).

13. Charles L. Taylor, *World Handbook of Political and Social Indicators*, 2d ed. (New Haven, Conn.: Yale University Press, 1972).

14. Arthur C. Banks, *Cross-Polity Time-Series Data* (Cambridge, Mass.: MIT Press 1971).

15. *Social Sciences Citation Index* (Philadelphia: Institute of Scientific Information, 1973-   ).

16. Marvin E. Wolfgang, et al., *Criminology Index: Research and Theory in Criminology in the United States, 1945-1972*, 2 vols. (New York: Elsevier, 1975).

17. Ibid., p. xii.

18. *Criminal Justice Abstracts* (New York: National Council on Crime and Delinquency, 1969-   ).

19. Sigmund Koch, ed., *Psychology: A Study of a Science*, 6 vols., (New York, McGraw-Hill, 1959-1963).

20. Carl M. White and associates, eds., *Sources of Information in the Social Sciences* 2d ed. (Chicago: American Library Association, 1973), p. 417.

21. George P. Murdock and Timothy O'Leary, eds., *Ethnographic Bibliography of North America* (New Haven, Conn.: HRAF Press, 1975), I, p. xxxv.

22. See Thelma Freides, *The Literature and Bibliography of the Social Sciences* (Los Angeles: Melville Publishing Co., 1973), pp. 221-3, 231-8. The quoted passage is on p. 221.

Part V

THE PRINCIPLES AND APPLICATIONS OF RESEARCH GUIDES IN AREA STUDIES

Part V focuses on the problems of relating the research literature on particular geographical areas (generally identified as area studies) to the research literature which forms the central core of literature of specific disciplines in the social sciences. Proper information about these relationships is especially important for inexperienced researchers for, once they become informed, the logic of structured inquiry becomes a valid mode of inquiry to employ.

Again, for research guides for area studies, organization and annotation are viewed as important in helping researchers understand the relationships between the research literature of a discipline in a particular geographical area and the larger body of literature of that discipline (Chapter 23). This chapter also notes the current stress on interdisciplinary studies, especially studies concerned with specific geographical areas. As a consequence, there is increased interdependency between the intermediary sources which give access to the research literature of area studies. By stressing the process of inquiry and the pattern of literature coverage among intermediary sources in these fields, researchers, especially those not well acquainted with either the subject matter or the intermediary sources available, are given greater awareness of the tasks involved.

As an aid to understanding why constructing research guides for particular geographical areas is problematical, attention is directed in Chapter 24 to two systems of classifying the research literature of geographical areas and to two standard research guides. Finally, by using examples, methods of organizing and annotating library-produced research guides for area studies are discussed (Chapter 25).

23 The Organization and Annotation of Research Guides for Area Studies

When confronted with the problem of constructing a research guide for a particular geographical area, the considerations discussed in the preceding introduction need to be taken into account. There are at least three other principles that should be considered. First, the social-scientific literature of a particular discipline for a geographical area is related to the larger body of literature of that same discipline, accumulated from the study of all geographical areas. Second, interdisciplinary research relating to specific geographical areas, particularly the so-called underdeveloped areas, is becoming very popular in higher education. As a result, the researchers' use of several types of sources treating intermediate forms of the literature of a particular topic on different levels takes on greater importance.[1] In addition to drawing on the larger body of literature of their respective disciplines, sociologists, anthropologists, and political scientists are making wide use of each other's records.

Not unexpectedly, the third principle derives from the first two. On the one hand, in preceding chapters it is argued that there are interdependent relationships between the intermediary sources that cover the larger body of literature of a particular discipline and those that cover the literature of narrow fields of inquiry in the same discipline. (This notion is illustrated in Figure 10) On the other hand, consideration should be given to those intermediary sources which cover both a particular geographical area and specific disciplines for that same area. (This notion is illustrated in Figure 9.) For example, all researchers should be able to recognize and appreciate the linkage (often implicit) between the portions of an article in Greenstein and Polsby's *Handbook on Political Science*,[2] which analyzes and compares political parties in Africa, and the large body of published articles and books on the same topic in Paden and Soja's *African Experience*.[3]

The organization of intermediary sources according to this scheme, which demonstrates these linkages, enables researchers to see that numerous intermediary sources (both bibliographic and substantive) provide treatment of the social-scientific literature on various levels. Just as it can be claimed that in a given discipline, intermediary sources assume natural patterns of coverage (directly related to the substantive-bibliographic continuum), it can be claimed that in relation to particular geographical areas, intermediary sources assume a natural pattern of coverage of the literature. (Qualifications of this statement are discussed in this chapter.) In addition, by employing this scheme of organizing intermediary sources of a given geographical area, research guides can elucidate the process of social-scientific inquiry and communication that occurs in area studies, that is, research guides for specific geographical areas can also perform important cognitive functions.

Patterns of Literature Coverage in Area Studies

Except for a few general statements, no attention is given here to the adequacy of (1) the coverage of the literature of particular geographical areas by the bibliographical and related instruments designed to collect and organize this literature, or (2) the acquisition of this same literature by academic libraries. In connection with the first point, suffice it to say that it is dangerous to discuss uncategorically either the patterns or the comprehensiveness of the coverage of the substantive literature concerned with geographical areas. Few studies have systematically attempted to determine how completely the literature of specific geographical areas is collected and organized. It is enough simply to acknowledge that there are gaps in the coverage of the literature of these areas, but that these gaps vary among geographical areas.

If my experience is typical, however, gaps in the completeness of the bibliographical coverage of area studies literature is less of a problem to researchers, particularly student researchers, than is the second point, the adequacy of area studies materials in academic libraries. Experience suggests, in this regard, that typically, to a greater or lesser degree, academic libraries are able to collect only a limited portion of the published research concerned with specific area studies. This condition applies particularly to the literature concerned with areas outside of Western Europe and the United States. It must be acknowledged, of course, that the pattern of collection development for the literature of particular geographical areas, including the United States, varies considerably among academic libraries. Libraries with stronger collections for certain geographical areas, because of particular interest by faculty researchers, continue to stress collection development in these areas, even in a period of reduced acquisitions programs.

At the same time, as reference librarians, we are still confronted with problems of assisting researchers in gaining access to the literature that *is* contained in academic libraries. In such a context, much of the reference librarian's time is occupied in finding materials for researchers, especially students, that are suitable substitutes for those materials the library does not hold. It is, in part, this latter issue that is being addressed here. More specifically, however, concern is directed toward modes of organizing for easier access those materials on particular geographical areas that are typically available in academic libraries for use in research.

It is instructive, in this connection, to examine the organizational schemes employed by the Human Relations Area Files and the American Geographical Society. Both schemes teach us important principles about the need for employing uniform patterns when attempting to organize the literature devoted to particular topics concerned with specific geographical areas.

Human Relations Area Files

The Human Relations Area Files (HRAF) comprises a vast collection of social-scientific literature on human cultures (historical, contemporary, and primitive). It consists of primary and secondary source materials (subject matter) on approximately 300 cultures throughout the world, and provides materials for undertaking research on individual cultures or for making cross-cultural comparisons. Essentially, it is a system of organizing subject matter about a people, the environment in which they live, their behavior, and their culture.

Two handbooks are used to direct users to particular cultural topics. On the one hand, the *Outline of World Cultures* classifies all known cultures, including extinct, historical, and prehistoric peoples, by geographical region.[4] The *Outline of Cultural Materials* is designed to be used jointly with the *Outline of World Cultures*.[5] It contains the topical classification system on which HRAF is based. All cultural and background information on world cultures is divided into 80-odd major divisions and over 600 minor divisions. Together, the two handbooks permit users to gain access to the literature about a particular cultural characteristic of a people.

Giving access to the literature occurs in a special way. In HRAF, appropriate pages (taken from the articles, books, and so forth, deposited in HRAF for a particular culture) are reproduced in sufficient numbers so that each subject discussed on those pages is represented in each topical division. No further attempt is made to synthesize, summarize, or otherwise treat the subject matter contained on the pages. In effect, when looking for information about marriage rites of the Kikuyu people of Kenya, what HRAF users find are pages from studies of the Kikuyu people, or Kenya in general, on which Kikuyu marriage rites are discussed. (One division, category 116, contains the full text of each source.) Thus, the HRAF system provides users a means of gaining access to subject matter with only incidental concern for the bibliographical aspects of the materials.[6] Indeed, the *HRAF Source Bibliography* was produced as a sort of afterthought, in response to the requests of HRAF users.[7] Thus, with qualification, it can be said that HRAF essentially gives access to subject matter.

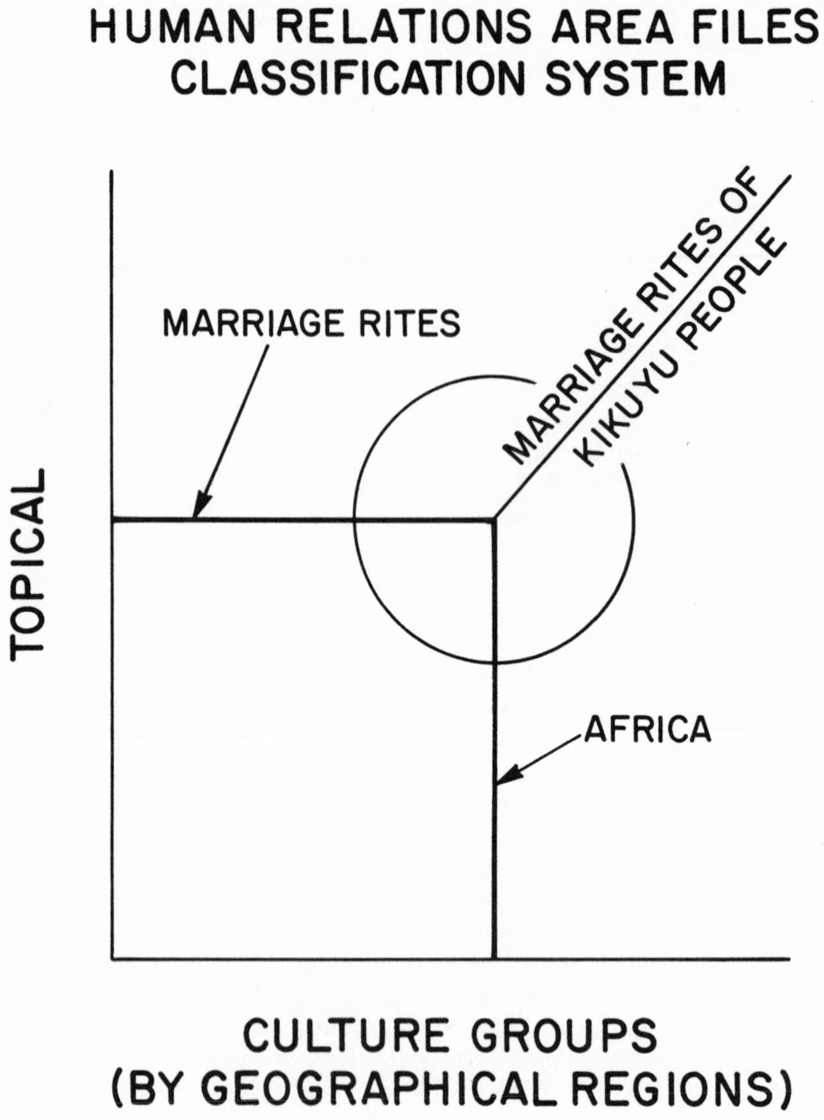

HUMAN RELATIONS AREA FILES CLASSIFICATION SYSTEM

Figure 20. Human Relations Area Files Classification System

By matching the alphanumeric symbol identifying a particular culture group (the symbol for the Kikuyu, for example) with a number corresponding to a particular cultural characteristic (topic), users can quickly expose the subject matter on that topic contained in the files. The system can be illustrated graphically (see Figure 20) by a vertical line (representing topics) perpendicular to a horizontal line (representing culture groups).

American Geographical Society

Although the characteristics of the American Geographical Society (AGS) scheme are the same as those of the HRAF, which organizes subject matter, the AGS scheme is designed to organize bibliogaphical citations of geographical and related literature. It applies to a particular geographical area as well as a particular research topic, and it exposes references to particular systematic or methodological themes, where general matters are considered. In the general or systematic section, classification is according to a decimal system. (Unlike that of HRAF, this section of the AGS classification system exposes citations to material dealing with particular themes, and not a particular geographical area.) For geographical areas, a regional classification system is used. The world is divided into fifty-two regions, each represented by a number, while subregions are identified by letters. (The western part of the United States, for example, is Region 10, and the states of Oregon and Washington are Subregion 10a.) By combining a decimal number derived from the topical or systematic classification scheme with a regional symbol, users of the AGS *Catalogue* are able to find the literature on a particular research topic for a particular geographical area.[8] (Except for specific topical considerations, Figure 21 illustrates how the AGS system works.)

Neither the HRAF nor the AGS system employs indexes in the conventional sense.[9] However, by coordinating numbers or symbols from the two separate classification schemes which each contains, users of both systems are led to the literature concerned with a particular topic on a particular geographical area.

Can Intermediary Sources Be Arranged by Discipline and Geographical Area?

It would be well indeed if it could be proposed that intermediary sources could be arranged according to a classification system based on that of HRAF or AGS. If such a system were possible, researchers, especially inexperienced ones, could be informed of a relatively simple pattern to which a research strategy could be applied to gain access to the needed literature on a particular geographical region. Unfortunately, it cannot be achieved.

AMERICAN GEOGRAPHICAL SOCIETY CLASSIFICATION SYSTEM

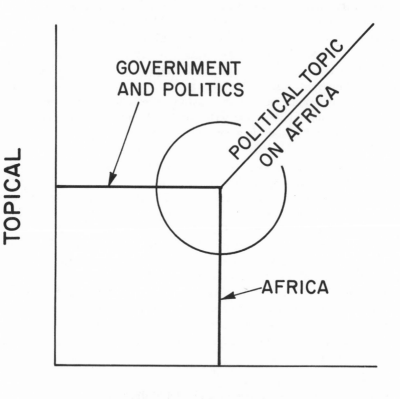

GOVERNMENT AND POLITICS

POLITICAL TOPIC ON AFRICA

TOPICAL

AFRICA

GEOGRAPHICAL

Figure 21. American Geographical Classification System.

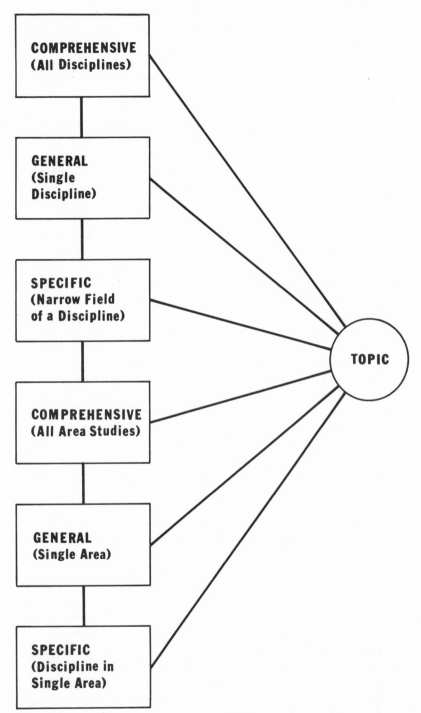

Figure 22. Conception of Suggested Levels of Specificity of Intermediary
Sources for Disciplinary Studies and for Area Studies (II)

Earlier, especially in Part III, it is argued that rather than giving discrete portions of the actual substantive literature, intermediary sources treat this literature in a special way, providing access to its substantive or bibliographic components (or various combinations of both) in a format which symbolically represents that literature. Thus, in this context, intermediary sources are considered as giving intermediate forms or stages of the substantive literature, and, further, these intermediate forms or stages occur as instruments which treat the literature according to either an analytical or synthetical format. Intermediary sources therefore perform *analytical functions* by exposing discrete elements of a body of literature (i.e., the individual studies of which it is made up) and *synthetical functions* by exposing synthesized portions of that same literature (i.e., the discrete contributions, cumulated in synthesized format, form a larger body of literature). Finally, it is argued that in order to conduct successful and satisfying inquiry, searchers should be acquainted with the processes and patterns which underly the function and structure both of social-scientific literature and of the instruments which give access to that literature.

Following this logic, the *HRAF Source Bibliography*, which lists the materials contained in HRAF, symbolically represents these materials. (The subject matter in HRAF, since it consists of portions of discrete, original research on specific culture groups, cannot be considered a special form or stage of that literature, in the manner argued above.) Likewise, the AGS *Catalogue*, which lists both the topical and regional literature held in the AGS library in New York, symbolically represents this literature.

The systems on which HRAF and AGS are based must not be confused with the materials which they classify. While the HRAF and AGS systems individually treat substantive information and bibliographic information, respectively, they do not treat both in the manner substantive and bibliographic components are treated (in relation to the substantive-bibliographic continuum) in intermediary sources. By adding a second element to either of the two individual components, it is impossible to use a matrix consisting of a simple vertical-horizontal axis as a means of organizing intermediary sources for area studies. Instead, in order to be epistemologically sound, it is necessary to show the relationship of intermediary sources for disciplines and for area studies in a hierarchical relationship. In effect, what is produced is a figure that can be described as a compound matrix or, more precisely, compound matrices, as illustrated in Figure 22.

Not unexpectedly, before this system of procedures can be employed as research strategy, researchers should achieve an understanding of what is occurring, especially in connection with the relationships between the substantive literature produced by researchers in the field and how this same substantive literature is treated in intermediary sources. As noted earlier, White states that gaining this facility requires "bibliographical expertise" which, according to Knapp, "must be taught" (see Chapter 14). By clearly describing the function and structure of intermediary sources, reference librarians can make researchers more aware of the research strategies that can be employed in conducting inquiry. How can this bibliographical expertise be achieved?

Let's review some of the principles noted above. Recall that intermediary sources provide intermediate forms or stages of substantive literature. Recall further that, in relation to the substantive-bibliographic continuum, these forms or stages which are exposed are either bibliographic or substantive components, or various combinations of both, of the literature. Finally, recall that coverage of the literature by intermediary sources can occur at more than one level of specificity—some sources expose discrete elements of a body of literature (i.e., the individual studies of which it is comprised) and perform synthetical functions by exposing synthesized portions of that same literature (i.e., the discrete contributions, cumulated in a synthesized format, form a larger body of literature). It is argued that in order to conduct successful and satisfying inquiry, researchers should be acquainted with the processes and patterns that underly the function and structure both of social-scientific literature and of the instruments (i.e., intermediary sources) which give access to that literature. Both the *HRAF Source Bibliography* and the AGS *Catalogue* symbolically represent the substantive literature listed. Neither contains material that can by itself be considered a special form or stage of the substantive portions of that literature. While the HRAF and AGS systems individually treat either substantive material or bibliographic information, neither treats *both* in the same way they are treated in intermediary sources. Thus, a simple vertical-horizontal axis (as in Figures 20 and 21) can be used to expose particular topics in both the HRAF and AGS systems. However, by adding a second element to either of these components, so that both substantive and bibliographic elements must be taken into consideration, it is impossible to use a matrix which consists of a simple vertical-horizontal axis.

For example, while Greenstein and Polsby's *Handbook of Political Science* examines aspects of African political parties, this topic is treated in relation to what is known about political parties in general. On the other hand, chapters in the first volume of Paden and Soja's *African Experience*, in Lystad's *The African World*[10] or, perhaps, a review article in *Current Bibliography on African Affairs*[11] examine the literature on African political parties. Similar analogies can be given, both for other geographical areas and/or other social science disciplines.

In this connection, it is important to consider (1) the changes in perspective that occur when researchers move from an analysis and comparison of the literature of African political parties, to an analysis and comparison of that literature with that in other parts of the world; and (2) the fact that a suitable treatment (either bibliographically or substantively) of the literature being examined by a researcher does not always exist on that level—when possible, a researcher should discover on another level where that literature is given the desired treatment. Indeed, in some instances, it is not possible to discover the desired treatment, in which case the researcher must employ alternative means of gaining access to the needed literature. If researchers, especially student researchers, are determined to employ the intermediary sources available to them and exploit them to their greatest potential, they should be aware of the different levels of intermediary sources in which it is possible to obtain a particular form or stage of that literature.

It is the second consideration that contrasts with the method of finding substantive literature in either the HRAF or the AGS classification systems. The difference, of course, is that where these two systems provide access to discrete studies concerned with the literature of a research topic (i.e., exclusively analytical treatment), this same literature is treated in intermediary sources either analytically or synthetically. An awareness that such treatment could be available, whether analytical or synthetical, would significantly affect both the direction and efficiency of inquiry.

If researchers are not aware of these characteristic patterns in which such intermediate forms or stages of the literature can be found, they cannot take advantage of these patterns. In such circumstances, research progresses at a slow, plodding, indecisive pace. In addition, significant considerations of the literature that can significantly alter either the course of inquiry or the conclusions derived often go unnoticed. By being aware of the function and structure of intermediary sources, particularly their characteristic pattern of providing treatments of literature on various levels, researchers can at least attempt to discover if a treatment fitting a particular need is available. This capability is of greatest importance to the researcher not well acquainted with a research topic; perhaps for this reason alone, it is important to consider the means of informing students of the process. It is most desirable if researchers can be informed of these patterns of literature coverage without the necessity of elaborate instructions in research materials, in the sense alluded to by O'Leary (see Chapter 19).

On the surface, standard research guides attempting general coverage are not very concerned about systematic coverage of the research instruments of all geographical areas. That is unfortunate.

In some cases, achieving a desirable systematic coverage of geographical areas is simply a matter of making a particular research guide more logically coherent and internally consistent. Such changes in organization would lead to the kind of coverage that would enable researchers, especially inexperienced ones, to quickly examine the intermediary sources in which a particular research topic is considered. In other cases, it is a matter of changing the patterns in which particular research guides are organized and, in the process, becoming aware of certain geographical areas that are not given the consideration they deserve.

Earlier (see Chapters 8 and 20), in a discussion of how Kaplan's distinction between logic-in-use and reconstructed logic applies to the construction of bibliographic research guides, it is suggested that the more closely the organization of a research guide reflects the course in which inquiry is conducted, the more useful it will be. In Chapter 14, reference is made to several conceptualizations of the process of inquiry. Knapp's system of "ways" and Freides' "tuning in" are particularly appropriate in this context. (An illustration of a method of progressing from a level of little or no prior acquaintance with a concept to a sophisticated understanding of it is given in Appendix A.) In this sense, stress is placed on the process in which inquiry is conducted rather than on specific library materials. Rather than considering that research is conducted according to specific prescribed patterns, it is assumed that tracing a course of inquiry requires following the patterns employed by experienced researchers in the field, patterns adjusted to the natural structure of the literature of a particular research topic (see the beginning of Chapter 10).

Research strategy is dependent to a large extent on how well individual researchers are acquainted with the subject matter. Tracing the course of inquiry requires an awareness of the pattern of bibliographic citations of the literature. Thus, in most cases, experienced researchers well acquainted with the subject matter of a topic begin research at a point in the network of literature at, or close to, its expanding frontiers, where the course of inquiry is not well defined. Inexperienced researchers begin at a more general level and slowly work toward assimilating a more sophisticated understanding of the subject matter (see Chapter 14).

Notes

1. Raymond G. McInnis and James W. Scott, *Social Science Research Handbook* (New York: Barnes and Noble, 1975), p. 141.

2. Fred I. Greenstein and Nelson W. Polsby, eds., *Handbook of Political Science*, 8 vols. and cumulative index (Reading, Mass.: Addison-Wesley, 1975).

3. John N. Paden and Edward W. Soja, eds., *The African Experience*, 3 vols. in 4 (Evanston, Ill.: Northwestern University Press, 1970).

4. George P. Murdock, *Outline of World Cultures*, 5th ed. (New Haven, Conn.: HRAF Press, 1975).

5. George P. Murdock, *Outline of Cultural Materials*, 4th ed. rev. (New Haven, Conn.: HRAF Press, 1967).

6. Not unexpectedly, these matters cause problems, especially among inexperienced researchers. See brief note and reference in McInnis and Scott, eds., *Social Science Research Handbook*, p. 152.

7. *HRAF Source Bibliography* (New Haven, Conn.: HRAF, 1976).

8. American Geographical Society, *Research Catalogue*, 15 vols. (Boston: G. K. Hall, 1962).

9. The *HRAF Source Bibliography* lists by culture group all sources deposited in HRAF. Using an abridged AGS classification scheme, *Current Geographical Publications* updates the AGS *Research Catalogue*, and it has monthly and annually cumulated author and subject indexes.

10. Robert Lystad, ed., *The African World* (New York: Praeger, 1965).

11, *Current Bibliography on African Affairs* (New York: Published by Greenwood Press, Inc., for the African Bibliographic Institute, 1962-   ).

24 Problems in Constructing Research Guides for Area Studies

Before examining methods employed by certain standard research guides for setting forth the intermediary sources relating to specific geographical areas, it is useful to review some of the problems encountered in attempts to construct area studies research guides. For example, most geographical areas are not as well represented as perhaps the United States and, to a lesser extent, Western Europe by some of the intermediary sources falling in the substantive divisions (toward the left end) of the tripartite matrix. In other words, political science dictionaries for specific areas such as Africa or Asia are rare while it is not unusual to find them for the United States or Western Europe. In numerous cases, too, political science dictionaries with general coverage have proportionally more material on Europe or North America than on other areas. Since the bulk of research in the social sciences is after all confined to these areas, such concerns are also reflected in intermediary sources.

Hence, when specific area studies outside either North America or Western Europe are considered in relation to the tripartite matrix, considerable attention must be given to how researchers will discover appropriate items that will provide needed information, if a pattern of structured inquiry is being recommended to them as a means of developing research strategies.

In area studies, linking the general intermediary sources such as dictionaries and encyclopedias with more specifically oriented bibliographic sources (i.e., geographical) presents certain difficulties. If inexperienced researchers are going to utilize these materials to their greatest potential, some means of drawing them to their attention must be devised. In Chapters 21-23, the importance of organization and annotation in integrating intermediary sources on general and specific levels (i.e., levels of specificity) of particular social-scientific disciplines is stressed. In area studies, the need to integrate through organization and annotation is much greater. With these points in mind, let's examine White's *Sources of Information in the Social Sciences* and Poulton's *The Historian's Handbook*.

White's *Sources of Information in the Social Sciences*

The second edition of *Sources of Information in the Social Sciences* was a long-awaited event among librarians and scholars in the social sciences.[1] The 1964 first edition justly achieved eminence as a valuable research guide. It received only minor criticisms, namely, that it had an occidental bias and that it failed to cover adequately the multitude of statistical sources available. In the second edition, the uneven coverage of statistical sources has largely been corrected. The occidental bias, however, remains but is manifested in a slightly different manner. The first edition emphasized European and U.S. materials, particularly in history, and gave uneven coverage of materials outside of these areas. In the current edition, the coverage of intermediary sources is nearly complete, but researchers in geographical areas outside of Western Europe and the United States will continue to quarrel with how these materials are treated.

Before examining the alleged weaknesses of White's work, it would be well to describe its organization and format, as these are the principal causes of its weaknesses. The preface describes the guidelines within which the contributors worked. White and fourteen specialists in various disciplines in the social sciences give a general treatment in nine chapters: the social sciences in general, history, geography, economics and business administration, sociology, anthropology, psychology, education, and political science. (In the first edition, geography was treated as a subdivision of history.) Each chapter consists of two sections: a bibliographic essay that reviews a substantial number of monographs and other types of published research on aspects of each discipline, which, "if they do not form the core, are at least representative of the core of the substantive literature in that field"[2]; and an annotated listing of intermediary sources and related materials presented according to an almost uniform format. According to White, contributors were allowed to organize the literature as "the discipline requires." Items are identified by a code combining letters (for chapters) and numerals, a system that allows the insertion of cross-references where necessary. (More liberal use of cross-references would have helped overcome some of the difficulties noted below and would have allowed less experienced researchers to make more effective use of the volume.) Finally, there is an expertly compiled index of over 130 pages including author, title, and subject entries. In short, it is a massive work attempting to cover the entire world literature in the social sciences.

For the purpose of this discussion, attention is directed to its perspective on history.[3] Historians will object to the work primarily on the basis that the sources for areas outside Western Europe, Russia, and the United States are spread unevenly and inconsistently throughout the other chapters. Historians will also question the work's narrow focus.

The history chapter begins with a fairly extensive account of the de-velopment and present status of history as a discipline. Particular stress is given to the need for history to absorb the methods of other disciplines. In examining the important monographic literature of history, historian Chodorow discusses only works on Europe, Russia, and the United States. Chodorow's characterization of his historiographical essay as "an annotated bibliography designed to introduce the student to the major fields of history" and his observation that these "works represent the main line of historical writing on each period"[4] will strike most historians as downright narrow-minded. Nonetheless, the 300-odd works included in the essay are discussed authoritatively.

The second section of the chapter maintains the European-American bias. For example, among the twenty-four "basic and general guides" and "spe-cialized guides," only five are concerned with areas outside Europe and the United States.[5] Particularly disappointing are the omission of Griffin's *Latin America: A Guide to Historical Literature* in the section on Latin America and the failure to provide a division for African history.

Bias is again evident in the Current Bibliographies section which lists such titles as *L'Annee Philologique, Bibliografia storica nazionale, Bibliographie annuelle de l'histoire de France, Bibliographie internationale de l'Humanisme et de la Renaissance, Indice historico espanol, International Medieval Bibli-ography, Writings on American History,* and *Writings on British History;* and, rather curiously, the series "Helps for Students of History," which resembles the American Historical Association's better known "Service Center for Teachers of History" series; the latter, as expected, is included in the preceding Reviews of the Literature section.[6] Such evidence suggests either that recurrent bibliographical publications of Western history are more numerous or that recurrent non-Western bibliographical publications tend to be multidisciplinary. (The preface notes that the anthropology chap-ter "bears the brunt of responsibility for area studies.")[7]

The difficulties noted above could be at least partially eliminated by arranging materials by geographical areas as well as by discipline. If the arrangement were in two main parts—the first consisting of chapters on each of the eight disciplines and the second of chapters dealing with each of the major areas of the world—the difficulty of locating required material would be reduced. By arranging intermediary sources according to both disciplines and geographical areas covered, all materials devoted exclusively to particular geographical areas would fall together in one chapter. As argued above, users can easily be informed of the logic of using chapters and subsections of chapters. Such a scheme would contain a general chapter; a chapter on each discipline; a chapter on materials concerned with area studies in general; and a chapter, subdivided appropriately by discipline, devoted to a specific geographical area. By identifying the subdivisions within chapters by small-case letters, the task of finding materials could be made more logically coherent and internally consistent (especially for those with little prior acquaintance with research materials) and the researcher could devote more attention to the basic organizational pattern of each chapter. Such an arrangement would make each chapter more explicitly an integral part of the whole book.

With such an arrangement, the researcher would not have to spend as much time hopping back and forth from chapter to chapter—or using the index, as is now the case. Central to the mode of inquiry being proposed, however, is the user's need to have easy familiarity with the characteristics and function of intermediary sources, particularly of how they provide access to the desired literature network.

Perhaps the following example will illustrate the point as well as any. The section in the history chapter which discusses retrospective bibliographies for North America lists about ten items, including Burr's *Critical Bibliography of Religion in America*, Griffin's *Bibliographies of American Historical Societies*, Nevins' *Civil War Books*, Trask, Meyer, and Trask's *Bibliography of U.S.-Latin American Relations Since 1810*, the *National Union Catalog of Manuscript Collections*, and Winther's *Classified Bibliography of the Trans-Mississippi West*.[8] These are all titles one would expect to encounter in such a work. One would also expect to encounter in the section discussing retrospective bibliographies at least cross-references to the *Harvard Guide to American History*, Bemis and Griffin's *Guide to the Diplomatic History of the U.S.*, and the Library of Congress's *Guide to the Study of the U.S.* On the contrary, these are listed in the following categories: the *Harvard Guide* and the *Guide to the Study of the U.S.* in the basic and general guides section of the history chapter's Guides to the Literature section;[9] and Bemis and Griffin in the International Relations section of the political science chapter (exactly where expected, but a cross-reference is still needed, particularly since the compilers recognized that Trask, Meyer, and Trask should be listed in the North American bibliography section, even though it deals with Latin America as well).[10] The index does, of course, provide access to all of these items under the entry *United States*.

The point of all this is neither to condemn nor to ridicule. On the contrary, in its first edition, *Sources of Information in the Social Sciences* became known among librarians and scholars as a superb research guide and, in its second edition, it achieves even greater excellence. The main purpose of my comments is to emphasize that disciplines in the social sciences are closely interrelated and that area studies consist largely of particular aspects of studies conducted within various disciplines. Further, as mentioned above, there is currently a powerful stimulus for area studies to become inter- or multidisciplinary.[11] Research guides which include area studies materials would become more widely and more effectively used if they reflected these same patterns.

Poulton's *The Historian's Handbook*

Poulton's *The Historian's Handbook*, a descriptive research guide for the history student and scholar which includes over 800 intermediary sources and related materials, is the most ambitious and informative general history volume currently available.[12] (It was recognized as one of the best reference works for 1972 by a committee of the American Library Association.) The chapters "Legal Sources" and "Government Publications" together occupy some eighty pages. The "Legal Sources" chapter alone represents one of the most valuable statements available on that topic, particularly because of the attention it gives Price and Bitner's *Effective Legal Research* and Schmecke-bier's *Government Publications*.

The bulk of the book is contained in Chapters 3-8: "Guides, Manuals and Bibliographies of History"; "Encyclopedias and Dictionaries"; "Almanacs, Yearbooks, Statistical Handbooks and Current Surveys"; "Serials and Newspapers"; "Geographical Aids"; and "Bibliographical Materials." Each chapter discusses works covering historical periods and geographical areas. Even though this treatment seems logical, it leads to some confusion. After a chapter discussing general historical material, it would be more logical (for the beginning student, for whom the volume is designed) to present a chapter which divides the material by geographical area and then by type of work, with an emphasis on the function of each work. Such treatment might have avoided the confusion such as results from introducing Martin and Lovett's *Encyclopedia of Latin American History* in the chapter "Guides, Manuals and Bibliographies," rather than in the chapter "Encyclopedias and Dictionaries."[13]

Even more disconcerting is the mix of geographical areas and periods in the third chapter, "Guides, Manuals and Bibliographies of History."[14] It is arranged in the following sequence: General; United States; Ancient; Medieval and Renaissance; Great Britain; Russia; Latin America; the Far East; and Modern. No attention is given Africa, the South Pacific, or the Middle East. Why distinguish only historical periods of the Western world? Further, the *International Bibliography of Historical Sciences* is discussed in the Modern subsection, even though this excellent source, as Poulton correctly notes, covers prehistory through modern periods. Likewise, Sauvaget's *Introduction to the History of the Muslim East* is discussed in the Modern subsection of the chapter, even though Sauvaget treats *only* premodern sources.[15]

Importance of Concern for Organization

If White, for the social sciences as a whole, or Poulton, for history, had directed more attention to the geographical coverage of the materials each describe, their research guides would be of greater assistance to those whose primary concerns are area studies, particularly area studies beyond North

America and Western Europe. Organization schemes with similar characteristics, reflecting similar conceptual oversight or lack of concern for area studies, are employed by other standard research guides.

Again, the intent of this discussion is neither to condemn nor ridicule. On the contrary, these suggestions are made to justify a conceptual reorientation in which the primary concern is to sharpen all researchers' perceptions of the patterns of literature coverage that prevail among intermediary sources in the social sciences for particular geographical areas. More importantly, they are offered as a means of making researchers more aware of specific strategies to employ in light of these patterns of literature coverage. In some cases, by simply reorganizing the materials described, the ideal of giving more systematically complete coverage could perhaps be more closely approximated. More significantly, gaps in the coverage of such research guides would be more easily detected.

The organization schemes of the AGS *Research Catalogue* and of the HRAF can be instructive in this context. At the very least, both inform us that it is worth considering different attitudes and perspectives toward our current conceptions of how reference materials in the social sciences are most effectively organized. By employing organization schemes in which the primary concern is systematic geographical coverage, gaps detected in such coverage are instructive to reference librarians, instructor-researchers, and students alike.

First, reference librarians know which the geographical areas are inadequately represented in their collections, and they also know the supporting reference materials. Thus, they have an opportunity for more deliberate, systematic development. Equally important, they can help researchers effectively exploit the existing collections.

Second, to instructor-researchers engaging in inquiry for their own purposes, acquaintance with the limited or inadequate coverage of their substantive fields by intermediary sources in library reference departments gives an opportunity for working jointly with the library in collection development. Informed of gaps in coverage by intermediary sources prevailing in their respective areas of substantive concern, instructor-researchers can collectively attempt to improve the coverage of the social-scientific literature in these areas. This goal can be achieved in several ways. Collective action by professional groups has resulted in the production of such excellent works as the multivolume *Handbook of Middle American Indians*,[16] the forthcoming *Handbook of North American Indians*,[17] and the volumes edited by Horecky on the U.S.S.R. and Eastern Europe,[18] to name just a few.

All of these suggested goals are, of course, part of the oft-repeated litany of the library profession, and to a greater or lesser degree, all reference librarians are engaged in promoting them. The greatest benefits, however, can accrue to students; it is for them that opportunities for integrating library research into courses in area studies are greatest. With these considerations in mind, the following chapter proposes a conceptual framework for library-produced research guides in area studies.

Notes

1. Carl M. White and associates, eds., *Sources of Information in the Social Sciences*, 2d ed. (Chicago: American Library Association, 1973). The discussion below of the works of White and Poulton are adapted from my article, "Integrating Classroom Instruction and Library Research: An Essay-Review," *Studies in History and Society* 6 (1974-1975):31-65.

2. White, *Sources of Information in the Social Sciences*, p. XVI.

3. Limiting an examination of this research guide to a single discipline may be questioned by some readers as unnecessarily harsh. My experience suggests, however, that, except for anthropology, a similar situation prevails generally in the other disciplines.

4. White, *Sources of Information in the Social Sciences*, p. 89.

5. Ibid., pp. 104-8.

6. Ibid., pp. 111-4.

7. Ibid., p. XVI.

8. Ibid., pp. 121-3.

9. Ibid., p. 104.

10. Ibid., p. 526.

11. A colleague, a specialist in Chinese history, has reminded me that area studies, at its best, is merely a restoration of the unity of humanistic studies, which both sinology (the old term for the multidisciplinary study of China) and classical studies have never really abandoned.

12. Helen Poulton, *The Historian's Handbook* (Norman, Okla.: University of Oklahoma Press, 1972).

13. Ibid., p. 48.

14. Ibid., pp. 30-60.

15. Jean Sauvaget's *Introduction to the History of the Muslim East* (Berkeley, Calif.: University of California Press, 1965) covers the Muslim world—the West (North Africa, Spain in the Middle Ages, and, for a time, Sicily) and the East (Arabia, Syria, Palestine and Mesopotamia, Egypt, Iran, and neighboring countries, and from the eleventh century on, Turkey). Most emphasis is given to the East. The two areas are treated differently because Islam originated in the East, and its center of gravity remained there; thus, for a well-founded understanding of Islam, a close study of the eastern part of the Muslim world is indispensable. It is further noted that, although the West is "less rich and less original," it has received greater scholarly attention. Thus, Sauvaget seeks to provide a more accurate perspective on the greater influence of the East, emphasizing historical development rather than geography. Although each country within the Islamic world varies in the time of its departure from the Middle Ages to modern times—"the moment when it was diverted from its

independent path by pressure from Europe"—each country is covered up to the modern period, "but [coverage] nowhere antedates the nineteenth century."

16. Robert Wauchope, ed., *Handbook of Middle American Indians*, 11 vols. (Austin, Tex.: University of Texas Press, 1964-1976).

17. William C. Sturtevant, ed., *Handbook of North American Indians* (Washington, D.C.: Smithsonian Institution Press, in press).

18. Paul L. Horecky, ed., *Basic Russian Publications* (Chicago: University of Chicago Press, 1965); *Russia and the Soviet Union* (Chicago: University of Chicago Press, 1965); *East Central Europe* (Chicago: University of Chicago Press, 1969); *Southeastern Europe* (Chicago: University of Chicago Press, 1969).

25 A Conceptual Framework for Research Guides in Area Studies

In proposing a conceptual framework for research guides in area studies, it becomes evident that greater emphasis should be given the integrative and analytical functions they can perform. It is assumed that under normal circumstances researchers can effectively examine the substantive literature in their field by limiting their searches to the bibliographic and substantive intermediary sources falling in divisions on the left side of Figure 10 or the top half of Figure 22. This assumption requires qualification.

First, much of the research conducted in the social sciences is concerned with the social phenomena of particular geographical areas (e.g., political institutions of Africa, social-demographic characteristics of Latin America). On the one hand, social scientists who concentrate on areas outside either North America or Western Europe are traditionally identified as Africanists or sinologists or Latin Americanists, even though these instructor-researchers pursue particular disciplinary specialties (e.g., political science) in these areas. On the other hand, instructor-researchers on the social institutions of either the United States or Western Europe are not identified as specialists in American Studies or European Studies. Instead, they are primarily identified by their general disciplinary specialty. There are, it is true, groups of scholars in North America and Europe which do indeed identify themselves as primarily engaged in American Studies or in European Studies. Further, a general shift toward an area studies orientation by greater numbers of researchers is occurring with increasing rapidity, stimulated primarily by the increased concern for interdisciplinary or cross-disciplinary inquiry.[1]

Second, the majority of social science research deals with American society, as is confirmed by examining the ratio of the number of empirical studies on American society to the total number of studies on the rest of the world. American social institutions are the most intensely examined institutions in the world, in part because there are far more social scientists in the United States than elsewhere.

Taken together, these two features of social inquiry have had, and continue to have, considerable influence on *how* research is conducted, on *what* research is conducted but, more significantly, on *how the literature resulting from this inquiry is organized and retrieved.* In such a context, as will be shown below, the integrative and analytical functions which research guides can perform become more fully evident.

Let's review some of the arguments with which the discussion about levels of specificity in research materials is concerned. Earlier in the discussion of Figure 10 it is suggested that to six levels of specificity of coverage by intermediary sources can be distinguished, given the bibliographic and substantive components of area studies literature. The idea of levels of specificity is further elaborated in Figure 22 which proposes that research strategy in a specific geographical area can instructively be based on a conceptual framework comprising a compound matrix of intermediary sources. The foundation of both notions is the tripartite matrix, which seeks to relate the functions of intermediary sources to the underlying structures and components of social-scientific literature.

The tripartite matrix can help students visualize and develop research strategy. (Often, too, individual instructors admit that the matrix sharpens their own perceptions of how best to conduct inquiry.) Admittedly, to some, the term *compound matrix* gives an abstruse, overly complex connotation to a concept that is epistemologically sound and not difficult to understand. Admittedly, too, difficulty can occur when the literature of a research topic is not pictured as being embedded within the structure of a larger body of social-scientific literature.

The important point, however, is that, the research procedure proposed here is not suggested as a rigid procedure to be imposed on researchers, but rather as a means of informing researchers about a conceptual framework that *can* be used as a mode of inquiry. It is important, then, that researchers understand how a topic's literature is embedded within the structure of a larger body of literature. (The structural characteristics of social-scientific literature is discussed in Part II.)

A third qualification is that the interrelated characteristics of intermediary sources, often implicit, both between and among the various levels of specificity, should be understood and appreciated.

One particularly difficult conceptual problem is that reference works conceptualized as intermediary sources exist on several levels of specificity. Seldom, at any given level of specificity, in each of the divisions of the tripartite matrix, are there always available representative intermediary sources. As noted in Chapter 24, this situation prevails to a greater extent in the lower or narrower sections of Figures 10 and 22. Indeed, it is perhaps unusual, at a given level of specificity, that *all* divisions of the tripartite matrix will contain representative intermediary sources.

The experienced reference librarian and the experienced researcher take such situations in stride. If, for example, a dictionary or encyclopedia of politics for a particular geographical area has not been produced or is otherwise not available, they recognize that alternative research means exist. It is then desirable that a similar intermediary source be sought out at another level of specificity, where a suitable substitute may *perhaps* be found. Polanyi's notion of a tacit dimension, or what is called tacit logic in this discussion, as well as the arguments of Ravetz, Koestler, Bruner, and others (discussed in Part II), touch on this creative aspect of research. Much of the "success" achieved by researchers in these situations depend upon their own intellectual creativity which, as noted in Parts II and III, is considered part of the craft of reference librarians and researchers alike.

In such circumstances, the integrative and analytical functions that research guides in area studies can perform are of particular importance, especially for inexperienced researchers. (Moreover, research guides are useful devices for reminding reference librarians themselves of what sources exist in a field.) The importance of stressing both the *pattern* of coverage of the bibliographic and substantive components of social-scientific literature, and the *process* of developing research strategies, becomes more fully evident in area studies. Library-produced research guides are especially useful for the special circumstances of local situations.

In both Figures 10 and 22, access to social-scientific literature is achieved by using research instruments which provide intermediate forms or stages— individually, or in various combinations—of the substantive and bibliographic components of that same literature. Among intermediary sources at any level of specificity is a matrix consisting of the substantive-bibliographic continuum and the functions of intermediary sources.

Intermediary sources at a given level of specificity—for example, that which is labeled comprehensive or general—provide access to the literature of a research topic, but this is achieved both in a special way and from a particular perspective. Greenstein and Polsby's *Handbook of Political Science*, for example, treats aspects of political instruments and customs in a general and comparative perspective.[2] That is, African political characteristics are compared or contrasted with similar characteristics in other parts of the world. Nevertheless, researchers, whether in bibliographic or substantive areas, are given a point of departure for more intensive inquiry, or quite simply, a clarification of an uncertainty.

By moving to another level of specificity of either Figure 10 or Figure 22— for example, that which is labeled specific geographical area or discipline in a specific geographical area—access to the empirical literature of that same topic is achieved, but from a more highly defined perspective. The chapter by Glickman in Lystad's *African World*, for example, examines the literature of Africa's political institutions in a very specific perspective.[3]

In each of the above examples, although the level of specificity and the matrix of intermediary sources changes, access is provided to the same body of social-scientific literature in which the topic is embedded.

This notion is made clearer and more concrete in Figure 23. This figure further demonstrates not only that intermediary sources expose the intermediate forms or stages of substantive and bibliographic components of social-scientific literature, but also that these intermediate forms or stages are exposed at various levels of specificity, depending on the perspective needed in a particular situation. Most importantly, the research topic is pictured as being embedded within the larger body of social-scientific literature. (The literature, which makes up two of the three parts of the tripartite matrix, comprises both bibliographic and substantive components of the literature; this notion is extensively outlined in Chapters 9 and 10.)

In Figure 23, intermediary sources giving access to substantive or bibliographic components are visualized as fixed apertures which give particular perspectives (i.e., levels of specificity) of the bibliographic and substantive components of the topic within the larger body of literature. (The intermediary sources portion of Figure 23 makes up the third part of the tripartite matrix.)

The researcher, the third part of Figure 23, is visualized as having available a variety of perspectives or specificities of the topic's literature. At the comprehensive level, for example, outlines of the topic are general, lacking clarity and definition. Detail about substantive content is brief, and only a few of the principal contributors are identified. In general, greater concern is directed toward how the literature of the topic is related to theoretical considerations within the larger body of social-scientific literature in which the literature of the topic is embedded.

As the researcher moves to a lower level (as illustrated in Figure 23), the specific outlines of the topic become more clearly defined. Intermediary sources at these levels make more direct reference to specific examples of the empirical literature. What is vital to this concept, of course, is that the researcher understands the underlying principle of moving from one level to another, in search of the intermediary source that most satisfactorily meets a need in a particular research problem.

To some reference librarians, the above arguments may seem arbitrary and unnecessarily confusing. Such would certainly be true if they attempted to transmit the entire concept to students and other researchers, without adequate development or qualification. This, however, is not intended in the foregoing discussion. On the contrary, the purpose is to establish a conceptual framework for the organization of area studies research materials that will acquaint researchers in area studies with the full range of materials available to them rather than only with those materials specifically related to particular disciplinary specialties or geographical areas. Moreover, the major concern is for the student, the inexperienced researcher.

If researchers become informed of the full range of available materials before less efficient research habits become rigidly ingrained, they will likely

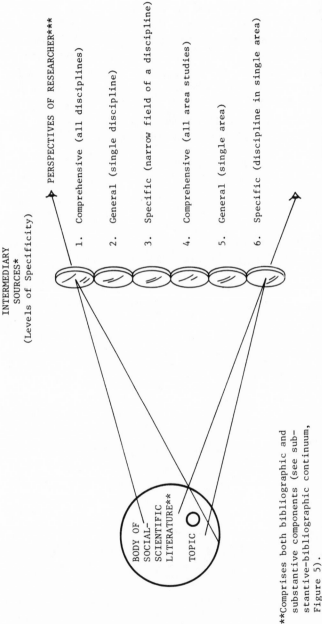

INTERMEDIARY
SOURCES*
(Levels of Specificity)

PERSPECTIVES OF RESEARCHER***

1. Comprehensive (all disciplines)

2. General (single discipline)

3. Specific (narrow field of a discipline)

4. Comprehensive (all area studies)

5. General (single area)

6. Specific (discipline in single area)

BODY OF
SOCIAL-
SCIENTIFIC
LITERATURE**

TOPIC

**Comprises both bibliographic and
substantive components (see substantive-bibliographic continuum,
Figure 5).

*Comprises third part of tripartite
matrix, (see Figure 5).

***At the comprehensive level,
outlines of topic lack clarity
and definition. As researcher
moves to a lower level (in
illustration) perspective of
topic through intermediary
sources becomes more clearly
defined.

Figure 23. Conception of Suggested Levels of Specificity of Intermediary
Sources for Disciplinary Studies and for Area Studies (III)

be more receptive to these suggestions and they will actually employ modes of inquiry that reflect an acquaintance with the levels of specificity among research materials discussed above. Similar arguments can be given for reference librarians, both in regard to how they are educated in library school and to the modes of operation adopted in their professional positions. More significantly, the foregoing considerations are parallel with the desires for improving instruction, especially undergradute instruction, noted in Chapter 2. By joining with groups of scholars, from among the disciplines, interested in promoting greater amounts of independent study and other library-related activities on national, regional, and local levels, reference librarians could realize definite progress toward achieving these ideals.

Notes

1. Cf. Thelma Freides, *The Literature and Bibliography of the Social Sciences* (Los Angeles: Melville Publishing Co., 1973), Chapter 2; and the Behavioral and Social Science Survey volumes noted at the beginning of Chapter 2.

2. Fred I. Greenstein and Nelson W. Polsby, eds., *Handbook of Political Science*, 8 vols. and cumulative index (Reading, Mass.: Addison-Wesley, 1975).

3. Harvey Glickman, "African Political Affairs," in Robert Lystad, ed., *The African World* (New York: Praeger, 1965).

Part VI

SUMMARY AND CONCLUSIONS

In this work, we have examined both the problems and the opportunities with which academic libraries are confronted when seeking closer working relationships between the classroom and the library. Some of the evidence presented is bleak and depressing, and tends to discourage reference librarians from becoming more actively engaged in promoting library research programs for undergraduates. Other evidence, however, points to opportunities which, if thoughtfully developed and skillfully implemented, can do much, in Knapp's words, "to make the library a more dynamic instrument of learning."

Because they possess both cognitive and heuristic qualities, the structural characteristics of social-scientific literature are suggested as a focus for developing library-oriented research programs in those disciplines. Specifically, they can encourage instructor-researchers to employ the library more directly in course-related activities.

As one means of achieving these ends, it is proposed that the epistemological foundations of reference materials become the nucleus around which research programs using library-produced research guides can be developed. The principles and applications of research guides in the social sciences present rich opportunities if organized on the foundations provided by the structural characteristics of the social-scientific literature to which they are related. In some respects, this notion has even greater validity within the narrower context of area studies research guides.

Motivating Instructors and Students

In connection with the opportunities for developing undergraduate library research programs that are more firmly grounded in classroom activities, it is suggested that the problem of motivating students to engage in serious research depends to a large extent on the attitude of instructors. Ironically, except for the very narrow aspects of their specialties, instructors in general have limited perceptions of the range and scope of research materials typically available in academic libraries. Their lack of awareness deters the development of well-grounded research-oriented programs for undergraduates. Hence, developing effective library programs becomes as much a problem of sharpening the perceptions of instructors, both as researchers and as teachers, as one of adequately grounding students in research skills and strategies.

Issues relating to the above considerations include the inseparability of teaching and research for enhancing the quality of instruction; and the concern among instructors for students' comprehension and retention of subject matter. With regard to the inseparability of teaching and research, Jencks and Riesman state: "Teachers cannot remain stimulating unless they also continue to learn. . . . When a teacher stops doing [research], he begins to repeat himself, and eventually loses touch with both the young and the world around him."[1] While some may consider this issue to be outside the traditional concerns of reference librarians, an acquaintance with it is an aid to developing proposals for library-oriented research programs.

As to concern about the comprehension and retention of subject matter among students, although much is speculative at the moment, Piaget, Bruner, Bell and others point to the importance of emphasizing the structure of the discipline as a means of improving comprehension and retention of subject matter. The structural orientation toward subject matter implicit in Epstein's "experience-based learning" and Washburn's "case studies method" seems to confirm this. Within the context of a rapidly expanding body of social-scientific literature and, concomitantly, the attendant obsolescence of portions of it—rather than merely seeking improved ways of imparting knowledge, as is the concern of many educators—improving instruction ideally includes a commitment to developing students' understanding of the processes and patterns of research in specific fields of inquiry and to having students engage in research as part of course requirements.

Implicit in these proposed reforms in instruction is that the emphasis in learning is shifting from *what* one learns to *how* one learns. As these changes become more clearly manifest, inevitably students will make greater demands on the library but, it is hoped, a different kind of demand than is characteristic today.

Given these anticipated realignments in the way courses are conducted and the expected requirements, if instructors and librarians can work together cooperatively, students, instructors, and librarians alike can achieve greater satisfaction and reward in matters relating to student research. Resolving certain problems associated with these research-oriented programs will not be easy. Merely acknowledging that problems exist is not enough. Reference librarians should consider what means are available—individual and collective—for effecting (or, perhaps, even fostering) changes and reforms in library policies and in instructor-librarian relationships.

The evidence of concern with problems of student comprehension and retention, as well as some attempts to implement innovative approaches to instruction and learning, augur well for increased library involvement. Among the most promising works in this area are those by Epstein, a biologist, and Weckstein, an economist, and the case-studies method proposed by Washburn.

Implicit in these newer approaches to learning is a desire to infuse in students the craft skills of the intellectual, skills which Bayley claims are almost entirely neglected today. By fusing the development of craft skills with students' learning, the problems of comprehension and retention acquire a different perspective and, in the end, are resolved in a different manner. Bayley, reacting to what he provocatively calls the "emptiness of curriculum reform," proposes courses designed to encourage students to independently, imaginatively, and purposefully investigate, reflect upon, and communicate lucidly the rich substantive contents of disciplines. Most of his suggestions are directed toward the social sciences.

Through such reforms, education would be visualized as learning a craft, where indeed the emphasis would shift from *what* one learns to *how* one learns. In such a context, craft is refined through practice and is undertaken not so much to demonstrate proficiency as to show what skills need to be improved so that greater proficiency can be achieved. Basically, learning a craft involves inquiry, reflection, discussion, writing, and a host of other skills which, although their underlying principles can be taught through precept, contain certain tacit dimensions, which are ultimately refined through practice and experience. The library's role in resolving these matters is secondary to the teacher's role, but even so, acquaintance with them is useful whenever library-oriented programs for students are being considered.

The faculty members' knowledge of the kind of support the library can give such programs often determines the extent of student activities in the library for particular courses. However, even the most well-informed faculty have curious gaps in their acquaintance with the library. Hence, no reference librarian should be too concerned about repeating himself about library services.

Other factors influencing instructors' attitudes toward teaching, research, and higher education in general must also be recognized. Perhaps the greatest influence on faculty behavior is the faculty reward system. According to one writer, since teaching is difficult to evaluate, it must be recognized that research, not teaching, is rewarded. "As a consequence, research flourishes at the expense of teaching."[2]

Perhaps some readers will see a contradiction between a concern, on the one hand, for the necessity of research to enhance teaching and a recognition, on the other hand, that research, not teaching, appears to carry more weight in matters of tenure and promotion. Perhaps there is some contradiction here. Experience suggests, however, that even though most faculty members recognize that tenure and promotion are tilted toward research, they are able to keep the matter in reasonable perspective. Further, since in most cases they enjoy teaching, considerable effort is directed toward refining it.

Students, as individuals, also enter these matters in unique ways. Among examples in Chapter 1 are problems associated, first, with the composition of student subcultures and, second, with different preferred learning styles among individuals. Clark and Trow, for example, suggest that there are four fairly distinct student subcultures on college campuses: the academic, the nonconformist, the collegiate, and the vocational. Of the four, the academic subculture holds the most promise for promoting effective library research programs. Grieneck's findings suggest that greater support and nurturing of the academic subculture, within and outside the library, would result in greater numbers of students retaining their initial preference for professional development. Not unrelated to the issues relating to student subcultures are the preferred learning styles of individuals. Learning styles among individuals, since they are dictated to a larger extent by personality characteristics than previously thought possible, also deserve to be given greater attention by instructors and librarians alike. (In this work, they are considered in connection with the psychological structure of a literature.)

Instructor-Researchers' Concern for Student Research

The concerns touched on above, as they apply to undergraduate instruction, acquire more validity when we examine the proposals by individuals and groups in the social sciences for reform in teaching and learning in higher education. Some groups and individuals within anthropology, economics, geography, history, political science, and sociology want to strengthen student learning by requiring more independent student research in undergraduate courses. It is appropriate that some exploratory efforts be directed toward organizing joint actitvities between these groups and like-minded librarians.

The Cognitive Functions of the Structures of Scientific Literature

In some respects, it appears almost ludicrous to suggest that an acquaintance with individual characteristics of inquiry in each discipline, as well as with definite parallel features among them, is important for instructor-researchers, students, and reference librarians alike. After all, such matters constitute the bulk of their day-to-day activities. However much of the foregoing may be assumed to be true, it is not. The fact that the characteristics of modes of inquiry of various disciplines are not well known is perhaps most forcefully demonstrated when we acknowledge how recently such phenomena as scientific revolutions, paradigms, and citation networks have been exposed in a perspective that allows taking advantage of them. Thus, in retrospect, it is quite easy for us both to lament the tortuously slow advances in these matters and to give lip service to an idealized conception of progress.

For reference librarians, an acquaintance with what is entailed in inquiry in their respective fields of responsibility enables them to realize how reference works are related to specific bodies of literature. This realization enhances their command of these materials, thereby enabling them to provide greater assistance to researchers. To this end, it is argued in Part II that reference librarians should have an acquaintance with the purpose, precepts, and conventions of the disciplines for which they are directly responsible. The discussion focuses primarily upon the social sciences, but certain of the principles that have been enunciated here apply to all areas of inquiry.

In the broadest sense, social scientists examine and explain human behavior and human institutions, both as a means of increasing society's understanding of the behavior of man in relation to his fellow men and the environment they share, and of providing a basis for planning and implementing social policies that meet human needs. This is a collective enterprise in which a group of researchers communicate to one another by various means what is known in a given field of inquiry.

The model for developing modes of inquiry and explanation in the social sciences is derived from the natural sciences, but because the precision of laboratory conditions characteristic of the natural sciences is difficult, or even impossible, to duplicate in the study of human behavior, necessarily many difficulties are encountered. Among these difficulties are (1) obtaining controlled conditions where human characteristics or activities being examined are not distorted either by the condition of the investigation or by the intrusion of the observer's values; (2) understanding and explaining how external manifestations of behavior are the result of, or are affected by, the internal or psychological component of human behavior; and (3) the social scientists' use of such terms as *sense of deprivation, morale,* and *role.* According to Nagel and others, such terms are derived from the current or popular vocabulary and are employed with little redefinition of "their vague common sense meanings."[3]

When explanations are constructed in the social sciences, the what, the why, and the how (or simply the cause) of social phenomena are considered. Explanation, it is suggested, in this book, is distinguished from description (which specifically concerns the what) by the addition of interpretation. Interpretation involves reducing the explanation of particular social phenomena to the smallest number of precepts that account for the specific facts considered.

Organized explanations are put forth as concepts which, among other things, identify, classify, and define attributes or characteristics of the social phenomena being investigated. Models for explanation called paradigms are shared by communities of researchers as part of a collective enterprise. Shared paradigms organize and guide inquiry, and insure that the results of these activities will be cumulative. Closely related to the conception of paradigms as shared models of inquiry and explanation among communities of researchers is the perception of knowledge as consensus. This perception means that the published results of research must be sifted and evaluated by the community of researchers in a specific field of inquiry. Ziman, among others, suggests that in the natural sciences the published results of research is first considered scientific information. After publication, there is a slow, erratic process of collectively assessing and integrating discrete findings into the existing body of literature. A similar process occurs in the social sciences. As this process occurs, the existing substantive content of the literature is also changing, where, through consensus, new findings displace previously agreed-upon formulations, indicating that the literature is fluid.

In this book, the subject matter of social scientists is identified as primary source material, or simply primary sources. It is recognized, however, that this material is also identified by such terms as *original documents, raw data,* or *primary data.* The published explanations of the meaning of this subject matter are called secondary source materials, or simply secondary sources. Primary sources are pictured as fixed or stable elements of inquiry, which is in contrast to the fluid quality of the explanation of them.

The different disciplines in the social sciences have different approaches to primary source materials, stemming from whether a discipline is primarily nomothetic or idiographic. If a generalizing mode of analysis is employed, where the intent is to construct laws which explain characteristic patterns in social processes and events, with little regard for the uniqueness of individual events, the discipline is said to be nomothetic. In contrast, if concern is directed toward explaining unique or individual social phenomena, the discipline is said to be idiographic. In this context, history is considered primarily idiographic, while other social science disciplines are considered primarily nomothetic. However, it is generally agreed that all social science disciplines deal with the unique and the general, the singular and the recurrent; the goals of the respective disciplines determine what combinations of these two perspectives are employed.

The production of social-scientific literature through disciplined inquiry is a creative act, requiring the craft skills of experienced researchers. Craft skills are acquired and refined from an association with more skilled researchers through apprenticeship and experience, by precept and imitation. Craft skills cannot be completely articulated or described in print. In this equation, intuition and tacit knowledge (or tacit logic) are as important as creativity. Polanyi used the terms *tacit knowledge* and *tacit logic* to explain those matters associated with inquiry which cannot be articulated which all the same have to be recognized as contributing to how individual social scientists are able to discover and understand social phenomena.

Kaplan addresses this problem by distinguishing between two types of logic with which he suggests a researcher operates: logic-in-use and reconstructed logic. Logic-in-use is not formalized, but by combining observation, imagination, intuition, and inspiration, researchers can derive specific conclusions. Reconstructed logic is the formalized procedure employed for setting forth what has been discovered through logic-in-use; it may bear little resemblance to the means by which certain discoveries were actually made, and in a sense it can be considered an idealization of the logic employed.

The form or structure assumed by a particular growing literature is influenced by several factors. For example, along with a so-called formal structure (i.e., ordering literature into hierarchical flowchart-like schemes), it can be argued that social-scientific literature has a natural structure. Natural structure relates both to the sequence in which a given literature was generated and to the mature researchers' mental images of it. Natural structure, in other words, relates both to the bibliographic and to the substantive structure of a literature.

Bibliographic structure refers both to the chronological sequence in which the secondary source literature was published and to the manner in which discrete studies are embedded in the existing literature of that same field. In order to obtain credibility, a given study refers (by a convention known as the footnote reference or bibliographic citation) to that material in the preexisting consensus which validates many of the claims made in it. In this manner, new contributions are considered to add to the cumulating body of literature in a particular field. A research front is indicated by the pattern assumed by citations.

The bibliographic structure is fixed; discrete contributions to a literature are permanently placed in the published records of research in the chronological sequence in which they appear. For instructional purposes, several attempts have been made to graphically depict the bibliographic structure of particular topics of inquiry. The most notable attempt is Garfield's use of historiographs. Others are Skelton's citation networks and MacGregor and McInnis's bibliographic network structures. All are based on the concept of a primordial citation, or key source—the first or base study which forms the foundation upon which all subsequent studies linked to it are built.

Implied in the concept of bibliographic structure is the idea that it forms the framework which supports and contains the substantive content of that body of literature. By substantive structure is meant the shape assumed by the cumulation of the substantive content of discrete contributions in a field as a consensus is achieved. Substantive structure is, therefore, the fluid component of scientific literature. The notion of substantive structure is necessarily a problem of conceptualizing subject matter concretely.

Conceptualizing subject matter concretely is made easier by the realization that, along with the formation of new configurations of the substantive content of a literature, both a diachronic and a synchronic structure of that same literature is formed. Synchronic structure refers to that body of substantive literature which at a particular moment, through consensus, is considered valid. In contrast, diachronic structure encompasses the entire corpus of discrete contributions to a body of literature.

The notion of the psychological structure of a literature gives some insight into how individuals become acquainted with the substantive structure of that literature. It refers to the cognitive processes (many of them tacit, learned from mature researchers through precept and imitation) by which an increasingly larger and more complex understanding of a literature that corresponds to the existing substantive structure of that literature is achieved. According to Kolb, individuals achieve this understanding in a variety of ways, which he calls preferred learning styles.

In this work, attention is directed to some examples of instruction which contain elements of inquiry as a mode of learning; under the right circumstances, these elements could be incorporated into library research programs. These modes of instruction are considered promising because, directly and indirectly, they introduce many of the skills, precepts, and conventions characteristic of the intellectual craft of mature researchers.

Reference Works as Intermediary Sources

Upon further analysis, in addition to the bibliographic and substantive, the literature of disciplined inquiry in the social sciences can be seen to have other characteristics of structure. These characteristics inform us of important considerations about understanding that literature and about retrieving portions of it. The instruments designed to inform us about this literature, to give order and coherence to particular bodies of literature, and to aid in the retrieval of portions of it are traditionally called reference works.

The function of reference works in these fields becomes more logical to potential researchers not acquainted with them if they are set forth as intermediate forms or stages of the literature to which they are related. Such an understanding is especially useful when giving instruction about their use. Ideally, the instruction is preceded with a grounding in the underlying structure of scientific literature. It must be acknowledged, however, that these instruments are produced because of a perceived need, not because of some preexisting grand design. In this sense, intermediary sources are artificial constructs, and necessarily their existence and function must be taught.

Because they are artificial constructs, produced by individuals and groups in largely unpremeditated fashion, situations often occur where, on the one hand, a particular field is saturated with intermediary sources, and where, on the other, another field has fragmented and uneven coverage.

The treatment given both the substantive and bibliographic components of a literature in intermediary sources occurs in special ways. It may be suggested then that intermediary sources in effect provide intermediate forms or stages of the larger bodies of literature which they represent. The substantive and bibliographic elements of a literature are almost always treated in a distilled or summary format. Here intermediary sources function either as instruments of analysis in which discrete elements of a given literature are considered individually (as they are in indexes, abstract journals, and bibliographies), or as instruments of synthesis, in which discrete elements of that same literature are considered in an integrated format (as they are in encyclopedias, dictionaries, and reviews of research).

The ideas of several writers on the structure and function of intermediary sources contain elements of the notions touched on above. Knapp, for example, suggests that considering the communication patterns in the published records of research as a system of "ways" substantially helps to overcome the obstacles that are encountered in libraries, where materials must be treated according to the format of publication. Building on Knapp's foundation, Freides proposes the idea of "tuning in," that is, once potential users become acquainted with the underlying communication patterns of the literature, as well as the parallel features of the structure and function of the instruments designed to give access to it, they can utilize them more effectively for both learning and research.

As a means of achieving these ends, it is argued that a research model, the tripartite matrix (Figure 5), and a mode of inquiry, tentatively called structured inquiry, hold considerable promise. In the tripartite matrix, the two structural components of scientific literature networks, bibliographic structure and substantive structure, are placed at either end of a continuum. A third component, reference works—conceptualized as intermediary sources—is superimposed on the continuum. The functions of intermediary sources create a matrix of five divisions. Intermediary sources in each division expose either substantive portions, bibliographic portions, or different combinations of these two components, of particular literature networks. An understanding of the function of the key source, the base study to which subsequent studies of a particular topic of inquiry are linked, is central to the notion of the tripartite matrix.

Divisions on the continuum serve as guides to developing research strategies by informing researchers of the functions of the different types of intermediary sources and of the relationships, largely tacit or implicit, that exist among them. Facility in using intermediary sources for the purpose for which they are intended requires an acquaintance with them, an acquaintance acquired by using them in research exercises. Structured inquiry is one means of providing a grounding in research procedures.

Actual examples of the results of structured inquiry are given. In the first example, the Clark and Trow typology of student subcultures, the relative efficiency of particular intermediary sources for exposing portions of a literature network are illustrated graphically (Figures 6, 7, 8, and 9). The second example comprises a set of actual pages of intermediary sources which expose increasingly complex formulations of both substantive and bibliographic portions of the literature on Katz and Braly's classic study of stereotypes and the conflicting explanations of kinship patterns in anthropology (Appendix A). These examples are keyed to library-produced research guides for psychology and sociology and to anthropology. Thus, it can be concluded that there is a tacit logic of research strategy, that this logic can be raised to the level of awareness, and that research strategy can be refined by intelligent and purposeful application.

Library-Produced Research Guides in the Social Sciences

Because they are artificial constructs, the principles and applications of intermediary sources must be taught. More satisfactory results in instructing students about sound research strategies occur if the materials they will be using are introduced in the context of an actual research problem related to their immediate research needs. Library-produced research guides which incorporate the principles of structured inquiry are one means of informing students about research strategies.

In constructing research guides in the social sciences (which includes area studies), the intent is to produce a research instrument that is logically integrated and internally coherent, so that definite patterns of inquiry are almost self-evident. How intermediary sources are arranged in research guides determines in large part how individual researchers, especially the inexperienced, approach a particular field of inquiry. Stress should be placed on the research process rather than on specific library matrials. Structured inquiry, as a mode of research, is an example in which process is the organizing principle of research guides.

Organization and annotation emerge as particular problems. Organization is the manner in which specific intermediary sources are arranged in relation to the substantive-bibliographic continuum so that their functions are made evident. Recognition must also be given the fact that, on the one hand, some intermediary sources attempt to cover an entire discipline (or disciplines), while, on the other hand, other intermediary sources limit their coverage to narrow subdivisions of these same disciplines. In constructing research guides, this means that several levels of specificity of literature coverage by intermediary sources must be considered. In area studies, it is suggested that it is possible to distinguish at least six levels of specificity of coverage in which intermediary sources give the substantive and bibliographic components of the literature.

Annotation, in contrast to organization, is the manner in which particular intermediary sources are explained in research guides, so that their specific functions and relative strengths, in relation to the substantive-bibliographic continuum, are made evident. This is called the analytical function of research guides. Equally significant in developing notions of sound research strategy are the recommended combinations in research guides in which specific intermediary sources can be used. This is called the integrative function of research guides. In effect, the amount of detail research guides give about the structure, function, and content of each item, and the recommended combinations for using them, are a problem of giving instruction about inquiry as a research process. The coverage by intermediary sources of the literature of alcoholism and of marriage and the family, for example, indicates the importance of specifying in research guides the patterns of literature coverage of those topics.

The problems of organization and annotation become more acute in area studies. Since the substantive literature of area studies should be considered part of the larger bodies of social-scientific literature which provides their foundation, it is seen that in area studies research guides intermediary sources can be set forth in a conceptual framework which comprises a compound matrix of intermediary sources consisting of more than two levels of specificity of coverage. This is simply an elaboration or extension of the organizing principles of research guides in the social sciences.

Notes

1. Christopher Jencks and David Riesman, *The Academic Revolution* (Garden City, N.Y.: Doubleday, 1968), p. 532, as cited by Charles D. Hadley, "Teaching Political Scientists: The Centrality of Research," *PS* 5 (Summer 1972):262.

2. Hadley, "Teaching Political Scientists: The Centrality of Research," p. 262. Hadley refers to proposals for improving teaching advanced by Jencks and Riesman and by Kerr. See Jencks and Riesman, *The Academic Revolution*, pp. 531-9; and Clark Kerr, *The Uses of the University* (Cambridge, Mass.: Harvard University Press, 1963), pp. 103-5, 118.

3. Ernest Nagel, *The Structure of Science* (New York: Harcourt, Brace and World, 1961), p. 506.

Appendix A

The following pages illustrate Wilson Library's method of demonstrating to a large class, first, how to use a library-produced research guide to discover intermediary sources (i.e., reference works) containing bibliographic and substantive information on a particular topic, and second, how to expose students to typical pages from specific intermediary sources containing material on that topic. Portions of pages from specific intermediary sources are, in each case, preceded by the annotation for that source contained in Western Washington University's library-produced research guides for psychology and anthropology. The method is tentatively called structured inquiry.

In actual practice, pages from the research guides included in this appendix are presented to students within the context of the research guides for psychology or sociology and for anthropology as organized guides to research materials on specific disciplines. Thus, two important aspects of developing research strategy in a particular field are demonstrated simultaneously.

First, in demonstrating how certain intermediary sources expose bibliographical and substantive information on a topic, students obtain a notion of how the research guide can be used to expose information on their own topic. (Particular attention is directed toward how the annotations give evidence of the function and scope of specific intermediary sources.)

Second, each student is given the opportunity to observe at close hand the kind of information typically available in several intermediary sources. This exercise most significantly demonstrates the largely implicit interrelatedness among intermediary sources.

Presentations on research guides are typically given in the classroom after some time is spent in the library so that students can become accustomed to where materials are located. When students are taken through the library first, they become better acquainted with the materials discussed in the lectures. The classroom presentations take from one to two hours, preferably two. In the first hour, the structure of social-scientific literature and the tripartite matrix are explained, and in the second hour, the research guide and the structured inquiry handout are presented as a mode of inquiry.

Each student is given a copy of the research guide and a copy of the structured inquiry handout. The research guide is introduced first. Such matters as its underlying organization and arrangement, the function of annotations, and the desirability of joint use of research guides are described.

Afterwards, the use of the research guide is demonstrated. For example, students are asked to turn to item I.c.14 in the psychology research guide. The annotation (or portions of it) is read aloud, and, if appropriate, other comments are made. While the actual volume is being held up in front of the class, students are asked to turn to page 1 of the structured inquiry handout on stereotypes, where they find an illustration taken from the volume. This procedure, that is, first examining an entry in the research guide and then looking at a sample entry from that intermediary source, is followed throughout.

In the library, smaller groups of students (the ideal size is ten or less) are taken on a loosely organized orientation tour that lasts an hour or more and more or less follows the sequence on the structured inquiry handout. Students are encouraged to be aware of the kind of problems they, as individual researchers, are apt to encounter in their own research. Such procedures enable them to view their own research strategy in relation to the items being discussed.

In Parts I and II the appropriate entry from a research guide is boxed. On the facing page is given the page from the structured inquiry handout which corresponds to the entry in the research guide. In some cases, because of the size of the annotation for the entry, only the bibliographical citations and the annotation for one entry is given (e.g., Lindzey and Aronson's *Handbook of Social Psychology*).

Part 1

AN ILLUSTRATION OF
STRUCTURED INQUIRY

The attached illustrations demonstrate how a student using "Psychology" Bibliography No. 25 or "Sociology" Bibliography No. 19 can locate information on a psychological or sociological research topic. By progressing in a step-by-step (i.e., structured) procedure, it is possible to advance from a point where little is known about a particular topic to the desired level of understanding of it.

Wilson Library
Reference Department
Western Washington State College
December 1976

I.c

which contains information on the topic. *See also* references, at the end of articles, direct users to related articles. "Subject maps," covering such topics as: abnormal and clinical psychology; emotion and motivation; intelligence; learning and memory; sensation and perception; and thinking and language, attempt to draw the reader's attention to the aggregate of articles which focus on aspects of these topics. The most useful feature, perhaps, is the frequent references to works to consult for more information. Profusely illustrated with photographs, charts, tables, etc. Joint use with Eysenck (I.c.15) is suggested.

Ref.
H41
.E6
[Ency.
Section]

13. *Encyclopedia of the Social Sciences.* Seligman, Edwin R.A. and Johnson, Alvin, eds. New York, Macmillan, 1930-35. 15 vols.

Attempts to present a synopsis or distillation of the progress made in the social sciences, to provide a repository of facts and principles useful to researchers in the subjects, and to create a body of authoritative knowledge to assist in promoting social progress and development. Includes articles on major topics in politics; economics, law, anthropology, sociology, penology and social work, with less attention given ethics, education, philosophy, psychology, and geography. There are some 4000 biographies of deceased persons whose work has been significant in these fields. Articles are of varying lengths, signed by the authors, and in an alphabetical arrangement. Cross-references to related articles are provided, and the final volume has a comprehensive index. Most articles have a brief bibliography.

Ref.
BF
31
.E58

14. English, Horace Bidwell. *A Comprehensive Dictionary of Psychological and Psychoanalytical Terms; a guide to usage.* 1st ed. New York, Longmans, Green, 1958.

"A useful reference (in crying need of updating) that includes in alphabetical order, terms denoting mental and behavioral phenomena and the constructs of concepts used in ordering these phenomena. Over 11,000 entries." (Marks)

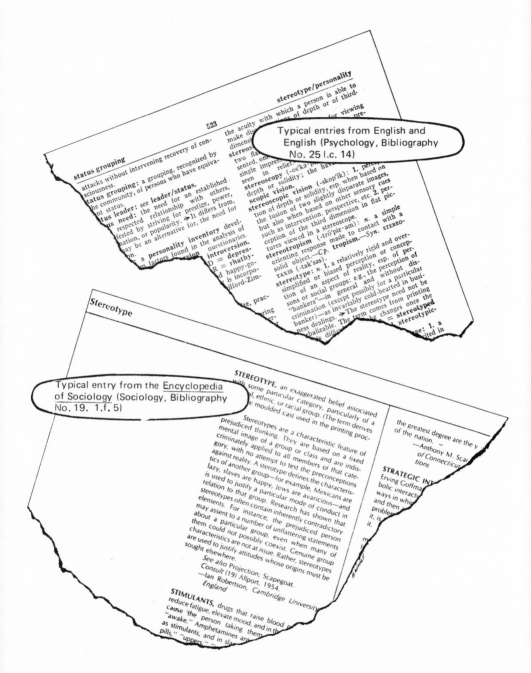

Typical entries from English and English (Psychology, Bibliography No. 25 l.c. 14)

status grouping

attacks without intervening recovery of consciousness.

status grouping: a grouping, recognized by the community, of persons who have equivalent status.

status leader: see **leader/status.**

status need: the need for an established, respected relationship with others, (tested by striving for prestige, power, domination, or popularity. → It differs from, and may be an alternative for, the need for ...

a personality inventory development ... factors found in the analysis of ... questionaries.
introversion.
D = depres-
R = rhathy-
... is incorpo-
...illford-Zim-

523

...the acuity with which a person is able to make dis...es of depth or of third-dimens...
stereo...
two fla...
single impres...
seen in relief...
stereoscopy (-os'ka-p... for viewing pre-
depth or solidity; the hav...
scopic vision.
stereoscopic vision (-skop'ik): **1.** perception of depth or solidity, esp. when based on the fusion of two slightly disparate images, but also when based on other sensory cues such as intervention, perspective, etc. **2.** perception of the third dimension in flat pictures viewed in a stereoscope. —*Syn.* STEREO-
stereotropism (-trō'piz·am): *n.* a simple orienting response made to contact with a solid object.—*Cp.* **tropism.**—*Syn.* STEREO-
TAXIS (-tak'sas).
stereotype: *n.* **1.** a relatively rigid and over-simplified or biased perception or conception of an aspect of reality, esp. of persons or social groups; e.g., the perception of "bankers"—in general and without discrimination (except possibly for a particular banker)—as invariably cold-hearted in business dealings. → The stereotype need not be ...balizable. The term comes from printing ...e changes once the ...e difficult ... = **stereotyped**
...stereotypic-
...ge: **1.** a
...ited in

Stereotype

Typical entry from the **Encyclopedia of Sociology** (Sociology, Bibliography No. 19. 1.f. 5)

STEREOTYPE, an exaggerated belief associated with some particular category, particularly of a ...al, ethnic, or racial group. (The term derives ...e moulded cast used in the printing proc-

Stereotypes are a characteristic feature of prejudiced thinking. They are based on a mental image of a group or class and are indiscriminately applied to all members of that category, with no attempt to test the preconceptions against reality. A stereotype defines the characteristics of another group—for example, Mexicans are lazy, slaves are happy, Jews are avaricious—and is used to justify a particular mode of conduct in relation to that group. Research has shown that stereotypes often contain inherently contradictory elements. For instance, the prejudiced person may assent to a number of unflattering statements about a particular group, even when many of them could not possibly coexist. Genuine group characteristics are not at issue. Rather, stereotypes are used to justify attitudes whose origins must be sought elsewhere.

See also Projection; Scapegoat.
Consult (19) Allport, 1954.
—Ian Robertson, *Cambridge University England*

STIMULANTS, drugs that raise blood ...reduce fatigue, elevate mood, and in th... cause the person taking them ... "awake." Amphetamines are ... as stimulants, and in sla... pills," "uppers," ...

the greatest degree are the y...
of the nation. -
—Anthony M. Sca...
of Connecticu...
tions

STRATEGIC IN...
Erving Goffma...
bolic interactio...
ways in whic...
and then ...
proble...
it, is...
it.

I.c

Ref.
BF
31
G6

16. Goldenson, Robert M. *The Encyclopedia of Human Behavior: Psychology, Psychiatry, and Mental Health.* 1st ed. Garden City, N.Y., Doubleday, 1970.

"Over 1,000 entries, from Aberration to Zen Buddhism, are dealt with in appropriate depth. The alphabetic arrangement is supplemented by a category index listing all articles by subject matter, a 5,000-item index including names and topics within articles, numerous cross references, and a lengthy list of references [for obtaining more information]. Illustration and illustrative cases enliven the text. The encyclopedia seems remarkably comprehensive and reasonably current." (*Personnel and Guidance Journal* 49:422 [1971])

Ref.
H41
.G6

17. Gould, Julius, and Kolb, William L., eds. *A Dictionary of the Social Sciences.* New York, Free Press of Glencoe, 1964.

Defines about one-fourth as many terms as Zadrozny (I.c.30), but the treatment of the terms is more intensive. There are more than 1,000 terms from anthropology and economics, but political science and sociological terms predominate; they are extensively defined by some 270 noted U.S. and British social scientists. With a few exceptions, entries are arranged as follows: A, the generally accepted meaning of the term; B, its historical background or a more extensive explanation. C, D, E, and so on are used where "controversies and divergencies of meaning have been explored and an attempt made to place them in their perspective." Many definitions are illustrated with quotes from authorities.

Ref.
BF
31
.H33
1965

18. Harriman, Philip Lawrence. *Handbook of Psychological Terms.* Totowa, New Jersey, Littlefield, Adams, 1965.

Brief definitions, some accompanied with illustrations and diagrams.

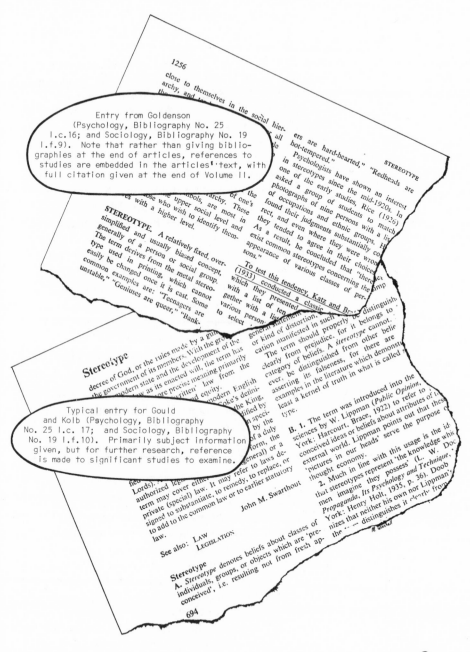

1256

close to themselves in the social hierarchy, and ...
the ...

*Entry from Goldenson
(Psychology, Bibliography No. 25
I.c.16; and Sociology, Bibliography No. 19
I.f.9). Note that rather than giving bibliographies at the end of articles, references to
studies are embedded in the articles' text, with
full citation given at the end of Volume II.*

ers are hard-hearted," "Redheads are
hot-tempered." ... STEREOTYPE

... of one's
... symbols, are most in
... ose who wish to identify them-
... with a higher level.

Psychologists have shown an interest
in stereotypes since the mid-1920s. In
one of the early studies, Rice (1926)
asked a group of students to match
photographs of nine persons with a list
of occupations and ethnic groups. He
found their judgments substantially correct, and even where they were wrong,
they tended to agree in their choices.
As a result, he concluded that "there
exist common stereotypes concerning the
appearance of various classes of persons."

STEREOTYPE. A relatively fixed, over-
simplified and usually biased concept.
The term derives from the metal stereotype used in printing, which cannot
easily be changed once it is cast. Some
common examples are: "Teenagers are
unstable," "Geniuses are queer," "Bank-

To test this tendency, Katz and Br...
(1933) conducted a classic ...
which they presented a ...
with a list of ten ...
gether with a li...
various person...
to select ...

... general statement ...
or kind of distortion. ...
cation manifested in such ... distinguish
clearly from prejudice, for it belongs to
category of beliefs. A *stereotype* cannot.
ever, be distinguished from other belie...
asserting its falseness, for there are
examples in the literature which demonstr...
least a kernel of truth in what is called
type.

Stereotype

decree of God, or the rules made by a gu...
the government of its members. With the gr...
modern state and the development of the
law as its enacted will, the term has
... ore precise meaning primarily
... written' law from the
... and equity.
... modern English
... oke's defini-
... the King,
... ified by
... speci-
... by the
... of a duly
... form, the
... general) or a
... refer to laws de-

*Typical entry for Gould
and Kolb (Psychology, Bibliography
No. 25 I.c. 17; and Sociology, Bibliography
No. 19 I.f.10). Primarily subject information
given, but for further research, reference
is made to significant studies to examine.*

Lords). ...
authorized leg...
term may cover either ...
private (special) law. It may refer to, replace, or
signed to substantiate, to remedy, to earlier statutory
to add to the common law or to ...
law.

John M. Swarthout

See also: LAW
         LEGISLATION

B. 1. The term was introduced into the
sciences by W. Lippman (*Public Opinion*,
York: Harcourt. Brace, 1922) to refer to
conceived ideas or beliefs about attributes of t...
external world. Lippman points out that these
'pictures in our heads' serve the purpose o...
thought economy.
   2. Much in line with this usage is the id...
that stereotypes represent 'the knowledge whic...
men imagine they possess' (L. W. Doo...
Propaganda, Its Psychology and Technique,
York: Henry Holt, 1935, p. 36). Doob
nizes that neither his own nor Lippman'...
the ... distinguishes it clearly from ...

Stereotype
A. *Stereotype* denotes beliefs about classes of
individuals, groups, or objects which are 'preconceived', i.e. resulting not from fresh ap-

694

Ref.   13. *Encyclopedia of the Social Sciences.* Seligman, Edwin
H41   R.A. and Johnson, Alvin, eds. New York, Macmillan,
.E6   1930-35. 15 vols.
[Ency.
Section]   Attempts to present a synopsis or distillation of the
                      progress made in the social sciences, to provide a
                      repository of facts and principles useful to researchers
                      in the subjects, and to create a body of authoritative
                      knowledge to assist in promoting social progress and
                      development. Includes articles on major topics in
                      politics, economics, law, anthropology, sociology,
                      penology and social work, with less attention given
                      ethics, education, philosophy, psychology, and
                      geography. There are some 4000 biographies of
                      deceased persons whose work has been significant in
                      these fields. Articles are of varying lengths, signed
                      by the authors, and in an alphabetical arrangement.
                      Cross-references to related articles are provided, and
                      the final volume has a comprehensive index. Most
                      articles have a brief bibliography.

Ref.   14. English, Horace Bidwell. *A Comprehensive Dictionary*
BF   *of Psychological and Psychoanalytical Terms; a guide*
31   *to usage.* 1st ed. New York, Longmans, Green, 1958.
.E58
                      "A useful reference (in crying need of updating) that
                      includes in alphabetical order, terms denoting mental
                      and behavioral phenomena and the constructs of
                      concepts used in ordering these phenomena. Over
                      11,000 entries." (Marks)

Ref.   15. Eysenck, H.J., et al, eds., *Encyclopedia of Psychology.*
BF   London, Herder and Herder, 1972. 3 vols.
31
E522   With over 300 contributors this work attempts to
                      provide international scope in its coverage. Among
                      the some 5000 articles are two kinds of entries: ordi-
                      nary definitions, occupying a line or two, which can
                      be found in most dictionaries; and, articles "covering
                      important terms and concepts, specially written by
                      well-known authorities, ranging up to 4000 words,"
                      (Foreword) and suggested sources of additional in-
                      formation. Numerous illustrations. A list of the main
                      articles in the set is given on pp. VII-XII of volume 1.
                      Use jointly with single-volume *Encyclopedia of Psy-*
                      chology (I.c.12).

Entry from Eysenck (Psychology, Bibliography No. 25 l.c.15) provides brief account of the concept "Stereotypes", what research has been conducted, and quite a large bibliography of sources of additional information.

273

way, monistic conception...
formalization form the basis...
experimental "mind-body" research.

Bibliography: Bechterewa, N. P., Bondartschuk, A. N., Smirnow, W. M. & Trochatschow, A. N.: ... und Pathophysiologie der tiefen Hirnstrukturen des Menschen. Berlin, 1969. Heath, R. G. & Mickle, W. A.: Evaluation of seven years experience with depth elec- trode studies in human patients. Electr. Studies on the unaesth. brain. New York, 1960. Riechert, T.: Die stereotaktischen Hirnoperationen zur Behandlung extrapyramidaler Bewegungsstörun- gen und ihre Resultate. Fortschr. Neurol. Psychiat., 1963, 3., 1-120. Spiegel, E. A. & Wycis, H. T.: Stereoeucephalotomy. New York, 1962. Umbach, W.: Elektrophysiol. und negative Phänomene bei stereo- taktischen Hirnoperationen. Berlin & New York, 1966.

M. Adler

STEREOTYPE

...classes of individuals, groups or objects which are "preconceived", i.e. which do not derive from new judgments of each single phenome- non but are pattern-like forms of percei... ing and judging. Accordingly, the Germa... for example, are hardworking and negro... musical, etc. But beyond this co... denominator, emphases differ.
Stereotypes can be examined as... when expressly defined as group ju... they are judgments on which... large number of the members o... or a social category are agree... Sherif & Sherif, 1969 call... stereotypes, and placed... relations between g... Emphasis can... of truth in the... types are... concer...

Stereotype. A term whose meaning varies. It is most commonly used in the sense formulated by M. Jahoda among others, and according to which a stereotype denotes opinions a...

STERBOTYPE

not due to race but, among other factors, to the conditions of life of the testees, for as a rule these are far more unfavorable for negroes. In this connection, Pettigrew (1964) speaks of a self-fulfilling prophecy: the opinion held about a population group influ- ences the behavior shown to this group, and this behavior in turn provokes in the group the alleged behavior. It is certain that every- one must generalize, for events or persons do not return in all their detail, but as long as we cannot discern any repetitions, we cannot plan for the future and anticipate it (Brown, 1965).

Empirical statistical studies as a rule are based predominantly on the approach of group psychology (Katz & Braly, 1933; Gilbert, 1951; Buchanan, 1953; Sodhi &

274

Bergius, 1953), which has nevertheless been heavily criticized.

(a) Eysenck (1950) showed (from a study on the lines of the classical work of Katz & Braly, 1933) that many subjects admit they only repeat clichés which do not represent their own opinion. And, in fact, even when a certain group are agreed about what they say, this cannot be taken as a proof that the corre- sponding judgment is widely shared.

(b) As Asch (1968) showed, an inquiry does not lead to any unequivocal pronouncement. It may be that the pronouncement is based on all the members of the category; it may, how- ever, for example, be based only on a higher percentage of the group in some particular respect. See Prejudice; Attitude.

Bibliography: Allport, G. W.: The nature of prejudice. Boston, 1955. Asch, S. E.: Social psychology. Engle- wood Cliffs, [8]1965. Brown, R.: Social psychology. ...w York, 1965. Buchanan, W. & Cantril, H.: How ...s see each other. Urbana, 1953. Duiker, H. & ...N.: National character and national ste... ...rdam, 1960. Katz, D. & Braly, K. ... ...of one hundred college stud... 1933. 28. Katz, D. & S...

3

Ref.   18.   Harriman, Philip Lawrence. *Handbook of Psychologi-*
BF   *cal Terms.* Totowa, New Jersey, Littlefield, Adams,
31   1965.
.H33
1965   Brief definitions, some accompanied with illustrations
                          and diagrams.

Ref.   19.   *International Encyclopedia of the Social Sciences.* Sills,
H41   David, ed. New York, Macmillan Co. and the Free
+.A215   Press, 1968. 17 vols.
[Ency.
Section]   Although this set has a marked resemblance to the
                          original (I.c.13) considerable changes in scope and
                          format were incorporated. Extensive articles on the
                          concepts, theories, and methods of psychology,
                          anthropology, economics, geography, history, law,
                          political science, sociology and statistics. Emphasis
                          is on analytical and comparative aspects of topics,
                          with historical and descriptive material used to illus-
                          trate concepts and theories. Article topics include
                          features of social processes (acculturation, coopera-
                          tion, and socialization); social and individual patholo-
                          gies (crime, poverty, blindness and drug addition);
                          economic processes and institutions; political doc-
                          trines and forms of government; forms of settlement
                          and social life; and methods of empirical research
                          and of setting forth research results. Statistics are
                          treated as an important auxiliary science. Contains
                          600 biographical articles, including social scientists
                          still living, but *born before 1890.* Bibliographies of
                          each article consist of works cited in text, suggestions
                          for further reading, sources of data, and related
                          journals.

STEREOTYPES   *259*

Hegel and the Rise
Humanities Pres~~
WEISS, JOHN 196~~
of Lorenz vor~~
History 8, no.

Boxed portions highlight important passages in first of 4 pages of article in IESS (Psychology, Bibliography No. 25 I.c.19; and Sociology, Bibliography No. 19 I.f.12) on Stereotypes. Bibliography on pp. 261-262 cites in full 18 studies, including Katz and Braly.

STEREOTYPES

The term "stereotype" originated in the technology of printing, where it has a clearly defined meaning. A body of type is set up; then a mold is made from this type, and a solid metal plate is cast in the mold. This metal plate is the stereotype. Its printing surface is precisely equivalent to that of the original type. The major purpose of stereotyping is to produce a printing surface that can be used for thousands and thousands of impressions without needing to be replaced. Thus, the adjective "stereotyped" has come to mean "mechanically repeated" or—in a broader usage—"hackneyed" or "trite."

During the past forty years the noun "stereotype" has been widely used as a social science concept without ever being precisely defined. Its usage was introduced by the American journalist Walter Lippmann in a book called *Public Opinion* (1922). The major thesis of this book is that in a modern democracy political leaders and ordinary citizens are required to make decisions about a variety of complicated matters that they do not understand.

Lippmann's book was much admired by social scientists, and in many of their writings (especially textbooks) the term "stereotype" has continued to have essentially the meaning Lippmann gave it. When a concept is referred to as a stereotype, the implication is that (1) it is simple rather than complex or differentiated; (2) it is erroneous rather than accurate; (3) it has been acquired secondhand rather than through direct experience with the reality it is supposed to represent; and (4) it is resistant to modification by new experience. [*See the biography of* LIPPMANN.]

~~here~~ ... few attempts to set up criteria for classifying individual's concepts in a particular area in "stereotypes" and "nonstereotypes." In empirical search the term "stereotype" has usually been employed simply as a pejorative designation for "group concept."

This "group concept" usage became established in a classic study by Katz and Braly (1933). A group of 100 white American college students were asked to select from a list of 84 traits those they considered characteristic of each one of ten ethnic groups; then they were asked to choose the five "most typical" traits for each group. An index of *definiteness of stereotype* was constructed by counting the least number of traits required to include 50 per cent of the 500 choices by all subjects.

The Katz and Braly procedure has been repeated many times, for many different ethnic groups, and in many different countries. In one of the more recent studies, a list of 99 adjectives was submitted to a group of 100 Arab students in Beirut, Leba~~non~~ (Prothro & Melikian 1954). These adjectives, Arabic, had been selected from a longer list d~~evel~~oped by other students at the same universi~~ty~~ characterize members of various ethni~~c~~ The Arab students characterized Negro~~es~~ ner similar to American students ~~as~~ earlier, but their rat~~ings~~ of Turks ferent. The six traits most ~~"most typical" of Turks~~ taristic (33), nation~~alistic~~ progressive (18) ~~...~~

Since 1933 ~~...~~ has been th~~e~~ ~~...~~ types. ~~...~~

LIPPMANN, ~~WALTER~~ ~~...~~ntipathy. *Social Forces* 15:232-237.
~~York:~~ Macmillan. (1922) 1944 *Public Opinion*. New ~~...~~lished in 1965 by the Free Press. → A paperback edition was published.
PROTHRO, EDWIN T.; and MELIKIAN, LEVON H. 1954 Studies in Stereotypes: III. Arab Students in the Near East. *Journal of Social Psychology* 40:237-243.
RATH, R.; and SIRCAR, N. C. 1960 The Mental Pictures of Six Hindu Caste Groups About Each Other as Reflected in Verbal Stereotypes. *Journal of Social Psychology* 51:277-293.
REIGROTSKI, ERICH; and ANDERSON, NELS 1959 National Stereotypes and Foreign Contacts. *Public Opinion Quarterly* 23:515-528.

~~There~~
~~gr~~oups—
~~Ch~~inese—
~~u~~s citizens
~~...~~ correct? A
~~t~~he "kernel of
~~...~~, which asserts
~~...~~ively and accu-

~~...~~ACE
~~...~~ian Personal-
~~l~~ Studies Series,
~~al~~ Stereotypes of
~~al of~~ Abnormal and
1933 Racial Stereo-
~~ll~~ege Students. *Journal of*
~~sychology* 28:280-290.
1936 Type-rationalizations of

4

II.g

5. Lindzey, Gardner and Aronson, Elliot, eds. *Handbook of Social Psychology*. 2nd ed. Reading, Mass., Addison-Wesley Pub. Co., 1968-70. 6 vols.

    In five volumes sixty-eight authorities in their respective fields examine and assess—in a compressed and distilled format—what is known in the broad area of social psychology. In all, the works of some 10,000 researchers are noted. After a chapter on the historical background of modern social psychology seven chapters in the first volume treat such "systematic positions" of the discipline as: stimulus-response theory, mathematical models, the relevance of Freudian psychology to the social sciences, organizations, cognitive, field, and role theories. "Research methods," taken up by volume two, is divided into nine chapters: experimentation; data analysis (including statistics); attitude measurement; stimulation of social behavior; systematic observational methods; measuring social choice and interpersonal attractiveness; interviewing; content analysis; cross-cultural research; and the social significance of animal studies. The third volume focuses on the individual in a social context where, in ten chapters, is set forth such topics of inquiry as psychophysiological approaches, social motivation, attitudes and attitude change, factors in perception, socialization, personality and social interaction, psycholinguistics, esthetics, and laughter, humor and play. Group psychology and phenomena of interaction receive attention in the eight chapters of volume four including: group problem solving; group structure (attraction, coalitions, communication, and power); leadership; cultural psychology of infrahuman animals. In the last volume are nine chapters on aspects of applied psychology, including prejudice and ethnic relations; effects of mass media; industrial social psychology; political behavior; psychology of religion; social psychology of mental health; and the social psychology of education. Where appropriate, discussion is supplemented with graphs, tables, formulas and such other illustrations

considered useful for clarification. All items mentioned in the text of a chapter are cited in full at the
end of the chapter, and significantly, there is a smaller,
sixth volume which provides access by author and
by subject to the five-volume set. In spite of the
highly distilled treatment given individual works,
researchers can acquaint themselves with the significant bibliographic and substantive details of specific
topics of this broad field of inquiry, and although
often it is the best point at which to start inquiry on
a topic, joint use with *IESS* (I.c.19), *SSCI* (I.a.14),
and *Psychological Abstracts* (I.a.9) is suggested.

The exhibit from the *Handbook of Social Psychology* is
given on page 275.

See pages 272-73 for the annotation that relates to the exhibit on the right.

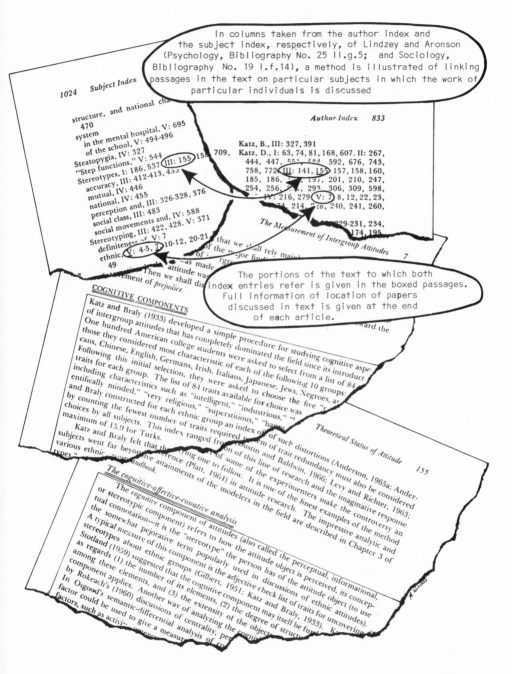

In columns taken from the author index and the subject index, respectively, of Lindzey and Aronson (Psychology, Bibliography No. 25 II.g.5; and Sociology, Bibliography No. 19 I.f.14), a method is illustrated of linking passages in the text on particular subjects in which the work of particular individuals is discussed

The portions of the text to which both index entries refer is given in the boxed passages. Full information of location of papers discussed in text is given at the end of each article.

5

I.c

5. Berelson, Bernard and Steiner, Gary A. *Human Be-
    havior: An Inventory of Scientific Findings.* New York,
    Harcourt, Brace and World, 1964.

    Intended to present a "simplified" distillation of the
    findings of 650 works in the behavioral sciences in
    language that can be comprehended by nonspecialists.
    The main chapters deal with the major aspects of
    human behavior to which scientific study has been
    devoted. Predominantly findings are based on west-
    ern culture, particularly the U.S. Included among
    chapter titles are: the individual (behavioral develop-
    ment, perceiving, learning and thinking, motiva-
    tion); the family; face-to-face relations; in small
    groups; organizations; institutions (religious, eco-
    nomic, political, educational, military); social strati-
    fication; ethnic relations; opinions, attitudes and
    beliefs; the society (demography, geography, social
    change, social conflict, social disorganization); and
    culture. In general, material in chapters is arranged
    uniformly: first, definitions of key terms; a major
    section on the findings, given as numbered state-
    ments followed by illustrative data; and a list of
    sources. Three approaches are possible: individual
    chapters on broad subjects; the subject index, re-
    ferring to narrower topics; or the "Bibliographical
    Index," indicating the pages where the findings of
    particular researchers are discussed. It can be sup-
    plemented with *Sociological Abstracts* (II.g.7), *In-
    ternational Bibliography of Sociology* ("Sociology,"
    Bibliography No. 19, I.b.4), and *Social Systems and
    Family Patterns* ("Sociology," Bibliography No. 19,
    II.a.6).

502 ETHNIC RELATIONS

Percentage of self-ratings on prejudice related to true prejudice score (percentages)

	Less prejudiced	More prejudiced
Much more or a little more than average	3.4	22.4
Average	13.0	38.1
A little less or much less than average	83.7	39.5

(Ibid., p. 35)

B2 People prejudiced against one ethnic group tend to be prej against others.

In other words, prejudice t

The research results to date i ported in that (1) individuals cific ethnic minority or minorities (2) prejudice toward one ethnic minority is companied by prejudice toward other ethnic minorities, and (3) th group is reified to the extent that patriotic and nationalistic sent related to rejection of ethnic minorities [Christie, 1954, p. 154].

That does not mean, of course, that prejudice is directed equ ethnic groups; that appears to be true only for the extreme ca Here are some illustrative correlations of attitudes towa minorities, as held by nonminority students at a California c

Entry from Berelson and Steiner (Psychology, Bibliography No. 25 I.c.5; and Sociology, Bibliography No. 19 I.f.2), giving a brief account of, and extracts from, important studies in "Stereotyping of ethnic groups".

	Negro	Japanese	Jewish	
Japanese	.72	.74	.66	
Jewish	.73	.70	.47	
Mexican	.75	.43		
English	.32			

(Campbell and McCandless, 1 THNIC RELATIONS 503

Values indicating relationships among ample evidence, were more needed in the psychological traits attributed to different ethnic toward any one group. Even a of varying personal experiences, needs, and cultural back- which because of their viduals et al., 1954, p. 1024]. the Anglophobe) [Harding et al., 1954, p. 1024].

B3 The ster example, here are the traits frequently assigned by college students, the society, a inly in the 1930's and 1940's, to a number of groups, e.g.: typed grou

Jews	shrewd, mercenary, industrious
Negroes	superstitious, lazy, happy-go-lucky
Italians	artistic, impulsive, passionate
English	sportsmanlike, intelligent, conventional
Americans	industrious, intelligent, materialistic
Irish	pugnacious, quick-tempered, witty

(Katz and Braly, 1933)

B3.1 The less contact or experience wi he less strongly held the stereotype ven so, stereotypes do not e with the group which one

6

SOURCE: Material reprinted from *Human Behavior: An Inventory of Scientific Findings* by Bernard Berelson and Gary A. Steiner, © 1964 by Harcourt Brace Jovanovich, Inc., by permission of the publishers.

I.a

Science   13. *Science Citation Index.* Philadelphia, Institute for
Periodical   Scientific Information, 1961-   .
Index

Periodical   14. *Social Sciences Citation Index.* 1973-   . Philadelphia,
Index   Institute for Scientific Information.

> Psychology, perhaps more than any other discipline, has forged strong links with other disciplines in the social sciences as well as some of the natural sciences. Thus these two similar intermediary sources, each covering broadly the natural and social sciences, but inevitably with considerable overlap from one area to the other, are most instructively considered together. The *SCI* is issued four times a year, the *SSCI* three times a year, with the final number of both titles being a cumulation of the whole year. Both present another dimension to research procedures. Based on the principle that the *names of people can be substituted for the subjects with which they are associated*, they provide the opportunity of advancing from earlier research to more recent studies on the same subject. Both the *SCI* and the *SSCI* consist of *three separate* but related indexes: the *Source Index*; the *Citation Index*; and the *Permuterm Subject Index*. Of the three, the *Citation Index* is the largest and the most useful, but for a clear understanding, it is better to describe first the *Source Index*. In the *Source Index* are arranged alphabetically by author's name, *articles* published in a given year in each indexed periodical. (In the *SCI* about 4,500 periodicals are indexed, in the *SSCI*, about 1,500). Along with author's names, information given includes *title of article, abbreviated* title of periodical, volume, date and page of issue, and number of footnote references. (Beginning with the 1974 cumulation, abbreviated citations of *all* references of each listed article are actually given in *SSCI*; this is *not* true of the *SCI*). In addition, when an article is *not* specifically a report of empirical research (e.g., a book review, a letter, or a review of research) letter symbols are used to indicate the type of information it contains.

(The table of symbols employed is part of the illustrated instructions in use inside the cover of each volume.) In the *Citation Index*, also arranged alphabetically by author's name, are articles *cited* by authors in the *Source Index*. Below each entry are names and brief bibliographical data, from the *Source Index*. Because authors in the *Source Index* ordinarily cite numerous studies, the *Citation Index* in both cases is several times larger than the *Source Index*. (About 80,000 citations are in the 1973 *SSCI*, while typically in the *SCI* there are 250,000 citations.) Although not as efficient as a device for research, the *Permuterm Subject Index* serves when researchers do not know a specific author concerned with a topic for which information is required. In general, the *SCI* and the *SSCI* are most useful for tracing the trends and developments which result from the publication of particular research studies. Melvin Weinstock's "Citation Indexes" in the *Encyclopedia of Library and Information Science* [Ref. Z1006./.E57] v. 5, pp. 16-40 (N.Y., Dekker, 1971) is an extensive discussion of the principles and uses of citation indexes.

The exhibit from the *Social Sciences Citation Index* is given on page 281.

See pages 278-79 for the annotation relating to the exhibit on the right. In an actual demonstration, this material is the same size was the publication, and thus (unlike this example) one has little difficulty in following the arrangement pattern or in reading the small print.

After having found that Katz and Braly (1933) is the "key" source in research literature associated with "stereotypes", researchers will want to find recent studies. Using the 1974 SSCI (Psychology, Bibliography No. 25 I.a.14; and Sociology, Bibliography No. 19 I.b.12) it is possible to advance from an older work to a more recent one, provided the older work is cited in the research literature. The illustrations show how the various portions of the SSCI and SCI are related to one another.

SOCIAL SCIENCE CITATION INDEX

CITATION INDEX	SOURCE INDEX	PERMUTERM INDEX

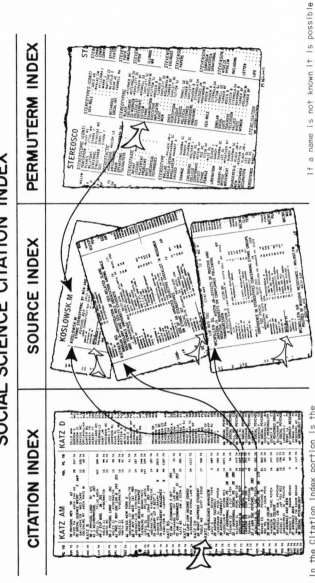

In the Citation Index portion is the entry for Katz and Braly's 1933 paper (only Katz's name, the date, abbreviated journal title, and first page of article are given). Listed directly below are those 1974 articles in which Katz and Braly (1933) is cited.

In the middle column are entries for Koslowski, Kutner, and McMillen, as they appear in the Source Index portion. Notice that in each case Katz and Braly (1933) is among the papers by the authors.

If a name is not known it is not possible using the Permuterm Subject Index portion to discover papers on a particular topic. This method is not as efficient as is using author's names in finding studies on a research topic.

(Note that the computer is only able to handle a certain number of letters in each name, meaning that occasionally a surname such as Koslowski is cropped.)

7

Science
Periodical
Index

8. *Monthly Bibliography of Medical Reviews.* Washington, National Library of Medicine, 1955-   . v. 1-   .

WWSC holds from 1966-   .

A subject index to authoritative articles which review what is known and what advances in research have occurred in a given field of biomedicine. Published monthly, with annual cumulations, fortunately for psychologists and those in such related fields as education and social psychology, biomedicine is interpreted broadly, and thus reviews of research advances in these fields can rapidly be found in this source. Since September, 1961, all articles in *Bibliography of Medical Reviews* are also listed in each monthly issue of *Index Medicus* (I.a.6). Annual cumulations also are published as part of the *Cumulated Index Medicus.* Note that the *Science Citation Index* (I.a.13) and the *Social Science Citation Index* (I.a.14) indicate the existence of review articles; an "R" symbol in a citation in either indicates a review article.

Periodical
Index

9. *Psychological Abstracts.* Lancaster, Pa., American Psychological Association, 1927-   .

Over 20,000 abstracts of books, parts of books (chapters), official documents and doctoral dissertations, as well as articles from periodicals from all over the world are published each year. Along with the general section at the beginning are sixteen broad sections (psychometrics and statistics; perception and motor performance; cognitive processes and motivation; animal psychology, and so forth), each having appropriate subdivisions. An author index is given in each monthly issue and there are half-yearly cumulated author and subject indexes. Also useful are the cumulative author and subject indexes, the author index including entries in the *Psychological Index* (1894-1935) as well as *Psychological Abstracts* since 1927, with coverage extending into the 1970's; and the cumulative subject index which covers from 1927 into the 1970's. A separately published alphabetical listing of the over 265,000 subject entries used in *Psychological Abstracts* is shelved closeby.

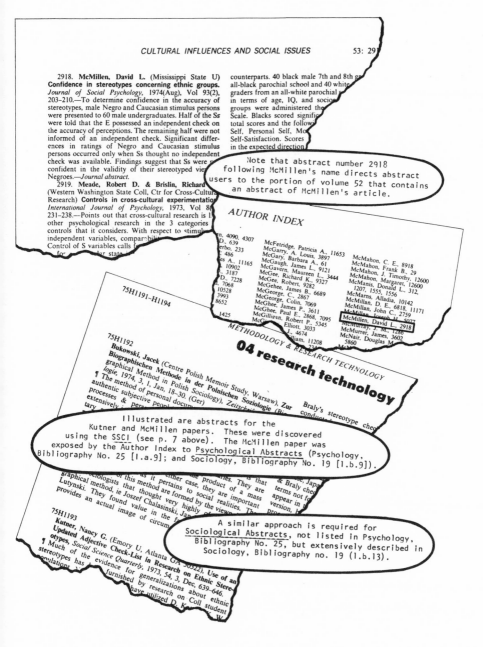

CULTURAL INFLUENCES AND SOCIAL ISSUES   53: 29

2918. McMillen, David L. (Mississippi State U) **Confidence in stereotypes concerning ethnic groups.** *Journal of Social Psychology,* 1974(Aug), Vol 93(2), 203–210.—To determine confidence in the accuracy of stereotypes, male Negro and Caucasian stimulus persons were presented to 60 male undergraduates. Half of the Ss were told that the E possessed an independent check on the accuracy of perceptions. The remaining half were not informed of an independent check. Significant differences in ratings of Negro and Caucasian stimulus persons occurred only when Ss thought no independent check was available. Findings suggest that Ss were more confident in the validity of their stereotyped views of Negroes.—*Journal abstract.*

2919. Meade, Robert D. & Brislin, Richard (Western Washington State Coll, Ctr for Cross-Cultural Research) **Controls in cross-cultural experimentation.** *International Journal of Psychology,* 1973, Vol 8(4), 231–238.—Points out that cross-cultural research is like other psychological research in the 3 categories of controls that it considers. With respect to stimulus independent variables, comparability of
Control of S variables calls for

counterparts. 40 black male 7th and 8th graders from an all-black parochial school and 40 white graders from an all-white parochial in terms of age, IQ, and socioeconomic groups were administered the Scale. Blacks scored significantly total scores and the following Self, Personal Self, Mo Self-Satisfaction. Scores in the expected direction

Note that abstract number 2918 following McMillen's name directs abstract users to the portion of volume 52 that contains an abstract of McMillen's article.

AUTHOR INDEX

...n, 4090, 4307
D., 639
erbo, 233
..; 486
es A., 11165
., 10902
., 3187
D., 7228
., 7068
10528
3993
8652

1425

McFetridge, Patricia A., 11653
McGarry, A. Louis, 3897
McGary, Barbara A., 61
McGaugh, James L., 9121
McGavern, Maureen L., 3444
McGee, Richard K., 9327
McGee, Robert, 9282
McGehee, James B., 6689
McGeorge, C., 2867
McGeorge, Colin, 7069
McGhee, James P., 3611
McGhee, Paul E., 2868, 7095
McGilligan, Robert P., 5345
McG... Elliott, 3033
...liam, 11208

McMahon, C. E., 8918
McMahon, Frank B., 29
McMahon, J. Timothy, 12600
McMahon, Margaret, 1207, 1555, 1556
McManis, Donald L., 312,
McMarns, Alladia, 10142
McMillan, D. E., 6818, 11171
McMillan, John C., 2759
McMillen, Joseph J., 5077
McMillen, David L., 2918
McMurray, J. M., 1286
McMurrer, James, 3602
McNair, Douglas M., 5860

METHODOLOGY & RESEARCH TECHNOLOGY

04 research technology

75H1191–H1194

75H1192

Bukowski, Jacek (Centre Polish Memoir Study, Warsaw) **Zur Biographischen Methode in der Polnischen Soziologie** (Biographical Method in Polish Sociology), *Zeitschr...* *logie,* 1974, 3, 1, Jan, 18–30. (Ger) ¶ The method of personal docum... authentic subjective personal docum... processes & per... extensively ; tary

Braly's stereotype chec conduct...

Illustrated are abstracts for the Kutner and McMillen papers. These were discovered using the SSCI (see p. 7 above). The McMillen paper was exposed by the Author Index to *Psychological Abstracts* (Psychology, Bibliography No. 25 [1.a.9]; and Sociology, Bibliography No. 19 [1.b.9]).

...es. They are ...that & Braly, Japa graphical method are formed by the views. The terms not fo... Lutynski. They found very highly in social realities. They appear in d... either case, they are important version, h... provides an actual image of circum... product of a mass pro... ...ciologists of this method as it pertains to social that Joszef Chalasinski, Jan...

A similar approach is required for *Sociological Abstracts,* not listed in Psychology, Bibliography No. 25, but extensively described in Sociology, Bibliography no. 19 (1.b.13).

75H1193

Kutner, Nancy G. (Emory U, Atlanta GA 30322), **Use of an Updated Adjective Check-List in Research on Ethnic Stereotypes,** *Social Science Quarterly,* 1973, 54, 3, Dec, 639–646. ¶ Much of the evidence for generalizations about ethnic stereotypes has furnished by research on Coll student populations ... have utilized D. K... W...

9. Chun, Ki-Taek, et al. *Measures for Psychological Assessment: A Guide to 3,000 Original Sources and Their Applications.* Ann Arbor, Michigan, Survey Research Center, Institute for Social Research, 1975.

A compilation of annotated references to the measures of mental health and related variables and the uses of these measures, published between 1960 and 1970 in 26 measurement-related journals in psychology and sociology. The intent, first, to provide a comprehensive bibliography relating to all measures of mental health and related concepts. Second, as an aid to selection, directions are given both to the original source where the measure was first described (there are 3,000) and to the 6,600-odd other studies in which the measure was subsequently used. Finally this volume provides access to quantitative research results in a particular substantive field. As well as an author index, there is a descriptor (i.e., subject) index, on pages 18-56, "a cross-referenced index of the main types of descriptors used for primary references. The great majority of the descriptors in the index describe the content of measures, i.e., the traits, characteristics, moods, attitudes, behaviors, and so forth, which they intend to assess." (Preface)

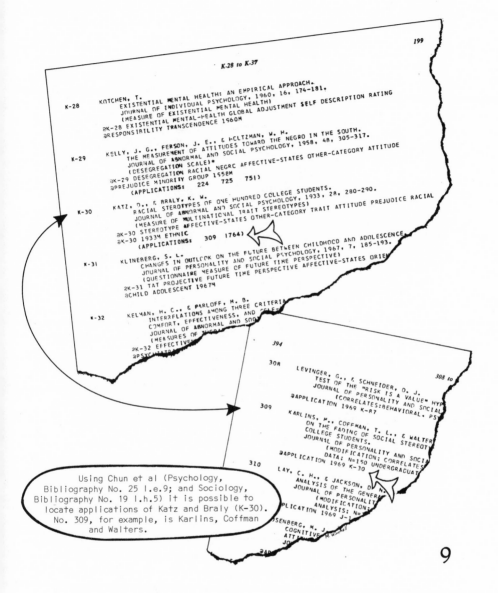

K-28 to K-37

K-28
KOTCHEN, T.
EXISTENTIAL MENTAL HEALTH: AN EMPIRICAL APPROACH.
JOURNAL OF INDIVIDUAL PSYCHOLOGY, 1960, 16, 174-181.
(MEASURE OF EXISTENTIAL MENTAL HEALTH) SELF DESCRIPTION RATING
∂K-28 EXISTENTIAL MENTAL-HEALTH GLOBAL ADJUSTMENT SELF DESCRIPTION RATING
∂RESPONSIBILITY TRANSCENDENCE 1960M

K-29
KELLY, J. G., FERSON, J. E., & HOLTZMAN, W. H.
THE MEASUREMENT OF ATTITUDES TOWARD THE NEGRO IN THE SOUTH.
JOURNAL OF ABNORMAL AND SOCIAL PSYCHOLOGY, 1958, 48, 305-317.
(DESEGREGATION SCALE)*
∂K-29 DESEGREGATION RACIAL NEGRO AFFECTIVE-STATES OTHER-CATEGORY ATTITUDE
∂PREJUDICE MINORITY GROUP 1958M
(APPLICATIONS: 224   725   751)

K-30
KATZ, D., & BRALY, K. W.
RACIAL STEROTYPES OF ONE HUNDRED COLLEGE STUDENTS.
JOURNAL OF ABNORMAL AND SOCIAL PSYCHOLOGY, 1933, 28, 280-290.
(MEASURE OF MULTINATIONAL TRAIT STEREOTYPES)
∂K-30 STEREOTYPE AFFECTIVE-STATES OTHER-CATEGORY TRAIT ATTITUDE PREJUDICE RACIAL
∂K-30 1933M ETHNIC
(APPLICATIONS: 309   1764)

K-31
KLINEBERG, S. L.
CHANGES IN OUTLOOK ON THE FUTURE BETWEEN CHILDHOOD AND ADOLESCENCE.
JOURNAL OF PERSONALITY AND SOCIAL PSYCHOLOGY, 1967, 7, 185-193.
(QUESTIONNAIRE MEASURE OF FUTURE TIME PERSPECTIVE)
∂K-31 TAT PROJECTIVE FUTURE TIME PERSPECTIVE AFFECTIVE-STATES ORIEN
∂CHILD ADOLESCENT 1967M

K-32
KELMAN, H. C., & PARLOFF, M. B.
INTERRELATIONS AMONG THREE CRITERIA
COMFORT, EFFECTIVENESS, AND SELF-
JOURNAL OF ABNORMAL AND SOC
(MEASURES OF PSYCHO
∂K-32 EFFECTIVE
∂PSYCHIATR

394

308

LEVINGER, G., & SCHNEIDER, D. J. "HYP
TEST OF THE "RISK IS A VALUE" HYP
JOURNAL OF PERSONALITY AND SOCIAL
(CORRELATES:BEHAVIORAL, PS
∂APPLICATION 1969 K-87

309

KARLINS, M., COFFMAN, T. L., & WALTER
ON THE FADING OF SOCIAL STEREOT
COLLEGE STUDENTS.
JOURNAL OF PERSONALITY AND SOCIA
(MODIFICATION; CORRELATES
DATA; N=150 UNDERGRADUAT
∂APPLICATION 1969 K-30

310

LAY, C. H., & JACKSON, D
ANALYSIS OF THE GENERA
JOURNAL OF PERSONALIT
(MODIFICATION:
ANALYSIS; N=
∂PLICATION 1969 J-

OSENBERG, M. J
COGNITIVE
ATTIT
JO

308 to

Using Chun et al (Psychology, Bibliography No. 25 I.e.9; and Sociology, Bibliography No. 19 I.h.5) it is possible to locate applications of Katz and Braly (K-30). No. 309, for example, is Karlins, Coffman and Walters.

9

I.e

Ref.   2. Barabas, Jean. *Assessment of Minority Groups, An*
Z   *Annotated Bibliography* (with subject index). New
1007   York, Science Associates, 1975. (Reader's Advisory
+R313   Service No. 84).
v.2
no.1   The materials [listed and annotated] represent in-
[Shelved   formation in articles, books, etc., on such diverse
in Ref.   and, at the same time, intertwining areas as: methods
Office]   of assessing achievement, intelligence, personality
                            factors, attitudes; effects of testing on self concept
                            and employment opportunities; prediction of aca-
                            demic success; reliability and validity of specific
                            tests; criticism of the methods and use of assessment
                            test construction; use of assessment for educational
                            placement and diagnosis; culture free and culture
                            fair tests; performance differences on tests between
                            majority and minority groups. (Preface) Arranged
                            by author, with subject index. There are a number
                            of citations which do not deal directly with minori-
                            ties. ERIC microfiche numbers are included where
                            appropriate.

Ref.   · 3. Bonjean, Charles M. *Sociological Measurement; An*
Z   *Inventory of Scales and Indices.* San Francisco, Chandler
7164   Pub. Co., 1967.
S68
B6   An inventory of scales and indices from *American*
                            Journal of Sociology, American Sociological Re-
                            view, Social Forces and Sociometry between 1954
                            and 1965. Although the distinctions are not rigidly
                            imposed, index is taken to mean combining several
                            indicators into one measurement and scale "a special
                            type of index designed to reflect only a single dimen-
                            sion of a concept." "Every use of a scale or index is
                            noted, categorized and, in some cases, the measuring
                            instrument is thoroughly described. The result is an
                            extensive bibliography which locates any use of any
                            scale or index during the period. Heavily used mea-
                            sures (achievement motivation, California F. Scale,
                            etc.) are described technically." (*Social Science Quar-*
                            terly, Sept. 1968, p. 392)

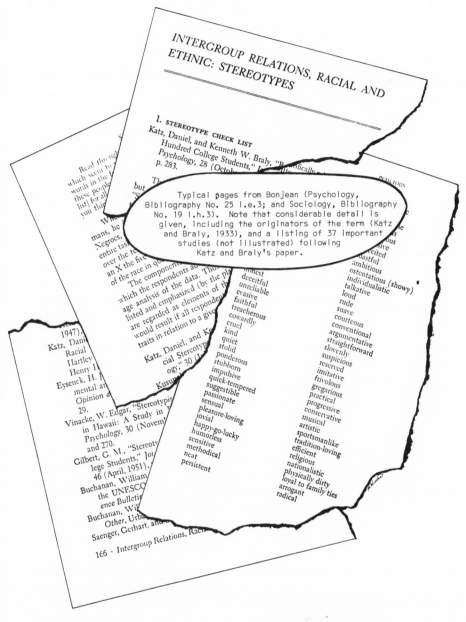

INTERGROUP RELATIONS, RACIAL AND ETHNIC: STEREOTYPES

1. STEREOTYPE CHECK LIST

Katz, Daniel, and Kenneth W. Braly, "R........ically.......
Hundred College Students," ....
Psychology, 28 (Octob........
p. 283.

Typical pages from Bonjean (Psychology, Bibliography No. 25 I.e.3; and Sociology, Bibliography No. 19 l.h.3). Note that considerable detail is given, including the originators of the term (Katz and Braly, 1933), and a listing of 37 important studies (not illustrated) following Katz and Braly's paper.

honest
deceitful
unreliable
evasive
faithful
treacherous
cowardly
cruel
kind
quiet
stolid
ponderous
stubborn
impulsive
quick-tempered
suggestible
passionate
sensual
pleasure-loving
jovial
happy-go-lucky
humorless
sensitive
methodical
neat
persistent

ostentatious (showy)
individualistic
talkative
loud
rude
suave
courteous
conventional
argumentative
straightforward
slovenly
suspicious
reserved
imitative
frivolous
gregarious
practical
progressive
conservative
musical
artistic
sportsmanlike
tradition-loving
efficient
religious
nationalistic
physically dirty
loyal to family ties
arrogant
radical

1947),
Katz, Dani........
Racial ....
Hartley ....
Henry I........
Eysenck, H. J........
mental an........
Opinion a........
29.
Vinacke, W. Edgar, "Stereotypi........
in Hawaii: A Study in ....
Psychology, 30 (Novem........
and 270.
Gilbert, G. M., "Stereoty........
lege Students," Jou........
46 (April, 1951), ...
Buchanan, William........
the UNESCO........
ence Bulletin........
Buchanan, Wil........
Other, Urba........
Saenger, Gerhart, and........

166 · Intergroup Relations, Racia........

10

Part 2

AN ILLUSTRATION OF
STRUCTURED INQUIRY

RESEARCH TOPIC

ALLIANCE and DESCENT as Conflicting KINSHIP
Paradigms in Social Anthropology.

The attached illustrations demonstrate how a student using
the research guide "Anthropology," Bibliography no. 1, can
locate information on a research topic in anthropology. By
progressing in a step-by-step (i.e., structured) procedure, it is
possible to advance from a point where little is known about
a particular topic to the desired level of understanding of it.

Wilson Library
Reference Department
Western Washington University
September 1977

Ref.   15.   Royal Anthropological Institute. *Notes and Queries on*
GN33   *Anthropology.*
R63   See I.i.3.
1957
[Shelved in
Ref. Office]

Ref.   16.   Williams, Raymond. *Keywords; a vocabulary of cul-*
PE   *ture and society.* New York: Oxford University Press,
1585   1976.
W5
                          While only a few entries in it apply directly to an-
                          thropology, the volume contains extensive discus-
                          sions of definitions and uses of special words in our
                          vocabulary which involve ideas and values. The
                          words range from Alienation and Community to
                          Myth and Native to Structural and Work. Concern
                          is directed to historical and current usage, especially
                          where "several disciplines converge but do not meet."
                          References to authoritative sources.

Ref.   17.   Winick, Charles. *Dictionary of Anthropology.* New
GN 11   York: Philosophical Library, 1956.
.W5
                          Approximately 7000 entries, including biographies.
                          Although coverage is not even, it consists of defini-
                          tions of terms not found in general dictionaries.
                          Occasional references to important contributors.

Ref.   18.   *Worldmark Encyclopedia of the Nations.* 5th ed. 5 vols.
G 63   New York: Worldmark Press, 1976.
+W67
[Shelved in   WWSC holds all editions. Earlier editions shelved in
Ref. Office]   general stacks.

                          Contains brief economic, political, historical, geo-
                          graphical, sociological and anthropological infor-
                          mation about countries and international organiza-

Typical entries from Winick's <u>Dictionary</u>
<u>of Anthropology</u> [I.g.17]. Although there
is no entry for "Alliance" (the reason is
not clear) there are several entries explaining various aspects of both "Descent"
and "Kinship". Note mention of Radcliffe-
Brown's name in "Kinship" entry; it will
be encountered below.

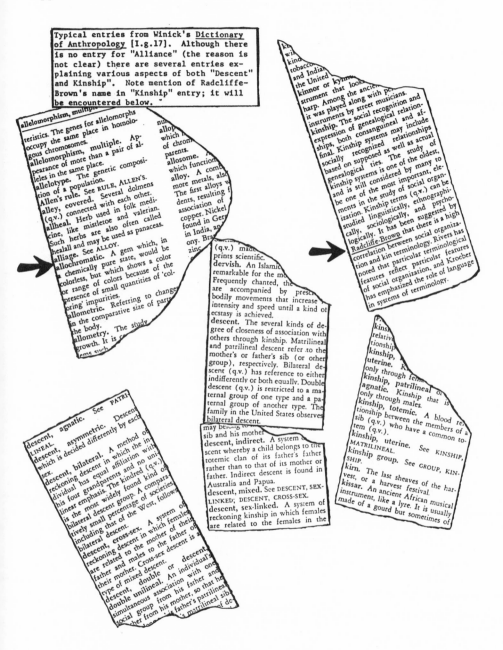

Ref.   11.   Hunter, David E., and Whitten, Phillip M., eds. *En-*
GN 11   *cyclopedia of Anthropology.* New York: Harper and
E52   Row, 1976. 411 p.

A compact, comprehensive work dealing with the
concepts and language, theories and leading figures
(both historical and contemporary), it consists of
some 1400 articles ranging from 25 to 3000 words.
Several hundred entries cover theories, concepts,
research findings, and individuals in such related
fields as linguistics, psychology, and sociology.
Articles of at least 20 lines are signed and, according
to the editors, the shorter unsigned articles were
written by the same people, some 100-odd authorities. Within the alphabetical sequence of entries, *see*
references direct users to the entries containing information on the topic. *See also references,* at the
end of articles, direct users to related articles. At the
end of all but the shortest articles is a bibliography
listing important books and articles on the subject.
Profusely illustrated with black and white photographs, charts, tables, etc. Joint use with such works
as *IESS* [I.g.6], Hultkrantz [I.g.10], and Honigmann
[II.g.11] is suggested.

Ref.   12.   *International Encyclopedia of the Social Sciences.*
H41
.E6 [Ency. Section]   See I.g.6.

Ref.   13.   *New Catholic Encyclopedia.* Prepared by an editorial
BX 841   staff at the Catholic University of America. New
+.N44   York: McGraw-Hill, 1967. 15 vols.
[Ency.
Stack]   Covers a broad range of secular as well as religious
topics, usually from a non-dogmatic point of view,
including such topics in anthropology as "kinship"
and "culture," and native peoples with whom the
Catholic Church established missions. Nearly all the
articles include a select bibliography of authoritative
works for further reference. Volume 15 is an index.

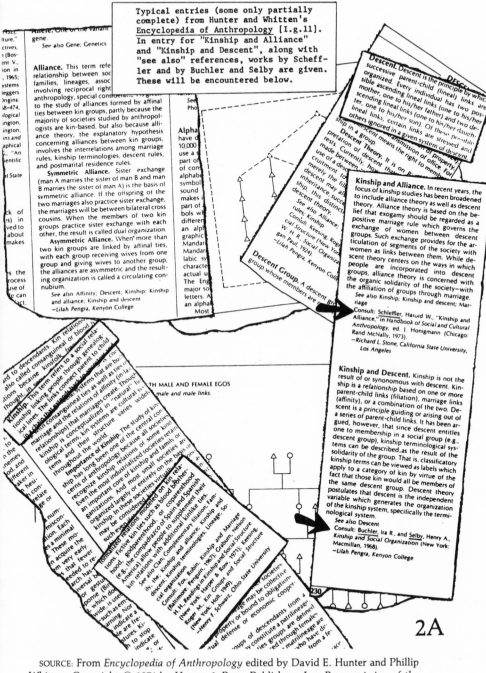

Typical entries (some only partially complete) from Hunter and Whitten's Encyclopedia of Anthropology [I.g.11]. In entry for "Kinship and Alliance" and "Kinship and Descent", along with "see also" references, works by Scheffler and by Buchler and Selby are given. These will be encountered below.

Allele. One of the variant gene.

See also Gene; Genetics

Alliance. This term refe... relationship between soc... families, lineages, assoc... involving reciprocal right... anthropology, special consi... to the study of alliances formed by affinal ties between kin groups, partly because the majority of societies studied by anthropologists are kin-based, but also because alliance theory, the explanatory hypothesis concerning alliances between kin groups, involves the interrelations among marriage rules, kinship terminologies, descent rules, and postmarital residence rules.

Symmetric Alliance. Sister exchange (man A marries the sister of man B and man B marries the sister of man A) is the basis of symmetric alliance. If the offspring of the two marriages also practice sister exchange, the marriages will be between bilateral cross cousins. When the members of two kin groups practice sister exchange with each other, the result is called *dual organization*.

Asymmetric Alliance. When more than two kin groups are linked by affinal ties, with each group receiving wives from one group and giving wives to another group, the alliances are asymmetric and the resulting organization is called a *circulating connubium*.

See also Affinity; Descent; Kinship; Kinship and alliance; Kinship and descent
—Lilah Pengra, Kenyon College

Descent. Descent is the principle by which successive parent-child (lineal) links are organized. Every individual has two possible ascending lineal links (one to his/her mother, one to his/her father) and two descending lineal links (one to his/her daughter, one to his/her son). Of these possible lineal links, certain links are ignored and others ignored in a given system of descent...

Descent Theory. It is on descent may...

Kinship and Alliance. In recent years, the focus of kinship studies has been broadened to include alliance theory as well as descent theory. Alliance theory is based on the belief that exogamy should be regarded as a positive marriage rule which governs the exchange of women between descent groups. Such exchange provides for the articulation of segments of the society by women as links between them. While descent theory centers on the ways in which people are incorporated into descent groups, alliance theory is concerned with the organic solidarity of the society—with the affiliation of groups through marriage.

See also Kinship; Kinship and descent; Marriage

Consult: Schleffler, Harold W., "Kinship and Alliance," in Handbook of Social and Cultural Anthropology, ed. J. Honigmann (Chicago: Rand McNally, 1973).
—Richard L. Stone, California State University, Los Angeles

Descent Group. A descent group whose members are...

Kinship and Descent. Kinship is not the result of or synonymous with descent. Kinship is a relationship based on one or more parent-child links (filiation), marriage links (affinity), or a combination of the two. Descent is a principle guiding or arising out of a series of parent-child links. It has been argued, however, that since descent entitles one to membership in a social group (e.g., descent group), kinship terminological systems can be described as the result of the solidarity of the group. That is, classificatory kinship terms can be viewed as labels which apply to a category of kin by virtue of the fact that those kin would all be members of the same descent group. Descent theory postulates that descent is the independent variable which generates the organization of the kinship system, specifically the terminological system.

See also Descent

Consult: Buchler, Ira R., and Selby, Henry A., Kinship and Social Organization (New York: Macmillan, 1968).
—Lilah Pengra, Kenyon College

...TH MALE AND FEMALE EGOS
...male and male links.

Kinship. This term refers to a social relationship... kinfolk... genealogical lines. The links connect parent to child... consanguineal ties as well as ties in... the relations of affinity (in la... marriage and the relations that marriages create. Though... kinship is conceptualized in "natural" te... ological terms, kin systems vary widely... tems and their structure varies... throughout the world.

Importance of Kinship. The study of kinship has long been one of the central concerns of anthropology because all societies recognize kinship relations of some kind. Even the most industrialized societies retain an important core of kinship and family organizations. And most small societies are organized largely or entirely on the basis of kin relations such as brother... may be considered virtually kin... such relations modeled on kin relations... godparenthood, or coparenthood (e.g., the compadrazgo of Spain and Spanish America) allow people to supplement their kin relations with additional fictive ties.

See also Clan, Complementary filiation Family, descent; Kinship and alliance; Kinship and cial organization; Kinship terminologies; Lineage; Social Structure
Consult: Fox, Robin, Kinship and Marriage (Baltimore: Penguin, 1967); Graburn, Nelson H. H., Readings in Kinship and Social Structure (New York: Harper & Row, 1971); Keesing, Roger M., Kin Groups and Social Structure (New York: Holt, 1949).
—Henry F. Schwarz, Ohio State University

The exhibit on the right is a follow up of information obtained from the exhibit on page 293.

[14] Kinship and Social Organization

Typical pages from Buchler and Selby's Kinship and Social Organization, referred to in the entry "Kinship and Descent" in the Encyclopedia of Anthropology (see p. 2A above).

and (4) the Sex Principle, whereby people respect those of opposite sex.

Thus Radcliffe-Brown's students attempted to summarize the behavioral and terminological universals of comparative sociology. They were later elaborated by Radcliffe-Brown in his *Introduction to African Systems of Kinship and Marriage* (1950), and it is this exposition that we utilize for discussion in Chapter Four. To anticipate slightly, it will be shown that these "rules" and "principles" are devoid of semantic and sociological significance. The rules are entirely *ad hoc*, mere verbal summaries, as Lowie calls them. They describe some data in some kinship systems, but nowhere is any attempt made (nor can it be) to indicate the scope of the rules, nor the conditions under which they may obtain. The application of the principles shows them to be tautological. An Omaha system, for example, is seen to recognize certain principles in its mergings, and the mergings are the validation of the ciracy of the principle. The reasoning is entirely circular. However, one of -Brown's teachings, which was never codified in any manner, did reat value. He insisted upon the close examination of kinship behavior in single societies, and upon the method of what alled the method of "controlled comparison." Kinship ican tribes were organized and analyzed with care and y absence of abstract theorizing. McAllister's work pache; Eggan's on Cheyenne and Arapaho (1937), 50); Tax' study (1937) of Fox; Gilbert's (1937) r's (1937) on Chiricahua Apache were all theoretical level, their simplistic organax, 1955, p. 254) was the inevitable aspect or level of terminology (the sociological) without admitting to d in the translation process. (See ach-Lounsbury controversy.) roke through an early preoccupation 's (1915, 1924) formulations. It was etermining factor in the morphology tly demonstrated by Murdock. In -Brown, however, it became a conceptual scheme, led to empirical studies of clarity and accuracy, led lations on the one hand, and tautological reifi- ce can be seen throughout this book, not he treatment on "Alliance Theory," and (Chapter Ten) and section systems

---

Chapter One
Introduction and Background

We can date the beginning of the scie about 100 years ago. Lewis Henry Morgan *sanguinity and Affinity of the Human Family*, a before its publication in 1870. It was a mon few in the history of science that have been As Lowie has stated (Lowie, 1937, p. 62), " lies in literally creating the study of kinship system tive sociology." In *Systems*, Morgan amassed an enor on kinship terminologies, "formulated a bold and original the various kinds of kinship systems he had discovered, . . . [and] out a classification of kinship systems that is at least as good as any today" (White, 1959, p. 10). Since Morgan's work, increasing numb scholars each decade have written about kinship and social organiza especially in the years after World War II. The tradition of study in the a of kinship systems is comparatively long for a social science, and the co tinuity of effort has been productive, sufficiently so to enable us to declare the study of kinship and social organization the most highly developed area of social anthropology.

This present book is a partial stock-taking of some of the more recent work that has taken place, particularly since World War II. This chapter serves, in the main, to introduce the reader to the issues that are to be presented for discussion, particularly in the follow ive chapters. No attempt is made here to write the intellectual history o ary discipline. Others have accomplished this at least in part (Fo an, 1937; Beattie, 1964; Murdock, 1949, 1951; Firth, 195 Linton, 1936; Lowie, 1920, 1937, 1948; Romney, 19 1965; and

[1]

Introduction and Background [15]

ALLIANCE THEORY Schneider (1965a) and Dumont (1953a, 1966) have made a convenient distinction between descent theory and alliance theory. By emphasizing the fact that the two are largely complementary, they have, perhaps, obscured the fact that Crow-Omaha systems, whereas alliance theory is more highly developed in the empirical study of what Lévi-Strauss has called developed systems, or elementary structures, where it has been able to attain to a greater degree of abstraction and generality than descent theory. In this section we survey of the antecedents of alliance theory, and thereby complete our survey of the background to the more basic substantive issues in this book. ss, and its realization to Durkheim, its advancement of *elementary* 1893) who first developed in an explicit fashion the notion of "organic which subsequently played a large part in the theory of social evolu- (Lévi-Strauss. So far as Durkheim was concerned, social relations) was o say, the development of complexity in penal methods and judicial ral order. Simple, homogeneous societies were charac- or signalled by a change in social relations directly. sanction. The collectivity punished members, for any offense against the common con- was based upon the "essential social the "mechanical solidarity" that arose egin, 1947, itudes ed

2B

I.g.

As well as archaeology, ethnography, kinship, linguistics, and race, both works feature articles on
cultural, economic, physical, political, social, and
applied anthropology, Among the several articles in
the entry "history" in *IESS* are ethnohistory and
culture history. The *IESS* has only 600 biographies,
compared with the over 4000 in *ESS*, but the articles
are longer and emphasize individuals not included in
the first work, including prominent social scientists
still living, but born before 1890.

Ref.   7.   Gould, Julius, and Kolb, William L., eds. *Dictionary*
H41   *of the Social Sciences.* New York: Free Press, 1964.
G6   761 pp.

Gould defines about one-fourth as many terms as
Zadrozny [I.g.19], but his treatment of the terms is
more intensive. There are more than 1000 terms
from anthropology and economics, but political-
science and sociological terms predominate; they are
extensively defined by some 270 noted U.S. and
British social scientists. With a few exceptions, entries are arranged as follows: A, the generally accepted meaning of the term; B, its historical background or a more extensive explanation. C,D,E, and
so on, are used where "controversies and divergencies of meaning have been explored and an attempt
made to place them in their perspective." Many
definitions are illustrated with quotes from authorities.

Ref.   8.   Heberer, Gerhard. *Anthropology A to Z.* New York:
GN 11   Grosset and Dunlap, 1963. Edited by Carleton Coon.
.H413
A translation of a work originally in German. According to its introduction, the work is designed to
"bring together knowledge of man's origins and
evolutionary history, his distribution into races, and
the biological aspects of human behavior." Since
Coon is a controversial figure among anthropologists,
students are cautioned that they might have to de-
fend the use of certain information included in this
book.

Kinship and Kinship System

A. In contemporary English (in Great Britain) *kinsman* is an aristocratic word for relative. *Kinship* in its technical sense follows naturally from the common understanding of words containing the element *kin* (*kindred, kinsman, kinsfolk*). The ordinary expression 'kith and kin', acquaintance and kinsfolk, sums up the world of intimate relationships. A *kinship system* is usually taken to refer to the complex of rules in any one society (or section of a society) which, by governing descent, succession, inheritance, marriage, extra-marital sexual relations, and residence, determines the status of individuals and groups in respect of their ties of consanguinity and marriage.

B. 1. Two people are kin(smen) when they share a common ancestor or one is descended from the other. The word 'ancestor' here means somebody standing in the social position of a father who had a child who had a child until the present generation is reached; or somebody standing in the social position of a mother, etc. An ancestor is not necessarily a forbear or progenitor in a biological sense, and the tracing of kinship links by genealogies (which are statements about social relationships) is a process different from that of the tracing of blood relationships by the geneticist. The facts of procreation provide men-in-society with certain elements which they use for the expression of social relations. Different societies perceive the facts of procreation differently (in a sense the facts differ); but even if the facts are perceived in the same way they may well be put to different social use. In their eagerness to dispel the wrong notion that the study of kinship is the study of blood relationships, anthropologists sometimes fall into the error of denying any connexion between the two things. The procreation and rearing of children form kernel around which a particular society its own system of allocating rights and Biology does not explain why any part kinship system exists, but the engenderin children is the natural key to the elabo social edifice known as kinship.

2. Kinship relations are sometimes calle

C. In formal analysis a primary distinction is made between *unilineal* and *non-unilineal* ship.

1. The first is a kind of tracing of descent males exclu sively)

In studying works on kinship written at different times during the last century the reader must grasp their underlying theoretical preoccupations. Much of the earlier work is concerned with the evolutionary sequence of forms of kinship and marriage, great reliance being placed upon kinship terminology. Contemporary interests in the subject and modern systems of analysis are exemplified in A. R. Radcliffe-Brown, 'Introduction' to A. R. Radcliffe-Brown & D. Forde, *African Systems of Kinship and Marriage* (London: Oxford University Press, 1950); C. Lévi-Strauss, *Les Structures élémentaires de la parenté* (Paris: Presses Universitaires de France, 1949); G. P. Murdock, *Social Structure* (New York: The Macmillan Co., 1949) and E. R. Leach, *Rethinking Anthropology* (London: Athlone Press, 1961). Maurice Freedman

See also: CONSANGUINITY
          DESCENT
          FAMILY
          MARRIAGE
          RESIDENCE

Kinship Terminology
A. Kinship *terminology* consists of terms which designate, in the first instance, social relation-
or persons occupying such relationships
by marriage and parenthood, and
ently extended to relation-

I.g.

Ref.   5.   *Encyclopedia of the Social Sciences.* New York: Mac-
H41   millan Co., 1930-1935. 15 vols.
.E6

Ref.   6.   *International Encyclopedia of the Social Sciences.* New
H41   York: Macmillan and Free Press, 1968. 17 vols. illus.
+.A215

> The two most prominent multivolume encyclopedias
> in the social sciences are the 15-volume *Encyclopedia
> of the Social Sciences (ESS)* and 17-volume *Interna-
> tional Encyclopedia of the Social Sciences (IESS).*
> The editorial policy on the later work was to com-
> plement rather than supersede the original. Together
> they represent excellent sources for information on
> a wide range of subjects within and related to disci-
> plines in the social sciences.
>
> As well as an article on anthropology, the *ESS* in-
> cludes articles on all major topics in politics, eco-
> nomics, law, sociology, and social work, with some
> attention directed toward what in the 1930's were
> considered peripheral subjects: ethics, education,
> philosophy, psychology, and geography. There are
> some 4,000 biographies of persons deceased when
> the *ESS* was published. Articles are of varying lengths,
> signed by their authors, and arranged alphabetically.
> Cross-references to related articles are provided,
> and the final volume has a comprehensive index and
> a classification of the articles in subject and biography
> groups. Most articles have brief bibliographies.
>
> The *IESS* has some difference in scope and format,
> but there is still a marked resemblance to the original.
> Along with anthropology, there are extensive articles
> on the concepts, theories and methods of economics,
> geography, history, law, political science, psychology
> and sociology. Articles on disciplines have cross-
> references to the related topical and biographical
> articles. Excellent—often extensive—bibliographies
> accompany each article. Emphasis in articles is on
> analytical and comparative aspects of topics, with
> historical and descriptive material added to illustrate
> concepts and theories.

As well as archaeology, ethnography, kinship, linguistics, and race, both works feature articles on cultural, economic, physical, political, social, and applied anthropology. Among the several articles in the entry "history" in *IESS* are ethno-history and culture history. The *IESS* has only 600 biographies, compared with the over 4,000 in *ESS*, but the articles are longer and emphasize individuals not included in the first work, including prominent social scientists still living, but born before 1890.

Ref.
H41
G6

7. Gould, Julius, and Kolb, William L., eds. *Dictionary of the Social Sciences*. New York: Free Press, 1964. 761 pp.

Gould defines about one-fourth as many terms as Zadrozny [I.g.19], but his treatment of the terms is

The exhibit from the *International Encyclopedia of the Social Sciences* is given on page 301.

See pages 298-99 for the annotation that relates to the exhibit on the right.

Because the treatment of "Kinship" and related topics is so extensive in IESS [I.g.6], only very brief portions can be illustrated in this format. Taken together, all major articles on "Kinship" occupy over 27 pages, with discussions of over 200 works. In particular, note the importance attached to the work of Radcliffe-Brown and Levi-Strauss, names that have been mentioned in preceding sources.

In England Malinowski and Radcliffe-Brown have been most influential figures in the development of kinship studies. Malinowski, as a result of his study The Family Among the Australian Aborigines (1913) and his extended field research in the Trobriand Islands, emphasized the importance of the family as the "initial situation" for the development of kinship, from which attitudes and terminology could be widely extended. He also called attention to the significance of "sociological fatherhood" in a matrilineal society that did not recognize the genetic role; but he was more concerned with the function of kinship and other social institutions in fulfilling individual needs. [See MALINOWSKI.] Radcliffe-Brown, an early student of Rivers, is the central figure in the modern study of kinship systems. He was the first to develop the conception of the kinship system as composed of both terminology and patterns of social behavior and to see kinship as an integral part of the larger social structure. As a functionalist he was concerned with the significance of institutions in maintaining the social system, but he went further and attempted to discover basic structural principles that were relevant to a variety of different terminological groupings and social usages. [See RADCLIFFE-BROWN.]

among those researches that have contributed to the development and modification of the structural–functional approach.

The clearest statement of this approach is found in Radcliffe-Brown's Introduction to African Systems of Kinship and Marriage (1950), in which he was concerned with the general comparative and theoretical study of kinship organization as an arrangement which enables persons to cooperate with one another in an orderly social life. In this discussion he compared and contrasted the cognatic system of the early Teutonic peoples with the agnatic lineage systems of ancient Rome and many modern African tribes and indicated the relevance of the principles of "the unity of the sibling group" and "the unity and solidarity of the lineage" for various aspects of social life. Here he was particularly concerned with the significance of unilineal descent in bringing about corporate kin groups that continue beyond the life of individual members and may control resources, exact vengeance, regulate marriage, and engage in ritual. He saw marriage as essentially a rearrangement of social structure and discussed in detail the significance of marriage in various African societies. For a worldwide classification of kinship systems he proposed four types: father-right, mother-right, cognatic systems, and double lineage systems, each of which

The contributions of Lévi-Strauss to the study of kinship systems are of a different character, and in Les structures élémentaires de la parenté (1949) and Structural Anthropology (1958) he presents some highly original views on the nature of social structure in general and kinship in particular. "Social structure," for Lévi-Strauss, is in itself concerned not with the empirical reality of social relations but with models which give rise to them, and he discusses the relevance of mechanical models (those on the same scale as the phenomena) and statistical models (where the elements of the model are on a different scale) for various problems, particularly those of communication. With regard to kinship he views the terminology and the system of attitudes as representing quite different orders

engendered considerable controversy. Homans and Schneider, in Marriage, Authority, and Final Causes (1955), essay an alternate explanation based on Radcliffe-Brown's theory of sentiments. Needham attacked this strongly in Structure and Sentiment (1962) and went on to make a number of reformulations of what he calls "prescriptive" marriage systems. Leach, in Rethinking Anthropology (1961), shows the considerable influence of Lévi-Strauss, as does Dumont, whose Hierarchy and Marriage Alliance in South Indian Kinship (1957) emphasizes the importance of treating certain categories of relatives as affinal rather than consanguineal.

[See MARRIAGE, articles on COMPARATIVE ANALYSIS and MARRIAGE ALLIANCE.]

4

II.g

11. Honigmann, John J., ed. *Handbook of Social and Cultural Anthropology.* Chicago: Rand McNally, 1973.

Broader in scope of coverage of the discipline than *IESS* [I.g.6], this is the first major assessment of what is currently known in social and cultural anthropology since Kroeber's *Anthropology Today* [I.g.2]. Individual chapters by authorities attempt to set forth objectively and comprehensively a review of relevant literature in 28 chapters, "including where relevant a history of what has been accomplished, major subdivisions or lines of work, unresolved issues, and future prospects." After a chapter on the history of cultural anthropology, subsequent chapters focus on such topics as: "the four faces—unilinear, universal, multilinear, and differential—of evolution"; "adaptation in biological and cultural evolution"; and "the structural anthropology of Claude Levi-Strauss." Other chapters examine such issues as "ecological anthropology and anthropological ecology"; "ethography (the field work enterprise)"; "genealogical methods as the foundation of structural demography"; "cross-cultural studies"; "mathematical anthropology"; "cognitive anthropology"; "sociolinguistics"; "belief systems"; "network analysis"; "identity, culture and behavior"; and "kinship, descent and alliance." Finally there are chapters devoted to topics which suggest interdisciplinary relations: "economic anthropology"; "political anthropology"; "urban anthropology"; and "anthropology and education." Some 2,400 anthropologists and others in related disciplines are included. Bibliographical information on each name is given in full at the end of the chapter in which the work is discussed. Often can be updated by *Social Sciences Citation Index* [I.c.12]. Author and subject indexes give access to the whole volume.

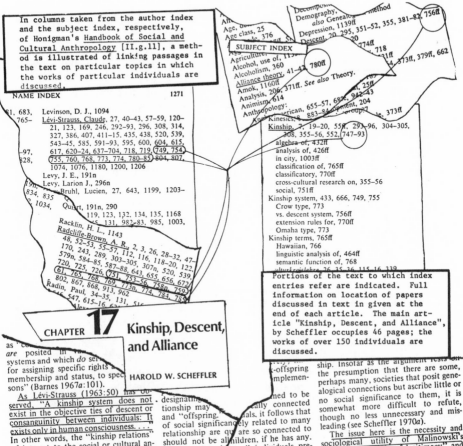

In columns taken from the author index
and the subject index, respectively,
of Honigman's Handbook of Social and
Cultural Anthropology [II.g.11], a method is illustrated of linking passages in
the text on particular topics in which
the works of particular individuals are
discussed.

NAME INDEX   1271

81, 683,   Levinson, D. J., 1094
  765—   Lévi-Strauss, Claude, 27, 40–43, 57–59, 120–
            21, 123, 169, 246, 292–93, 296, 308, 314,
            327, 386, 407, 411–15, 435, 438, 520, 539,
            543–45, 585, 591–93, 595, 600, 604, 615,
—97,   617, 620–24, 637–704, 718, 719, 749, 754,
828,   755, 760, 768, 773, 774, 780–85, 804, 807,
            1074, 1076, 1180, 1200, 1206
           Levy, J. E., 191n
19n,   Levy, Larion J., 296n
834, 835   Bruhl, Lucien, 27, 643, 1199, 1203–
            1034,   Quirt, 191n, 290
                    119, 123, 132, 134, 135, 1168
           Racklin, H. L.,   131, 983–83, 985, 1003,
           Radcliffe-Brown, A. R., 1143
            48, 52–53, 55–57, 112, 116, 2, 3, 26, 28–32, 47–
            170, 243, 289, 303–305, 118–20, 122,
            579n, 584–85, 587–88, 643, 307n, 520, 539,
            720, 725, 726, 753, 655, 656, 672,
            61, 765, 768, 769, 773n, 756, 758, 759,
            802, 867, 868, 913, 962   774, 784, 789,
           Radin, Paul, 34–35, 131, 51
            547, 615–16,   131,

SUBJECT INDEX

Age, 207
Age class, 25
Agriculture,
Alcohol, use of,
Alcoholism, 360
Alliance theory, 41–42, 780ff
Amok, 206, 371ff. See also Theory.
Analysis, 614
Animism, 614
Anthropology:
    American, 655–57, 682, 942–43
    883–84
Kinesics,   le, 373ff
Kinship, 7, 19–20, 55ff, 293–96, 304–305,
    308, 355–56, 552, 747–93
    algebra of, 432ff
    analysis of, 426ff
    in city, 1003ff
    classification of, 765ff
    classificatory, 770ff
    cross-cultural research on, 355–56
    social, 751ff
Kinship system, 433, 666, 749, 755
    Crow type, 773
    vs. descent system, 756ff
    extension rules for, 770ff
    Omaha type, 773
Kinship terms, 765ff
    Hawaiian, 766
    linguistic analysis of, 464ff
    semantic function of, 768

Decomposi
Demography,
    also Genealo
Depression, 1139ff
Descent, 20, 295, 351–52, 355, 381–82, 756ff
                                    718
                                    373ff, 379ff, 662

Portions of the text to which index
entries refer are indicated. Full
information on location of papers
discussed in text in given at the
end of each article. The main article "Kinship, Descent, and Alliance",
by Scheffler occupies 46 pages; the
works of over 150 individuals are
discussed.

CHAPTER 17
Kinship, Descent, and Alliance

HAROLD W. SCHEFFLER

as
are   posited
systems and which do se
for assigning specific rights
membership and status, to spec
sons" (Barnes 1967a:101).

As Lévi-Strauss (1963:50) has observed, "A kinship system does not
exist in the objective ties of descent or
consanguinity between individuals: It
exists only in human consciousness. . . ."
In other words, the "kinship relations"
of interest to the social or cultural anthropologist are those "genealogical"
connections whose existence is pre-
sumed by or "known" to any people,
not those posited by or known to any
scientific discipline. Thus the foundation of any kinship system consists in a
        ltural theory designed to ac-
                at women give
                heory of hu-
            we know,
            t such a
            es are

designati
tionship may
and "offspring.
of social significan
relationship are q
should not be al
fact that the rel
tural universal
    The poss
some so
se
category. The verbal label for this category, where such a label exists, is appropriately glossed as "kin" or "kindred."

**III. THE CONCEPT OF
SOCIAL KINSHIP**

It has often been argued that a
cross-culturally useful definition of kin-

-offspring
mplemen-

ned to be
lly connected
als, it follows that
ly related to many
are so connected to
ildren. if he has any.
ies all individuals pre-
genealogically connected
ther individual, though per-
within a limited range, are
conceptually aggregated into a single

ship. Insofar as the argument rests on
the presumption that there are some,
perhaps many, societies that posit genealogical connections but ascribe little or
no social significance to them, it is
somewhat more difficult to refute,
though no less unnecessary and misleading (see Scheffler 1970a).
    The issue here is the necessity and
sociological utility of Malinowski's
(1930a) "principle of legitimacy" and
of his and Radcliffe-Brown's concept of
"social kinship" as something greater
than, though inclusive of, social relations ascribed on the basis of genealogical connection.
    Malinowski argued (1930a [1962:
65] that although the existence of geni-
tors is not always posited, and although
it may confer no rights or duties on the
reputed genitor even when it is posited, it still is possible to maintain that

[7] That is, given by male informants to anthropologists. Powell (1956:278) notes that he was told
that the Trobriand sexual theory of reproduction

"was 'women's and children's talk' . . . what fathers or
their sisters told children as they became old enough
to take more than a childish sexual interest in the
opposite sex" (emphasis added).

5

12. *Social Sciences Citation Index*. Philadelphia: Institute
     for Scientific Information, 1972-   .

    Issued three times a year, the *SSCI* gives another
dimension to research procedures in the social sciences. Based on the principle that the names of people
can be substituted for the subjects with which they
are associated, it provides the opportunity for advancing from earlier research to more recent studies
on the same subject. As well as anthropology, such
subjects as area studies, demography, sociology,
history and political science are covered. *SSCI* consists of three separate but related indexes: the *Source
Index*; the *Citation Index*; and the *Permuterm Subject Index*. Except in unusual cases, the object is to
converge on the *Source Index* from either the *Citation
Index* or the *Permuterm Subject Index*.

    Of the three, the *Citation Index* is the largest and
most useful, but for a clear understanding it is better
to describe first the *Source Index*. In the *Source Index*
are arranged alphabetically by author's name articles
that appear in 1000-odd periodicals within a specific
interval (e.g., one year). Along with the names,
information given includes article title, abbreviated
title of periodical, volume, date, page of issue and
number of footnote references. In addition, since
1974, the works cited in each article are listed in
abbreviated citation format in the *Source Index*. In
the *Citation Index*, also arranged alphabetically by
author's name, are all works cited by the authors
listed in the *Source Index*, with the citing author's
name (from the *Source Index*) listed below. Because
authors appearing in the *Source Index* ordinarily cite
numerous studies, the *Citation Index* is several times
larger than the *Source Index*, and gives an efficient
means of exposing new articles on the subjects covered
by known authors. (Approximately 100,000 citations
are listed annually.) Finally, in the *Citation* and
Source Indexes, any type of communication other
than an ordinary article that reports research (e.g.,
bibliography, review of research, book review,

letter, editorial, etc.) is distinguished by a set of symbols. The symbols and other aspects of using *SSCI* are described inside the front cover of each volume.

The *Permuterm Subject Index* serves when researchers do not know a specific author concerned with a topic for which information is required. By pairing *two* words derived from the titles of articles listed in the *Source Index*, users are led to articles in the *Source Index* which *may* be on those subjects. (As a method, it is not as efficient as using names of people.)

In general, the *SSCI* is useful for tracing trends and developments resulting from the publication of particular research studies, but it is also useful for exposing reviews of research in such titles as the *Annual Review of Anthropology* [I.g.1], *Current Anthropology*, specialized articles listed in *Social Science Information* [I.i.4], and book reviews.

The exhibit for the *Social Sciences Citation Index* is given on page 307.

See pages 304-5 for the annotation relating to the exhibit on the right. In an actual demonstration, this material is the same size as the publication, and thus (unlike this example) one has little difficulty in following the arrangement pattern or in reading the small print.

After having found that Radcliffe-Brown and Levi-Strauss are, respectively, the key sources for "Descent" and for "Alliance" theories of Kinship in the research literature, researchers will want to find recent studies. Using the 1976 SSCI [I.c.12?], it is possible to advance from an older work to a more recent one provided the older work is cited in the research literature. The illustrations show how the various portions of the SSCI are related to one another.

SOCIAL SCIENCE CITATION INDEX

| CITATION INDEX | SOURCE INDEX | PERMUTERM INDEX |

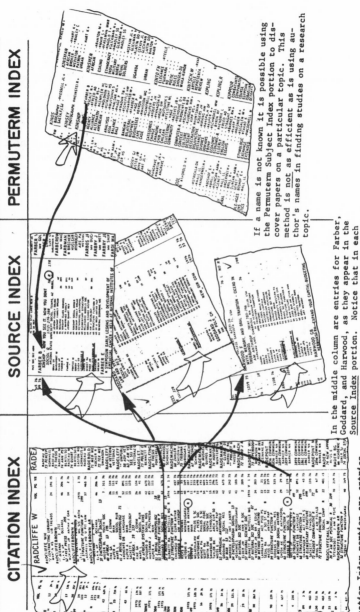

In the Citation Index portion are entries for Radcliffe-Brown's 1950 and 1952 publications (or subsequent editions). Listed directly below are those 1975 or 1976 articles in which these works are cited.

In the middle column are entries for Farber, Goddard, and Harwood, as they appear in the Source Index portion. Notice that in each case articles are selected in which both Radcliffe-Brown and Levi-Strauss are among the papers cited by the authors, strongly suggesting that these studies are concerned with both "Descent" and "Alliance."

If a name is not known it is possible using the Permuterm Subject Index portion to discover papers on a particular topic. This method is not as efficient as is using author's names in finding studies on a research topic.

6A

1. *Annual Review of Anthropology.* Palo Alto, Calif.:
    Annual Reviews, Inc., 1959-

    Formerly entitled *Biennial Review of Anthropology.*
    Each of the approximately 15 articles in a volume is
    the work of a specialist, and provides in a synthe-
    sized, distilled format a survey of recent advances in
    narrow fields within the discipline. Although not
    settled, the policy of coverage of particular topics is
    loose and flexible, and is to be reviewed every five
    years. Titles of recent articles include: "Environment,
    Subsistence, and Society"; "Adaptation"; "Anthro-
    pology of the Middle East and North Africa: a Criti-
    cal Assessment"; "Mythology and Folklore"; "Cross-
    Cultural Analysis: Methods and Scope"; "Theories
    of Culture"; "Comparative Studies of Socialization";
    "Social Networks"; "Fifty Years of Physical Anthro-
    pology: the Men, the Material, the Concepts, the
    Methods, and Aims"; "Social Stratification"; and
    "Kin Groups: Structural Analysis and the Study of
    Behavior." These articles should be used to discover
    trends and developments that have occurred since
    the publication of earlier surveys in such works as
    IESS [I.g.6] or Honigman [I.g.9], or in individual
    volumes devoted to a narrow field of anthropology.
    For example, the article "Mythology and Folklore"
    at least partially updates the 1961 survey, *Folklore
    Around the World* [II.d.9]. References for the ap-
    proximately 3,000 items noted in each volume are
    given at the end of articles in which they are dis-
    cussed. Each volume has an author and subject in-
    dex; authors discussed are also indexed in *SSCI*
    [I.c.12].

Holy's article in the 1976 *Annual Review of Anthropology*
(the exhibit on the right) is listed among the entries under
Radcliffe-Brown's name (the top circles "R" in the Citation
Index portion of the exhibit) on page 307.

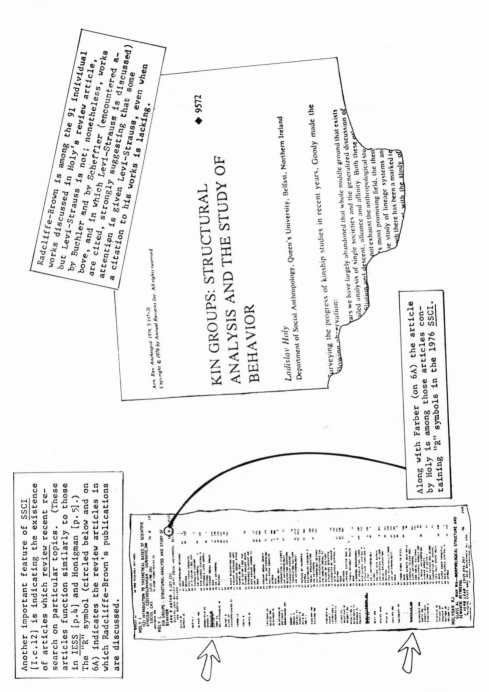

Radcliffe-Brown is among the 91 individual
works discussed in Holy's review article,
but Levi-Strauss is not; nonetheless, works
by Buchler and by Scheffler (encountered a-
bove, and in which Levi-Strauss is discussed)
are cited, strongly suggesting that some
attention is given Levi-Strauss, even when
a citation to his works is lacking.

◆ 9572

Ann. Rev. Anthropol. 1976. 5:107–31
Copyright © 1976 by Annual Reviews Inc. All rights reserved

KIN GROUPS: STRUCTURAL
ANALYSIS AND THE STUDY OF
BEHAVIOR

Ladislav Holy
Department of Social Anthropology, Queen's University, Belfast, Northern Ireland

surveying the progress of kinship studies in recent years. Goody made the

Another important feature of SSCI
[I.c.12] is indicating the existence
of articles which review recent research on particular topics. (These
articles function similarly to those
in IESS [p.4] and Honigman [p.5].)
The "R" symbol (circled below and on
6A) indicates the review articles in
which Radcliffe-Brown's publications
are discussed.

Along with Farber (on 6A) the article
by Holy is among those articles containing "R" symbols in the 1976 SSCI.

6B

David M. Schneider

Some Muddles in the Models: Or, How the System really Works[1]

PART ONE. ALLIANCE

1. The phrase 'alliance theory' and its opposition to what has been called 'descent theory' was first suggested by Dumont (1961a). ... Alliance theory, with roots clearly in Durkheim and Mauss, has specifically arisen out of Lévi-Strauss's *Structures élémentaires* ... and Needham. Descent theory also has its roots in Durkheim and Mauss, but its development has been through Radcliffe-Brown to Fortes, Goody, Gough, Gluckman, and, in certain respects, Firth.

(1940) and has been developed by Lévi-Strauss's *Structures élémentaires* ...

This is an oversimplified picture, of course, but one which provides a reasonable beginning. It would oversimplify matters, too, but also be useful to point out, that where Durkheim tried to bridge the gap between positivism and idealism and ended up as an ... alist in the remnants of some positiviz) ... Needham's ...

Portions of Schneider's article, "Some Muddles in the Models: Or, How the System Really Works." Along with Radcliffe-Brown and Lévi-Strauss some 150 works on "Kinship" are discussed.

1940) it is the enduring social groups, the concrete lineages.[2] For alliance theory, the problem is not what the concrete patterns of social relations actually are, although these are not neglected; it is not the actual organization of any specific group like a lineage. It is, instead, that construct of ... as a lineage. [Illinois Studies in ... fabricated by the anthropol... Chin Society, as is Firth... The Structure of ...

LEHMAN, F. K. 1963. *The Structure of ...*

LÉVI-STRAUSS, c. 1945. L'Analyse structurale en linguistique et en Anthropology No. 3.

LÉVI-STRAUSS, c. 1945. *Word* 1 (also in *Anthropologie Structurale*. Paris: Presses anthropologie. *Anthropologie élémentaires de la parenté*.

1940. *Les Structures* de France. In Kroeber, A. L. (ed.), *Anthropology* Univeritaires de France.

Social Structure. In Kroeber, A. L. (ed.), *Anthropology* 68.

1953. Chicago: University of Myth. *J. Am. Folklore* 68.

Chicago: University of Chicago Press. Structural Study of Myth. *J. Am. Folklore* 68. Bijdragen 116.

POSPISIL, L. 1958. ... dualistes existent-elles? Univermitaires. Social Change and ... Models. Bijdragen 116.

RADCLIFFE-BROWN, A. R. 1952. *Structure and Function in Primitive Society*. London: Cohen & West.

1953. Dravidian Kinship Terminology. *Man* 53, No. 169.

(Traus...

♦ 9572

As exposed by the SSCI [I.c.12], Holy's article occupies pp. 107-31 of the 1976 *Annual Review of Anthropology* [I.g.1]. Among the **87 works** discussed are no. 10, Buchler (see **p.23 above**), no. 77, Schneider, **and** no. 76, Scheffler (see **p.5 above**).

Ann. Rev. An...
Copyright © 19.. by Annual ...

KIN GROUPS: STRUCTURAL ANALYSIS AND THE STUDY OF BEHAVIOR

Ladislav Holy

Department of Social Anthropology, Queen's University, Belfast, Northern Ireland

... of ... or descent as the main structural principle derives directly from African ethnography accumulated during fieldwork carried out in the 1940s and early 1950s. When new ethnography became extensively available from India, Burma, Ceylon, Indonesia, and South America, it became increasingly obvious that in explanation of the social structure of many societies in these areas, the main structuring importance could not be ascribed to the principle of descent. New structuring principles were sought and found in enduring alliances between groups. As a result of this development, the anthropological study of kin groups in the 1960s was dominated by the discussion between the proponents of the 'alliance theory,' developed mainly by Lévi-Strauss, Dumont, Leach, and Needham, and the proponents of 'descent theory,' developed mainly by Radcliffe-Brown, Evans-Pritchard, Fortes, Goody, Gough, Gluckman, and, to a certain extent, Firth (for a review of the discussion see references, c[10], [77]).

On the ethnographical level, the discussion between ... 'scent'' theorists was basically the discussion between ... predominantly in Southeast Asia on the ... ... cation with the Australian Natl. Univ.

9. Brown, A., Brookfield, H. C. 1959-60. Chimbu land and society. *Oceania* 30: 1-75

10. Buchler, I. R., Selby, H. A. 1968. *Kinship and Social Organization: An Introduction to Theory and Method*. New York: Macmillan

11. Caplan, P. 1969. Cognatic descent groups on Mafia. *Man* (NS) ...

... vironment ...

7.5-11

6. Newman, P. L. 1965. *Knowing the Gururumba*. New York: Holt Rinehart & Winston

57. Pouwer, J. 1960. Loosely structured societies in Netherlands New Guinea. *Bijdragen* 116:109-18

58. Pouwer, J. 1964. ... *Volkenkunde* ... Mountains: toward a reorientation of a social system in ... the Star Mountains ...

59. Radcliffe-Brown, A. R. 1952. *Structure and Function in Primitive Society*. London: Cohen & West

60. Read, K. E. 1951. ... Gama of the Central Highlands.

KIN GROUPS   129

Social Order: The Legacy of Lewis Henry Morgan. Chicago: Aldine

26. Freeman, J. D. 1961. On the concept of kindred. *J. R. Anthropol. Inst.* 91:192-220

27. Glasse. R. M. 1968. See Ref. 4

28. Glickman, M. 1971. Kinship and credit among the Nuer. *Africa* 41: 306-19

29. Glickman, M. 1972. The Nuer and the Dinka: a further note. *Man* (NS) 7: 586-... Glue... ...ture. Ber...

75. Scheffler, H. W. 1966. Ancestor worship in anthropology: observation on descent and descent groups. *Curr. Anthropol.* 1966: 541-51

76. Schneider and alliance. In *Handbook of Social and Cultural Anthropology*, ed. J. J. Honigman, 747-93. Chicago: Rand McNally

77. Schneider, D. M. 1965. Some muddles in the models: or, how the system really works. In *The Relevance of Models for Social Anthropology*, 25-85. A.S.A. Monogr. 1. London: Tavistock... On segmentary

In the exhibit on the left, an attempt is made to show how following up the information in the text and bibliography of the article on the preceding page supplements and expands the topic.

Items are identified by a code combining letters (for chapters) and numerals—not unlike the system employed in this research guide. There are over 130 pages of expertly compiled indexes of author, title and subject entries.

I.c.   BIBLIOGRAPHIES AND ABSTRACTS

Periodical
Index

1.   *Abstracts in Anthropology.* Westport, Conn: Greenwood Publications, 1970-   .

WWSC has V. 1, No. 1, Feb. 1970-   .

Annually about 4,000 abstracts of articles from some 200 periodicals are published in four categories (each appropriately subdivided): archaeology; linguistics; physical anthropology; and cultural anthropology. Author and subject indexes for each issue.

Ref.
Z 7128
.W6A4

2.   Albert, Ethel M. *Selected Bibliography on Values, Ethics, and Esthetics in the Behavioral Sciences . . .* Glencoe, Illinois: Free Press, 1959.

A classified arrangement that includes 303 briefly annotated items on anthropology. A "Guide to the Bibliography" on pages 3-41 indicates, by numbers, items on Topical Studies (such as Cross-Cultural Comparisons of Values, Culture and Personality), Area Studies, Methodology, etc. Author index.

Ref.
Z6009
+A48

3.   American Geographical Society. *Research Catalogue.* 15 vols. Boston: G. K. Hall, 1962.

For a more detailed description see item I.b.1, in the research guide "Geography," No. 2. For anthropology, Section 5, Human Geography, is the most useful. This section includes such subdivisions as: Relation of Man and the Geographical Environment (Anthro-Geography); Physiological Geography; Geography of Population; Economic Geo-Political Geography; Social and Cultural Geography; and Military Geography. In turn, each of these is further subdivided into such divisions as: adjustment of man to the geographical environment; nomadic anthropology; nomadism; tribal migration; rural settlements; food supply; linguistic geography;

religions; material culture (e.g., clothing, shelter, implements); customs, folklore; and slavery. An excellent bibliographic complement to the *HRAF Source Bibliography* [I.c.8] and the HRAF system [III]. Kept up-to-date by *Current Geographical Publicatons*. [I.c.5].

Periodical
Index

4. *Anthropological Index to Current Periodicals in the Library of the Royal Anthropological Institute.* London: 1963-   .

WWSC holdings begin V. 7, 1969-   .

Considered one of the most complete current indexes in anthropology. Section I contains general articles, while each of the five sections that follow is devoted to a geographical area. Each section has five cate-

Periodical
Index

6. *Ethnic Studies Bibliography.* Pittsburgh: Published by University Center for International Studies, University of Pittsburgh, in conjunction with the Pennsylvania Ethnic Heritage Studies Center, 1975-   .

Although "ethnic" is not necessarily anthropological (evidently only selective coverage is given anthropology journals) many of the articles included are of interest to anthropologists. This annual computer-produced bibliography contains abstracts of 400 articles of worldwide concern published in some 120 U.S. social and ethnic studies journals. Expanded coverage is promised for future volumes.

The bulk of the volume consists of the Document Description Listing, where each entry contains: an accession number (entries are listed in numerical order); bibliographical information; an abstract of the article; special features (the titles of all tables, charts, figures, maps and the like); cited people (the names of all people whose work is cited in the article); and the subject headings (descriptors) under which the article is listed in the various indexes.

There are five indexes: Author/Contributor; Subject; Geographic Area; Proper Name; and Journal Title.

Appendix A

If an author's name is not known, the Subject and Proper Names Indexes are the most useful.

The Subject Index should be used jointly with the Rotated Subject Descriptor Display (which precedes the Subject Index) in which, by computer, all words contained in each descriptor are arranged alphabetically. The Rotated Subject Descriptor Display allows users to become acquainted with the terminology used in the Subject Index, and to determine where a particular descriptor is located in the Subject Index. (For example, a descriptor such as "Social System Structural Characteristics" appears in a *single* place in the Subject Index, alphabetically by the first word, but in the Rotated Subject Descriptor Display, there are entries for this descriptor under each of the four words.) It is suggested that once an appropriate article is located, by examining the other index entries under which the article is listed, given at the end of the abstracts, other related articles can be located. The Proper Names Index provides access to articles about notable events, organizations, and smaller geographic areas not represented in the Geographic Index. Occasionally a subject not contained in the Subject Index (e.g., busing), and the names of people treated alphabetically in articles, will appear here.

Although there is no index to the names included in Cited People section of particular entries, this feature suggests joint use of *ESB* with *SSCI* [I.c.12].

Attentive readers will have noted that there is no entry I.C.5 on page 313. It was deleted because of space limitations.

Illustrated are abstracts of an article by Elam in a 1975 issue of _Ethnology_ as they appeared in Abstracts in Anthropology [I.c.1] and Ethnic Studies Bibliography [I.c.6].

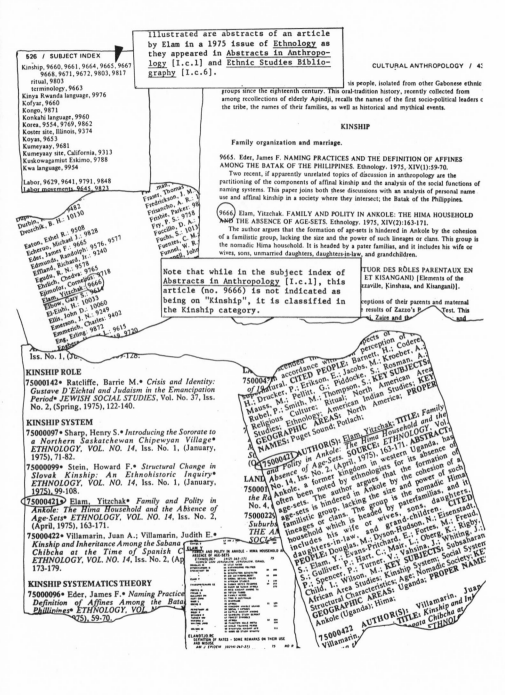

CULTURAL ANTHROPOLOGY / 4:

...his people, isolated from other Gabonese ethnic groups since the eighteenth century. This oral-tradition history, recently collected from among recollections of elderly Apindji, recalls the names of the first socio-political leaders c the tribe, the names of their families, as well as historical and mythical events.

KINSHIP

Family organization and marriage.

9665. Eder, James F. NAMING PRACTICES AND THE DEFINITION OF AFFINES AMONG THE BATAK OF THE PHILIPPINES. Ethnology, 1975, XIV(1):59-70.

Two recent, if apparently unrelated topics of discussion in anthropology are the partitioning of the components of affinal kinship and the analysis of the social functions of naming systems. This paper joins both these discussions with an analysis of personal name use and affinal kinship in a society where they intersect; the Batak of the Philippines.

9666. Elam, Yitzchak. FAMILY AND POLITY IN ANKOLE: THE HIMA HOUSEHOLD AND THE ABSENCE OF AGE-SETS. Ethnology. 1975, XIV(2):163-171.

The author argues that the formation of age-sets is hindered in Ankole by the cohesion of a familistic group, lacking the size and the power of such lineages or clans. This group is the nomadic Hima household. It is headed by a pater familias, and it includes his wife or wives, sons, unmarried daughters, daughters-in-law, and grandchildren.

Note that while in the subject index of Abstracts in Anthropology [I.c.1], this article (no. 9666) is not indicated as being on "Kinship", it is classified in the Kinship category.

...TUOR DES RÔLES PARENTAUX EN ...ET KISANGANI) [Elements of the ...zzaville, Kinshasa, and Kisangani)].

...ceptions of their parents and maternal ...e results of Zazzo's P... Test. This ...i, Zaire and th...   and

Dup... 9482
Durbin, B. H.: 10130
Dvorchik, J...
Eaton, Ethel R.: 9508
Echeruo, Michael J.: 9828
Eder, James F.: 9665, 9576, 9577
Edmunds, Randolph: 9240
Effland, Richard, Jr.:
Egudu, R. N.: 9578
Ehrlich, Chedva: 9765
Ejimofor, Cornelius: 9718
Elam, Yitzchak: 9666
Elbow, Gary S.: 961...
El-Eishi, H.: 10033
Ellis, John D.: 10060
Emerson, J. N.: 9249
Emmerich, Charles: 9402
Eng, Erling: 9872
Engberg...: 9615
...: 9720

...man,
Fraser, Thomas J. M....
Fredrickson, A. R.:...
Frisancho, A. R.:...
Frisbie, Parker: 98...
Fry, P. S.: 9758
Fuccillo, D. A.:
Fuchs, S.: 1013...
Fuentes, C. M...:
Funnel, W. R...
...ell, John...

Iss. No. 1, (Ju... ...-128.

KINSHIP ROLE

75000142• Ratcliffe, Barrie M.• _Crisis and Identity: Gustave D'Eichtal and Judaism in the Emancipation Period_• _JEWISH SOCIAL STUDIES_, Vol. No. 37, Iss. No. 2, (Spring, 1975), 122-140.

KINSHIP SYSTEM

75000097• Sharp, Henry S.• _Introducing the Sororate to a Northern Saskatchewan Chipewyan Village_• _ETHNOLOGY, VOL. NO. 14_, Iss. No. 1, (January, 1975), 71-82.

75000099• Stein, Howard F.• _Structural Change in Slovak Kinship: An Ethnohistoric Inquiry_• _ETHNOLOGY, VOL. NO. 14_, Iss. No. 1, (January, 1975), 99-108.

75000421• Elam, Yitzchak• _Family and Polity in Ankole: The Hima Household and the Absence of Age-Sets_• _ETHNOLOGY, VOL. NO. 14_, Iss. No. 2, (April, 1975), 163-171.

75000422• Villamarin, Juan A.; Villamarin, Judith E.• _Kinship and Inheritance Among the Sabana Chibcha at the Time of Spanish C_ _ETHNOLOGY, VOL. NO. 14_, Iss. No. 2, (Ap 173-179.

KINSHIP SYSTEMATICS THEORY

75000096• Eder, James F.• _Naming Practice_ _Definition of Affines Among the Bata_ _Phillipines_• _ETHNOLOGY, VOL. N_...975), 59-70.

750004?... in accordance with ...of l9...ural. CITED PEOPLE: Barnett, H.; Coderc H.; Drucker, P.; Erikson, E.; Jacobs, M.; Kroeber, A.; Mauss, M.; Pellitt, G.; Piddocke, S.; Rosman, A.; Rubel, P.; Smith, M.; Thompson, S. KEY SUBJECTS: Religious Culture; Ethnology; American Indian Studies; KEY Studies; Ritual; North America; PROPER NAMES: Puget Sound; Potlach. GEOGRAPHIC AREAS: North America;

75000421• AUTHOR(S): Elam, Yitzchak; TITLE: Family and Polity in Ankole: The Hima Household and the Absence of Age-Sets. SOURCE: ETHNOLOGY, Vol. No. 14, Iss. No. 2, (April, 1975), 163-171. ABSTRACT: Ankole, a former kingdom in western Uganda, has often been noted by ethnologists for its absence of age-sets. The author argues that the formation of age-sets is hindered in Ankole by the cohesion of such familistic group, lacking the size and power of such lineages or clans. The group is the nomadic Hima household which is headed by paterfamilias, and it includes his wife or wives, sons, daughters, daughters-in-law, and grand-children. CITED PEOPLE: Douglas, M.; Dyson-Hudson, N.; Eisenstadt, S.; Elam, Y.; Evans-Pritchard, E.; Fortes, M.; Freud, S.; Gulliver, P.; Hart, C.; Mair, L.; Oberg, K.; Rigby, P.; Spencer, P.; Turner, V.; Vahsina, J.; Whiting, J.; Child, I.; Wilson, M.; KEY SUBJECTS: Kinship System; Social System; African Area Studies; Age; Nomadic Society; KE... Structural Characteristics; Age; PROPER NAME... GEOGRAPHIC AREAS: Uganda; Hima; Ankole (Uganda); Hima;

75000422 AUTHOR(S): Villamarin, Jua... Villamarin, ...TITLE: Kinship and In... ...ata Chibcha at ...ETHNOL...

APPENDIX B

Citation Relationships of a Bibliography on Staining Nucleic Acid

1. Rabinowitz, E., and Epstein, L. F. "Polymerization of Dyestuffs in Solution." *Journal of the American Chemical Society* 63 (1941):69-78.
2. Michaelis, L. "The Nature of the Interaction of Nucleic Acids and Nuclei with Basic Dyes." *Cold Spring Harbor Symposium on Quantitative Biology* 12 (1947):131-42.
3. _____. "Reversible Polymerization and Molecular Aggregation." *Journal of Physical and Colloid Chemistry* 54 (1950):1-17.
4. Zanker, V. "The Proof of Definite Reversible Association of Acridine Orange by Absorption and Fluorescence Measurements in Aqueous Solution." *Zeitschrift für Physikalische Chemie* 199 (1952):225-58.
5. Morthland, F. W. et al. "Spectrophotometric Studies on the Interaction of Nucleic Acids with Aminoacridines and Other Basic Dyes." *Experimental Cell Research* 7 (1954):201-14.
6. Lawley, P. D. "Interaction Studies with Deoxyribonucleic Acid." *Biochimica et Biophysica Acta* 19 (1956):160-7, 328-32.
7. Peacocke, A. R., and Skerrett, J.N.H. "Interaction of Aminoacridines with Nucleic Acids." *Transactions of the Faraday Society* 52 (1956):261-79.
8. Appel, W., and Zanker, V. "Metachromism and the Formation of a Reversible Complex Between Acridine Orange and Heparin." *Zeitschrift für Naturforschung* 13B (1958):126-34.
9. _____, and Scheibe, G. "Reversible Association of Pseudosocynanine Caused by Polar Polymers (Heporin)." *Zeitschrift für Naturforschung* 13B (1958):356-64.
10. Steiner, R. F. "Enzymical Produced Polynucleotides." *Journal of Polymer Science* 30 (1958):17-28.
11. _____, and Beers, R. F. "Polynucleotides. V. Titration and Spectrometric Studies on the Interaction of Synthetic Polynucleotides with Various Dyes." *Archives of Biochimica and Biophysica Acta* 81 (1959): 75-92.
12. Bradley, D. F., and Felsenfeld, G. "Aggregation of an Acridine Dye on Native and Denatured Deoxyribonucleates." *Nature* 184 (1959):1920-2.

13. _____, and Wolf, M. K. "Aggregation of Dyes Bound to Polyanions." *Proceedings of the National Academy of Science of the U.S.* 45 (1959): 944-52.
14. _____, and _____. "Neurochemistry of Polynucleotides." In R. O. Brady and D. B. Tower, eds., *Symposium on the Neurochemistry of Nucleotides and Amino Acids*, Philadelphia, 1958. New York: John Wiley, 1960.
15. Loeser, C. N., et al. "Absorption and Fluorescence Studies on Biological Systems—Nucleic Acid Dye Complexes." *Anatomical Record* 138 (1960): 163-78.

APPENDIX C

Short-term Memory
Citation Network

1. Peterson, L. R., and Peterson, M. J. "Short-term Retention of Individual Verbal Items." *Journal of Experimental Psychology* 58 (1959):193-8.
2. Lloyd, K. E., Reid, L. S., and Feallock, J. B. "Short-term Retention as a Function of the Average Number of Items Presented." *Journal of Experimental Psychology* 60 (1960):201-7.
3. Murdock, B. B., Jr. "Short-term Retention of Single Paired Associates." *Psychological Reports* 8 (1961):280.
4. Keppel, G., and Underwood, B. J. "Proactive Inhibition in Short-term Retention of Single Verbal Items." *Journal of Verbal Learning and Verbal Behaviour* 1 (1962):153-61.
5. Merton, A. W. "Implications of Short-term Memory for a General Theory of Memory." *Journal of Verbal Learning and Verbal Behaviour* 2 (1963): 1-21.
6. Murdock, B. B., Jr. "Short-term Retention of Single Paired Associates." *Journal of Experimental Psychology* 65 (1963):433-43.
7. _____. "Short-term Memory and Paired Associate Learning." *Journal of Verbal Learning and Verbal Behaviour* 2 (1963):320-8.
8. Schumsky, D. A., Grasha, D. G., and Allen, C. K. "Proactive Inhibition and Item Similarity in Short-term Memory." *Journal of Verbal Learning and Verbal Behaviour* 2 (1963):440-5.
9. Wickens, D. D., Born, D. G., and Allen, C. K. "Proactive Inhibition and Item Similarity in Short-term Memory." *Journal of Verbal Learning and Verbal Behaviour* 2 (1963):440-5.
10. Conrad, R. "Acoustic Confusions in Immediate Memory." *British Journal of Psychology* 55 (1964):75-84.
11. Loess, H. "Proactive Inhibition in Short-term Memory." *Journal of Verbal Learning and Verbal Behaviour* 3 (1964):362-8.
12. Murdock, B. B., Jr. "Proactive Inhibition in Short-term Memory." *Journal of Experimental Psychology* 68 (1964):184-9.
13. Postman, L. "Short-term Memory and Incidental Learning." In A. Melton, ed., *Categories of human learning.* Academic Press, 1964.

14. Howe, M.J.A. "Intra-list Differences in Short-term Memory." *Quarterly Journal of Experimental Psychology* 17 (1965):338-42.
15. Keppel, G. "Problems of Method in the Study of Short-term Memory." *Psychological Bulletin* 63 (1965):1-13.
16. Murdock, B. B., Jr. "Effects of a Subsidiary Task on Short-term Memory." *British Journal of Psychology* 56 (1965):418-9.
17. Posner, M. I., and Rossman, E. "Effect of Size and Location of Informational Transforms upon Short-term Retention." *Journal of Experimental Psychology* 70 (1965):496-505.
18. Rohrmen, N. L., and Jahnke, J. C. "Effect of Recall Condition, Presentation Rate and Retention Interval on Short-term Memory." *Psychological Reports* 16 (1965):877-83.
19. Wickelgren, W. A. "Acoustic Similarity and Retroactive Interference in Short-term Memory." *Journal of Verbal Learning and Verbal Behaviour* 4 (1965):53-61.
20. Crawford, J., Hunt, E., and Peak, G. "Inverse Forgetting in Short-term Memory." *Journal of Experimental Psychology* 72 (1966):415-22.
21. Goggin, J. "Retroactive and Proactive Inhibition in Short-term Retention of Paired Associates." *Journal of Verbal Learning and Verbal Behaviour* 5 (1966):526-34.
22. Peterson, L. R. "Short-term Verbal Memory and Learning." *Psychological Review* 73 (1966):193-207.
23. Posner, M. I., and Konick, A. F. "On the Role of Interference in Short-term Retention." *Journal of Experimental Psychology* 72 (1966):221-31.
24. Wickelgren, W. A. "Phonemic Similarity and Interference in Short-term Memory for Single Letters." *Journal of Experimental Psychology* 71 (1966):396-404.
25. Aarsonson, D. "Temporal Factors in Perception and Short-term Memory." *Psychological Bulletin* 67 (1967):130-44.
26. Bjork, R. A. *The Effect of Instructions to Selectively Forget During Short-term Memory.* (Memorandum Report No. 3.) Ann Arbor, Mich.: University of Michigan, Human Performance Centre, 1967.
27. Loess, H. "Short-term Memory, Word Class, and Sequence of Items." *Journal of Experimental Psychology* 74 (1967):556-61.
28. Loess, H., and Waugh, N. C. "Short-term Memory and Intertrial Interval." *Journal of Verbal Learning and Verbal Behaviour* 6 (1967):544.
29. Talland, G. A. "Short-term Memory with Interpolated Activity." *Journal of Verbal Learning and Verbal Behaviour* 6 (1967):144-50.
30. Bjork, R. A., Laberge, D., and Legrand, R. "The Modification of Short-term Memory Through Instructions to Forget." *Psychonomic Science* 10 (1968):55-6.
31. Jahnke, J. C. "Delayed Recall and the Serial-Position Effect of Short-

term Memory." *Journal of Experimental Psychology* 76 (1968):618-22.

32. Martin E., Roberts, K. H., and Collins, A. M. "Short-term Memory for Sentences." *Journal of Verbal Learning and Verbal Behaviour* 7 (1968): 560-6.

33. Murdock, B. B., Jr. "Serial Order Effects in Short-term Memory." *Journal of Experimental Psychology* 76 (No. 4, pt. 2) (1968):1-15.

34. Wickens, D. D., and Clarke, S. F. "Osgood Dimensions as an Encoding Class in Short-term Memory." *Journal of Experimental Psychology* 78 (1968):580-4.

35. Dickens, D. D., Clarke, S. F., Hill, F. A., and Willinger, R. P. "An Investigation of Grammatical Class as an Encoding Class in Short-term Memory." *Journal of Experimental Psychology* 78 (1968):599-604.

36. Baddeley, A. D., Scott, D., and Drynan, R. "Short-term Memory and Limited Capacity Hypothesis." *British Journal of Psychology* 60 (1969): 51-5.

37. Blount, W. R. "Short-term Memory in Retardates as a Function of Direction and Delay of Recall." *Psychonomic Science* 14 (1969):69-70.

38. Cermak, L. S. "Repetition and Encoding in Short-term Memory." *Journal of Abnormal Psychology* 92 (1969):321 [citation inaccurate].

39. Dillon, R. F., and Reid, L. S. "Short-term Memory as a Function of Information Processing During Retention Interval." *Journal of Experimental Psychology* 81 (1969):261-9.

40. Doll, T. J. "Short-term Retention: Preparatory Set as Covert Rehearsal." *Journal of Experimental Psychology* 82 (1969):175-82.

41. Ellis, N. R. "Effects of Interpolated Recall on Short-term Memory." *Journal of Experimental Psychology* 79 (1969):568-9.

42. Elmes, D. G. "Role or Prior Calls and Storage Load in Short-term Memory." *Journal of Experimental Psychology* 79 (1969):468-72.

43. Gilson, E. Q. "Tactile Short-term Memory." *Quarterly Journal of Experimental Psychology* 21 (1969):180-4.

44. Lachar, B., and Goggin, J. "Effects of Changes in Word Length on Proactive Interference in Short-term Memory." *Psychonomic Science* 17 (1969):213-4.

45. Landauer, T. K. "Relation Between Short and Long-term Memory— Effect of Order on Retroactive Interference." *Psychonomic Science* 17 (1969):116.

46. Martin, E., and Walter, D. A. "Subject Uncertainty and World-class Effects in Short-term Memory for Sentences." *Journal of Experimental Psychology* 80 (1969):47.

47. Nelson, T. O., and Batchelder, W. H. "Forgetting in Short-term Recall— All or None on Decremental." *Journal of Experimental Psychology* 82 · (1969):96-106.

48. Ryan, J. "Temporal Grouping Rehearsal and Short-term Memory." *Quarterly Journal of Experimental Psychology* 21 (1969):148-55.
49. Ryan, J. F. "Short-term Memory and Rehearsal in Educable Subnormals." *American Journal of Mental Deficiency* 74 (1969):218-22.
50. Schumsky, D. A., Grasha, A. F., Trinder, J., and Richman, C. "List Length and Single-trial Short-term Memory." *Journal of Experimental Psychology* 82 (1969):238-41.
51. Schwartz, F. "Some Problems and Notes About Short-term Memory." *Psychological Reports* 24 (1969):71-80.
52. Stanners, R. F., and Meunier, G. F. "Pronunciability and Rehearsal Time in Short-term Memory with Controlled Acquisition." *Journal of Experimental Psychology* 80 (1969):359-63.
53. Stanners, R. F., Meunier, G. F., and Headley, D. B. "Reaction Time as an Index of Rehearsal in Short-memory." *Journal of Experimental Psychology* 82 (1969):566-70.
54. Tarpy, R. M. "Motivation and Short-term Retention—evidence for Covert Rehearsal." *American Journal of Psychology* 82 (1969):111-6.
55. Tarpy, R. M. "Effects of Interference in STM with Minimum Covert Rehearsal." *Psychological Reports* 24 (1969):723-6.
56. Turvey, M. T., et al. "Connotative Classification and Proactive Interference in Short-term Memory." *Psychonomic Science* 16 (1969):223-4.
57. Turvey, M. T., and Wittlinger, R. D. "Attenuation of Proactive Interference in Short-term Memory as a Function of Cueing to Forget." *Journal of Experimental Psychology* 80 (1969):295-8.

APPENDIX D

Bibliography of Clark and Trow Typology of College Student Subcultures

Apostal, Robert A. *College Student Subcultures and Personal Values. Orono,* Me.: University of Maine, 1966. (Report R-22) ERIC Document 011669.
_____. "College Subcultures and Peer Independence." *College of Education Record* 54 (March 1969):114-9.
_____. *Personality Type and Preferred College Subculture.* Paper read at APGA Annual Meeting, Las Vegas, April 1969. ERIC Document 033 393.
_____. "Student Subcultures and Personal Values." *Journal of College Student Personnel* 9 (January 1968):34-9.
Bolton, C. D., and Kammeyer, K.C.W. *The University Student.* New Haven, Conn.: College and University Press, 1967. [Chapter VI: "Campus Cultures, Role Orientations, and Social Types."]
Brainard, Stephen R. *Personality Characteristics of Leaders Identifying with Different Student Subcultures.* Washington, D.C.: NDEA Institute, 1969. ERIC Document 031 236. (Also published as article in *Journal of College Student Personnel,* May 1971).
_____, and Dollar, Robert J. "Personality Characteristics of Leaders Identifying with Different Student Subcultures." *Journal of College Student Personnel* 12 (May 1971):200-3.
Brown, Jerry W. *Student Subcultures on the Bowdoin Campus.* Brunswick, Me.: Bowdoin College, 1969. ERIC Document 031 745.
Brown, Robert D. "An Investigation of the Relationship Between the Intellectual and the Academic Aspects of College Life." *Journal of Educational Research* 61 (1968):439-41.
Clark, Burton R. "College Image and Student Selection." In *Selection and Educational Differentiation.* Berkeley, Calif.: University of California, Center for the Study of Higher Education, 1960.
_____. *Educating the Expert Society.* San Francisco: Chandler Publishing Co., 1962.
_____. "The New University." *American Behavioral Scientist* 11 (May-June 1968):1-4.
_____, and Trow, Martin A. "College Subcultures." In Leonard Broom and P. Selznick, eds., *Sociology.* 3d ed. New York: Harper and Row, 1963.
_____, _____. *Determinants of College Student Subcultures.* Berkeley,

Calif.: Center for the Study of Higher Education, University of California, 1960. [mimeo]

_____, and _____. "Determinants of College Student Subcultures." Berkeley, Calif.: University of California, Center for Research and Development in Higher Education, 1963.

_____, and _____. "The Organizational Context." In Theodore M. Newcomb and Everett K. Wilson, eds., *College Peer Groups*. Denver, Colo. WICHE, 1966.

Coleman, James S. "Peer Culture and Education in Modern Society." In Theodore Newcomb and Everett K. Wilson, eds., *College Peer Groups*. Denver, Colo.: WICHE, 1966.

Duster, T. "Student Interests, Student Power and Swedish Experience." *American Behavioral Scientist* 11 (May 1968):21-7.

Ellis, Robert A., Parelius, Robert J., and Parelius, Ann P. "The Collegiate Scholar: Education for Elite Status." *Sociology of Education* 44 (Winter 1973):27-58.

Farber, I. E., and Goodstein, L. D. "Student Orientation Survey." Preliminary Report, Public Health Service Research Grant M-226, 1964.

Fiore, Neil A., and Sedlacek, William E. "An Empirical Description of University Student Subcultures." *College Student Journal* (April-May 1972):142-9.

Frantz, Thomas T. "Student Subcultures." *Journal of College Student Personnel* 10 (January 1969):16-20.

_____, and Snider, B. "Dimensions of Student Behavior." *Journal of Educational Research* 63 (December 1969):181-4.

Gallessich, J. "An Investigation of Correlates of Academic Success of Freshmen Engineering Students." *Journal of Counseling Psychology* 17 (1970):173-6.

Gottlieb, David. "College Climates and Student Subcultures." In W. B. Brookover, et al., eds., *The College Student*. New York: Center for Applied Research in Education, 1965, pp. 78-99.

_____, and Hodgkins, Benjamin. "College Student Subcultures: The Structure and Characteristics in Relation to Student Attitude Change." *School Review* 71 (Autumn 1963):266-89.

_____, and Ramsey, Charles. *The American Adolescent*. Homewood, Ill.: Dorsey Press, 1964, pp. 188-96.

Grande, P. P., Simons, J. B., and Pallone, N. J. "The Perception of College Experience and Academic Motivation." *Journal of Educational Research* 61 (October 1967):65-7.

Grieneeks, Laura E. "Changes in Student Role Orientation Toward College." *Proceedings of the 77th Annual Convention of American Psychological Association* (1969):655-6.

Hartnett, R. T. "Differences in Selected Attitudes and College Orientation Between Black Students Attending Traditionally Negro and Traditionally White Institutions." *Sociology of Education* 43 (1970):419-36.

Hassenger, R., and Weiss, R. "The Catholic College Climate." *School Review* 74 (1966):419-45.

Hoge, D. R. "College Students' Value Patterns in 1950s and 1960s." *Sociology of Education* 44 (1970):170-97.

Holland, J. L. "Explorations of a Theory of Vocational Choice: A Longitudinal Study Using a Sample of Typical College Students." *Journal of Applied Psychology* 52 (No. 1, pt. 2) (1968):1-31.

Kees, Donald J., and McDougall, William P. "A Validation Study of the Clark-Trow College Subculture Typology." *Journal of College Student Personnel* 12 (May 1971):193-8.

Keniston, Kenneth. "The Faces in the Lecture Room." In Robert S. Morrison, ed., *The Contemporary University: USA.* Cambridge, Mass.: Houghton, Mifflin, 1966, pp. 315-49.

Lewis, Lionel S. "The Value of College to Different Subcultures." *School Review* 77 (March 1969):32-40.

Mauss, Armond L. *Toward an Empirical Typology of Junior College Student Subculture.* Pleasant Hill, Calif.: Social Sciences Department, Diablo Valley College, 1967. ERIC Document 013 076.

Maw, Ian E. L. "Student Subcultures and Activity Involvement." *Journal of College Student Personnel* 12 (January 1971):62-6.

_____. "Student Subcultures and Their Future Time Perspectives." *National Association of Student Personnel Administrators (NASPA) Journal* 8 (January 1971):160-7.

Michael, W. B., and Boyer, E. L. "Campus Environments." *Review of Educational Research* 35 (1965):264-76.

Newcomb, Theodore M., et al. *Persistence and Change: Bennington College and Its Students After 25 Years.* New York: John Wiley, 1967.

Pemberton, W. A. *Ability, Values and College Achievement.* Newark, Del.: University of Delaware, 1963.

Peterson, Richard E. *College Student Questionnaire (Technical Manual).* Rev. ed. Princeton, N.J.: Educational Testing Service, 1968.

_____. *On a Typology of College Students.* (Research Bulletin 65-9). Princeton, N.J.: Educational Testing Service, 1965.

Reinhold, John E. "Users and Nonusers of College Counseling and Psychiatric Services." *Journal of American College Health Association* 21 (February 1973):201-8.

Sauicki, Victor, Schumer, Harry, and Stanfield, R. E. "Student Role Orientations and College Dropouts." *Journal of Counseling Psychology* 17 (1970):559-66.

Segal, B. E., and Phillips, D. L. "Work, Play and Emotional Disturbance. An Examination of Environment and Disturbances." *Archives of General Psychiatry* 16 (February 1967):173-9.

Segal, S. J. "Student Development and Counseling." *Annual Review of Psychology* 19 (1968):497-508.

Sugarman, Michael. "Vocationalism in Higher Education: A Review." *Vocational Guidance Quarterly* 18 (1969):103-9.

Trow, Martin. "Administrative Implications of Analyses of Campus Cultures." In Terry F. Lunsford, ed., *The Study of Campus Cultures.* Denver, Colo.: WICHE, 1963.

_____. "The Campus Viewed as a Culture." In Hall T. Sprague, ed., *Research on College Students.* Denver, Colo.: WICHE and Center for the Study of Higher Education, 1960.

_____. "Cultural Sophistication and Higher Education." In *Selection and Educational Differentiation.* Berkeley, Calif.: University of California, Center for the Study of Higher Education, 1960.

_____. "Social Research and Educational Policy." In *Research in Higher Education; Guide to Institutional Decisions.* New York: College Entrance Examination Board, 1965.

_____. "Student Cultures and Administrative Action." In Robert L. Sutherland, et al., eds., *Personality Factors on the Campus.* Austin, Tex.: Hogg Foundation for Mental Health, 1962.

_____, and Clark, Burton R. "Varieties and Determinants of Undergraduate Subcultures." New York: 1960. (Paper read at the annual meeting of the American Sociological Society.)

Walker, Jimmy R. *College Student Subcultures: Implications for Student Personnel Administration.* Washington, D.C.: APGA, 1968.

Warren, Jonathan R. "College Student Subcultures as Dimensions of Behavior." (Paper read at the meeting of the American Educational Research Association, February 1967.)

_____. *Patterns of College Experiences.* Claremont, Calif.: College Personnel Institute, 1966. ERIC Document 010 100.

_____. "Student Perception of College Subcultures." *American Educational Research Journal* 58 (1968):213-32.

Whitaker, David. "Student Subcultures Reviewed and Revisited." *National Association of Student Personnel Administrators (NASPA) Journal* 7 (July 1969):23-34.

_____. *Student Subcultures Reviewed and Revisited.* Berkeley, Calif.: University of California, Center for Research and Development in Higher Education, 1969. ERIC Document 026 003.

William, Gerald D. *The Clark-Trow Viewpoints: Associated Personality Traits and Changes During the Freshman Year.* University Park, Penn.: Pennsylvania State University, Student Affairs Research Office, 1971.

Bibliography

Aldous, Joan, and Hill, R., eds. *International Bibliography of Research on Marriage and the Family, 1900-1972*. 2 vols. Minneapolis: University of Minnesota Press, 1967-1974.

American Geographical Society. *Research Catalogue.* 15 vols. Boston: G. K. Hall, 1962.

Amsden, Diana. "Information Problems of Anthropologists." *College and Research Libraries* 29 (1968):117-31.

"ASLIB Social Sciences Group Conference on Primary Materials in the Social Sciences." *ASLIB Proceedings* 23 (1971):166-206, 412-34.

Association of College and Research Libraries. Bibliographic Instruction Task Force. "Toward Guidelines for Bibliographic Instruction in Academic Libraries." *College and Research Libraries News* 36 (1975):137-9, 169-70.

Ausubel, David P. "Some Psychological Aspects of the Structure of Knowledge." In *Education and the Structure of Knowledge* (Fifth Annual Phi Delta Kappa Symposium on Educational Research). Chicago: Rand McNally, 1964.

Axelrod, Joseph, et al. *Search for Relevance: The Campus in Crisis.* San Francisco: Jossey-Bass, 1969.

Bach, G. L., and Saunders, Phillip. "Economic Education: Aspirations and Achievements." *American Economic Review* 55 (June 1965):329-56.

_____, and _____. "Lasting Effects of Economics Courses at Different Types of Institutions." *American Economic Review* 56 (June 1966):505-11.

Ball, John M. "Toward a Humanistic Teaching of Geography." In Nicholas Helburn, ed., *Challenge and Change in College Geography*. Washington, D.C.: Association of American Geographers, Commission on College Geography, 1973.

Barron, Paul, and Narin, Francis. *Analysis of Research Journals and Related Research Structure in Education.* Chicago: Computer Horizons, 1972. ERIC Document 072 787.

Bartlett, F. C. *Thinking.* New York: Basic Books, 1958.

Bates, Marcia J. "Rigorous Systematic Bibliography." *RQ* 16 (Fall 1976):7-26.

Bayley, David H. "The Emptiness of Curriculum Reform." *Journal of Higher Education* 43 (November 1972):591-600.

Bechtel, Joan. "A Possible Contribution of the Library College Idea to Modern Education." *Drexel Library Quarterly* 7 (July-October 1971):189-201.

The Behavioral and Social Sciences: Outlook and Needs. Englewood Cliffs, N.J.: Prentice-Hall, 1969.

Bell, Daniel. *The Reforming of General Education*. New York: Columbia University Press, 1966.

Ben-David, Joseph. *American Higher Education, Directions Old and New*. New York: McGraw-Hill, 1972.

Bergen, Daniel B. "Foreword." In Edward B. Montgomery, ed., *The Foundation of Access to Knowledge: A Symposium*. Syracuse, N.Y.: School of Library Science Syracuse University, 1968.

Berkhofer, Robert. *A Behavioral Approach to Historical Analysis*. New York: Free Press, 1969.

Birkos, Alexander S., and Tombs, Lewis A. *Historiography, Method, History Teaching: A Bibliography of Books and Articles in English, 1965-1973*. Hamden, Conn.: Linnet Books, 1975.

Blackburn, Robert T. "College Libraries—Indicated Failures: Some Reasons and a Possible Remedy." *College and Research Libraries* 29 (March 1968):171-7.

Bok, Derek. "On the Purposes of Undergraduate Education." *Daedalus* 103 (Fall 1974):159-72.

Borko, Harold, and Bernier, Charles L. *Abstracting Concepts and Methods*. New York: Academic Press, 1975.

Borrowman, Merle. "'Performance-based' Evaluation of History Teaching." *AHA Newsletter* 11 (May 1973):18-21.

Boulding, Kenneth. *Eiconics*. Ann Arbor, Mich.: University of Michigan Press, 1961.

Brittain, J. M. *Information and Its Users*. Bath, England: Bath University Press, 1970.

_____. and Line, M. "Sources of Citations and References for Analysis Purposes: A Comparative Assessment." *Journal of Documentation* 29 (March 1973):72-80.

Broadus, Robert N. *Selecting Materials for Libraries*. New York: Wilson, 1973.

Brookes, B. C. "Jesse Shera and the Theory of Bibliography." *Journal of Librarianship* 5 (October 1973):233-45, 258.

Broom, Leonard, and Selznick, Philip, eds. *Sociology*. 3rd ed. New York: Harper and Row, 1963.

Bruner, Jerome S. "Going Beyond the Information Given." In *Contemporary Approaches to Cognition*, A Symposium held at the University of Colorado. Cambridge, Mass.: Harvard University Press, 1957.

_____. *On Knowing*. Cambridge, Mass.: Belknap Press of Harvard University Press, 1964.

Bry, Ilse, and Afflerbach, Lois. "Bibliographic Foundations for Emergent History of the Behavioral Sciences." *Mental Health Book Review Index*, 5 (1970):I-VIII.

_____, and _____. "'Intensive Bibliography' and the Growth Pattern of the Literature" *Mental Health Book Review Index* 4 (1969):I-VI.

Burns, Shannon, et al. *An Annotated Bibliography of Texts on Writing Skills*. New York: Garland Publishing Co., 1976.

Buros, Oscar K., ed. *Seventh Mental Measurements Yearbook*. Highland Park, N.J.: Gryphon Press, 1972.

Cahnman, Werner J., and Boskoff, Alvin. "Sociology and History: Reunion and Rapprochement." In Werner J. Cahnman and Alvin Boskoff, eds., *Sociology and History: Theory and Research*. New York: Free Press of Glencoe, 1964.

Calvin, Allan D. "A Psychologist Looks at the 'Teaching' of Economics at the Undergraduate Level." In Keith G. Lumsden, ed., *Recent Research in Economics Education*. Englewood Cliffs, N.J.: Prentice-Hall, 1970.

Carnegie Commission on Higher Education. *Reform on Campus; Changing Students, Changing Academic Programs.* New York: McGraw-Hill, 1972.

Casagrande, Joseph B. "The Relations of Anthropology with the Social Sciences." In David G. Mandelbaum, ed., *The Teaching of Anthropology.* (American Anthropological Association Memoir 94.) Berkeley, Calif.: University of California Press, 1963.

Cassidy, Harold G. "Liberation and Limitation." In Francis Sweeney, ed., *The Knowledge Explosion.* New York: Farrar, Straus and Giroux, 1966.

Caws, Peter. "Instruction and Inquiry." *Daedalus* 103 (1974):18-24.

Charters, W. W. "Knowledge and Intelligent Behavior: A Framework for the Educative Process." In J. Shaver and H. Berlak, eds., *Democracy, Pluralism and the Social Studies.* Boston: Houghton, Mifflin, 1968.

Chorley, R. J., and Haggett, P. E., eds. *Frontiers of Geography.* London: Methuen, 1970.

Christ, John. *Toward a Philosophy of Educational Librarianship.* Littleton, Colo.: Libraries Unlimited, 1972.

Christensen, Harold T., ed. *Handbook of Marriage and the Family.* Chicago: Rand McNally, 1964.

Clark, Burton R. *Educating the Expert Society.* San Francisco: Chandler Publishing Co., 1962.

_____, and Trow, Martin. "Determinants of College Student Subcultures." Berkeley, Calif.: Center for the Study of Higher Education, University of California, 1960. (mimeo)

_____, and _____. "The Organizational Context." In Theodore Newcomb and E. Wilson, eds., *College Peer Groups: Problems and Prospects for Research.* Chicago: Aldine, 1966.

Clark, Kenneth E., and Miller, George A., eds. *Psychology.* Englewood Cliffs, N.J.: Prentice-Hall, 1970.

Cochran, Thomas C. "History and the Social Sciences." In A. S. Eisenstadt, ed., *The Craft of American History.* Volume II. New York: Harper and Row, 1966.

Cohan, Arthur M., et al. "Teaching Technology and Methods." In Robert M. Travers, ed., *Second Handbook of Research on Teaching.* Chicago: Rand McNally, 1973.

Collison, Robert L. *Abstracts and Abstracting Services.* Santa Barbara, Calif.: ABC Clio, 1971.

Committee on the Requirements of the Academic User, ed. *Use, Mis-use and Nonuse of Academic Libraries; Proceedings of the New York Library Association, College and University Libraries Section Spring Conference.* [Albany, N.Y.]: College and University Libraries Section, New York Library Association [n.d.].

Criminal Justice Abstracts. New York: National Council on Crime and Delinquency, 1969- .

Current Bibliography on African Affairs. New York: Published by Greenwood Press, Inc., for the African Bibliographic Institute, 1962- .

Current Index to Journals in Education. New York: CCM Corporation, 1969- .

Currier, Margaret. "Problems in Anthropological Bibliography." *Annual Review of Anthropology* 5 (1976):15-34.

Dawson, George, and Bernstein, Irving. *The Effectiveness of Introductory Economics Courses in High Schools and Colleges.* New York: Center for Economic Education, New York University, 1967.

Deighton, L. C., ed. *Encyclopedia of Education.* 10 vols. New York: Macmillan, 1971.

DeLorme, Roland L., and McInnis, Raymond G., eds. *Antidemocratic Trends in Twentieth Century America.* Reading, Mass.: Addison-Wesley, 1969.

Dennis, Lawrence E., and Kauffman, J. F., eds. *The College and the Student.* Washington, D.C.: American Council on Education, 1966.

Diller, Ann. "On Tacit Knowing and Apprenticeship." In *Philosophy of Education 1974; Proceedings of the Thirtieth Annual Meeting of the Philosophy of Education Society,* Boston, 1974. Edwardsville, Ill.: Philosophy of Education Society, 1974.

Di Renzo, Gordon J. "Toward Explanation in the Behavioral Sciences." In Gordon J. Di Renzo, ed., *Concepts, Theory and Explanation in the Behavioral Sciences.* New York: Random House, 1966.

Dolby, R.G.A. "Sociology of Knowledge in Natural Science." *Science Studies* 1 (1971):3-21.

Doyle, James M., and Grimes, George H. *Reference Resources: A Systematic Approach.* Metuchen, N.J.: Scarecrow Press, 1976.

Dubin, Robert, and Taveggia, Thomas C. *The Teaching-Learning Paradox; A Comparative Analysis of College Teaching Methods.* Eugene, Ore.: Center for the Advanced Study of Educational Administration, University of Oregon, 1968.

Dyson, Allan J. "Organizing Undergraduate Library Instruction: The English and American Experience." *Journal of Academic Librarianship* 1 (March 1975):9-13.

Ebel, R. L., ed. *Encyclopedia of Educational Research.* 4th ed. New York: Macmillan, 1969.

Eble, Kenneth E. *Professors as Teachers.* San Francisco: Jossey-Bass, 1972.

Ehrman, Edith, and Morehouse, Ward. *Students, Teachers and the Third World in the American College Curriculum: A Guide and Commentary on Innovative Approaches in Undergraduate Education.* (Occasional Paper No. 19.) Albany, N.Y.: Foreign Area Materials Center, University of the State of New York, 1972.

Ekistics Index. Athens, Greece: Athens Center of Ekistics, 1955- .

Ellis, Robert A., et al. "The Collegiate Scholar: Education for Elite Status." *Sociology of Education* 44 (Winter 1971):27-58.

Elton, G. R. *The Practice of History.* New York: Crowell, 1969.

Encyclopedia of World Art. 15 vols. New York: McGraw-Hill, 1959-1968.

Epstein, Herman T. *A Strategy for Education.* New York: Oxford University Press, 1970.

Eulau, Heinz, and March, James G., eds. *Political Science.* Englewood Cliffs, N.J.: Prentice-Hall, 1969.

Faris, R.E.L., ed. *Handbook of Modern Sociology.* Chicago: Rand McNally, 1964.

Fletcher, John, ed. *The Use of Economics Literature.* Hamden, Conn.: Archon Books, 1971.

Flynn, George Q. "History and the Social Sciences." *History Teacher* 7 (May 1974): 434-47.

Ford, Geoffrey. "Research on User Behavior in University Libraries." *Journal of Documentation* 29 (March 1973):85-106.

Foskett, D. J. "Problems of Indexing and Classifiction in the Social Sciences." *International Social Science Journal* 23 (1971):244-55.

Freedman, Alfred M., and Kaplan, H. I., eds. *Comprehensive Textbook of Psychiatry.* Baltimore: Williams and Wilkins, 1967.

Freidel, Frank, ed. *Harvard Guide to American History.* Rev. ed., 2 vols. Cambridge, Mass.: Belknap Press of Harvard University Press, 1974.

Freides, Thelma. "Bibliographic Gaps in the Social Science Literature." *Special Libraries* 67 (February 1976):68-74.

_____. *The Literature and Bibliography of the Social Sciences.* Los Angeles: Melville Publishing Co., 1973.

French, David H. "The Anthropologist in the Methodology of Teaching." In David G. Mandelbaum, et al., eds., *The Teaching of Anthropology.* (American Anthropological Association Memoir 94.) Berkeley, Calif.: University of California Press, 1963.

Frick, Elizabeth. "Information Structure and Bibliographic Instruction." *Journal of Academic Librarianship* 6 (September 1975):12-4.

Friedrichs, Robert W. *A Sociology of Sociology.* New York: Free Press, 1972.

Gardiner, G. L. "Empirical Study of Reference." *College and Research Libraries* 30 (March 1969):130-55.

Gardner, James. "Strategies for Relevant Learning Situations in Physical Geography." In Nicolas Helburn, ed., *Challenge and Change in College Geography.* Washington, D.C.: Association of American Geographers, Commission on College Geography, 1973.

Garfield, Eugene. "Citation Indexing, Historio-Bibliography and the Sociology of Sciences." In *Proceedings of the 3rd International Congress of Medical Librarianship.* Amsterdam: Excerpta Medica, 1970.

_____. "Historiographs, Librarianship, and the History of Science." In Conrad Rawski, ed., *Toward a Theory of Librarianship.* Metuchen, N.J.: Scarecrow Press, 1973.

_____. "Primordial Concepts, Citation Indexing, and Historio-Bibliography." *Journal of Library History* 2 (1967):235-49.

_____. *The Use of Citation Data in Writing the History of Science.* Philadelphia: Institute for Scientific Information, 1964.

Gill, Jerry H. "The Case for Tacit Knowledge." *Southern Journal of Philosophy* 9 (Spring 1971):48-59.

Goode, William J. *Social Systems and Family Patterns: A Propositional Inventory.* Indianapolis, Ind.: Bobbs-Merrill, 1971.

Gould, Julius, and Kolb, William A., eds. *Dictionary of the Social Sciences.* New York: Free Press of Glencoe, 1964.

Gration, Selby U., and Young, Arthur P. "Reference-Bibliographers in the College Library." *College and Research Libraries* 35 (January 1974):28-34.

Graubard, Stephen R. "University Cities in the Year 2,000." *Daedalus* 96 (1967): 817-22.

Gray, Richard A. [Review of *Social Sciences Citation Index.*] *American Reference Books Annual 1976* 7 (1976):151.

Greenstein, Fred I., and Polsby, Nelson W., eds. *Handbook of Political Science.* 8 vols. and cumulative index. Reading, Mass.: Addison-Wesley, 1975.

Greenwald, Douglas, ed. *McGraw-Hill Dictionary of Modern Economics.* 2d ed. New York: McGraw-Hill, 1973.

Gregory, Robert G. "Africana Archives and Innovative Teaching: The Teacher-Scholar's New Need for Research Materials." *Africana Library Journal* 2 (Winter 1971):18-20.

Grieneeks, Laura E. "Changes in Student Role Orientation Toward College." In *Proceedings of the 77th Annual Convention of the American Psychological Association, 1969.* Washington, D.C.: American Psychological Society, 1970.

Gurin, Gerald. "The Impact of the College Experience." In Stephen B. Withey, ed., *A Degree and What Else; Correlates and Consequences of a College Education.* New York: McGraw-Hill, 1971.

Hadley, Charles D. "Teaching Political Scientists: The Centrality of Research." *PS* 5 (Summer 1972):262-70.

Harmon, Glynn. "Opinion Paper on the Evolution of Information Sciences." *ASIS; Journal of the American Society for Information Science* 22 (July-August 1971): 235-41.

Harvey, David. *Explanation in Geography.* London: Arnold, 1969.

Havelock, Ronald G. *A Comparative Study of the Literature on the Dissemination and Utilization of Scientific Knowledge.* Ann Arbor, Mich.: Center of Research on Utilization of Scientific Knowledge, Institute for Social Research, University of Michigan, 1969.

Heilprin, L. B., and Goodman, F. L. "Analogy Between Information Retrieval and Education." *American Documentation* 16 (1965):163-9.

Helburn, Nicholas, ed. *Challenge and Change in College Geography.* Washington, D.C.: Association of American Geographers, Commission on College Geography, 1973.

Henning, P. A., and Stillman, M. E., eds. "Integrating Library Instruction in the College Curriculum." *Drexel Library Quarterly* 7 (July-October 1971) [whole issue].

Hewes, Gordon W. "Course Design." In David G. Mandelbaum, et al., eds., *The Teaching of Anthropology.* (American Anthropological Association Memoir 94.) Berkeley, Calif.: University of California Press, 1963.

Hill, A. David. "Geography and Geographic Education: Paradigms and Prospects." In Nicholas Helburn, ed., *Challenge and Change in College Geography.* Washington, D.C.: Association of American Geographers, Commission on College Geography, 1973.

Hillard, James M. *Where to Find What: A Handbook to Reference Services.* Metuchen, N.J.: Scarecrow Press, 1975.

Hobbs, Nicholas. "The Art of Getting Students into Trouble." In L. E. Dennis and J. F. Kauffman, eds., *The College and the Student.* Washington, D.C.: American Council on Education, 1966.

Holler, Frederick. "Library Material Without Instruction—A Disaster?" *Journal of Education for Librarianship* 8 (Spring 1967):38-49.

———. "Toward a Reference Theory." *RQ* 14 (Summer 1975):301-9.

Hollinger, David A. "T. S. Kuhn's Theory of Science and Its Implications for History." *American Historical Review* 78 (1973):370-93.

Holroyd, Gileon. "On the Sociology of Knowledge." *Journal of Librarianship* 4 (January 1972):48-56.

Horecky, Paul Louis, ed. *Basic Russian Publications*. Chicago: University of Chicago Press, 1965.

_____. *East Central Europe*. Chicago: University of Chicago Press, 1969.

_____, et al. *Russia and the Soviet Union*. Chicago: University of Chicago Press, 1965.

_____, et al. *Southeastern Europe*. Chicago: University of Chicago Press, 1969.

Hoselitz, Bert F., ed. *A Reader's Guide to the Social Sciences*. 2d ed. Glencoe, Ill.: Free Press, 1970.

_____. "The Social Sciences in the Last Two Hundred Years." In Bert F. Hoselitz, ed., *A Reader's Guide to the Social Sciences*. Glencoe, Ill.: Free Press, 1970.

House, David E. "Reference Efficiency or Reference Deficiency." *Library Association Record* 76 (November 1974):222-3.

HRAF Source Bibliography. New Haven, Conn.: HRAF, 1976.

Hughes, H. Stuart. "The Historian and the Social Scientist." *American Historical Review* 66 (October 1960):20-46.

Hultkrantz, Ake, ed. *General Ethnological Concepts*. Copenhagen: Rosenkilde and Bagger, 1960.

International Bibliography of Sociology. Paris: UNESCO, 1959-   .

Jones, Clyve, et al. "The Characteristics of the Literature Used by Historians." *Journal of Librarianship* 4 (1972):137-56.

Journal of Studies on Alcohol. New Brunswick, N.J.: Rutgers Center of Alcohol Studies, 1940-   .

Kaplan, Abraham. *The Conduct of Inquiry*. Scranton, Penn.: Chandler Publishing Co., 1964.

Kaplan, N. "The Norms of Citation Behavior: Prolegomena to the Footnote." *American Documentation*, 16 (1965):179-84.

Katz, William A. *Introduction to Reference Work*. 2 vols. New York: McGraw-Hill, 1974.

Kauffman, Joseph F. "College Student Profile." In L. C. Deighton, ed., *Encyclopedia of Education*. New York: Macmillan, 1971, Vol. 2, pp. 217-21.

Keller, Mark, ed. *International Bibliography of Studies on Alcohol*. New Brunswick, N.J.: Rutgers University Press, 1960-   .

_____, and McCormick, Mairi, eds. *A Dictionary of Words About Alcohol*. New Brunswick, N.J.: Rutgers Center on Alcohol Studies, 1968.

Kemp, D. A. *The Nature of Knowledge: An Introduction for Librarians*. London: Clive Bingley and Linnet, 1976.

Kernig, C. D., ed. *Marxism, Communism and Western Society*. 8 vols. New York: Herder and Herder, 1972.

Knapp, Patricia. *The Library, the Undergraduate and the Teaching Faculty*. San Diego: The University Library, University of California, 1970. ERIC Document 042 475.

_____. "The Meaning of the Monteith College Library Program for Library Education." *Journal of Education for Librarianship* 6 (1965):111-27.

_____. *The Monteith College Library Experiment*. New York: Scarecrow Press, 1966.

Koch, Sigmund, ed. *Psychology: A Study of a Science*. 6 vols. New York: McGraw-

Hill, 1959-1963.

Kochen, Manfred. *Principles of Information Retrieval.* Los Angeles: Melville Publishing Co., 1974.

———. "Stability in the Growth of Knowledge." *American Documentation* 20 (1969):186-97.

Koestler, Arthur. "Evolution and Revolution in the History of Science." *Encounter* 25 (December 1965):32-8.

Kohn, Clyde F. "The 1960's: A Decade of Progress in Geographical Research and Instruction." *Annals of the Association of American Geographers* 60 (June 1970):211-9.

Kolb, David A. "Individual Learning Styles and the Learning Process." Cambridge, Mass.: 1971. (mimeo)

Krevitt, Beth I., and Griffith, Belver C. *Evolution of Information Systems: A Bibliography, 1967-1972.* Washington, D.C.: ERIC Clearinghouse on Library and Information Sciences, 1973.

Krier, Maureen. "Bibliographic Instruction: A Checklist of the Literature, 1971-75." *Reference Services Review* 4 (January-March 1976):9-26.

Kruskal, William, ed. *Mathematical Sciences and Social Sciences.* Englewood Cliffs, N.J.: Prentice-Hall, 1970.

Kubie, Lawrence S. *Neurotic Distortion of the Creative Process.* Lawrence, Kan.: University of Kansas Press, 1958.

Kuhn, Thomas S. *The Structure of Scientific Revolutions.* 2d ed. Chicago: University of Chicago Press, 1970.

Landes, David S., and Tilly, Charles, eds., *History as Social Science.* Englewood Cliffs, N.J.: Prentice-Hall, 1971.

Langford, Thomas A., and Poteat, William H., eds. *Intellect and Hope.* Durham, N.C.: Duke University Press, 1968.

Lasker, Gabriel W. "The Introductory Course." In David G. Mandelbaum, et al., eds., *The Teaching of Anthropology* (American Anthropology Association Memoir 94). Berkeley, Calif.: University of California Press, 1963.

Laughlin, William S. "Concepts and Problems." In David G. Mandelbaum, et al., eds., *The Teaching of Anthropology.* (American Anthropological Association Memoir 94.) Berkeley, Calif.: University of California Press, 1963.

Lavalle, Placido. "Recent Trends in Undergraduate Geographic Training in American Universities and Colleges." In R. J. Chorley and P. E. Haggett, eds., *Frontiers in Geography Teaching.* London: Methuen, 1970.

Lee, Sul H. *Library Orientation; Papers Presented at the First Annual Conference on Library Orientation.* Ann Arbor, Mich.: Pierian Press, 1972.

Lewis, Ben H. "A Retrospective Look at Undergraduate Economics." *American Economic Review* 60 (May 1970):370-9. (Papers and proceedings of 82d annual meeting.)

Lewis, Darrell R., and Orvis, Charles C. *Research in Economic Education: A Review, Bibliography and Abstracts.* New York: Joint Council on Economic Education, 1971.

Lindzey, Gardner, and Aronson, E., eds. *Handbook of Social Psychology.* 5 vols. and index. Reading, Mass.: Addison-Wesley, 1968-1970.

Line, Maurice. "Information Requirements in the Social Sciences." In *Access to the Literature of the Social Sciences and Humanities: Proceedings.* Conference on

Access to Knowledge and Information in the Social Sciences and the Humanities, New York, 1972. Flushing, N.Y.: Queens College Press, 1974.

_____. *Information Requirements of Researchers in the Social Sciences.* Bath, England: University Library, Bath University of Technology, 1971. ERIC Document 054 806.

_____. "Information Services in Academic Libraries." In *Educating the Library User; Proceedings of the Fourth Triennial Meeting of the International Association of Technology Libraries.* Loughborough, England: University of Technology Library, 1970.

_____. "Social Scientists' Information." *SSRC Newsletter* 3 (1968):2-5.

Lipset, Seymour W., and Hofstadter, Richard, eds. *Sociology and History: Methods.* New York: Basic Books, 1968.

Lubans, John, ed. *Educating the Library User.* New York: Bowker, 1974.

Lystad, Robert, ed. *The African World.* New York: Praeger, 1965.

McEwen, William P. *The Problem of Social-Scientific Knowledge.* Totowa, N.J.: Bedminster Press, 1963.

MacGregor, John, and McInnis, Raymond G. "Integrating Classroom Instruction and Library Research: The Cognitive Functions of Bibliographic Network Structures." *Journal of Higher Education* 48 (January-February 1977):17-38.

Machlup, Fritz. "Are the Social Sciences Really Inferior?" *Southern Economic Journal* 27 (January 1961):173-84. (Reprinted in Maurice Natanson, ed., *Philosophy of the Social Sciences.* New York: Random House, 1963.)

McInnis, Raymond G. "Integrating Classroom Instruction and Library Research." *Studies in History and Society* 6 (Winter 1974-1975):31-65.

_____, and Scott, James W. *Social Science Research Handbook.* New York: Barnes and Noble, 1975.

McKellar, Peter. *Imagination and Thinking.* New York: Basic Books, 1957.

Madge, John. *The Tools of Social Science.* London: Longmans, Green, 1953.

Mandelbaum, David G. "The Transmission of Anthropological Culture." In David G. Mandelbaum, et al., eds., *The Teaching of Anthropology.* (American Anthropological Association Memoir 94.) Berkeley, Calif.: University of California Press, 1963.

_____, Lasker, Gabriel, and Albert, Ethel M., eds. *The Teaching of Anthropology.* (American Anthropological Association Memoir 94.) Berkeley, Calif.: University of California Press, 1963.

Margenau, Henry. *Open Vistas.* New Haven, Conn.: Yale University Press, 1961.

Maslow, Abraham H. *The Psychology of Science, A Reconnaissance.* New York: Harper and Row, 1966.

Mead, Margaret. "Why Is Education Obsolescent?" *Harvard Business Review* 36 (1958):30-4.

Meehan, Eugene J. *Explanation in Social Science, A System Paradigm.* Homewood, Ill.: Dorsey Press, 1968.

Miller, Elizabeth, and Truesdell, Eugenie. "Citation Indexing: History and Applications." *Drexel Library Quarterly* 8 (April 1972): 159-72.

Millis, Charlotte Hickman. "The Wabash Project: A Centrifugal Program." *Drexel Library Quarterly* 7 (1971): 371-4. [Appendix: "Suggested Readings to Orient Librarians to Today's Students and Their Search for Self in a Context of Change and Anomaly."]

Mills, C. Wright. *The Sociological Imagination.* New York: Oxford University Press, 1959.

Mitchell, G. Duncan. *Dictionary of Sociology.* Chicago: Aldine, 1968.

Mitra, A. C. "The Bibliographic Reference: A Review of Its Role." *Annals of Library Science and Documentation* 17 (1970):117-23.

"Model Statement of Criteria and Procedures for Appointment, Promotion in Academic Rank, and Tenure for College and University Librarians." *College and Research Libraries News* 34 (1973): 192-5.

Mohamed, Oli. "Structure of Knowledge and 'Resources' Programs in Librarianship." *Journal of Education for Librarianship* 16 (1975):3-17.

Morgan, Kathryn P. "Some Philosophical Difficulties Concerning the Notion 'Structure of a Discipline.'" *Educational Theory* 23 (Winter 1973):74-88.

Murdock, George P. *Outline of Cultural Materials.* 4th ed. rev. New Haven, Conn.: HRAF Press, 1967.

_____. *Outline of World Cultures.* 5th ed. New Haven, Conn.: HRAF Press, 1975.

_____, and O'Leary, Timothy. *Ethnographic Bibliography of North America.* New Haven, Conn.: HRAF Press, 1975.

Nagel, Ernest. *The Structure of Science.* New York: Harcourt, Brace and World, 1961.

Oakeshott, Michael. "Learning and Teaching." In R. S. Peters, ed., *The Concept of Education.* New York: Humanities Press, 1967, pp. 156-76.

Olson, David H. L., and Dahl, Nancy S., eds. *Inventory of Marriage and Family Literature.* St. Paul, Minn.: Family Social Science, University of Minnesota Press, 1975- .

Overhage, Carl F. J. "Science Libraries: Prospects and Problems." *Science* 155 (1967): 802-6.

Palmer, John R. "Using Historical Research in the Teaching of American History." *Social Education* 36 (March 1972):271-9.

Perelman, Chaim. "Polanyi's Interpretation of Scientific Inquiry." In Thomas A. Langford and William H. Poteat, eds., *Intellect and Hope.* Durham, N.C.: Duke University Press, 1968.

Perkins, Dexter. "And We Shall Gladly Teach." *American Historical Review* 62 (January 1957):291-309.

Perry, William G. *Forms of Intellectual and Ethical Development in the College Years, A Scheme.* New York: Holt, Rinehart and Winston, 1968.

Peterson, Richard. *College Student Questionnaire and Technical Manual.* Princeton, N.J.: Educational Testing Service, 1965.

_____. *College Student Questionnaire (Technical Manual).* Rev. ed. Princeton, N.J.: Educational Testing Services, 1968.

Phenix, Philip H. "The Architeconics of Knowledge." In *Education and the Structure of Knowledge.* Chicago: Rand McNally, 1964.

Phillips, Derek L. *Abandoning Method.* San Francisco: Jossey-Bass, 1973.

Plano, Jack C., and Riggs, Robert E. *Dictionary of Political Analysis.* Hinsdale, Ill.: Dryden Press, 1973.

Pois, Robert A. "The Lecture-Textbook Syndrome and Library Use." In John Lubans, ed. *Educating the Library User.* New York: Bowker, 1974.

Polanyi, Michael. *Knowing and Being: Essays.* Chicago: University of Chicago Press, 1969.

_____. *Personal Knowledge.* Chicago: University of Chicago Press, 1958.

_____. *The Study of Man*. Chicago: University of Chicago Press, 1959.

Popescu, Oreste. "On the Historiography of Economic Thought: A Bibliographical Survey." *Cahiers d'histoire mondiale (Journal of Modern History)* 64 (1964): 168-209.

Poulton, Helen. *The Historian's Handbook*. Norman, Okla.: University of Oklahoma Press, 1972.

Price, Derek J. de Sola. *Little Science, Big Science*. New York: Columbia University Press, 1963.

_____. "Networks of Scientific Papers." *Science* 149 (1965):510-5.

Psychological Abstracts. Washington, D.C.: American Psychological Association, 1927- .

Ravetz, Jerome R. *Scientific Knowledge and Its Social Problems*. New York: Oxford University Press, 1971.

Rawski, Conrad H. "Subject Literature and Librarianship." In L. R. Bone, ed., *Conference on Library School Teaching Methods*. Urbana, Ill.: University of Illinois, Graduate School of Library Science, 1969.

Reader's Guide to Periodical Literature. New York: Wilson, 1900- .

Research in Education. Washington, D.C.: U.S. Government Printing Office, for the Educational Resources Information Center, 1966- .

Roberts, Marc J. "On the Nature and Condition of Social Science." *Daedalus* 103 (1974):47-64.

Rowe, John Holland. "Library Problems in the Teaching of Anthropology." In David G. Mandelbaum, ed., *The Teaching of Anthropology*. (American Anthropological Association Memoir 94). Berkeley, Calif.: University of California Press, 1963.

Ruggles, Nancy D., ed. *Economics*. Englewood Cliffs, N.J.: Prentice-Hall, 1970.

Rundell, Walter, "Clio's Ways and Means: A Preliminary Report on the Survey." *Historian* 30 (1967):20-40.

_____. *In Pursuit of American History*. Norman, Okla.: University of Oklahoma Press, 1970.

Sauvaget, Jean. *Introduction to the History of the Muslim East*. Berkeley, Calif.: University of California Press, 1965.

Saveland, Robert N., and Pannell, Clifton W. *Inventory of Recent U.S. Research in Geographic Education, 1975*. (Geography Curriculum Project. Occasional Paper No. 4.)

Saveth, Edward N., ed. *American History and the Social Sciences*. New York: Free-Press, 1964.

Schein, Edgar H. *Professional Education, Some New Directions*. New York: McGraw-Hill, 1972.

Schwab, Joseph J. "The Concept of the Structure of a Discipline." *Educational Record* 43 (1962):197-205.

_____. "Problems, Topics, and Issues." In *Education and the Structure of Knowledge*. Fifth Annual Phi Delta Kappa Symposium on Education. Chicago: Rand McNally, 1964.

_____. "Teaching Science as Enquiry." *Science* 170 (1970):1394. [Review of Epstein's *A Strategy for Education*.]

Schwartz, Fred, ed. *Scientific Thought and Social Reality: Essays by Michael Polanyi*. New York: International Universities Press, 1974.

Scott, William T. "The Gentle Rain—A Search for Understanding." In T. A. Langford and W. H. Poteat, eds., *Intellect and Hope*. Durham, N.C.: Duke University Press, 1968.

———. "Tacit Knowing and *The Concept of Mind*." *Philosophical Quarterly* 21
(June 1971):22-35.

Scrivener, Jeffrey E. "Instruction in Library Use: The Persisting Problem." *Australian
Academic and Research Libraries* 2 (June 1972):87-118.

Shera, Jesse. "An Epistemological Foundation for Library Science." In Edward B.
Montgomery, ed., *The Foundations of Access to Knowledge: A Symposium*.
Syracuse, N.Y.: School of Library Service, Syracuse University, 1968.

———. *Foundations of Education for Librarianship*. New York: Becker and Hayes,
1972.

Siegfried, John J., and White, Kenneth J. "Teaching and Publishing as Determinants
of Academic Salaries." *Journal of Economic Education* 4 (1973):90-9.

Sills, David L., ed. *International Encyclopedia of the Social Sciences*. 17 vols. New
York: Macmillan, 1968.

Skelton, Barbara, et al. *The Use of Citation Linkages and Networks for Information
Retrieval in the Social Sciences*. Bath, England: Bath University of Technology
Library, 1973. ERIC Document 078 868.

Skinner, G. William, ed. *Modern Chinese Society: An Analytical Bibliography*.
3 vols. Stanford, Calif.: Stanford University Press, 1973.

Smelser, Neil J., and Davis, James A., eds. *Sociology*. Englewood Cliffs, N.J.: Prentice-Hall, 1970.

Smith, Allen H., and Fischer, John L., eds. *Anthropology*. Englewood Cliffs, N.J.:
Prentice-Hall, 1970.

Social Sciences Citation Index. Philadelphia: Institute of Scientific Information,
1973- .

Social Sciences Citation Index Guide and Journal Lists. Philadelphia: Institute for
Scientific Education (Annual).

Sociological Abstracts. New York: American Sociological Association, 1952- .

Sociology of Education Abstracts. London: Pergamon, 1965- .

Stephens, Lester D. *Historiography: A Bibliography*. Metuchen, N.J.: Scarecrow
Press, 1975.

Sturtevant, William C., ed. *Handbook of North American Indians*. 20 vols. Washington, D.C.: Smithsonian Institution Press (in press).

Taafe, Edward J., ed. *Geography*. Englewood Cliffs, N.J.: Prentice-Hall, 1970.

Taylor, Alan R. "A Model for Academic Library Service." In *Papers Delivered at
the Indiana University Library Dedication, Bloomington Campus, Bloomington
Campus, October 9-10, 1970*. Bloomington, Ind.: Indiana University Library,
1971.

Taylor, Charles L. *World Handbook of Political and Social Indicators*. 2d ed. New
Haven, Conn.: Yale University Press, 1972.

Textor, Robert B. *A Cross-Cultural Summary*. New Haven, Conn.: HRAF Press,
1967.

Theodorson, George A. *Modern Dictionary of Sociology*. New York: Crowell-
Collier-Macmillan, 1969.

Trow, Martin. "The Campus Viewed as a Culture." In Hall T. Sprague, ed., *Research on College Students.* Boulder, Colo.: Western Interstate Compact for Higher Education, 1960.

_____. "Cultural Sophistication and Higher Education." In *Conference on Selection and Educational Differentiation.* Berkeley, Calif.: Field Service Center and Center for Higher Education, University of California, 1960.

Wagener, James W. "The Philosophy of Michael Polanyi as a Source of Educational Theory." Ph.D. Dissertation, University of Texas, 1968.

_____. "Toward a Heuristic Theory of Instruction: Notes on the Thought of Michael Polanyi." *Educational Theory* 20 (1970):46-53.

Walford, Arthur J., ed. *Guide to Reference Materials.* 3d ed. 3 vols. London: Library Association, 1973.

Wall, C. Edward, ed. *Author Index to Poole's Index to Periodical Literature.* Ann Arbor, Mich.: Pierian Press, 1971.

Walshe, Francis. "Personal Knowledge and Concepts in the Biological Sciences." In T. A. Langford and W. H. Poteat, eds., *Intellect and Hope.* Durham, N.C.: Duke University Press, 1968.

Warren, Jonathan. "Student Perceptions of College Subcultures." *American Educational Research Journal* 5 (March 1968): 213-32.

Washburn, S. L. "Evolution and Education." *Daedalus* 103 (1974):221-8.

Wauchope, Robert, ed. *Handbook of Middle American Indians.* 11 vols. Austin, Tex.: University of Texas Press, 1964-76.

Weckstein, Richard S. *A Report on an Experiment in Teaching Introductory Economics.* Waltham, Mass.: n.d. (mimeo)

Weingartner, Rudolph H. "The Quarrel About Historical Explanation." *Journal of Philosophy* 58 (1961):29-45. (Reprinted in Ronald H. Nash, ed., *Ideas of History.* New York: Dalton, 1969.)

Weinstock, Melvin. "Citation Indexes." In Allen Kent and Harold Lancour, eds., *Encyclopedia of Library and Information Science.* Vol. 5. New York: Marcel Dekker, 1971, pp. 16-40.

White, Carl M., and associates, eds. *Sources of Information in the Social Sciences.* 2d. Chicago: American Library Association, 1973.

White, Morton. *Foundations of Historical Knowledge.* New York: Harper and Row, 1965.

Whittaker, Kenneth. "Towards a Theory for Reference and Information Services." *Journal of Librarianship* 9 (January 1977):49-63.

Whitten, Benjamin. "Social Science Bibliography Course: A Client-oriented Approach." *Journal of Education for Librarianship* 16 (Summer 1975):25-32.

Wilson, Patrick. *Two Kinds of Power.* Berkeley, Calif.: University of California Press, 1968.

Winchell, Constance M., and Sheehy, Eugene P., eds. *Guide to Reference Books.* 8th ed. Chicago: American Library Association, 1967.

Winick, Charles. *Dictionary of Anthropology.* New York: Philosophical Library, 1959.

Winn, V. A. "A Case Study of the Problems of Information Processing in a Social Science Field: The OSTI: *SEA* Project." *ASLIB Proceedings* 23 (February 1971): 76-88.

Wise, Gene. *American Historical Explanations.* Homewood, Ill.: Dorsey Press, 1973.

Withey, Stephen B., ed. *A Degree and What Else; Correlates and Consequences of a College Education.* New York: McGraw-Hill, 1971.

Wolfe, Gary K., and Williams, Carol. "All Education Is 'Adult Education': Some Observations on Curriculum and Profession in the Seventies." *AAUP Bulletin* 60 (1974):291-5.

Wolfgang, Marvin E., et al. *Criminology Index: Research and Theory in Criminology in the United States, 1945-1972.* 2 vols. New York: Elsevier, 1975.

Ziman, John M. "Information, Communication Knowledge." In T. Saracevic, ed., *Introduction to Information Science.* New York: Bowker, 1971.

_____. *Public Knowledge.* Cambridge, Mass.: Cambridge University Press, 1968.

Index

Page numbers in italic indicate Notes sections.

About the Author

Raymond G. McInnis is Head of the Reference Department and Social Sciences Librarian at the Wilson Library, Western Washington University, Bellingham. He has coedited *Anti-democratic Trends in Twentieth Century America*, coauthored *Social Science Research Handbook*, and published in such journals as *Studies in History and Society*, and *Journal of Higher Education*.